SERVICE AND
DEVICE DISCOVERY

Service and Device Discovery

Protocols and Programming

Golden G. Richard III, Ph.D.
Department of Computer Science
University of New Orleans

McGraw-Hill
New York · Chicago · San Francisco · Lisbon
London · Madrid · Mexico City · Milan · New Delhi
San Juan · Seoul · Singapore
Sydney · Toronto

Cataloging-in-Publication Data is on file with the Library of Congress.

McGraw-Hill

A Division of The McGraw·Hill Companies

Copyright © 2002 by The McGraw-Hill Companies, Inc. All rights reserved. Printed in the United States of America. Except as permitted under the United States Copyright Act of 1976, no part of this publication may be reproduced or distributed in any form or by any means, or stored in a data base or retrieval system, without the prior written permission of the publisher.

1 2 3 4 5 6 7 8 9 0   DOC/DOC   0 8 7 6 5 4 3 2

ISBN 0-07-137959-2

The sponsoring editor for this book was Marjorie Spencer, the editing supervisor was Caroline Levine, and the production supervisor was Sherri Souffrance. It was set in New Century Schoolbook by Joanne Morbit of McGraw-Hill Professional's Hightstown, N.J., composition unit.

Printed and bound by R. R. Donnelley & Sons Company.

McGraw-Hill books are available at special quantity discounts to use as premiums and sales promotions, or for use in corporate training programs. For more information, please write to the Director of Special Sales, Professional Publishing, McGraw-Hill, Two Penn Plaza, New York, NY 10121-2298. Or contact your local bookstore.

CONTENTS

Preface   ix

Acknowledgments   xi

Chapter 1   Introduction to Service Discovery   1

Introduction   2
Service Discovery Features   4
Common Characteristics   6
Service Discovery Suites   8
    Jini   9
    Service Location Protocol (SLP)   10
    Universal Plug and Play (UPnP)   10
    Bluetooth SDP   11
Applications   11
Interoperability, or Why Learn a Bunch of Protocols?   14

Chapter 2   Jini Works Its Magic   17

    What Is Jini?   18
    Goals of the Chapter   19
    Jini Overview   19
    Object Serialization   21
    Code Downloading   22
    Distributed Objects: RMI   23
    More on Requirements   27
    Jini Entities   28
Leasing   31
    Basic Leases   32
    Automatic Lease Renewal   34
Clients, Services, and Registries   37
    Lookup Services   37
    Controlling a Lookup Service: The ServiceRegistrar Interface   51
    Jini Services   53
    Jini Clients   84
Jini Security   125

Other Jini Components   127
  JavaSpaces   127
  Transactions   138
  Firing It All Up   146

Chapter 3   SLP: An IETF Protocol for Service Discovery   149

Overview of Service Location Protocol   150
Goals of the Chapter   152
Essential Details   152
  Specifying a Service Type   153
  Naming Authorities   159
  Message Formats   159
  Message Retransmission Policies   162
SLP Agents   163
  Directory Agents   163
  Service Agents   166
  User Agents   170
  Scope and SLP Agents   174
Designing SLP Applications: The SLP API   176
  The C API   177
  Callbacks in the C API   184
  A Concrete Example: An SLP Echo Service   187
  The Client Side: An SLP Echo Client Implementation   199
Configuration   212
  Configuration File   212
DHCP Issues   215
Security   215
  Introduction   215
  Authentication Blocks   216
  Security and SLP Messages   217

Chapter 4   Universal Plug and Play: Extending Plug and Play
to the Network   221

Overview of Universal Plug and Play (UPnP)   222
  What Is UPnP?   222
  Goals of the Chapter   222
  UPnP Protocols in Brief   223
  Requirements   224
Universal Plug and Play Protocols in Detail   226
  Describing Devices and Services in UPnP   226

Addressing: Auto-IP		236
Discovery: The Simple Service Discovery Protocol (SSDP)		237
Description: Moving Description Documents		242
Control: The Simple Object Access Protocol (SOAP)		243
Eventing: The General Event Notification Architecture (GENA)		250
Presentation: Getting Visual		257
Where's the Code?		257
Here's the Code: The UPnP Blender Device		260
And Here's More: A Control Point for the UPnP Blender		289
Code for the "common.c" Library		336
Code for the "prioque.c" Queue Package		346

Chapter 5 Bluetooth Service Discovery Protocol **359**

Bluetooth Overview	360
What Is Bluetooth?	360
Goals of the Chapter	363
Bluetooth Basics	364
Our Focus: Bluetooth SDP	370
Bluetooth SDP Operations	373
A Sample API: Digianswer's Bluetooth Software Suite	376

Index	381

To Lois Besemer (1919—1999) and
Gerrod Richard (1967—2001)

PREFACE

Service and Device Discovery: Protocols and Programming was written in response to my frustration with existing documentation on service discovery protocols and a lack of freely available, documented examples of clients and services. In my opinion, much of the existing documentation is either too terse, or far too wordy. The material has its roots in a tutorial I gave at the IEEE International Performance, Computing, and Communications Conference; the tutorial was created at the request of Dr. Sumi Helal of the University of Florida, who was charged with organizing the conference. Subsequently, versions of the tutorial were given at Mobicom and other conferences. With much massaging, expansion, and mutilation, the present volume was born.

I feel that the format of this book is rather unorthodox. Rather than writing a series of short chapters, as is typical, I chose to write very fat "chapters," each of which (aside from the introduction) might be considered a "mini-book" on a particular service discovery protocol. My intention is that each chapter be relatively stand-alone. If the only thing you care about is Service Location Protocol, it should be possible to read that section independently. That said, the book is divided as follows:

Chapter 1 provides general background on service discovery, covering the common components of service discovery protocols, looking at interesting applications and surveying some of the roadblocks.

Chapter 2 covers Jini, a popular service discovery protocol developed by Sun Microsystems. Jini is a Java-based technology, which relies extensively on Java's Remote Method Invocation (RMI). A comprehensive example of a service implementation as well as use of additional Jini features such as Javaspaces and the Jini Transactions are highlights of this chapter.

Chapter 3 examines Service Location Protocol (SLP), an open standard for service discovery in IP-based networks. SLP defines both C and Java APIs, though the examples in this book are in C.

Chapter 4 covers Universal Plug and Play (UPnP), an XML-based service discovery architecture developed by the UPnP Forum (headed by Microsoft). UPnP is language neutral, though current implementations target Java, C, and C++. Working examples in C for both clients and services are provided in this chapter.

Chapter 5 briefly covers Bluetooth's Service Discovery Protocol (Bluetooth SDP). Bluetooth is an exciting short range radio system, and while it's not yet mature it's a technology to watch.

The book is aimed at several classes of readers. First, I expect the book to serve well as a textbook in an applied senior undergraduate or graduate course on networking, distributed computing, or mobile computing. Supplemented with material providing additional background on computer networking, the current book motivates development of dynamic client/server applications.

Developers working in, or considering working in, service discovery should also find the book useful. The specifications for the various service discovery protocols can be quite terse, and I've made every effort to condense the material into a manageable form, paying special attention to the topics that will most concern developers. It's my hope that developers will find the material in the book sufficient to fuel some really cool client/server applications.

Finally, for the technically curious, I hope *Service and Device Discovery: Protocols and Programming* provides a reasonable introduction to service discovery. Readers unfamiliar with Java or C (or programming in general) can carefully navigate around these sections, concentrating instead on the motivations behind each service discovery architecture.

Golden G. Richard III
New Orleans, LA

ACKNOWLEDGMENTS

Many people helped me to write this book, both directly and indirectly. First, I'd like to thank my graduate student, Minoo Singh, who assisted me in many ways, including writing some of the code, testing other code, and proofreading. Sumi Helal of the University of Florida raised my interest level in service discovery several notches, opening the path that led to my agreeing to write this book. My editor at McGraw-Hill, Marjorie Spencer, has made the process as painless as possible. I hope we will remain friends. Jeremie Allard, Paul Gonin, and Lizhe Xu read early drafts of the Jini and UPnP chapters and provided extensive comments on the text and discovered some minor errors in the code. Students in my Fall 2001 Principles of Distributed Systems course were kind enough to complain only modestly as they grappled with early drafts of some of the chapters.

Mahdi Abdelguerfi, the Chair of the Computer Science Department at the University of New Orleans, was very understanding and allowed me to dedicate a lot of time to writing. My other UNO colleages were also very supportive. My remote colleagues (and dear friends) Frank Adelstein of Odyssey Research Associates, Sandeep Gupta of Arizona State, Darrell Long of University of California/Santa Cruz, and Loren Schwiebert of Wayne State were often willing to listen to me complain.

I live in New Orleans because of the wonderful people, great food, and fantastic jazz scene. I know few of the local musicians personally, but they provide a service that is more valuable than my modest means can ever reward—I wish them success beyong imagining. Thanks for the nonstop music, which has broken a tough writing schedule, and thanks for enduring what can be a very tough lifestyle.

Mom, dad: it's done. You can stop asking. And now my excuses for being so terrible at staying in touch have dried up. Thanks for being so patient.

My friends are my second-most-valued resource, and at least the local ones tend to spend a lot of time on my deck—eating, thinking, drinking mint juleps, and arguing (and agreeing) on a wide range of topics. It's simply too dangeous to list them for fear of forgetting somone. You know who you are. See you on the deck.

Most of all, my wife/writer/friend Christine Ciarmello Richard (resource #1) makes everything worthwhile. Thanks for putting up with me.

Introduction to Service Discovery

Introduction

Broadly, a service discovery framework is a collection of protocols for developing dynamic client/server applications. Client/server is nothing new, and in fact many of the concepts in service discovery are not ground-breaking. Instead, the advantages provided by service discovery arise because a number of important features are bundled and standardized. Highly dynamic interactions between clients and services is the norm—service discovery-enabled clients seek needed services based on their type (e.g., printing, file storage) and based on descriptive attributes that identify the manufacturer, the cost of using the service, or other interesting facts. Enabled services announce their presence when they enter the network and (if possible) announce their demise when they leave the network. Catalogs track available services. Garbage collection facilities rid the system of outdated information. Applications which display some of these characteristics already exist in networked environments—a client in need of an IP address, for example, might seek a DHCP server, communicate with the server, and finally be granted one. But these clients and services are typically developed from scratch, with little support for the developer other than "Here's a C compiler. Get to work." Service discovery technologies generalize and standardize the environments in which client/server applications are developed and used, and implementations of the various service discovery protocols provide software tools that make the development effort much easier and interactions between clients and services more dynamic than usually seen in today's systems.

There is a lot of common ground among the various choices in service discovery frameworks. All support the concepts of *client* and *service,* which are simply entities that need and offer some functionality (e.g., printing), respectively. Clients perform *discovery* in order to find needed services. In some cases, they may directly seek the needed services themselves; in others, they may contact one or more *service catalogs,* which maintain directories of available services. A discovery attempt generally classifies the service by type, and may optionally include requirements such as a manufacturer, serial number, or other service attributes. Whether services are sought directly or a catalog is consulted, a client needs very little information about its environment—it can locate services (or service catalogs) dynamically, with little or no static configuration. Multicast is typically used to support discovery. When a service enters the network, it will perform *service advertisement,* either directly to clients or to one or more service catalogs. The advertisement includes necessary contact information, and will also include either descriptive attributes or information that will allow these attributes to be discovered. Figure 1-1 illustrates a small service discovery world in the abstract.

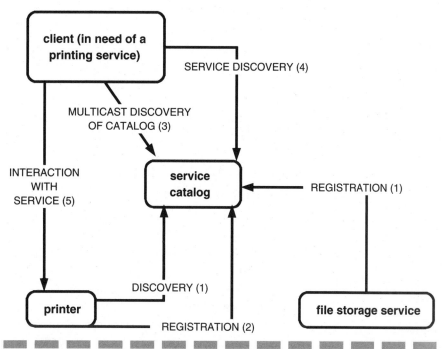

Figure 1-1

A small service discovery world is depicted. At time (1), a file storage service knowing the location of a service catalog comes online and registers its availability. Simultaneously, a printer that has not been configured with the location of a service catalog dynamically discovers the catalog (using multicast) and registers at time (2). A time (3), a client in need of a printer discovers the service catalog, then searches the catalog for an available printer (4), and finally interacts with the printer (5).

Service discovery is cool, but things aren't all sunshine and roses. Until interoperability efforts mature or the field is narrowed down, the presence of half a dozen competing technologies will limit the usefulness of service discovery "in the large." Even so, individual service discovery frameworks provide many features that facilitate client/server development. The developed applications will more easily support dynamic behavior such as insertion into the network, location changes, or removal. In turn, users of the developed applications will be faced with fewer administrative headaches.

Service Discovery Features

Service discovery technologies provide standards-based frameworks in which to solve a variety of client/server-based problems. Central questions (aside from security issues) in the design of client/server systems include

- What types of services are available?
- Where are the services?
- What's necessary for a client to use the service?
- What protocol is spoken between client and service?

Service discovery technologies provide most of the pieces for building dynamic, distributed communications systems, assisting developers in attacking both the design and administrative issues of deploying client/server applications. These technologies allow services introduced into a network to be discovered, configured, and used with a minimum of manual intervention. In a service discovery-based network, virtually anything can be a client or a service—clients need things, and services provide them. For example, a word processor in need of a printer is a typical client, and the printer, in turn, is a typical service. But a digital camera might participate in a network as a service, at once providing pictures and also engaging an enabled light (i.e., the service) if the picture is too dark. Connecting the needy—clients—and the providers—available services—is the point of service discovery. Service discovery technologies directly attack the "I don't know where you are" and "I don't know how to talk to you" issues.

One problem users encounter with increasing frequency and severity is the installation, configuration, and management of peripherals. This is a client/server problem in disguise. The complexity of this problem is becoming more serious as laptops, handheld computers, printers, scanners, wireless devices, external storage devices, digital cameras, and other peripherals are integrated into networked environments in the home and office. Inexperienced computer users may become quite frustrated in dealing with the configuration and interaction of such a multitude of devices. Introducing a new device can include physical installation, removing device drivers for a device being replaced, installation of device drivers included with the new device, determining that the included device drivers are outdated or designed for a different operating system, necessitating downloading and installing new device drivers, and unexpected (usually negative) interactions with existing devices. Concrete evidence of users' frustration with these situations can be seen in the red faces and angry tones of customers standing in any large computer store's technical support/merchandise return line. I fear to approach these places! Even for very experienced computer users, who are *capable* of dealing with complex configuration issues, the whole experience really seems like a waste of time. Configuration headaches can be compounded many times over in environments with numerous computers (e.g., a corporation or a computer laboratory at a university). Service discovery technologies take an important step toward eliminating manually installed device drivers, relying instead on standard interfaces to put devices in touch.

With service discovery technologies, clients and services are designed to support dynamic interaction, of which the peripheral installation problem discussed above is a specific case. Increasing use of mobile devices creates many instances where highly dynamic behavior is the norm, not the exception. Many people are purchasing a variety of mobile devices, since discovering that one size doesn't fit all. Cellular phones are great for communicating, but their tiny screens and awkward input mechanisms make wireless e-mail or web browsing difficult. Laptops are increasingly powerful, but difficult to carry about. Palm-size computers are somewhere in between—more powerful than cellular phones, less powerful than typical laptops. Most of these mobile devices are necessarily "peripheral-poor" because they trade functionality for suitable form factors and low power consumption, so they must rely on nearby services for storage, faxing, high-speed network access, and printing. Certainly some of these services may be provided by a user's own equipment—for example, a cellular phone might provide a network connection to a palm-size computer—but in many cases the services will provided by a third party (e.g., a printer in a coffee shop). The interaction between a mobile device and a needed peripheral will often be fleeting; for example, a consultant who needs to print a contract stored on a palm-size computer on a client's printer during a site visit shouldn't have to spend much time getting the two devices to cooperate. In fact, the printing activity should do nothing more than consume a sheet of paper—the consultant *mustn't* appear to tamper with the client's devices at all! A similar situation arises for a user who's keyboarding over a decaffeinated soy latte (cough, cough) in a futuristic coffee shop. The coffee shop provides printing services, storage, high-speed network access, etc. Such an environment could be a high-tech utopia, but downloading appropriate device drivers and installing them on the spot would quickly dampen enthusiasm. Moreover, having to manually determine what services (e.g., printing, faxing) are available is inconvenient. In general, people *do* seem to want to work and play in diverse environments—but not if it's too painful. Service discovery can make things more convenient by allowing the types of available services to be discovered easily. Further, since the interfaces between clients and services are standardized, the client can get to work quickly without manual configuration.

I often use the terms *server, service,* and *device* when referring to "the things that clients need." In most cases, at least from a high-level point of view, these terms are interchangeable in a service discovery world. Devices typically provide services (e.g., a printer provides a printing service), but in many cases services are just software, running on general-purpose computer systems. A polygon rendering service, which accepts specifications of polygons (including geometry and shading information) and outputs streams of pixel colors, is an example of such a service. A translation service that accepts sentences in one language and outputs them in another language is another example. A high-performance computer service that can execute code embodied in arbitrary Java classes is another. In the rest of the book, except where it is necessary to clarify the meaning of the terms as used in a specification (as in the case of UPnP, where *service* and *device* have specific meanings), the terms *server, service,* and *device* will be used interchangeably.

Common Characteristics

While at a low level the service discovery technologies covered in this book (and others, e.g., Salutation [1]) have incompatible design philosophies, at a high level they are relatively similar. Taking a look at the common characteristics of service discovery technologies gives a good idea of what they provide for end users and for programmers. Not all service discovery technologies embody all these concepts, but most include a majority of the features listed below. The next section discusses the specific technologies described in this book; in that section, you'll begin to see the divergent philosophies emerge. For now, the common ground:

- *Discovery of services.* Needed services may be discovered on demand, with minimal prior knowledge of the network. This is really the point of service discovery. Typically, clients can search for services by type ("scanner") or by descriptive attributes ("manufactured by Scan-o-magic, Inc.") or by both. The richness of search facilities varies widely by technology. For example, Service Location Protocol (SLP) provides very powerful searching facilities, while Bluetooth SDP allows only integer-valued attributes to be targeted in a search for services.

- *Service "subtyping."* Clients may occasionally be interested in a very specific type of service; for example, a high-resolution color laser printer with duplex capability might be needed to print a slick advertisement. Other types of printers just won't do. In other cases, only basic printing services are required and "any old printer will do." A client needing basic printing should be able to discover one without knowing many details. A client needing sophisticated services should be able to make these needs known. Service subtyping allows the bare essence of a printer to be defined and more elaborate printing services to provide supersets of the basic functionality. A client needing to print can be as specific (or as nonspecific) as she wishes, and she will find services with the needed features.

- *Service insertion and advertisement.* Services slip into a network with a minimum of manual configuration and advertise their availability, directly either to clients or to servers maintaining a catalog of services. Conversely, services leaving a network in an orderly fashion (as opposed to crashing) can advertise their demise. A primary difference between service discovery technologies and static information services is that service discovery technologies allow highly dynamic updates—services appearing or disappearing result in immediate updates. In contrast, services such as DNS and DHCP rely on static files or databases that are configured by systems administrators with higher levels of authority than those of typical users. Service discovery technologies also (typically) provide more powerful searching capabilities than static schemes.

- *Service browsing.* Clients can browse the list of available services. This information might be presented to a user in a graphical user interface, and the user could then choose services of interest.

- *Catalogs of available services.* Some service discovery technologies, such as UPnP, are inherently peer-to-peer, allowing clients and services to directly address each other for the purposes of advertisement and discovery. Others, such as Jini, implement catalogs that track available services. Still others, such as SLP, can operate either with or without service catalogs. In service discovery protocols that do support service catalogs, services register their availability with the catalogs and clients obtain contact information for interesting services directly from the catalogs. On one hand, service catalogs can dramatically reduce multicast traffic, since they relieve clients of the need to use multicast to discover service locations; on the other hand, in so doing they add another component to be administered. Catalogs also allow service discovery beyond the local multicast radius, allowing much larger service discovery domains to be created.

- *Eventing.* Eventing allows asynchronous notification of interesting conditions (e.g., a needed service becoming available, a service leaving the network, or an important change in the state of a service, such as a printer running out of paper). Eventing makes the developer's job much easier, eliminating the need to use polling to watch for service state changes.

- *Garbage collection.* A mechanism is normally included in the service discovery framework to expire service availability information, to expunge outdated information from catalogs of available services, and to terminate client-initiated eventing. Without such a mechanism, outdated information would abound, and performance would suffer when, for example, clients tried to contact nonexistent services or services continued to perform operations on behalf of crashed clients. Leases are a popular garbage collection mechanism. The concept is simple: Rather than grant the right to use a resource (e.g., storage of contact information in a catalog by a service) indefinitely, a lease is assigned. The grantor of the lease (e.g., a service catalog) cancels the lease and discards related information if the lease is allowed to expire. To avoid expiration, the party that is using the resource (e.g., a service that has registered with the catalog) must periodically request a renewal.

Service Discovery Suites

This book examines a number of leading service discovery technologies, including Jini, Universal Plug-and-Play, Service Location Protocol, and

Bluetooth SDP. The emphasis is on understanding the protocol specifications and in developing real software. Each of the included technologies was chosen because its specification is relatively mature and at least one complete implementation is available. Other worthy service discovery technologies, of which Salutation is perhaps the most obvious, are not addressed in this book because no widely available implementation existed as I wrote this edition. For each technology included, with the notable exception of Bluetooth, fully documented source code for a representative client and service is provided and examined in detail. Some of the examples are more complicated than others, because in some cases (as for Jini) the service discovery technology provides mechanisms for client/service communication, for example, Remote Method Invocation. To explore these mechanisms properly requires more code. In others (e.g., SLP), client/server communication is completely an application-specific issue, and sockets or similar (and familiar) mechanisms are used.

Although most of these "service discovery suites" promise similar functionality, namely, reduced configuration hassles, improved device cooperation, and automated discovery of required services, they come at the problem from different philosophical and technical approaches. In this book, a (long) chapter is dedicated to each technology. Here, a brief overview of each service discovery technology is presented.

Jini

Jini is a service discovery technology based on Java, developed by Sun Microsystems. Because of the platform-independent nature of Java, Jini can rely on mobile code to control services. *Lookup services* provide catalogs of available services to clients in a Jini network. Jini services register their availability by uploading proxy objects to one or more of these lookup services. The proxy objects are essentially "device drivers" written in Java—they allow interaction with the service. Clients can dynamically discover lookup services, search for interesting services, and then download these proxy objects. Searching is based on the type of proxy object and on sets of descriptive attributes. Note that Jini specifically requires at least one accessible lookup service—there is no "directory-less" mode where clients and services directly discover each other. Jini also includes associated tools, such as a transaction service and a JavaSpaces implementation, which provides a Linda-like bag-of-objects abstraction. Code mobility allows the creation of very interesting services in Jini—the proxy object downloaded by a client may perform computation on the client side, on the service side, or on both. Examples in this book are developed against the standard Jini distribution v1.1 from Sun Microsystems.

Service Location Protocol (SLP)

SLP is an IETF standards-track protocol for IP-based networks. It is language-neutral, although APIs are defined for C and Java. In SLP, User agents (UAs) search for needed services on behalf of clients. Service agents (SAs) advertise the availability of services, either directly to UAs or to Directory agents (DAs), if at least one DA is available. Directory agents serve some of the purposes of lookup services in Jini by cataloging available services, but they store only service contact information—*not* code. Service location information in SLP is encoded in service URLs, which contain all information necessary for contacting a service. In contrast to Jini, SLP is concerned primarily with putting clients in touch with services—the specific protocols spoken between clients and services are outside the jurisdiction of SLP. Service templates are used to standardize particular service types (such as printer and scanners); they provide the syntax of service URLs for a specific type and also standardize the set of descriptive attributes. UAs locate interesting services by service type, further narrowing searches by the values of descriptive attributes or by specifying scopes, which group services into location-based or administrative domains. SLP examples in this book were developed under OpenSLP v1.0.5, an open source SLP implementation.

Universal Plug and Play (UPnP)

Universal Plug and Play is a set of protocols for service discovery under development by the Universal Plug and Play Forum, an industry consortium led by Microsoft. UPnP standardizes the protocols spoken between clients (called control points in UPnP lingo) and services rather than relying on mobile code (like Jini). Device and service descriptions are coded in XML; and a number of protocols for local autoconfiguration, discovery, advertisement, client/service interaction, and eventing—Auto-IP, SSDP, SOAP, GENA—are included in the specification. These protocols tend to be based loosely on existing standards (say, HTTP). Unlike Jini and SLP, UPnP does not support service directories—communication between devices and clients is always direct. Thus UPnP is aimed at smaller environments, such as the home, where the benefits of directories are reduced due to the small number of devices typically found in the network. UPnP examples in this book were developed using Intel's UPnP SDK v1.0.4, an open source implementation of the UPnP protocols.

Bluetooth SDP

The Bluetooth specification is a design for a low-cost, low-power radio system, designed as a cable replacement, and short-range, personal area networking technology. Bluetooth devices search their environment (within the 10-m or so range of the transmitter) to find other devices providing services and to offer services. Bluetooth Service Discovery Protocol (SDP) is a simple service discovery mechanism used to locate other Bluetooth devices offering interesting services and to facilitate offering services. Bluetooth devices maintain sets of *service records,* each of which describes an available service. Service records consist entirely of descriptive attributes, describing the type of service, the necessary protocols for communication with the service, the location of appropriate documentation, etc. To find references to services of interest, Bluetooth devices search the available space of services for those with matching attribute values (one attribute is the service's type). For example, a Bluetooth client might search for a nearby ColorDuplexPrinter. Bluetooth SDP is lightweight, because it's intended primarily for personal area networks—devices on your desk or within tens of feet. But other service discovery protocols can be mapped to Bluetooth SDP, or more sophisticated service discovery protocols such as SLP might be run over Bluetooth, using Bluetooth as a wireless transport.

Applications

Proponents of service discovery have a bag of applications, from relatively mundane to quite exotic. Of course there's a lot of hype, and some of the applications projected will be hampered by both technical problems and human behavioral issues. But the advantages provided to both developers and end users are real—if I didn't firmly believe this, you wouldn't be reading this book. A survey of some of these applications, along with the benefits and perceived problems (whether technical or otherwise), is presented below. This list is not meant to be exhaustive by any means, but instead to spark the reader's imagination.

Services can be provided directly by a hardware device (e.g., a Jini-enabled printer); they can be provided by a hardware device via a general-purpose computing device (e.g., a printer attached to computer running Jini software); or they can be software-only (e.g., a language translation service). While direct support for service discovery by commercially available devices (e.g., printers, digital cameras, LCD projectors) is desirable because it provides service discovery functionality "right out of the box," in the near term it is likely that many service discovery capabilities will be provided by general-purpose computers. For example, an LCD projector could be attached to a small desktop computer running UPnP in order to make projection services available. As the technologies mature and market pressures narrow the field, enabled $69 printers will become more likely.

Service discovery will make networked devices significantly less tedious to deploy and use than they are currently. In a UPnP network, for example, an enabled printer becomes usable as soon as it is plugged in. A word processor in need of a printing service can discover the printer, download configuration information directly from the printer, and then begin to print almost immediately. If the printer is removed—say, in order to upgrade it to a model with greater capacity—and replaced with another, the new printer will integrate into the network just as easily. Used in this way, service discovery extends the "plug and play" technology that (usually) works in Windows environments to the network *and* between different platforms (Linux, Windows, Solaris, MacOS, etc.). This naturally makes device mobility less painful—moving a device from home to an office and then to a friend's home requires no configuration *if* the same service discovery framework is running in all the locations.

Services that are more interesting than the usual examples—printing, scanning, etc.—can also be enabled by service discovery technologies. A Bluetooth wireless dongle[1] in a user's purse could turn on lights, transfer desktop settings, or adjust stereo systems as they move about. The same device might also suck up electronic business cards automatically when the user attends a meeting, or make a copy of a diagram scribbled on an enabled whiteboard. These ideas are not revolutionary, but service discovery technologies standardize the software environment

---

[1] I hate this word.

(and in the case of Bluetooth, part of the hardware environment), making both implementation and compatibility more straightforward.

Data synchronization is a much-hyped application. High-tech users accumulate bits of data on a variety of mobile devices—PDAs, laptop computers, cellular phones, pagers, etc. Keeping the data in synchronization is a tedious and error-prone process. A simple data synchronization scenario involves the exchange of business cards, calendar entries, etc., between PDAs. This is already a common operation among users of Palm organizers, but interoperability among different platforms is sometimes a problem. A more elaborate synchronization scenario involves laptops, PDAs, cellular phones, and other devices discovering each other and automatically synchronizing data—these data might include updated contact lists or recently edited files. Clearly it would be wonderful if you could just toss your PDA on the desk and of its own accord, have it find other devices and synchronize information. But there are serious technical and nontechnical issues to consider. First, handling conflicts automatically isn't trivial. If users update contact lists or files on multiple devices that are not in synchronization range, then update conflicts can occur. Resolving such conflicts automatically is error-prone, so a manual component to synchronization is introduced. Second, in most cases you don't want *your* PDA synchronizing with a neighbor's PDA just because you visit his home! You also don't want other users maliciously sucking data out of your mobile devices. Crypto can help, but to help it has to be used. Witness results of one of the latest crazes, "war driving"[2], where people equipped with a laptop and a wireless network card roam the streets searching for wireless networks. War driving by users all over the world has revealed that the vast majority of 802.11 wireless LANs are being deployed "out of the box," with encryption and access controls off. If it works out of the box, users are less likely to pay attention to critical security configuration. Security issues will require serious attention for service discovery applications that handle sensitive data.

An example we'll revisit in the Jini chapter (Chap. 2) is the remote file storage service, which allows users to store and retrieve files on remote servers. This kind of service could significantly (though temporarily) increase the storage capacity of small mobile computers such as PDAs. Of course, remote file storage is hardly a revolutionary idea—people do it all the time via file transfer protocol (ftp). But with service discovery, the client in need of file storage need not know the locations of remote file storage services—they can be discovered automatically, and limits on file storage, cost, etc., can be determined dynamically. Cost and other parameters are easily represented by using descriptive attributes in most service discovery technologies, and searches can be tailored accordingly (e.g., to avoid using a $2/page printer). None of the current service discovery technologies address billing; they assume that such issues will be handled by an add-on protocol. Of course billing may be a substantial concern for "public" services.

Interoperability, or Why Learn a Bunch of Protocols?

None of the technologies covered in this book is a superset of the others, and none is mature enough to dominate the market. The fact that none dominates isn't a sign of poor engineering, or an excuse to sit down and wait for the "next big thing"—it just indicates the existence of different approaches. Smart people will all identify a problem, but they won't necessarily tackle it in the same way. In the long term, market pressures may result in the field being trimmed substantially—small devices in particular can't be built to support a variety of service discovery technologies in a cost-effective manner. Of course, the service discovery approach that succeeds in the marketplace may do so for reasons quite unrelated to "best technical approach." In any event, in this book the service discovery technologies stand on their own merit, the advertising budgets (or lack thereof) of their proponents ignored. In the short term, there are options, and developers have to choose among them.

Despite the high-level similarities between various service discovery protocols, interoperability turns out to be quite difficult. The language-centric nature of some of the protocols, and distinct differences in *what* has to be standardized to define a service, are substantial obstacles. For example, Jini services can make use of a wide spectrum of Java technologies, including support for audio, video, and the transfer of complex Java objects through object serialization. Since Jini relies heavily on mobile code, the thing to be standardized is an interface, which specifies the methods that a Java client can expect a service implementation to provide. Complicated types (sets, hash tables, queues, queues of queues of queues!) can bleed over into these interfaces, making interaction with non-Java applications quite daunting. In UPnP, on the other hand, the thing to standardize is the XML device and service descriptions. The protocols spoken between UPnP clients and services tend to be based on simple, primitive types such as strings, booleans, and integers. Bridging Jini and UPnP, especially if the interface to which a Java service adheres includes references to complex Java classes, is nontrivial, and difficult to automate. In general, interoperability among the technologies discussed in this book will require bridging mechanisms.

At the University of New Orleans, we've made substantial progress on Jini/UPnP interoperability, and we have designed and implemented a UPnP/Jini bridging framework [3]. Our initial architecture introduces service-specific, Java-based proxies that allow services of either type to be used by both Jini and UPnP clients. For each new service type, a modest implementation effort is required. The framework ensures that appropriate objects are registered with Jini lookup services to accommodate Jini clients, and that appropriate UPnP advertisements are made so that UPnP clients can find Jini services. Our goal, as might be expected, is to reduce the per-service implementation effort as much as possible.

A white paper [4] describes mapping the Salutation architecture for service discovery to Bluetooth SDP. Bluetooth is an attractive target for interoperability efforts because it brings low-cost wireless to mobile devices, eliminating cables. Salutation interoperability with SLP is described in the Salutation specification. A complete description of Salutation will be included in a future edition of this book. None of the other groups developing service discovery technologies rule out Bluetooth interoperability; and mapping Jini, UPnP, and SLP to Bluetooth is possible because PPP (and thus IP) can be run over Bluetooth. Current implementations of Jini, UPnP, and SLP all target IP-based networks, since IP is ubiquitous.

Some work on bridging Jini and SLP has also been done. A Jini/SLP bridge has been proposed that allows Jini clients to make use of SLP services [5]. Properly equipped service agents advertise the availability of Java driver factories that may be used to instantiate Java objects for interacting with an SLP service. A special SLP user agent discovers these service agents and registers the driver factories with available Jini lookup services. An advantage of this architecture is that the service agents do not need to support Jini—in fact, they do not even need to run a Java virtual machine. Bridges of this sort seem to be the most appropriate way to foster operability between the various service discovery technologies. Some extra programming effort will always be required—the client/service interfaces are quite different between the various approaches.

The importance of interoperability is an especially good reason for understanding more than one service discovery technology. If you're currently working in service discovery or considering service discovery technologies to support a new application, it's likely that interoperability concerns will enter the picture at some point. In addition, understanding the intricacies of several service discovery protocols will help you to choose the right primary technology. This book aims to provide a guidebook for most of the popular service discovery technologies, and I hope it will ease your way.

Pointers

1. Salutation Service Discovery Architecture. www.salutation.org.
2. R. Cowell, "War Dialing and War Driving: An Overview," SANS Institute, http://rr.sans.org/wireless/war.php.
3. J. Allard, V. Chinta, L. Glatt, S. Gundala, and G. G. Richard, III, "Jini Meets UPnP: An Architecture for Jini/UPnP Interoperability," submitted for publication.
4. B. Miller and R. Pascoe, "Mapping Salutation Architecture APIs to Bluetooth Service Discovery Layer," www.salutation.org/whitepaper/BtoothMapping.PDF.
5. Erik Guttman and James Kempf, *Automatic Discovery of Thin Servers: SLP, Jini and the SLP-Jini Bridge*, IECON, San Jose, CA, 1999.

Jini Works Its Magic

What Is Jini?

At its introduction, Jini was variously heralded as a revolution in distributed computing, the death of the hard drive, the successor to the operating system, and a technology that would allow systems administrators to spend a lot more time on the beach and less time worrying over configuration issues. Like most things, Jini doesn't quite live up to the hype, but it's a solid technology for developing and deploying services that plug into the network with a solid "click." Jini is a service discovery technology, based on Java, which promotes a service-based architecture capable of supporting network plug-and-play for clients and services.

The Jini model allows clients and services to be "plugged in" and "unplugged" from the network at any time; it is a realization of the Sun Microsystems slogan "The network is the computer." Services that are plugged in become available to clients, and services that are unplugged simply disappear. When connected to the network, clients can discover and search catalogs (called lookup services) of available services and then select and use those they need. Before interacting with a service, Jini clients download an object that provides methods for invoking interesting operations [e.g., for a PrinterService, print(), ejectPage()]. At this point it's too early for a compilable example, but the following bit of code illustrates a simple Jini client that searches for and obtains an instance of a PrinterService and then invokes the print() method to output "Hello, world":

```
public class SimpleJiniClient {
  public static  void main(String args[]) {
    try {
      ServiceDiscoveryManager catalog =
        new ServiceDiscoveryManager(null, null);
      ServiceTemplate printerTemplate =
        new ServiceTemplate(null,
          new Class[] {PrinterService.class}, null);
      PrinterService printer = (PrinterService)
        catalog.lookup(printerTemplate);
      printer.print("Hello, world");
    }
    catch (Exception e) {
      System.out.println("Failed to obtain a printer service: " + e);
    }
  }
}
```

Goals of the Chapter

The goal of this chapter is to provide a solid introduction to the Jini specification, paying special attention to the design of Jini clients and services.
Given that there are several Jini books approaching 1,000 pages, it is
obviously impossible in this book, which covers several service discovery
technologies, to discuss every nuance of Jini. Instead, the most important
components are covered—the ones that Jini developers will most likely
need in developing useful clients and services. We also cover typical
design patterns for Jini services. Because of limited space, familiarity
with Java is assumed. The Pointers section lists some recommended
books on Java and a reference to the Jini specification, which is included
in electronic form in the Jini distribution. Throughout this chapter, Java
code is presented to illustrate important concepts.

Jini Overview

The Jini model allows a much more maintenance-free and spontaneous
computing paradigm than most users see today. With Jini, networks
become very dynamic environments freed from the administrative
penalties associated with introducing and removing services. But Jini
goes much further than simply making printers, scanners, and digital
cameras easier to install, configure, and access. It is a common miscon-
ception that Jini is simply another way to hook up devices so that application software can find and use them. In fact, Jini blurs the line
between hardware and software, providing a very flexible definition of
service.

Services can be mostly hardware, as are printing and fax, or completely software (e.g., a service that accepts specifications of 3D environments and returns a rendered image). The actual implementation of the
service need not be revealed to a client at all, so the details of a proprietary polygon-rendering algorithm, for example, need never be exposed.
Moreover, clients are usually not aware of either the locations or soft-
ware/hardware makeup of services. Because of this transparency to the
client, implementations can be modified and services can be relocated
without affecting client code. All the client cares about is the *interface* to
which a service conforms—a Java specification of the API adhered to by
a service.

Upon initialization, a Jini service uploads a proxy object to one or
more lookup services to announce its availability to other Jini entities.

Jini lookup services contain catalogs of these proxy objects, which are really software "remote controls" for services, and present them to interested clients. In Jini a proxy might be only a wrapper that communicates with the guts of the service remotely, or it might implement the entire service—these details are hidden from the client. Clients discover catalogs, provide the interfaces that define needed services, and download matching proxy objects. Methods in the proxy object allow the client to use the service. When downloading the proxy, clients can also access class files as needed. (We will talk more about this shortly.)

A rather exaggerated example helps illustrate the strong separation between service interface and implementation in Jini. Imagine that a client is searching for a Jini service that returns the current outdoor temperature. The interface for such a service might be called TemperatureService and might provide at least one method for determining the current temperature. An initial implementation of this service involves alerting a human being who is monitoring a console. He then rushes outside, reads the temperature displayed by a thermometer, and returns to the console to type the thermometer reading into a text-based service-to-proxy interface. On initialization, this simplistic version of the service contacts a lookup service and uploads its proxy object. When the client searches for a TemperatureService, the proxy object is downloaded from a lookup service and the client is able to check temperatures. The particular protocol spoken between service proxy and the service backend is private.

Subsequently a more sophisticated implementation develops, which queries a thermometer directly. When the client searches for a TemperatureService, the proxy object for this new implementation is downloaded, and again temperatures can be checked. The interesting thing is that the client simply requests access to a TemperatureService instance—the actual wire protocol that is spoken between the service's proxy and the implementation of the service is completely arbitrary, and the client has no reason to care about it. Of course the implementor of the service needs to care very much!

Jini is the only service discovery technology discussed in this book that relies on *code mobility*—moving pieces of executable code around the network. As mentioned above, clients search lookup services by interface, meaning that clients know which operations the desired service will perform, but may not have the class files for the service's implementation. Java objects and associated Java class files are moved around the network automatically as necessary to facilitate interaction between clients and services. Code mobility allows clean design and permits interesting service implementations, but also results in a set of fairly stringent requirements for the developer, not the least of which is that generally Jini clients and services must be written in Java.

Requirements.   Jini is heavily dependent on the platform-independent nature of Java and Java's inherent support for distributed computing. In particular, Jini relies on Java's object serialization and code downloading facilities and on Remote Method Invocation (RMI).[1] Jini clients interact with lookup services to find interesting services, while Jini services interact with lookup services to register their proxy objects. In both cases, the communication between client or service and a lookup service is via an instance of ServiceRegistrar, obtained when the lookup service is discovered. Several pieces of Java magic are at work here. The ServiceRegistrar uses RMI for communication between client/service and lookup service. Object serialization allows a copy of the proxy object to be migrated to the client. Code downloading allows class files required by the client (or by the service) to be downloaded as necessary. Object serialization, code downloading, and RMI are discussed quite briefly below, but these treatments are intended primarily as refreshers. Discussion of these topics in any depth would require another book!

Object Serialization

Java's object serialization facility allows objects that implement the Serializable interface to be flattened ("serialized") into a stream of bytes and then stored or transmitted over a stream. Upon retrieval from storage or reception at the other end of a stream, the object is reconstituted ("deserialized") into its original form. This facility makes development of complex client/server applications in Java easier than in languages such as C/C++, primarily because complex data structures are much easier to transfer. Transmission of data structures over a socket connection in C/C++ is perfectly doable, but custom marshaling and unmarshaling code must be developed for each data type. If a data structure contains linked structures, each of the linked structures must be traversed and converted to a form proper for transport. On the other side, the data structures are reconstituted. A key difficulty is that pointers are almost always used in the development of C data structures, and local pointers are meaningless outside the current execution context. This means that custom marshaling code is almost always needed. Contrast this with object serialization in Java: marshaling objects is almost embarrassingly easy. For example, a class declared as follows

```
public class VeryComplicatedClass implements Serializable {

   <<fields>>
   <<methods>>
}
```

is made serializable simply by including Serializable in the implements list. Instances of the object may then be transferred over a stream or stored in a file, using the readObject() and writeObject() methods of ObjectInputStream and ObjectOutputStream. The following code snip reads and writes an instance of VeryComplicatedClass over a socket connection:

```
. . .
VeryComplicatedClass instance;
ObjectInputStream input =
   new ObjectInputStream(socket.getInputStream());
ObjectOutputStream output =
   new ObjectOutputStream(socket.getOutputStream());
. . .
instance = (VeryComplicatedClass)input.readObject();
. . .
output.writeObject(instance);
. . .
```

The ObjectInputStream and ObjectOutputStream will typically be wrapped around another stream associated with a file or network connection (as in the example above, where the underlying stream is associated with a socket connection). There are restrictions on the serializability of objects, most notably that Thread objects and objects representing streams are not Serializable. (See Ref. 2 in the Pointers section for some work-arounds.) In Jini, the proxy objects exported by services to lookup services and available for download to clients must be Serializable, since they will be transmitted over a network connection. For readers who need more discussion, most good Java books discuss serialization in some detail.

Code Downloading

One of the most powerful features of Java is the ability to load Java bytecode from arbitrary locations. It's common knowledge that each Java Virtual Machine contains an embedded class loader responsible for loading trusted Java classes, typically from the local file system. These include the built-in Java classes and classes that appear in locations listed in the CLASSPATH. In addition to this so-called "primordial" class loader, class loaders may be present that can load Java code from arbitrary locations. The target of such a class loader can be either a local file system or a remote machine.

In Jini, clients search for services by interface. Thus the client definitely has the *specification* of the desired service's proxy object, but it is unlikely that Java code for the *implementation* of the service is available at the client (particularly if the service has not been used previously). Java clients obtain an *instance* of a Java object that controls a service from a lookup service, but the bytecode, which is the executable code for the class, is also required. Web servers running at the various entities in a Jini system allow clients to download Java bytecode as needed.

Distributed Objects: RMI

Java's RMI provides remote method invocation for Java objects, permitting objects to be physically distributed across the network. RMI is supported by a registry running on each machine where remotely accessible objects are hosted. Typically server applications will register one or more remote objects with the local RMI registry, and then client applications will request references to needed objects, using the lookup() method in the Naming interface. Lookup is via a String identifier, which is provided by the service when it registers object instances. Once remote object references are obtained via lookup(), they can be passed as parameters to other code, enabling other objects to perform remote references.

Classes from which remote objects will be created must be passed through the RMI compiler (rmic) to generate the stub that provides the client endpoint for remote method invocation. This endpoint handles serialization and deserialization of arguments and also handles return values when remote method calls are executed. Once the stubs are generated, the programmer won't need details of how RMI performs the remote references—the remote method calls work similar to local ones, with a caveat that remote references are typically orders of magnitude slower than local ones.

Figure 2-1 illustrates the various components in an RMI interaction. Here a service registers remote objects with an RMI registry. A client obtains remote references to the registered objects and makes remote method calls. Java code missing from either the client or the service is

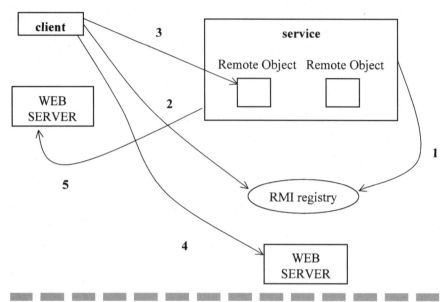

Figure 2-1
A schematic illustrating RMI operations. In (1), a service registers an object with the local RMI registry. In (2), a client searches for a remote object reference by contacting the RMI registry. Note that the location of the RMI registry must be known to the client, as must the String-based "tag" attached to the remote object reference when it is registered by the service. In (3) the client invokes a remote method on a remote object. In (4) and (5), web servers running on the client and service allow bytecode for needed classes to be downloaded. This code downloading is crucial, because the client might only have the *interface* which a remote object implements, but not the actual class file. The class file is downloaded as needed. It is also possible for the service to be missing class files corresponding to objects passed as arguments in a remote method call. Again, the needed class files will be downloaded by RMI automatically, as needed.

downloaded from web servers running on the client and service. Note that web servers are typically needed on both client and service (assuming they are running on different machines) because the client might be missing class files related to the implementation of a particular interface, while the service might be missing class files corresponding to arguments provided to a remote method call.

The use of RMI will be illustrated with a simple example. Here is a "meaning of life" (MOL) service interface that provides a single method. The method reveals the meaning of life in String form:

```
import java.rmi.*;

public interface RMI_MOLServerInterface extends Remote {
```

```
        // reveal the meaning of life
        public String reveal() throws java.rmi.RemoteException;
}
```

A client obtaining a reference to an object implementing this interface will be able to determine the meaning of life (or a facsimile thereof) by invoking reveal(). The following implementation registers a meaning-of-life object that lets clients determine the meaning of life through RMI. The textual meaning of life is specified as a command line argument (e.g., "Jazz is Life") when the service is started, and Naming.rebind() is used to register the object with the RMI registry. The registry is assumed to be running on the local host:

```
// Simple RMI server which implements the
// RMI_MOLServerInterface—registers itself, then awaits the
// chance to reveal the meaning of life.

import java.io.*;
import java.rmi.*;
import java.rmi.server.UnicastRemoteObject;

public class RMI_MOLServer extends UnicastRemoteObject
   implements RMI_MOLServerInterface {

    private String mol = null;
    public RMI_MOLServer(String mol) throws RemoteException {
        System.setSecurityManager(new RMISecurityManager());
        this.mol = mol;
    }

    public String reveal() throws java.rmi.RemoteException {
        return mol;
    }

    public static void main (String args[]) throws Exception {
        if (args.length != 1) {
            throw new RuntimeException(
              "Usage: java RMI_MOLServer <string>");
        }//end if
        RMI_MOLServer us = new RMI_MOLServer(args[0]);
        Naming.rebind("MOL", us);
    }
}
```

Here is a simple client that invokes methods on the MOL service to determine the meaning of life. It is started with a single command line parameter, the host on which the MOL service should be found. Naming.lookup() provides a reference to the remote MOL service's object. The reveal() method of this instance is then used to discover the meaning of life.

```
// Simple RMI client—requests a reference to an object
// implementing the "meaning of life" interface, then
// determines meaning of life and displays it.

import java.io.*;
import java.rmi.*;

public class RMI_MOLClient {
  public static void main (String args[]) throws Exception {
    if (args.length != 1) {
        throw new RuntimeException("Usage: java RMIMOLClient <host>");
    }//end if
    System.setSecurityManager(new RMISecurityManager());
    RMI_MOLServerInterface mol = null;
    try {
      mol = (RMI_MOLServerInterface)Naming.lookup("rmi://"+
        args[0] + "/MOL");
    }
    catch (java.rmi.NotBoundException e1) {
      System.out.println("No MOL service object bound on that host.");
    }//end catch
    catch (java.rmi.ConnectException e2) {
      System.out.println("Either the RMI registry or the" +
        " MOL service is dead on that host.");
    }//end catch

    if (mol != null) {
      System.out.println("The meaning of life is: " +  mol.reveal());
    }//end if
    else {
      System.out.println("Couldn't determine the meaning of life."+
        " Keep searching!");
    }//end else
  }
}
```

As threatened, this overview of RMI is very abbreviated and omits many important details. The complete RMI specification is available on the Javasoft website. It contains explanations of all the interfaces as well as details of the wire protocol. (See Ref. 1 in the Pointers section for details.) Because Jini is built over RMI, understanding RMI is crucial to programmers. You will see that Jini provides far more powerful mechanisms for service implementation and discovery than does RMI. Most importantly, clients don't need to know the locations of objects in the network.

More on Requirements

Jini's reliance on advanced Java facilities such as object serialization creates an expectation that clients and services will be written in Java. Thus Jini requires each device to either run a Java Virtual Machine (JVM) or to associate itself with an entity that can execute a JVM on its behalf. The JVM must be able to access the standard Java packages and all the Java packages needed to support Jini. To support the downloading of Java code, each entity must also provide a mechanism for serving Java classes. A simple web server suffices for this, and a rudimentary web server, written in Java, is included in the standard Jini distribution.

In situations where it is neither cost-effective nor practical for a device to contain its own JVM, a *device chassis* can be used. A device chassis can enable a number of "dumb" devices, making their services available to Jini clients. This is illustrated in Fig. 2-2, where a device

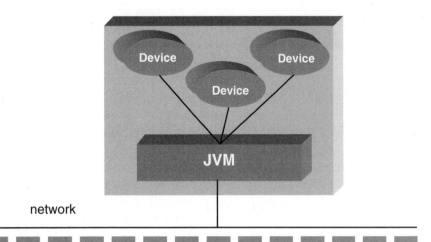

network

Figure 2-2
A Jini device chassis amortizes the cost of a Java Virtual Machine (JVM) over several devices. The device chassis can recognize insertion and deletion of devices and speak native device protocols in order to make the devices available to Jini clients.

chassis speaks the native protocols of several non-Jini-enabled devices, so they can participate in a Jini federation. The device chassis is also responsible for detecting events such as insertion and removal of devices, so that device capabilities can be advertised and removed as appropriate. (The Jini specification discusses a number of techniques for accommodating non-Jini devices and services.)

The current Jini implementation from Sun is based on TCP and UDP, but other network protocols could be used as transports. Jini's major requirements of the network stack are reliable, stream-oriented communication and a multicast facility. Currently, UDP multicast is used for dynamic discovery and advertisement of Jini lookup services. Beyond this, most communication is point-to-point. TCP handles communication between clients/services and lookup services (after the initial discovery). Jini expects that clients and services either have a fixed, static IP address or can obtain an IP address through some external protocol such as DHCP. In that respect it is typical of service discovery protocols, with the exception of Universal Plug and Play (UPnP), whose specification contains a simple protocol for "inventing" a nonrouteable IP address. Except for custom protocols between a service proxy and the service itself, the particular transport and the multicast facility are completely encapsulated by Jini—programmers developing Jini clients and services don't need to lie awake at night, worrying about what they are. Thus typical Jini programmers require only passing familiarity with TCP and UDP to be effective, unless they need to develop socket-based protocols between service proxies and service backends.

There are pros and cons to Jini's language-centric approach. On one hand, a common language allows code mobility and very flexible definition of *service*. On the other hand, the need for standardization is taken to an extreme, since Jini requires of each device either that it run a Java Virtual Machine or that it associate with a device that can run a JVM on its behalf. Jini clients and services are fairly easy to design and code for someone familiar with Java (after reading the rest of this chapter, of course!), but for the Java neophyte, the situation is not as bright. Jini relies on other fairly complicated Java mechanisms, including RMI, and understanding these is important to fully understand Jini.

Jini Entities

There are three primary classes of entities in Jini: clients, services, and lookup services. Let's quickly review the nature of each. Lookup services are themselves a special type of service, and protocols are provided for clients (and other types of services, including lookup services) to discover them. Lookup services catalog available services, and all interactions between Jini clients and services initially involve one. Jini services advertise their availability by registering proxy objects with one or more lookup services. Clients query the lookup services for needed services and are provided with copies of the proxy objects for matching services. These proxy objects either implement the services entirely or serve as "remote controls" for communication with the backends of the services.

A service can also be a client. A telescope, say, might provide pictures to a PDA as a service, but look for printing services as a client. Jini clients and services are illustrated in Fig. 2-3. Since all advertisements and requests for service go through a lookup server in Jini, discovery of lookup services is critical. Clients and services either are statically configured with the location of lookup services or discover them dynamically or do both. Jini provides several protocols for discovery of lookup services, which will be explored in the upcoming section on clients, services, and registries.

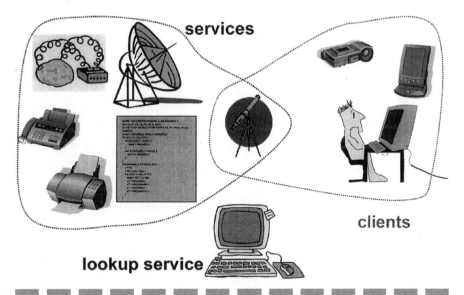

Figure 2-3
Members of a collection of Jini clients and services interact with the assistance of a Jini lookup service. Jini provides for very flexible service architectures—services can be completely software (e.g., the algorithmic service shown as computer code above) or combinations of hardware and software. In this example a telescope is both a client and a service, requiring printing services as a client, but providing images to other clients.

Figure 2-4 illustrates the discovery and registration process for Jini clients and services. In this example, a printing service that knows the location of a lookup service communicates with it and registers its proxy object, which will serve as a remote control for clients using the service.

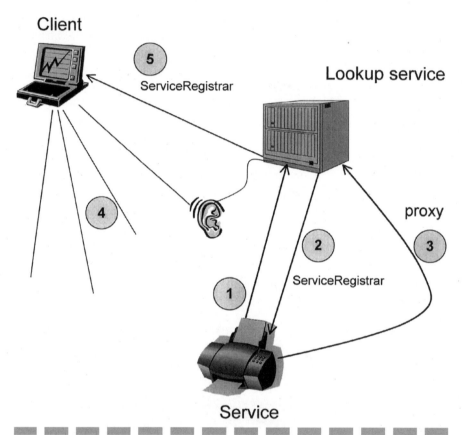

Figure 2-4

Jini's three entities are clients, services, and lookup services. In this example, a printing service that knows the location of a lookup service contacts the lookup service directly (1). In response, the lookup service provides a Java object that allows the service to interact with the lookup service (2). In (3), the printing service uses the object that was transferred, an instance of **ServiceRegistrar,** to register its proxy object. This object will allow clients to use the service. In (4), a client that does not know the location of any lookup services sends a multicast message to discover nearby lookup services. In (5), a lookup service that hears the multicast responds with an instance of ServiceRegistrar, as it did for the printing service. The client will then be able to use ServiceRegistrar methods to search for services and to obtain their proxy objects. Once the proxy object for a service is available to the client, it can control the service.

The client, who does not know the location of a lookup service, sends multicast messages to search for one. The lookup service observes the discovery attempt and establishes a TCP connection to the client using the port specified in the discovery multicast message. The lookup service then passes an instance of ServiceRegistrar, which will allow the client to search for services and obtain their proxy objects. Of course the devil is in the details, and that's why you'll enjoy reading the rest of this chapter.

In this chapter, a temporary file storage service and a GUI-based client for using the service will be used as examples (along with other bits and pieces of Java code). The file storage service allows clients to connect, establish an account, and then store and retrieve files. This type of service is useful for extending the storage capacities of resource-limited devices, for short-term backup, etc.

Leasing

Before we discuss Jini clients and services in detail, the leasing facilities in Jini are worth a look. Leasing is a well-known design tool in building resilient distributed software. The parties in a lease relationship, as in real life, are the grantor of the lease (the *lessor*) and the holder of the lease (the *lessee*). Each party has specific responsibilities with respect to the lease relationship and promises to abide by the terms of the lease. In general, the lessor makes some resource available for a specified amount of time, and the lessee uses the resource to some advantage during this time. The duration of the lease can be fixed, determined by one of the parties, or negotiated. A lease may be renewed if this is agreeable to both parties, and the lease may be canceled. Lease expiration is similar to an explicit cancellation, except that no communication is required.

A good example of leasing is found in the 4.4BSD Unix [3] variant of NFS, the Network File System. The NFS is a deliberately stateless protocol, in which servers do not maintain information about files currently being used by clients. This makes file locking difficult, however. In 4.4BSD, leases are used to enforce a form of file locking for NFS, without the messy stateful semantics of a "real" locking mechanism. It works as follows: Clients request read or read/write permission on files from an NFS server and are granted leases. For the duration of the lease, clients may access file blocks without worrying about stale data or conflicting updates. The leases require clients to renew or face revocation of consistency guarantees and permission to change blocks. As a result, design of the NFS server is simplified because, on a crash, it won't have to recover any state associated with file locking—it simply stays down long enough to allow all leases to expire and then resumes normal operation. Client crashes and network partitions are also handled easily, because in the case of a conflicting lease (say, the server wants to grant an outstanding lease to a different client, but the current lease is unreachable or dead), the server can simply wait for one lease to expire before granting the new one.

The previous example illustrates a key concept for leases in a distributed system: They simplify design. Crashes, neglect, and communication failures can be handled in a uniform manner.

Leases are used in Jini for a number of purposes, typically for maintenance of "persistent" state, of which there can be quite a bit. In Jini, lookup services maintain a set of proxy objects, one object for each registered service. Clients may register their interest in hearing about lookup services, or in the appearance or expiration of specific services. Jini entities can place objects in a JavaSpace. Each of these requires a Jini entity to remember interesting things about another entity. Over a long time, the amount of persistent state in the system multiplies. Partial failures could result in explicit cleanup being skipped, which would result in the accumulation of a substantial amount of electronic "junk." Jini could have been designed so that cleanup of stale service registrations, etc., was delegated to a human systems administrator; but for a large, long-running system such administration would be extremely inconvenient, if not completely impossible. Instead, leases are used.

With leases, maintenance of persistent state becomes much easier. Clients register their interest in hearing of new services in the context of a lease. Lookup services handle service registration in the same way. JavaSpaces lease storage. When leases are not renewed in a timely manner, information associated with the lessee (e.g., a proxy object registered by a service, or an object in a JavaSpace) can be discarded. Jini provides a basic leasing mechanism and some associated machinery to facilitate handling. These are discussed in the next two sections. I'll concentrate on the API here, deferring concrete code examples for leasing until we've established a bit more context.

Basic Leases

The basic Lease interface in Jini (Fig. 2-5) defines several constants associated with lease durations, including FOREVER, which is used to request a lease of the longest possible duration, and ANY, which

```
package net.jini.core.lease;
import java.rmi.RemoteException;
public interface Lease {
    long FOREVER = Long.MAX_VALUE;
    long ANY = -1;
    int DURATION = 1;
    int ABSOLUTE = 2;
    long getExpiration();
    void cancel() throws UnknownLeaseException, RemoteException;
    void renew(long duration) throws LeaseDeniedException,
        UnknownLeaseException, RemoteException;
    void setSerialFormat(int format);
    int getSerialFormat();
    LeaseMap createLeaseMap(long duration);
    boolean canBatch(Lease lease);
}
```

Figure 2-5
Lease.

states that the requestor of the lease will be satisfied with any duration. Unless there are compelling reasons to do otherwise, the use of Lease.ANY is recommended as a requested duration, because it allows the lessor maximum flexibility in assigning leases. Methods in the Lease interface allow one to determine the expiration time of a lease, cancel an existing lease, and renew a lease.

In general, the Jini leasing mechanism is based on durations of time rather than absolute time. This design decision is described in detail in the Jini specification, but the key observation is that although clocks in a distributed system are unlikely to be tightly synchronized, individual clocks tend to measure the *rate* at which time elapses fairly accurately. The single long parameter to renew() is a requested lease duration in milliseconds. If a renewal attempt succeeds, the lease expiration time becomes at most *duration* in milliseconds, but possibly less. Note that renew() has no return value—it is necessary to call getExpiration() to determine the actual expiration time. The return value from getExpiration() is an absolute time in milliseconds from January 1, 1970. This is meant as a convenience for the programmer, but it is important to keep in mind that conversion to a duration is necessary before one compares the return value of getExpiration() to a requested lease renewal period. This is most commonly done as follows:

```
long actuallease = lease.getExpiration() -
   System.currentTimeMillis();
```

Two constants defined in the Lease interface, DURATION and ABSOLUTE, are used with the serialization control methods, setSerial-Format() and getSerialFormat(). These control how the duration is stored in a serialized Lease. A call of setSerialFormat(DURATION) causes the remaining lease time to be stored as a duration from the serialization time, while setSerialFormat(ABSOLUTE) stores the remaining lease time as an offset from the local clock. The former should be used for a Lease to be migrated to another virtual machine, while the latter is appropriate when a Lease will be stored for eventual retrieval within the same virtual machine. The remaining methods, createLeaseMap() and canBatch(), are used to batch leases so they can be renewed or canceled as a group. Not all leases can be batched—under many circumstances, only leases from the same lessor can be grouped in a LeaseMap. Whether or not leases are batchable is implementation-specific, and so methods are provided to determine if leases are "compatible." These methods are rarely used in client/service code, because the LeaseRenewalManager utility can handle lease renewal. Thus we won't get into these methods here.

Three different exceptions can be thrown when calling Lease methods: LeaseDeniedException, UnknownLeaseException, and Remote Exception. LeaseDeniedException is thrown when a renewal or request for a lease is denied, for whatever reason. UnknownLeaseException is thrown when the supposed grantor of the lease has no knowledge of the lease being in effect, and RemoteException can be thrown if the particular Lease implementation has trouble communicating with a remote object.

Finally, note that Jini entities interested in being lessors must implement the Lease interface and handle lease renewals, cancellations, etc. Currrently there is little support in the specification for lease management on the lessor side, even though a Landlord and related classes are being shipped with the distribution. Since these are not yet officially part of the specification, they can't be covered here. Luckily there is help for the lessee in the form of utility classes that make automatic lease renewal less tedious. These are covered next.

Automatic Lease Renewal

A common pattern is for entities to hold leases until the leased resources are no longer needed, renewing the leases as frequently as necessary. To assist in automatic renewal of leases, Jini provides a utility class called the LeaseRenewalManager. This class handles lease renewal duties for an arbitrary number of leases on behalf of a Jini client or service. The LeaseRenewalManager API is shown in Fig. 2-6. Some of the methods have rather involved semantics, but a higher-level look suffices for all but the most complicated Jini needs, so that's what we'll take here. The reader is referred to the Jini specification for gory details.

```
package net.jini.lease;
public class LeaseRenewalManager {
    public LeaseRenewalManager() {...}
    public LeaseRenewalManager(Lease lease,
        long desiredExpiration, LeaseListener listener) {...}
    public void renewUntil(Lease lease, long desiredExpiration,
        long renewDuration, LeaseListener listener) {...}
    public void renewUntil(Lease lease, long desiredExpiration,
        LeaseListener listener) {...}
    public void renewFor(Lease lease, long desiredDuration,
        long renewDuration, LeaseListener listener) {...}
    public void renewFor(Lease lease, long desiredDuration,
        LeaseListener listener) {...}
    public long getExpiration(Lease lease)
        throws UnknownLeaseException {...}
    public void setExpiration(Lease lease, long desiredExpiration)
        throws UnknownLeaseException {...}
    public void remove(Lease lease)
        throws UnknownLeaseException {...}
    public void cancel(Lease lease) throws UnknownLeaseException,
        RemoteException {...}
    public void clear() {...}
}
```

Figure 2-6
LeaseRenewalManager.

There are two constructors and nine other public methods in LeaseRenewalManager. The no-argument constructor creates a quiescent LeaseRenewalManager, involved in no lease renewals. The other constructor creates a LeaseRenewalManager that initially manages a single lease, exactly as if the renewUntil() method had been called immediately after the no-argument constructor.

The renewUntil() method is used to add a single lease to the set of leases managed by a LeaseRenewalManager. There are two versions. The first accepts a lease to be managed, a desired expiration, a renewal duration, and an instance of LeaseListener. LeaseListeners are notified of important events such as a lease renewal failure or a lease expiration. (The LeaseListener interface is discussed below.) The other version of renewUntil() doesn't require that a renewal duration be specified—instead, a reasonable renewal duration is chosen that will avoid premature expiration of the lease. The desired expiration *desiredExpiration* should be the absolute local time at which the lease expires. Take note, in case it isn't obvious from the name of the parameter, that this is the *desired* expiration time. The lessor may not allow the lease to be extended through this time. If the lease expiration granted by the lessor is earlier than the time *desiredExpiration,* then the Lease RenewalManager will repeatedly attempt to renew the lease (as many times as necessary) until *desiredExpiration* is reached. If specified, the *renewDuration* should be the lease renewal duration, in milliseconds.

The renewFor() method behaves much as renewUntil() does, but it specifies a desired lease duration instead of an absolute desired expiration time. Lease.ANY is not useful as a duration for renewFor()—in fact, if Lease.ANY is specified, the lease expires immediately and is removed from the set of managed leases! The *lease* parameter for renewUntil() and renewFor() can refer to a Lease already managed by the Lease RenewalManager—in this case, the renewal information—and LeaseListener is updated.

In addition to the constructors and renewUntil()/renewFor(), several methods allow you to maintain the set of managed leases and the expiration times of individual leases.

- The getExpiration() and setExpiration() methods allow the desired expiration for a lease to be queried and set, respectively. Note that these methods operate on the desired lease times, not the actual lease times granted by the lessor.

- remove() deletes a particular lease from the set of managed leases, but it does *not* cancel the lease.

- cancel() has a similar effect, except that the lease is also canceled.

- clear() has the same effect as if remove() were called on each managed lease; namely, the leases are not canceled.

We will now return to the LeaseListener interface, used by the LeaseRenewalManager to deliver renewal failure events to the holder of a managed lease. If the *listener* argument for either renewUntil() or renewFor() is null, then no lease-related events are delivered. Otherwise, when a lease renewal fails or a lease is terminated, a Lease RenewalEvent is sent to the instance of LeaseListener. Lease renewals fail when the LeaseRenewalManager realizes that the lease has actually expired (before the next renewal event) and that a lease renewal will not be accepted. Lookup services cancel leases when a duplicate service registration is discovered, and this is a common reason for lease cancellation. Renewals can also fail when exceptions occur, preventing the renewals to the extent that the actual lease expiration time passes. The LeaseListener interface is straightforward, having only one method with the form

```
void notify(LeaseRenewalEvent e) { }
```

The LeaseRenewalEvent class has only three methods:

- getLease() returns the Lease object associated with the event.
- getExpiration() returns a long integer that expresses the expiration time of the associated lease.
- getException() returns a Throwable. This method allows diagnosis of the last lease renewal-related exception.

LeaseListener also has a subinterface called DesiredExpirationListener. It adds one additional method to LeaseListener:

```
void expirationReached(LeaseRenewalEvent e) { }
```

This method is called when a lease's desired expiration is reached and the LeaseRenewalManager has dropped the lease from the set of managed leases. Note that DesiredExpirationListeners also receive the renewal events that LeaseListeners receive.

Clients, Services, and Registries

Lookup Services

Lookup services, as we've mentioned, have several important responsibilities. They are catalogs of available services, and they store the proxy object associated with each registered service. They allow clients to find services of interest and download code to interact with the services. They also assign globally unique identifiers to services that register for the first time. Although Jini entities can be statically configured with the location of lookup services, at the core of Jini's dynamicity is its ability to power up with little or no static configuration (except possibly an IP address), obtain services, and do useful work. Thus Jini provides extensive support for dynamically discovering lookup services.

Jini provides a mechanism for segmenting lookup services into *groups*. Each lookup service has an associated (possibly empty) set of group names, which are simply string identifiers. The default group is the *public* group, which comes into play if no group identifiers are associated with a lookup service. When a lookup service advertises its availability, it includes the set of group identifiers in the advertisement. Similarly, when clients and services attempt to discover lookup services, a list of interesting group identifiers can be included. Only lookup services that are members of the specified groups will respond. This is a simple scheme, but it enhances the dynamic nature of Jini significantly. Clients can be configured with lists of group names rather than the *locations* of services. For example, a client might discover a lookup service in the group "Golden's Office" to find the printer on my desk, which has previously registered with this lookup service. If attempts to discover this lookup service fail, then "University of New Orleans Department of Computer Science" might be chosen as a group, which will reveal less-local lookup services in my department. Note that in either case, the specific machines running the lookup services need not be known (and thus a systems administrator is blissfully free to choose different machines to run the services without causing a nightmare!).

Jini lookup services use Java's Remote Method Invocation (RMI) facility for all interactions between either a client or service and a lookup service (after the initial discovery of the lookup service). These interactions are through an instance of ServiceRegistrar, obtained when a lookup service is discovered. Methods in ServiceRegistrar allow services to register their availability, and allow clients to search for needed services. Therefore we'll consider the mechanisms for discovering lookup services before we look at ServiceRegistrar in greater detail.

Finding Lookup Services. Since lookup services always handle the initial association between a client and service, finding them is critical for both Jini clients and services. There are three primary protocols associated with discovery and advertisement of lookup services in Jini:

- Multicast request protocol
- Multicast announcement protocol
- Unicast discovery protocol

Jini provides extensive class support for these protocols at two levels: with default implementations and with protocol utility packages that support the default implementations. Jini application developers will *not* code implementations of these protocols, but understanding how the protocols work is nonetheless important. We'll examine the protocols at a conceptual level before turning to a discussion of the Jini classes and interfaces that implement and support them.

MULTICAST REQUEST PROTOCOL. The *multicast request protocol* is used by clients and services to discover lookup services and is based on UDP multicast. Initially, a client looking for services—or a service wishing to advertise its availability—may not know the location of a Jini lookup service. To discover one within multicast range, the discovering entity first sets up a local TCP-based server. It then multicasts a UDP packet containing the port of this TCP server and the identities of any lookup services that are already known. Other fields in the packet identify the current protocol version (currently always 1) and a set of group identifiers that target specific groups of lookup services. The multicast packet is limited to 512 bytes to ensure that it fits within a single UDP datagram. If the number of known lookup services exceeds this limit, then an incomplete list is used to avoid violating the 512-byte limit. A set of groups that causes the byte limit to be exceeded is handled differently—in this case, multiple multicasts are performed so that the entire set of group identifiers is represented. Repetition prevents lookup services from falling through the cracks. The packet format for the multicast message is shown in Fig. 2-7. The multicast can be repeated periodically to ensure that new lookup services are contacted. The Jini specification recommends a 5-s delay between

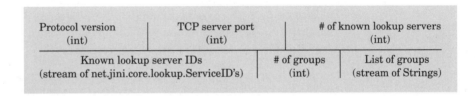

Protocol version (int)	TCP server port (int)	# of known lookup servers (int)
Known lookup server IDs (stream of net.jini.core.lookup.ServiceID's)	# of groups (int)	List of groups (stream of Strings)

Figure 2-7
Multicast request protocol packet format.

multicasts and a TTL (time to live) of 15. The specification requires that multicast address 224.0.0.85 and port 4160 be used for multicast discovery.

A lookup service receiving a discovery multicast that is not in the list of known lookup services and *is* in the set of groups connects to the TCP server on the discovering entity and transfers a Java object—an instance of ServiceRegistrar—which serves as a remote control for the lookup service. The ServiceRegistrar class provides methods for finding and registering services and is discussed in the sections on Jini clients and services later in this chapter. If the responding lookup service is indeed known to the discovering entity, but the lookup service's ID was not included in the multicast packet due to a space constraint, then the contact can be ignored. The multicast request protocol is illustrated in Fig. 2-8.

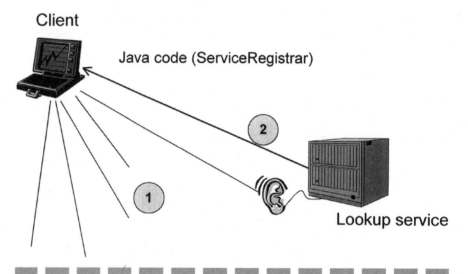

Figure 2-8

A client or service that does not know the location of Jini lookup services must go through several rounds of communication to find at least one lookup service before it can discover needed services. These rounds of communication comprise the *multicast request protocol*. In (1), the client sends a UDP multicast message to discover lookup services. The information that is multicast includes the identities of known lookup services and the groups in which the client wants to participate. It also includes the port on which the client will listen for responses. A lookup service hearing the multicast that is not one of the lookup services already known to the client, and that belongs to the proper groups, will establish a TCP connection to the client using the port specified in the multicast message (2). It passes an instance of ServiceRegistrar to the client over this TCP connection. This completes the multicast request protocol. The client can then invoke ServiceRegistrar methods to search for needed services.

MULTICAST ANNOUNCEMENT PROTOCOL. The *multicast announcement protocol* allows a lookup service to take an active role in advertising its presence. This protocol is particularly useful when lookup services are brought back up after maintenance or a crash, or are introduced into a system for the first time. It is based on a simple UDP multicast, containing contact and descriptive information for the advertising lookup service. The fields in the UDP datagram include the protocol version number (currently required to be 1), the host name and TCP port of the lookup service (used in contacting the lookup service via the unicast discovery protocol, discussed below), and a set of group identifiers (one for each of the groups of which the lookup service is a member. The packet format for the multicast message is shown in Fig. 2-9.

Protocol version (int)	Lookup server hostname (String)	Lookup server port (int)
Lookup server ID (net.jini.core.lookup.ServiceID)	# of groups (int)	List of groups (stream of Strings)

Figure 2-9
Multicast announcement protocol packet format

As in the multicast request protocol, the UDP datagram to be multicast is limited to 512 bytes. If all the groups of which a lookup service is a member cannot be accommodated in a single datagram, then multiple datagrams with disjoint sets of group names are multicast. The advertisement should be repeated periodically. While there is no mandated interval, the specification recommends a 120-s delay between announcements. The specification requires that multicast address 224.0.1.84 and port 4160 be used for advertisement of lookup services. The multicast announcement protocol is illustrated in Fig. 2-10.

UNICAST DISCOVERY PROTOCOL. The *unicast discovery protocol* allows Jini clients and services to contact a lookup service whose location is already known. This location might have been learned through the multicast request protocol or through some other source (e.g., a human operator). Since it is currently not feasible to do multicast discovery on a scale much beyond the local network, the ability to statically configure the locations of remote lookup services is very important.

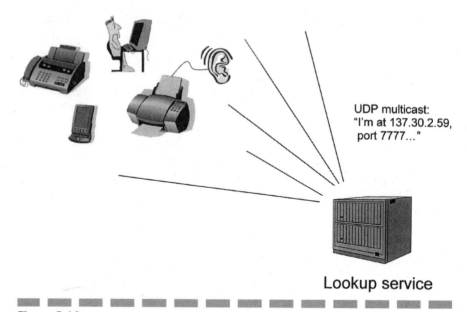

UDP multicast:
"I'm at 137.30.2.59,
port 7777..."

Lookup service

Figure 2-10

In the *multicast announcement protocol,* a lookup service periodically sends UDP multicasts to make other Jini entities aware of its presence. The multicast contains location information as well as the set of groups to which the lookup service belong.

The required contact information for unicast discovery includes the host name of the lookup service and the TCP port on which the lookup service is listening for connections. In the unicast discovery protocol, a Jini client or service initiates a TCP connection to the lookup service to begin the relationship. The lookup service responds with a ServiceRegistrar object, which provides methods for interacting with the lookup service. Once a ServiceRegistrar object is available, it can be used to search for services and to register services.

Jini Class Support for Discovery of Lookup Services. To register service availability or to discover needed services, a service or client must first locate one or more lookup services. That process relies on the advertisement and discovery protocols discussed above. Fortunately, Jini provides such extensive class support for discovery of lookup services, as we explained earlier in this chapter, that programmers rarely have to worry about the protocol details. Not all the related interfaces and classes are covered here, but the ones most often used by programmers are discussed. We will first discuss support for multicast discovery of lookup services, useful when the exact locations of lookup services are unknown. A subsequent section will address unicast lookup service discovery. The lookup service implementation provided in the Jini distribution, called reggie, implements the advertisement protocol.

MULTICAST LOOKUP SERVICE DISCOVERY.   The multicast discovery protocol is made available to clients and services through a number of classes and interfaces. These are used when the locations of lookup services are unknown and include the DiscoveryManagement, DiscoveryGroupManagement, and DiscoveryListener interfaces and the LookupDiscovery implementation of the first two of these interfaces. The DiscoveryManagement interface is shown in Fig. 2-11. There are five public methods:

- The addDiscoveryListener( ) takes a single argument, an instance of DiscoveryListener, which will receive notifications when new lookup services are discovered or old ones disappear. An implementation of the DiscoveryListener must be provided by a client or service wishing to use DiscoveryManagement.

- The removeDiscoveryListener( ) causes a particular DiscoveryListener to stop receiving notifications.

- The getRegistrars( ) method returns an array of ServiceRegistrar objects, one for each lookup service that has been discovered.

- The discard( ) method allows user code to "assist" in discovery management—a discovering entity should call discard( ) whenever a particular lookup service is determined to be unavailable, most likely as a result of a failed attempt to communicate with the lookup service. These communication failures will manifest themselves as RemoteExceptions when methods in an instance of ServiceRegistrar are called.

```
package net.jini.discovery;
public interface DiscoveryManagement {
    public void addDiscoveryListener(DiscoveryListener listener);
    public void removeDiscoveryListener(DiscoveryListener listener);
    public ServiceRegistrar[] getRegistrars();
    public void discard(ServiceRegistrar proxy);
    public void terminate();
}
```

Figure 2-11
The DiscoveryManagement interface.

- Finally, the terminate( ) method stops the discovery process completely.

The DiscoveryGroupManagement interface (Fig. 2-12) provides methods to constrain the discovery of lookup services to those belonging to select groups. The methods are straightforward.

- The setGroups() method takes a single argument, an array of group names, and constrains discovery to the specified groups.
- The addGroups() and removeGroups() allow the initial set of group names to be expanded and trimmed.
- Two constants are provided in the class: ALL_GROUPS and NO_GROUPS. These may be used in place of the array of group names for setGroups() and addGroups() methods.
- Finally, getGroups() returns the current set of group names as an array of Strings.

```
package net.jini.discovery;
public interface DiscoveryGroupManagement {
    public static final String[] ALL_GROUPS = null;
    public static final String[] NO_GROUPS = new String[0];
    public String[] getGroups();
    public void addGroups(String[] groups) throws IOException;
    public void setGroups(String[] groups) throws IOException;
    public void removeGroups(String[] groups);
}
```

Figure 2-12
The Discovery GroupManagement Interface.

LookupDiscovery (Fig. 2-13), an implementation of the DiscoveryManagement and DiscoveryGroupManagement interfaces, provides the default implementation of the multicast request protocol. It adds a single constructor that accepts an array of group names as a parameter. ALL_GROUPS should be specified if a Jini entity wants to discover all available lookup services in multicast range.

The following code fragment creates a LookupDiscovery instance charged with discovering lookup services belonging to all groups. After

```
package net.jini.discovery;
public class LookupDiscovery implements DiscoveryManagement,
DiscoveryGroupManagement {
    public static final String[] ALL_GROUPS =
        DiscoveryGroupManagement.ALL_GROUPS;
    public static final String[] NO_GROUPS =
        DiscoveryGroupManagement.NO_GROUPS;
    public LookupDiscovery(String[] groups) throws IOException {...}
}
```

Figure 2-13
The LookupDiscovery class.

creation of the LookupDiscovery instance, an event listener is registered to receive discovery-related events—since 'this' is specified as a target object for the event notifications, the calling object must implement the DiscoveryListener interface.

```
LookupDiscovery discover = null;

try{
    discover = new LookupDiscovery(LookupDiscovery.ALL_GROUPS);
}catch(Exception e){
    System.out.println("Error in lookup discovery: "+e.toString( ));
}//end catch

discover.addDiscoveryListener(this);
```

The DiscoveryListener interfaces are shown in Fig. 2-14. The basic DiscoveryListener provides two methods, discovered() and discarded(), which are called when new lookup services are discovered and previously discovered lookup services become unavailable, respectively.

An extension of DiscoveryListener called DiscoveryChangeListener is also available, which adds a method changed(). This method is called when a discovered lookup service experiences a change in group membership.

Extensive code illustrating DiscoveryListeners will be presented in the section on service registration, since ServiceRegistrar methods are used heavily and these have not yet been explored. For now, a simple example displays location information about each lookup service as it is discovered:

```
package net.jini.discovery;
public interface DiscoveryListener extends EventListener {
    public void discovered(DiscoveryEvent e);
    public void discarded(DiscoveryEvent e);
}

package net.jini.discovery;
    public interface DiscoveryChangeListener extends
DiscoveryListener {
    public void changed(DiscoveryEvent e);
}
```

Figure 2-14
The DiscoveryListener interfaces.

```
public void discovered(DiscoveryEvent e){

 /**
  * Gets ServiceRegistrar objects for all discovered lookup services
  */

 ServiceRegistrar[ ] registrars = e.getRegistrars( );
 System.out.println("Number of lookup services discovered:"
   +registrars.length);

 /**
  * Iterates through all discovered lookup services
  */

 for(int i=0; i < registrars.length; i++){
   ServiceRegistrar registrar = registrars[i];
   try{
     System.out.println("The registrar is at: "+
       registrar.getLocator( ).getHost( ));
   }catch(Exception ex){    /* an error occurred */ }

   // at this point, would typically search lookup service
   // for matching services using ServiceRegistrar methods...
   // ...and possibly register interest in getting events related
   // to matching services appearing in the future
 }//end for
```

Note that discovered() is passed an instance of DiscoveryEvent, shown in Fig. 2-15. Instances of DiscoveryEvent provide information about new lookup services, lookup services becoming unavailable, and lookup

```
package net.jini.discovery;
public class DiscoveryEvent extends EventObject {
    public DiscoveryEvent(Object source, Map groups) {...}
    public DiscoveryEvent(Object source,
    ServiceRegistrar[] regs) {...}
    public Map getGroups() {...}
    public ServiceRegistrar[] getRegistrars() {...}
}
```

Figure 2-15
DiscoveryEvent.

services changing their group membership. For discovery of lookup services, only the getRegistrars( ) and getGroups( ) methods are of interest. The getRegistrars( ) method returns a reference to an array of objects of type ServiceRegistrar, each corresponding to a lookup service that has been involved in an interesting event. The getGroups( ) method returns a Map between ServiceRegistrars and their associated groups. Plugging a ServiceRegistrar key into the Map returns an array of Strings, each element of which identifies a group to which the lookup service belongs.

UNICAST LOOKUP SERVICE DISCOVERY. Unicast discovery is used when the location of a lookup service is known and is supported by the LookupLocator class. For the public methods in this class, see Fig. 2-16. There

```
package net.jini.core.discovery;
public class LookupLocator implements Serializable {
    public LookupLocator(String host, int port) {...}
    public LookupLocator(String url)
    throws MalformedURLException {...}
    public String getHost() {...}
    public int getPort() {...}
    public ServiceRegistrar getRegistrar()
    throws IOException, ClassNotFoundException {...}
    public ServiceRegistrar getRegistrar(int timeout)
    throws IOException, ClassNotFoundException {...}
}
```

Figure 2-16
LookupLocator.

are two constructors, which differ in the way they specify the location of a lookup service. Both specify the IP address and TCP port where a lookup service is expected, but one uses separate IP and port parameters while the other uses a URL scheme. Jini URLs for lookup services look like "jini://nowhere.cs.uno.edu" or "jini://nowhere.cs.uno.edu:8888". The default TCP port is 4160 and is assumed if not specified.

There are also two versions of the getRegistrar() method in LookupLocator. These initiate the discovery process and return the ServiceRegistrar object associated with a lookup service. The first variety of getRegistrar() waits up to 60 s by default for a response from the lookup service. The second variety, which takes a single integer parameter *timeout,* blocks only for *timeout* milliseconds before giving up. Use of this class is straightforward. The following example obtains the ServiceRegistrar instance for a lookup service at IP "lookup.cs.uno.edu", port 4160. It does nothing further with the instance of ServiceRegistrar.

```
import net.jini.core.discovery.LookupLocator;
import net.jini.core.lookup.ServiceRegistrar;
import java.rmi.*;

public class UnicastLookup {

   public static void main(String[ ] args)
      throws java.rmi.RemoteException {
      System.setSecurityManager(new RMISecurityManager( ));
      new UnicastLookup();
   }

   public UnicastLookup() {
      LookupLocator discover = null;
      try{
         discover = new LookupLocator("lookup.cs.uno.edu", 4160);
         ServiceRegistrar reg = discover.getRegistrar();
      }
      catch(Exception e){
         System.out.println("Error in lookup discovery: "
            +e.toString( ));
      }//end catch
   }
}
```

Note that the unicast discovery protocol is not invoked until one of the getRegistrar() methods is called. Finally, the getHost() and getPort() methods simply return the host name and port specified in one of the LookupLocator constructors.

MANAGING UNICAST DISCOVERY OF MULTIPLE LOOKUP SERVICES. Jini provides an additional utility class that's helpful when unicast discovery will contact more than one lookup service. This class is called the LookupLocatorDiscovery (see Fig. 2-17). It implements the DiscoveryManagement interface, discussed in the section on multicast discovery (above) and also the DiscoveryLocatorManagement class, illustrated in Fig. 2-18.

```
package net.jini.discovery;
public class LookupLocatorDiscovery implements DiscoveryManagement,
   DiscoveryLocatorManagement {
       public LookupLocatorDiscovery (LookupLocator[] locators) {...}
       public LookupLocator[] getDiscoveredLocators() {...}
       public LookupLocator[] getUndiscoveredLocators() {...}
}
```

Figure 2-17
LookupLocatorDiscovery.

```
package net.jini.discovery;
public interface DiscoveryLocatorManagement {
       public LookupLocator[] getLocators();
       public void addLocators(LookupLocator[] locators);
       public void setLocators(LookupLocator[] locators);
       public void removeLocators(LookupLocator[] locators);
}
```

Figure 2-18
DiscoveryLocatorManagement.

Implementing DiscoveryManagement allows listeners to be added and removed, so applications can receive notifications when lookup services are successfully contacted. The DiscoveryLocatorManagement interface provides methods that allow particular lookup services to be added and removed from a contact list. The addLocators(), setLocators(), and removeLocators() methods each take an array of LookupLocators, each element of which defines contact information for a specific lookup service. These methods have obvious semantics, adding more locators, completely changing the list of lookup services to be contacted, and removing specific lookup services, respectively. In all cases, duplicate entries in the array of LookupLocators are silently ignored. If setLocators() is passed a null argument, the discovery of lookup services is interrupted until a subsequent call of setLocators() or addLocators() inserts lookup services into the contact list. The getLocators() returns the entire contents of the current contact list, regardless of whether the individual lookup services have been successfully contacted.

Unicast discovery begins immediately when a new instance of LookupLocatorDiscovery is created. The single constructor takes an array of LookupLocators, each element of which defines contact information for a single lookup service. The getDiscoveredLocators() and getUndiscoveredLocators() methods allow the sets of lookup services that have and have not been successfully contacted to be determined, respectively. Note that until one or more listeners is added via the methods associated with DiscoveryManagement, events corresponding to lookup service discovery will not be delivered.

MANAGING UNICAST AND MULTICAST DISCOVERY OF LOOKUP SERVICES.
Often clients and services will be interested in both contacting known lookup services (through the unicast discovery protocol) and discovering other lookup services dynamically (via the multicast discovery protocol). The utility class LookupDiscoveryManager (Fig. 2-19) implements all three lookup service management interfaces discussed above: DiscoveryManagement, DiscoveryGroupManagement, and DiscoveryLocatorManagement. As such, it provides the ability to specify the locations of known lookup services that should be contacted, to discover additional lookup services using multicast, constrained by a set of group names,

```
package net.jini.discovery;
public class LookupDiscoveryManager implements DiscoveryManagement,
  DiscoveryGroupManagement, DiscoveryLocatorManagement  {
    public LookupDiscoveryManager(String[] groups,
      LookupLocator[] locators, DiscoveryListener listener)
        throws IOException {...}
}
```

Figure 2-19
LookupDiscoveryManager.

```
package net.jini.discovery;
public interface DiscoveryLocatorManagement {
    public LookupLocator[] getLocators();
    public void addLocators(LookupLocator[] locators);
    public void setLocators(LookupLocator[] locators);
    public void removeLocators(LookupLocator[] locators);
}
```

Figure 2-20
DiscoveryLocatorManagement.

and allows listeners to be used to watch for interesting discovery-related events.

LookupDiscoveryManagement is illustrated in Fig. 2-20.

The constructor is the only new method added to the set of methods defined in the three interfaces. It accepts the set of groups that the discovered lookup services should belong to, an array of LookupLocators defining known lookup services, and a DiscoveryListener instance. The methods in DiscoveryManagement, DiscoveryGroupManagement, and DiscoveryLocatorManagement behave as described previously.

The following code snip instantiates a LookupDiscoveryManager that dynamically finds locally available lookup services and also discovers a known lookup service at "lookup.cs.uno.edu." The known lookup service is assumed to be listening on the default port, 4160. Lookup services belonging to any group are considered, and the calling code ("this") will receive events related to discovery.

```
LookupDiscoveryManager discovery =
  new LookupDiscoveryManager(LookupDiscovery.ALL_GROUPS,
    new LookupLocator("lookup.cs.uno.edu", 4160), this);
```

Controlling a Lookup Service: The ServiceRegistrar Interface

Discovery of lookup services allows a client or service to obtain instances of classes implementing the ServiceRegistrar interface. Methods in this class allow interaction between a Jini entity and a Jini lookup service. The ServiceRegistrar is a fairly complicated interface and requires careful

```
public interface ServiceRegistrar {
  ServiceRegistration register(ServiceItem item,
    long leaseDuration) throws RemoteException;
  Object lookup(ServiceTemplate tmpl) throws RemoteException;
  ServiceMatches lookup(ServiceTemplate tmpl, int maxMatches)
    throws RemoteException;
  int TRANSITION_MATCH_NOMATCH = 1 << 0;
  int TRANSITION_NOMATCH_MATCH = 1 << 1;
  int TRANSITION_MATCH_MATCH = 1 << 2;
  EventRegistration notify(ServiceTemplate tmpl, int transitions,
    RemoteEventListener listener, MarshalledObject handback,
    long leaseDuration) throws RemoteException;
  Class[] getEntryClasses(ServiceTemplate tmpl)
    throws RemoteException;
  Object[] getFieldValues(ServiceTemplate tmpl,.int setIndex,
    String field) throws NoSuchFieldException, RemoteException;
  Class[] getServiceTypes(ServiceTemplate tmpl, String prefix)
    throws RemoteException;
  ServiceID getServiceID();
  LookupLocator getLocator() throws RemoteException;
  String[] getGroups() throws RemoteException;
}
```

Figure 2-21
Public Interface ServiceRegistrar.

study, because it is arguably the most important in Jini. The public methods are shown in Fig. 2-21. Three of the methods are *generic,* in that they are not targeted specifically at clients or services. The getServiceID() method returns the lookup service's unique ID. The getLocator() method returns a LookupLocator (essentially, an IP address and port) that indicates how to contact this lookup service directly by using the unicast discovery protocol. The last of the generic methods is getGroups(), which identifies the groups to which the lookup service belongs.

The register() method in ServiceRegistrar is used by a service to register its availability. Most of the remaining methods are of interest only to clients seeking services. The register() method takes two parameters. The first parameter is a ServiceItem that encapsulates the proxy object for the service, its attributes, and ServiceID. The second parameter is a requested lease duration. A ServiceRegistration instance is returned. This object allows the registration of the service to be controlled and provides vital information concerning the actual lease duration and assigned ServiceID (find more information on ServiceID in the section on universally unique identifiers). The semantics of register() and the details of ServiceItem and ServiceRegistration are covered under "Service Registration."

Clients use the lookup() methods in ServiceRegistrar to find needed services. Both of the lookup() methods accept an instance of ServiceTemplate, which describes the services of interest. The first lookup() method returns a single Object, which is the proxy for a matching service. If no matching service is found, then null is returned. The other lookup() takes an additional parameter *maxMatches,* the maximum number of matches that should be returned. At most *maxMatches* matching service proxies are returned in a ServiceMatches object. ServiceMatches is just a wrapper for an *items* array (containing the proxies for the matching services) and *totalMatches,* the number of actual matches (which may exceed the length of the *items* array). If the proxy object for a particular service can't be deserialized, then the associated array element is null. Clients can also be notified when certain services become available or disappear. The notify() method allows a client to register interest in important transitions in the state of the lookup service. When services become available or disappear, a RemoteEventListener, specified by the client, is notified. Client interactions with lookup services, including the methods described briefly above and the getEntryClasses(), getFieldValues(), and getServiceTypes() methods, are revisited in some detail in "Searching for Services."

Jini Services

Services in Jini provide benefits to clients, such as file storage, printing, faxing, and access to high-performance computing facilities. In Jini, each service instance has an associated proxy object, which allows clients to interact with the service. A Jini service registers its proxy object with one or more lookup services to advertise its availability. A client can then obtain a copy of this proxy from a lookup service and can invoke methods in the proxy to interact with the service. Unlike in service discovery technologies such as SLP, a client associating itself with an advertised service does not merely obtain the necessary contact information for the service—a copy of the proxy object is *migrated* to the client. This offers some interesting possibilities for service implementation, as discussed in the introduction to this chapter. In general, clients neither know nor care about the actual implementation of the proxy object or how it communicates with the remote service. Clients simply retrieve a proxy object, invoke the methods, and enjoy the benefits. Clients need not know the actual location of the service, although in some cases it is important that the service reveal its physical location (e.g., in the case of a printing service—otherwise, how would you know where to pick up the printout?).

Entry Objects.   In addition to their remote implementation (if there is one) and proxy object (which may in fact implement the entire service), services can have associated attributes. Attributes provide additional information about services, such as specific capabilities, an e-mail address of the maintainer, pointers to documentation, or even an implementation of a GUI for the service. In Jini, attributes are classes that implement the empty (no methods) interface net.jini.core.entry.Entry. As we'll see later, Entry objects are also used in JavaSpaces. Implementing the Entry interface serves as a tag that causes a special object serialization technique to be used which is optimized for quick comparisons between Entry objects. This is useful since *template* Entry objects will be used to search for matching attributes associated with services and for discovering matching Entry objects in a JavaSpace. A pattern must be followed when Entry classes are created. The following rules must be observed:

■ Each Entry object must consist only of public object references.

■ Primitive types are not allowed in Entry objects.

■ A default constructor that takes no arguments must be supplied.

■ Object references that are final, static, or transient are ignored when Entry objects are transmitted.

When an Entry object is used as a template to match other Entry objects, a field in one Entry object matches the corresponding field in another if their serialized forms match or if the field in the template is null. The equals() method is *not* used for comparison. While it is permissible that fields in a class implementing the Entry interface have null values, it is not possible to search for such values, since a null value indicates a wild card. More on this when we discuss how clients search for services and then again when JavaSpaces are considered at the end of the chapter.

A number of classes implementing Entry are included in Jini. They address commonly needed service descriptions and reduce the need to create custom Entry classes. They include the following:

■ *Address.* This class represents the physical location of an entity. Fields include country, street, organization, etc.

■ *Comment.* This class contains a single String field suitable for generic commentary about a particular service.

- *Location.* This is a smaller-scale version of Address. Location contains building, floor, and room fields.

- *Name.* This class represents a human-readable name of a service. It contains a single String field.

- *ServiceInfo.* This describes the hardware particulars of a service and contains manufacturer, model, vendor, etc.

- *ServiceType.* This class contains information about the type of a service, including an icon representing the service, a short description of the service, and a name.

- *Status.* This is a base class useful for creating status objects, which reveal the current status of the service (e.g, ERROR, NORMAL).

- *StatusType.*

For complete details on these Entry classes and others, see the Jini specification and API documentation. The following code illustrates the definition of a custom attribute Environment, which describes whether an entity's environment allows smoking, requires ties, and has live music available. We will return to this example later when we explore the mechanisms that allow clients to discover needed services.

```
import net.jini.core.entry.Entry;
public class Environment implements Entry {

  public Boolean smoking=new Boolean(false);
  public Boolean tiereqired = new Boolean(false);
  public Boolean livemusic = new Boolean(true);
  public Environment() {}    // no argument constructor is required

  public Environment(boolean smoking, boolean tierequired,
     boolean livemusic) {
    this.smoking = new Boolean(smoking);
    this.tierequired = new Boolean(tierequired);
    this.livemusic = new Boolean(livemusic);
  }
}//end of class Environment
```

Universally Unique Identifiers.   Each Jini service should be assigned a universally unique identifier, either when the service is created or on its first contact with a lookup service. This identifier is an instance of net.jini.core.lookup.ServiceID, illustrated in Fig. 2-22, and is used in all future registrations.

```
public final class ServiceID implements Serializable {
    public ServiceID(long mostSig, long leastSig) {...}
    public ServiceID(DataInput in) throws IOException {...}
    public void writeBytes(DataOutput out)
    throws IOException {...}
    public long getMostSignificantBits() {...}
    public long getLeastSignificantBits() {...}
}
```

Figure 2-22
ServiceID

Assigning unique identifiers to services has several benefits: It allows clients to search for a specific service by its identifier, and it allows clients to determine when services registered on different lookup services are in fact the same. Since a client might remember a service's ID for an indefinite period of time, it is very important that Jini services use the same ID each time they register, even if the service is migrated to a new location (either physically or with a different network address). In fact, clients can be statically configured to look for *specific* services by ID. Unique identifiers are also assigned to lookup services themselves, and are used in the discovery and advertisement protocols to find unique lookup instances.

At first it might seem difficult to generate universally unique identifiers without global infrastructure, but in fact if an extremely slim possibility of duplication is permissible, the process is straightforward. Unique identifiers in Jini are 128 bits long and are created by using a combination of randomness, a measure of the current time, and in some cases a MAC address. The most significant 64 bits of the identifier are composed of a 32-bit *time_low* field, a 16-bit *time_mid* field, a four-bit *version* number, and a 12-bit *time_hi* field. The least significant 64 bits of the identifier are composed of a 4-bit *variant* field, a 12-bit *clock_seq* field, and a 48-bit *node* field. The variant is always 0x2. The version field can contain either 1 or 4. If the version field contains 1, then the *node* field is set to a 48-bit IEEE MAC address, the *clock_seq* field is set to a random number, and the three time fields are set to a 60-bit measure of elapsed time (in 100-ns increments) from midnight, October 15, 1582. If the version field is 4, then the other fields (except for variant) are set to a random number.

Unique service identifiers can be created automatically for a service when it initially registers with a lookup service. If the ServiceID field in the ServiceItem (discussed in "Service Registration") registered with a lookup service is null, then a unique identifier is created for the service. The JoinManager, which handles many of the tedious day-to-day chores of being a Jini service, can also arrange for a service identifier to be generated. JoinManager is also discussed a bit later. In other instances, e.g., for commodity devices such as printers and digital cameras, it may make more sense for the device to be preconfigured with a unique ID or to generate its own ID prior to registering with a lookup service. The ServiceID class can be used to generate unique identifiers (see Fig. 2-22).

Unfortunately the only constructor intended for creation of new ServiceIDs simply accepts most significant and least significant 64-bit quantities—it does *not* cook a ServiceID using the recipe given above. The reason is that a crucial portion of one ServiceID version is an IEEE MAC address, which is not accessible through any supplied classes. To access the MAC address, native code or user intervention is required. Of course, it is possible to create universally unique identifiers for *version* = 4 completely within Java, since the MAC address is not required. In addition to the constructor discussed above, the ServiceID class provides a constructor that reads a ServiceID from a DataInput stream. This ServiceID should have been written by a previous call to writeBytes(), which takes a DataOutput stream as a parameter. The final two methods, getMostSignificantBits() and getLeastSignificantBits(), allow the most and least significant 64 bits of an initialized ServiceID to be extracted.

Designing a Jini Service.   There are several issues involved in designing a new Jini service. These include designing a public interface that defines the operations available to a client via the service's proxy object, defining the client-to-service communication protocol, implementing the operations themselves (e.g., for a remote file storage service, methods to store and retrieve files, obtain listings of stored files, etc.), and being careful to be a good Jini service[1] all the while. The first is largely a standardization issue—since clients must have a copy of the interface that a service's proxy object implements, a standards body will have to define interfaces for common service types to enable widespread use of Jini.

Clients search for services based on a class or interface name, so the client will always have access to at least the interface which a service's proxy object implements. From the client perspective, the proxy object for a service, downloaded from a lookup service, appears to be a remote

---

[1] A Jini federation is an agnostic anarchy—there are no guard dogs, but deep thought about the effects of your own bad behavior generalized keeps you in line—sort of a Jini categorical imperative.

control for the service. The client executes methods and things happen. What actually occurs "behind" the methods in the proxy object is generally not the client's concern, but of course is a major concern to the implementer of the service. Most of the registration and leasing issues that a service must deal with can be easily automated by using supplied Jini classes, leaving the implementation of the service and proxy ↔ service backend communication as the major programming tasks. There are at least four different patterns for design of a service's proxy object:

■ The proxy object can be a complete implementation of the service. This is appropriate for software-only services. Services of this kind will exclusively use the client's computational resources. Examples range from simple services such as a mortgage payment calculator to a software suite that performs advanced 3D rendering services. An interesting point about software-only services is that the entity registering the service proxy may have very limited resources. For example, a software-only 3D rendering service's backend might have only enough resources to run Java, enabling it to register its proxy objects with lookup services. All the 3D rendering might be done on the client side.

■ The proxy object can be an RMI stub, so that all computation is actually performed in the virtual machine storing the remote object. In this case all proxy methods are executed in a remote object.

■ Some of the implementation of the service may be present in the proxy object, but the proxy communicates with the service backend through RMI.

■ A private, non-RMI protocol may be spoken between the proxy object and the remote service. This private protocol would most likely be based on UDP or TCP. Aside from communication with the remote service, some portion of the computation might be performed in the proxy object.

We will now consider an example to illustrate development of a Jini service. An RMI-based temporary file storage service (which is in the second category above) will be used. The file storage service provides methods for establishing or reestablishing a connection; for temporarily closing a connection; for permanently terminating a relationship (and thus deleting all stored files); for storing, retrieving, deleting, and listing stored files; and for retrieving a unique name of the service. The name() method offers a nice guarantee to clients—that two temporary file storage services are the same if and only if name() returns exactly the same value for each. The interface for this service is contained in StorageService.java, illustrated here:

```
package server;

import java.rmi.Remote;
import java.rmi.RemoteException;
import java.rmi.server.*;
import java.util.*;

/**
 * Description: Interface for Temporary File Storage Service.  This
 * defines the proxy object methods available to the
 * client.   Communication between proxy object on the client and the
 * service proper is through RMI.  All methods except name()
 * require a username and password to be supplied, for authentication.
 */

public interface StorageService extends Remote {
  // establish communication with the server.  If 'newAccount'
  // is true, then a new account is created, otherwise an
  // existing account is assumed.
  public boolean open(String username, String password,
    boolean newAccount) throws RemoteException;
  // close communication with the server, but don't destroy the account
  public boolean close(String username, String password) throws
    RemoteException;
  // close communication with the server, and destroy the account,
  // deleting all remotely stored files
  public boolean shutdown(String username, String password) throws
    RemoteException;
  // store the 'contents' of a file with name 'pathname'
  public boolean store(String username, String password,
    byte[] contents, String pathname) throws RemoteException;
  // return the contents of a stored file identified by 'pathname'
  public byte[] retrieve(String username, String password,
    String pathname)throws RemoteException;
  // remove a file with name 'pathname' from remote storage
  public boolean delete(String username, String password,
    String pathname) throws RemoteException;
  // return an array containing the pathnames of remotely stored files
  public String[] listFiles(String username, String password)
    throws RemoteException;
  // returns the hostname + serviceID of the temporary file storage
  // service.  We guarantee that this name is unique for distinct
  // storage services.
  public String name() throws RemoteException;
}
```

To use a file storage service, clients are required to have access to the interface above. The clients typically know nothing about the implementation of the service, however. A sample implementation of this interface is provided below (contained in StorageServiceImpl.java). Commentary on this code is at a high level, since there are few Jini-specific issues in the implemention of the methods in the proxy. Most of the Jini-specific code is contained in the backend, which handles discovery of lookup services, registration of the proxy object, and leasing issues. A subsequent section discusses the backend of the storage service example.

```java
package server;

import java.util.*;
import java.io.*;
import java.net.*;
import java.rmi.*;
import java.rmi.server.UnicastRemoteObject;
import net.jini.core.lookup.ServiceID;

/**
 * Description: Implementation of StorageService interface.
 */

public class StorageServiceImpl extends UnicastRemoteObject
  implements StorageService, Serializable{

  private Users members = null;       // the list of users
  private String hostName = null;     // the hostname of this service
  public ServiceID id = null;         // service ID for this service
```

The proxy is provided with a ServiceID and the host name of the machine running the service so it can create a unique, human-readable name that identifies this service. The users argument contains a list of users who already have accounts and the files they are currently storing.

```java
  /**
   * Creates an implementation of this StorageService interface with
   * the given hostname and the given list of users.
   */

  public StorageServiceImpl(ServiceID id, String hostName,
    Users users) throws RemoteException{
    this.id = id;
    this.hostName = hostName;
    this.members = users;
  }
```

Before a user can interact with a file storage service, it must open an account, supplying a user name and password. The account can be preexisting or a new account. The value of the boolean parameter determines whether a brand-new account must be created.

```
/**
 * This is the implementation of the method that opens/creates
 * an account for the user with the given username and
 * password. The boolean indicates whether or not the account is
 * new.
 */

public boolean open(String username, String password,
  boolean newAccount){
  boolean ok = false;

  // A new account has been requested.
  System.out.println("Remote OPEN invocation from " + username);
  if(newAccount && ! members.exists(username) &&
    ! username.equals("")) {
    members.addUser(new User(username,password));
    ok = true;
  }//end if(newAccount)
  else{//if it is an existing member
    if(members.verify(username, password)) {
      ok = true;
    }//end if
  }//end else
  return ok;
}
```

The service provides two mechanisms for severing connectivity with a client. The close( ) method terminates the connection but does not delete the user's account. Upon a subsequent rediscovery of the service, the user can use the open( ) method to reestablish communication, having lost no stored files. This method is included in the interface so that additional processing might be done when a user disconnects (perhaps for time or storage-based billing) but currently just returns true if the authentication succeeds.

```
/**
 * Stop communicating with client but don't delete the account.
 * The client is free to connect with the same username and
 * password later to resume using the file storage service.
 */

public boolean close(String username, String password ){
  System.out.println("Remote CLOSE invocation from " + username);
  if (members.verify(username, password)) {
```

```
      return true;
    }//end if
    else {
      return false;
    }//end else
  }
```

The shutdown() method also terminates connectivity, but deletes the user's account (including all stored files).

```
/**
 * Stop communicating with the client, but also terminate the
 * user's account.   All files associated with this user are
 * deleted.
 */

public boolean shutdown(String username, String password ){
  System.out.println("Remote SHUTDOWN invocation from "
    + username);
  if (members.verify(username, password)) {
    members.removeUser(username);
    return true;
  }//end if
  else {
    return false;
  }//end else
}
```

The store( ) method allows a user to store a file on the storage service. The file is represented by a path name argument and a byte array. The User class handles file storage issues for a particular user.

```
/**
 * Stores the 'contents' of a file with the given 'pathname'
 * for a given user 'username'.   Return value indicates success
 * of the operation.
 */

public boolean store(String username, String password,
  byte contents[], String pathname) {
  System.out.println("Remote STORE invocation from " + username);
  if (members.verify(username, password)) {
    User user = members.getUser(username);
    user.putFile(pathname, contents);
    return true;
  }//end if
  else {
```

```
      return false;
  }//end else
}
```

The retrieve() method complements store() by allowing a user to retrieve a stored file. The file contents are returned as a byte array.

```
/**
 * Retrieves and returns the contents of a file specified by
 * the given 'pathname'.  null is returned if the
 * operation fails.
 */

public byte[] retrieve(String username, String password,
   String pathname){
   System.out.println("Remote RETRIEVE invocation from "
     + username);
   if (members.verify(username, password)) {
     User user = members.getUser(username);
     return user.getFile(pathname);
   }//end if
   else {
     return null;
   }//end else
}
```

The following allows a user to permanently delete a stored file by referencing its path name.

```
/**
 * Deletes the given file from the list of files available for
 * this user.  Return value indicates success of the operation.
 */

public boolean delete(String username, String password,
   String pathname){
   System.out.println("Remote DELETE invocation from " + username);
   if (members.verify(username, password)) {
     User user = members.getUser(username);
     user.removeFile(pathname);
     return true;
   }//end if
   else {
     return false;
   }//end else
}
```

The listFiles( ) method provides a rudimentary directory facility. The list of path names of files currently stored for the specified user is returned as an array of Strings.

```java
/**
 * Returns an array of Strings containing the pathnames of
 * the files currently stored for the specified user.  null
 * is returned if the operation can't be completed.
 */

public String[] listFiles(String username, String password){
  System.out.println("Remote LISTFILES invocation from " + username);
  if (members.verify(username, password)) {
    User user = members.getUser(username);
    return user.listFiles( );
  }//end if
  else {
    return null;
  }//end else
}
```

The name() method allows a client to obtain a unique name for this service instance. The name is human-readable, in that the initial portion is the host name of the machine executing the file storage service.

```java
/**
 * Returns a unique name for this service
 */

public String name(){
  return (this.hostName + " " + id);
}

/**
 * We're equal to another StorageServiceImpl iff our ServiceIDs
 * are the same
 */

public boolean equals(Object obj) {
  if (obj instanceof StorageServiceImpl) {
    StorageServiceImpl other = (StorageServiceImpl)obj;
    return id.equals(other.id);
  }
  return false;
}

public int hashCode() {
  return id.toString().hashCode();
}
```

```
}//end of class StorageServiceImpl
```

The User and Users classes are presented here for completeness. They contain no Jini-specific code or advanced Java features and are (hopefully) self-documenting.

```java
package server;

import java.util.*;
import java.io.*;

/**
 * Description:Representation of a single user's account.
 * Contains authentication information and all stored files.
 */

public class User {

    private String username   = null;   // the member's username
    private String password   = null;   // the member's password
    // a collection of the member's files stored as a
    // hashtable, with pathnames as keys and file contents as
    // targets
    private Hashtable files    = null;

    /**
     * Creates a new user of the service with
     * the given username and password and an
     * empty list of files.
     */

    public User(String uname, String passwd){
      this.username = uname;
      this.password = passwd;
      files = new Hashtable( );
    }

    /**
     * Returns the username of this user
     */

    public String getUsername( ){
      return username;
    }

    /**
     * Returns the password of this user
     */
```

```java
public String getPassword( ){
  return password;
}

/**
 * Changes the username of this user
 */

public void changeUsername(String newUsername){
  username = newUsername;
}

/**
 * Changes the password of this user
 */

public void changePassword(String newPassword){
  password = newPassword;
}

/**
 * Returns an array of string containing the pathnames
 * of all files currently stored for this user.
 */

public String [] listFiles( ){
  Enumeration e = files.keys();
  String list[] = new String[files.size()];
  int i=0;
  while (e.hasMoreElements()) {
    list[i++] = (String)e.nextElement();
  }
  return list;
}

/**
 * Adds the file to the list of the user's files. If the
 * file already exists then the older version is replaced
 * by the new one.
 */

public void putFile(String path, byte [] contents){
  files.put(path, contents);
}

/**
 * Returns the contents of stored file 'path'.
 */
```

```
    public byte [] getFile(String path) {
      return (byte [])files.get(path);
    }

    /**
     * Removes a file from the list of the
     * user's files.
     */

    public void removeFile(String path) {
      files.remove(path);
    }

    /**
     * Removes all files
     */

    public void removeAll() {
      files.clear();
    }

}//end of class User
```

The Users class is shown below. An instance of Users handles the entire collection of users who have accounts on a temporary file storage service.

```
package server;

import java.util.*;
import java.io.*;

/**
 * Description:Collection of all users with accounts on the
 * temporary file storage service.
 */

public class Users extends Hashtable {

    /**
     * Creates a list of users initially empty.  Hashtable is
     * synchronized, so don't have to worry about concurrent
     * access.
     */

    public Users() {
      super();
    }
```

```
/**
 * Add a user
 */

public void addUser(User user) {
  put(user.getUsername(), user);
}

/**
 * Given a username and password, this method authenticates
 * the user by  verifying that the username exists and
 * has a matching password
 */

public boolean verify(String uname, String passwd){
  User user = (User) get(uname);
  if (user == null || ! user.getPassword().equals(passwd)){
    return false;
  }
  else {
    return true;
  }//end if
}

/**
 * Given a username, this method checks to see if the
 * username is already in use.
 */

public boolean exists(String uname) {
  return containsKey(uname);
}

/**
 * Returns the User object associated with username.
 */

public User getUser(String uname) {
  return (User) get(uname);
}

/**
 * Deletes a user's account (which also deletes all files stored
 * for this user)
 */

public void removeUser(String uname) {
  User user = (User) get(uname);
```

```
    if (user != null) {
      user.removeAll();
      remove(uname);
    }//end if
  }


}//end of class
```

Service Registration. Services must be registered with a lookup service before they become available to clients. Registration is performed via the register() method of ServiceRegistrar, which accepts a ServiceItem and requested lease duration and returns a ServiceRegistration object. The ServiceRegistration instance is subsequently used to manipulate the registration. Before we examine register() further, the ServiceItem class, shown in Fig. 2-23, and ServiceRegistration interface, shown in Fig. 2-24, require a closer look.

ServiceItem describes a service instance to a lookup service. The constructor for ServiceItem takes a ServiceID, which uniquely identifies the service, the service's proxy object, which is downloaded by clients to interact with the service, and an array of Entry objects, which describe the service's attributes. If this is the first time that the service has registered with any lookup service, then ServiceID in the ServiceItem should be set to null. This causes the lookup service to generate a unique ServiceID for the service, which is returned in an instance of ServiceRegistration.

The getServiceID() method of the ServiceRegistration instance can be used to determine the service's new ServiceID if a null ServiceID

```
public class ServiceItem implements Serializable {
    public ServiceItem(ServiceID serviceID,Object service,
        Entry[] attributeSets) {...}
    public ServiceID serviceID;
    public Object service;
    public Entry[] attributeSets;
}
```

Figure 2-23
ServiceItem.

```
public interface ServiceRegistration {
  ServiceID getServiceID();
  Lease getLease();
  void addAttributes(Entry[] attrSets) throws UnknownLeaseException,
    RemoteException;
  void modifyAttributes(Entry[] attrSetTemplates, Entry[] attrSets)
    throws UnknownLeaseException, RemoteException;
  void setAttributes(Entry[] attrSets) throws UnknownLeaseException,
    RemoteException;
}
```

Figure 2-24
ServiceRegistration.

was passed; it is the responsibility of the service to save the ServiceID for use in future registrations. The getLease() method in ServiceRegistration allows a service to determine the actual lease duration of its registration. This value is always less than or equal to the value requested in the registration request. The modifyAttributes() and setAttributes() methods allow the attributes associated with a service to be modified after the initial registration. Since ServiceRegistration is only an interface, each lookup service must provide an implementation.

We'll begin examining the class StorageServiceServer, which contains the server-side guts of the temporary file storage service. This class is responsible for discovering lookup services, registering the proxy object, and handling leases. The header of the class looks like this:

```
package server;

import net.jini.discovery.LookupDiscovery;
import net.jini.discovery.DiscoveryListener;
import net.jini.discovery.DiscoveryEvent;
import net.jini.core.discovery.LookupLocator;
import net.jini.core.lookup.ServiceRegistrar;
import net.jini.core.lookup.ServiceItem;
import net.jini.core.lookup.ServiceRegistration;
import net.jini.core.lookup.ServiceID;
import net.jini.core.lease.Lease;
import net.jini.lease.LeaseRenewalManager;
import net.jini.lease.LeaseListener;
```

```
import net.jini.lease.LeaseRenewalEvent;
import java.rmi.*;
import java.net.*;
import java.io.*;

/**
 * Description: Main Temporary File Storage Server class.
 * Handles proxy registration, leasing, etc.
 */

public class StorageServiceServer implements DiscoveryListener,
  LeaseListener {

  // proxy object, interface to client
  private StorageServiceImpl storage = null;
  // renews leases
  private LeaseRenewalManager leaseManager = null;
  // list of members
  private Users members = null;
  // unique identifier for this service
  private ServiceID id = null;
  // registered at each discovered lookup service
  private ServiceItem item = null;
```

The first step in initializing the file storage service's backend is to instantiate a security manager. Security issues are deferred until a later section, but all nontrivial Jini applications will typically register a security manager as an initial step. The main() method then creates an instance of StorageServiceServer.

```
  /**
   * The server first sets a security manager.
   */

  public static void main(String[ ] args){
    System.setSecurityManager(new RMISecurityManager( ));
    new StorageServiceServer( );
  }

  /**
   * The server creates the lookup discovery object that
   * initiates the discovery of different lookup service locators.
   * The server also listens for future locators by implementing
   * the DiscoveryListener interface.
   */

  public StorageServiceServer() {
```

```
// for simplicity, we don't store the list of users across
// invocations—that is, when the server is taken down,
// all accounts and files are deleted (thus  "temporary"
// file storage really means it!).  A more elaborate
// implementation would  retrieve the previous list of user
// accounts here.
```

The Users class maintains information about the clients of the file storage service. This class was presented earlier in this section.

```
members = new Users( );
```

Next a LeaseRenewalManager instance is created. This object will handle renewing the leases on our registrations with discovered lookup services. The LeaseRenewalManager class was discussed earlier in this chapter in the section on leasing.

```
leaseManager = new LeaseRenewalManager( );
```

The following code determines the host name of the machine executing the service. This is used in conjunction with the ServiceID of the service to produce a unique, human-friendly name for the service.

```
String host = null;
try{
  InetAddress address = InetAddress.getLocalHost( );
  host = address.getHostName( );
}catch(Exception e){
  System.out.println("Localhost not found "+e.toString( ));
  System.exit(1);
}//end catch
```

If this is the first time the service has been executed on this machine, then no ServiceID is known. Before assuming we should use null for a ServiceID when we register (and thus be granted a new ServiceID), we try to read a previously assigned ServiceID from a known location in the local file system. The ServiceID constructor that takes an input stream as a parameter is used:

```
// Try to retrieve our ServiceID from the same directory where
// we started—if we can't, then this is our first invocation
// and we'll get assigned one shortly.

try {
  FileInputStream is = new FileInputStream("SERVICEID");
  id = new ServiceID(new DataInputStream(is));
```

```
    is.close();
}catch (Exception e) {
  id = null;
}// end catch
```

Next an instance of the proxy object for the temporary file storage service is created. This instance will be registered with all discovered lookup services once it is wrapped inside a ServiceItem instance. No attributes are registered.

```
try{
   storage = new StorageServiceImpl(id, host, members);
}catch(RemoteException e){
   System.out.println("Error in creating the service "
     +e.toString( ));
   System.exit(1);
}//end catch
```

The following creates the ServiceItem that is passed to each lookup service. Either the ID is still null because we failed to read a ServiceID from disk, or it contains our unique identifier:

```
// Create the ServiceItem we'll register at each discovered
// lookup service.  null == we have no attributes to register.
item = new ServiceItem(id, storage, null);
```

Now an instance of LookupDiscovery is created to dynamically discover local lookup services. LookupDiscoveryManager is used because we have no information on the locations of known lookup services. LookupDiscovery.ALL_GROUPS signifies that we don't care to which groups the discovered lookup services belong. Once the LookupDiscovery instance has been created, we add ourselves as a listener for discovery-related events. Each time we are notified of discovery of a lookup service, the proxy object will be registered. To receive discovery events, we must implement the DiscoveryListener interface, which requires that a discovered() method be provided, through which events will be delivered. The implementation of discovered() and the rest of the StorageServiceServer appear shortly, after we have discussed the register() method of ServiceRegistrar.

```
LookupDiscovery discover = null;

try{
   discover = new LookupDiscovery(LookupDiscovery.ALL_GROUPS);
}catch(Exception e){
```

```
    System.out.println("Lookup discovery not started"
        + e.toString( ));
    System.exit(1);
}//end catch

discover.addDiscoveryListener(this);
}
```

The semantics of the register() method in ServiceRegistrar are now discussed in detail. The following description assumes that the parameters passed to register() are *item* (a ServiceItem) and *lease* (a requested lease duration). The lookup service acts on a registration request via the register() method in the following way. If item.serviceID is null, then the lookup service compares item.service (the proxy object for the service) with all other registered proxy objects. If there is no match, then a new ServiceID is generated and returned in the ServiceRegistration instance. If there is a match, then the matching service's lease is canceled, the proxy object is removed, and the new service is assigned the deleted service's ServiceID. Again, this ServiceID is returned in the ServiceRegistration instance.

If item.serviceID is not null, then this service has registered previously with one or more lookup services. The ServiceID in item contains the value previously assigned to the service. If the lookup service currently has a service registered under this ServiceID, then that service's lease is canceled, the service's proxy object is deleted, and the new service is registered. For both new and reregistrations, the registration is guaranteed by the lookup service implementation to be persistent across lookup service restarts while the lease is in effect. Finally, the lookup service is free to adjust or ignore the requested lease time, but the actual lease duration must not exceed the requested duration. The use of register() is illustrated concretely below.

The discovered() method in the DiscoveryListener interface, shown below, is called whenever a lookup service is discovered. This is our chance to register the ServiceItem *item,* which contains our service proxy.

It is possible that a number of lookup services have been discovered and are being reported in a single event. The discovered() method retrieves the array of ServiceRegistrars associated with this event; then for each ServiceRegistrar object, a register() call is made.

```
/**
 * One of the methods in the DiscoveryListener interface.
```

```
 * This method is invoked every time a lookup service is
 * discovered.  This is the perfect opportunity to register
 * our service.
 */

public void discovered(DiscoveryEvent e){
  ServiceRegistrar[ ] registrars = e.getRegistrars( );
  System.out.println("Number of lookup servers found:"
    +registrars.length);
```

We ask for a fairly small lease because it's easier to debug the service in this way. Ordinarily it is a bad practice to ask for very short leases, because lookup services maintain stable state to survive crashes. High lease renewal activity can result in substantial load on the lookup services; therefore before deployment it's a good idea to adjust the lease time if it was deliberately kept short during development.

```
// Iterates through all discovered lookup services

for(int i=0; i < registrars.length; i++){
  ServiceRegistrar registrar = registrars[i];
  try{
    System.out.println("Service Registrar found at:"
      +registrar.getLocator().getHost( ));
  }catch(RemoteException ex){}

  ServiceRegistration receipt = null;
  // Attempts to register the ServiceItem created above with
  // the lookup server and begs the lookup server for a short
  // lease.  The  lease duration could have been
  // Lease.FOREVER, but for debugging purposes it's easier
  // if it's short.
  try{
    receipt = registrar.register(item, 15000L);
```

Once the registration is performed, if a unique ServiceID wasn't available before, now one is assigned, and it is written to the local file system for safekeeping. Should this storage fail, the service silently ignores the error.

```
  // if we didn't have a unique service ID before, we do
  // now...try to write it to disk
  if (id == null) {
    id = receipt.getServiceID();
    storage.id = id;
    try {
```

```
          FileOutputStream os = new FileOutputStream("SERVICEID");
          id.writeBytes(new DataOutputStream(os));
          os.close();
        }catch (Exception ignore) {
          /* if we can't store it, well...  */
        }
      }//end if
    }catch(RemoteException ex){
      System.out.println("Error in receiving receipt "
        +ex.toString( ));
    }//end catch
```

At this point, the LeaseRenewalManager instance is assigned the
duty of renewing the registration on this lookup service. Then the whole
process is repeated for the next discovered lookup service.

```
  // The ServiceRegistration object obtained above is
  // queried for the lease and a lease manager is used
  // to renew our lease as long as we're around.
  leaseManager.renewUntil(receipt.getLease( ),
    Lease.FOREVER, 10000L, this);
 }//end for
}

/**
 * This method is invoked when a lookup service has left or
 * has "died". The lookup server is removed from the list of
 * locators available and there are no more attempts made at
 * registering the service to the discarded server.
 */

public void discarded(DiscoveryEvent e){ }

/**
 * This method is invoked whenever there is an error in renewing
 * the lease of the service at the lookup service or if the
 * lease of a service has expired because it was not renewed.
 * The latter could happen if a duplicate service is registered
 * at a lookup service—the lease of the earlier registrant is
 * terminated in favor of the "new" version of  the service.
 */

public void notify(LeaseRenewalEvent e){
   System.out.println("Lease Expired : "+e.toString( ));
}

}//end of class StorageServiceServer
```

A client to use the storage service will be discussed shortly, but first a few words on being a good Jini citizen, if you happen to be born a service.

Well-Behaved Jini Services.   The Jini specification outlines a number of responsibilities for a well-designed Jini service. Some of these qualities are present in the temporary file storage service described in the previous section, but there is room for improvement. These responsibilities comprise the Jini Join Protocol and address the "good behavior" aspect of being a Jini service. They include maintaining persistent state across restarts, updating the set of lookup services with which the service is registered in a consistent fashion, and taking steps to avoid "melting down" the network. A full description of these responsibilities appears in the Jini Technology Core Platform Specification, under the section "The Join Protocol." The state that a service must maintain includes the following items:

■ *The service's unique identifier.* As discussed earlier, this may be obtained from a lookup service on the first registration; it may be statically configured; or it may be generated by the service before its first registration.

■ *A possibly empty set of lookup services with which the service should register.* For some services, lookup services will always be discovered dynamically, while for others this statically configured list will be used in conjunction with multicast discovery.

■ *A set of attributes that describe the service.* Service Entry objects were discussed earlier in this section.

■ *A set of groups in which the service intends to participate.*

The set of consistency requirements outlined in the specification ensures that compliant sevices will present a consistent view of themselves to all discovered lookup services. First, a service is required to register with each discovered lookup service using the same ServiceID. This ensures that clients using multiple lookup services can determine whether service instances are in fact the same. The specific order of registrations is not mandated; e.g., a service can register with discovered lookup services and those it is statically configured to register with in any order. But if changes are made to the set of groups that a service participates in or to the values of a service's attributes, then these situations must be handled in a consistent fashion. If changes to these service characteristics are made, then the service is required to adjust the set of lookup service registrations and either unregister or register with additional lookup services as appropriate. Changes to the set of attributes for a service must be propagated to *all* the lookup services with which a service has registered. The service is required to renew its leases until it is removed from duty. If lookup services on the statically configured list become unavailable, the service should periodically try to renew these registrations.

Finally, a service should pause for a random period of time on initialization before discovering or contacting lookup services. This prevents a network meltdown in the event that a large network of Jini entities is restarted (e.g., after a power failure). The specification recommends a maximum pause duration on the order of 15 s. These requirements would seem to make creating a properly behaved Jini service quite tedious, but the Jini architects foresaw this concern and provided substantial class support (in the form of the JoinManager) to make the job much easier.

The JoinManager utility class, a part of the standard Jini distribution, brings lease renewal, lookup service discovery, registration, attribute modification, and ServiceID assignment under centralized control. In short, JoinManager makes being a well-behaved Jini service much easier. The JoinManager class is shown in Fig. 2-25.

Before the instantiation of a JoinManager instance, some initial preparation must be done—this is so because JoinManager relies heavily on the services of other utility classes that provide lease and lookup service management support. The first constructor requires five parameters and is used when the service does not have a unique ServiceID. This is commonly the case for a service that has never before registered in a Jini network. The first and second parameters are the service's proxy object and set of Entry (attribute) objects, respectively. If the attrSets parameter is null, then no attributes are associated with the service. The third parameter, an instance of ServiceIDListener, is used to assist the service in obtaining a ServiceID. The ServiceIDListener interface has a single public method that must be implemented. This method is called when a ServiceID is assigned by a lookup service. A sample implementation of ServiceIDListener is given below. Typically the serviceIDNotify() method will take steps to save the ServiceID in nonvolatile storage. The nature of the storage is service-dependent; e.g., it might be stored on disk, in nonvolatile RAM, or on some other media. In the following example, as in the implementation of the temporary file storage service's backend, the ServiceID is simply stored in a local file.

```
public class GotServiceID implements ServiceIDListener {
  public void serviceIDNotify(ServiceID serviceID) {
```

```
package net.jini.lookup;
public class JoinManager {
  public JoinManager(Object obj, Entry[] attrSets,
    ServiceIDListener callback,
    DiscoveryManagement discoveryMgr,
    LeaseRenewalManager leaseMgr) throws IOException {...}
  public JoinManager(Object obj, Entry[] attrSets,
    ServiceID serviceID, DiscoveryManagement discoveryMgr,
    LeaseRenewalManager leaseMgr) throws IOException {...}
  public DiscoveryManagement getDiscoveryManager() {...}
  public LeaseRenewalManager getLeaseRenewalManager() {...}
  public ServiceRegistrar[] getJoinSet() {...}
  public Entry[] getAttributes(){...}
  public void addAttributes(Entry[] attrSets) {...}
  public void addAttributes(Entry[] attrSets, boolean checkSC) {...}
  public void setAttributes(Entry[] attrSets) {...}
  public void modifyAttributes(Entry[] attrSetTemplates,
    Entry[] attrSets) {...}
  public void modifyAttributes(Entry[] attrSetTemplates,
    Entry[] attrSets, boolean checkSC) {...}
  public void terminate() {...}
}
```

Figure 2-25
JoinManager.

```
// store unique ID in a local file "SERVICEID"
try {
  FileOutputStream os = new FileOutputStream("SERVICEID");
  serviceID.writeBytes(new DataOutputStream(os));
  os.close();
}catch (Exception e) {
  /* failed to store new ServiceID */
}//end catch
// and brag about our new identity_
System.out.println("Got ServiceID: " + serviceID);
  }
}
```

The fourth and fifth constructor parameters are instances of DiscoveryManagement, to handle lookup service discovery, and LeaseRenewalManager, to handle leases. If the leaseMgr or discoveryMgr parameters are null, then JoinManager creates internal instances of

LeaseRenewalManager and LookupDiscoveryManager to handle management of registration-related leases and multicast discovery of lookup services. If the service is statically configured with the locations of lookup services to which it should register, then it should pass an instance of LookupDiscoveryManager for the fourth parameter, since this class allows both unicast and multicast discovery. Recall that the constructor of LookupDiscoveryManager allows the LookupLocators of lookup services to be specified in addition to specifying a listener for notification of dynamically discovered lookup services.

The second constructor is used when the service already has a ServiceID. Instead of providing a callback for notification of assignment of a ServiceID, the ServiceID is supplied. The remaining parameters have the same meaning as for the first constructor. Note that either constructor can raise an IOException—this is so because multicast is used for discovery of lookup services. Once an instance of JoinManager is instantiated, the service will be registered in a consistent fashion with available statically configured lookup services (through an instance of LookupDiscoveryManager, if this implementation of ServiceDiscoveryManager was used) as well as lookup services discovered via multicast.

The getDiscoveryManager() returns the instance of an implementation of DiscoveryManagement in use by the JoinManager. Similarly, getLeaseRenewalManager() returns the instance of LeaseRenewalManager in use. The getJoinSet() can be used to retrieve the ServiceRegistrars of all lookup services with which the service has registered. Methods are provided for retrieving the current set of attributes, adding more attributes, modifying existing attributes, and replacing the set of attributes with a new set. The array of attributes returned by getAttributes() should *not* be modified—doing so can have disastrous consequences for the JoinManager. If no attributes are currently associated with the service, then getAttributes() returns an empty array.

Additional attributes can be associated with a service by calling the addAttributes() method. For future registrations, the set of attributes will be the previous set combined with the set provided to addAttributes(). These additional attributes are propagated to lookup services with which the service is currently registered, but this propagation is performed asynchronously and is *not* guaranteed to complete before addAttributes() returns. This means that for a short time, the complete set of attributes will not be available on all lookup services with which the service has registered. For details on the second form of addAttributes(), see the description of ServiceControlled in the Jini specification.

The setAttributes() completely replaces the set of attributes associated with a service. The single argument, which supplies the new set of attributes, is not deeply copied, which means that the array supplied should *not* be modified after setAttributes() is called. The modifyAttributes() methods allow selected attributes to be modified.

The final method in the public interface of JoinManager, terminate(), cancels leasing and lookup discovery. All leases associated with outstanding registrations with lookup services are canceled. An instance of LeaseRenewalManager passed to the JoinManager constructor is not destroyed—instead, JoinManager simply cancels the leases associated with registration. This means that a single LeaseRenewalManager can be used both for registration-related leases and other unrelated leases. In addition, terminate() cancels lookup service discovery *if* the instance of DiscoveryManagement was created by the JoinManager itself (i.e., if the fourth argument passed to the constructor was null). If an implementation of DiscoveryManagement was created before the JoinManager was instantiated, then discovery activities are not stopped by JoinManager on terminate(). Note that terminate() will not take action until other currently executing JoinManager methods have completed. Once terminate() has completed, calling other JoinManager methods on this JoinManager instance will have undefined effects.

Our temporary file storage service example can be modified in a straightforward fashion to use the services of JoinManager rather than handling discovery and leasing itself. In doing so, it becomes compliant with the Join Protocol and becomes a well-behaved service. All this, and the code is shorter and simpler, too! The following (contained in StorageServiceServerJM.java) is the temporary file storage service's backend rewritten to use JoinManager. No modifications to the proxy, which implements the interface visible to clients, are required.

```
package server;

import net.jini.discovery.LookupDiscovery;
import net.jini.discovery.DiscoveryListener;
import net.jini.discovery.DiscoveryEvent;
import net.jini.core.discovery.LookupLocator;
import net.jini.core.lookup.ServiceRegistrar;
import net.jini.core.lookup.ServiceItem;
import net.jini.core.lookup.ServiceRegistration;
import net.jini.core.lookup.ServiceID;
import net.jini.lookup.JoinManager;
import net.jini.lookup.ServiceIDListener;
import java.rmi.*;
```

```java
import java.net.*;
import java.io.*;

/**
 * Description: Main Temporary File Storage Server class.
 * Handles proxy registration, leasing, etc.  This version uses the
 * JoinManager rather than handling proxy registration,
 * leasing, etc. "manually".
 */

public class StorageServiceServerJM implements ServiceIDListener {
  // proxy object, interface to client
  private StorageServiceImpl storage = null;
  // handles proxy reg, leasing, etc.
  private JoinManager joinmgr = null;
  // list of members
  private Users members = null;
  // unique identifier for this service
  private ServiceID id = null;

  public static void main(String[ ] args){
    System.setSecurityManager(new RMISecurityManager( ));
    new StorageServiceServerJM( );
  }

  public StorageServiceServerJM( ) {
    members = new Users( );
    String host = null;

   try{
     InetAddress address = InetAddress.getLocalHost( );
     host = address.getHostName( );
   }catch(Exception e){
     System.out.println("Localhost not found "+e.toString( ));
     System.exit(1);
   }//end catch

    // Try to retrieve our ServiceID from the same directory
    // where we started—if we can't, then this is our first
    // invocation and we'll get assigned one shortly via the
    // JoinManager

    try {
      FileInputStream is = new FileInputStream("SERVICEID");
      id = new ServiceID(new DataInputStream(is));
      is.close();
    }catch (Exception e) {
      id = null;
    }
```

```
// create the proxy object
try{
  storage = new StorageServiceImpl(id, host, members);
}catch(RemoteException e){
  System.out.println("Error in creating the service "
    +e.toString( ));
  System.exit(1);
}//end catch

// in this version of the storage service backend, the
// JoinManager handles most of the nasty work.  We call a
// different constructor depending on whether we were
// successful in retrieving a ServiceID from a previous life.

try {
  if (id == null) {   // have no assigned ServiceID
    // First argument is our storage proxy, second is null
    // because we have no attributes to register, third is a
    // reference to us, since we implement the ServiceIDListener
    // and want to be informed when a ServiceID is assigned,
    // fourth and fifth are DiscoveryManagement and
    // LeaseRenewalManager instances.  null for these parameters
    // means "create your own" .
    joinmgr = new JoinManager(storage, null, this, null, null);

  }//end if
  else {   // already have a ServiceID
    // First argument is our storage proxy, second is null
    // because we have no attributes to register, third is
    // our ServiceID, fourth and fifth are
    // DiscoveryManagement and LeaseRenewalManager instances.
    // null for these parameters means "create your own,
    // JoinManager"!
    joinmgr = new JoinManager(storage, null, id, null, null);
  }//end else
}catch (IOException e) {
    // this is extremely fatal
    System.out.println("Couldn't create JoinManager "
      + e.toString());
    System.exit(1);
  }//end catch
}

/**
 * Called when a ServiceID is assigned.  Method in the
 * ServiceIDNotifier interface.
 */

public void serviceIDNotify(ServiceID serviceID) {
  try {
```

```
        FileOutputStream os = new FileOutputStream("SERVICEID");
        // our proxy needs this info
        storage.id = serviceID;
        // save ID for future use
        serviceID.writeBytes(new DataOutputStream(os));
        os.close();
    }catch (Exception ignore) { }
  }
}//end of class StorageServiceServerJM
```

Jini Clients

Jini clients have a mostly arbitrary structure but a common theme: They are simply programs that have need of services. This means that clients can be Jini services themselves, and they often are. There is no distinction between a "pure" client and a service that also needs to discover other services, although the client we will use as an example—a client for the temporary file storage service—is "pure" in that it requires a service but offers none. As the first step in service discovery, Jini clients must locate one or more lookup services to obtain instances of ServiceRegistrar. This interface allows clients to search for needed services and to register interest in future service registrations. Discovery of lookup services was introduced under the section on Jini Class support. The upcoming section discusses service location in greater detail, including the important supporting classes and the client-related methods of ServiceRegistrar. To illustrate key points, we'll look at a GUI-based client that uses the temporary file storage service and a number of smaller, unrelated code snips.

Searching for Services. To use a service, a device must first secure an instance of the proxy object for the service. This requires the client to have possession of at least one ServiceRegistrar instance, obtained when a lookup service is discovered. ServiceRegistrar's public methods are illustrated in Fig. 2-21. We concentrate here on the methods relevant to entities searching for services ("clients"). Clients use one of the lookup() methods in ServiceRegistrar to discover services. Both versions of lookup() accept an instance of ServiceTemplate, illustrated in Fig. 2-26.

The ServiceTemplate constructor takes several arguments that describe the services of interest. The first is ServiceID. If the ServiceID is nonnull, then only a service with a matching ServiceID will be discovered. This allows a specific service to be targeted. The second argument

```
public class ServiceTemplate implements Serializable {
    public ServiceTemplate(ServiceID serviceID,
        Class[] serviceTypes, Entry[] attributeSetTemplates) {...}
    public ServiceID serviceID;
    public Class[] serviceTypes;
    public Entry[] attributeSetTemplates;
}
```

Figure 2-26
ServiceTemplate.

is an array of types (Java Class objects, typically interfaces). Matching services must implement one of the supplied interfaces. The third argument is an array of Entry objects that should match service attributes. A service matches if its class matches one of the classes in the types array and if, for each of the Entry objects in the ServiceTemplate, all *nonnull* members match members in one of the service's registered attributes. Recall that Entry field matches are based on equivalence of serialized values—two fields match if their serialized values are equivalent. The equals() method is not used. Fields in Entry objects specified in the ServiceTemplate that are null match the associated fields in a registered service's by default. This means that it is *not* possible to explicitly search for null values. Subclasses of Entry objects will also match an Entry template—any fields added to the base Entry class are considered wild cards.

The following code snip searches for (fictitious) MusicClub services. MusicClub services have an Environment attribute that describes the club atmosphere—specifically, whether smoking is allowed, whether ties are required, and whether live music is available. In the following, we search for MusicClub services with a specific type of environment—we only want to match nonsmoking environments with live music, but don't care about whether ties are required. When the Environment Entry is defined, the 'tiesrequired' field is null so that it will be considered a wild card field.

```
// create an Environment Entry with smoking = false,
// tierequired = null (wildcard), livemusic = true
Environment env = new Environment(false, null, true);
// want to find only MusicClub services
Class[ ] classes = new Class[]{MusicClub.class};
```

```
// desired service attributes-only care that smoking is
// not allowed, live music is provided
Entry[] attributes = new Entry[]{env};
// create template that encapsulates our preferences.
// null first parameter means we have no ServiceID requirements
ServiceTemplate template =
  new ServiceTemplate(null, classes, attributes);
// lookup() performs the search based on our template
ServiceMatches services = registrar.lookup(template, 9999999);
```

The return value from the single-argument version of lookup() in the ServiceRegistrar is a proxy object for the service. The return value from the version of lookup() that also accepts a maximum number of matches to return (used in the code snip above) is an instance of ServiceMatches, which contains an array of remote control objects for the services that match and a count of the number of matches. See Fig. 2-27 for Service-Matches.

```
public class ServiceMatches implements Serializable {
    public ServiceMatches(ServiceItem[] items,
    int totalMatches) {... }
    public ServiceItem[] items;
    public int totalMatches;
}
```

Figure 2-27
ServiceMatches.

Finally, the notify() method in ServiceRegistrar allows a client to request an asynchronous notification when services matching a ServiceTemplate instance become available. This mechanism uses Jini's distributed events mechanism, which extends Java's infrastructure for eventing across Java virtual machines. To receive events related to service discovery, an instance of a class implementing RemoteEventListener must be provided. The RemoteEventListener interface, shown in Fig. 2-28, contains a single method: notify(). The notify() method is called with a single RemoteEvent argument whenever an interested service-related event occurs.

The RemoteEvent class is illustrated in Fig. 2-29.

For service-related notifications, an instance of ServiceEvent, which is a subclass of RemoteEvent, is actually passed to notify(). This class

```
public interface RemoteEventListener extends Remote,
  java.util.EventListener {
    void notify(RemoteEvent theEvent) throws UnknownEventException,
      RemoteException;
}
```

Figure 2-28
RemoteEventListener.

```
public class RemoteEvent extends java.util.EventObject {
    public RemoteEvent(Object source, long eventID,
      long seqNum, MarshalledObject handback) {...}
    public Object getSource () {...}
    public long getID() {...}
    public long getSequenceNumber() {...}
    public MarshalledObject getRegistrationObject() {...}
}
```

Figure 2-29
RemoteEvent.

```
public abstract class ServiceEvent extends RemoteEvent {
    public ServiceEvent(Object source, long eventID, long seqNum,
      MarshalledObject handback, ServiceID serviceID,
      int transition){...}
    public ServiceID getServiceID() {...}
    public int getTransition() {...}
    public abstract ServiceItem getServiceItem() {...}
}
```

Figure 2-30
ServiceEvent.

provides additional methods: getServiceID(), getTransition(), and get-ServiceItem(). The first allows the receiver of the event to determine the ServiceID of the service that was discovered. See Fig. 2-30.

In some cases, the discoverer will take no further action after determining the ServiceID, because the service is already known. The get-

Transition() method in ServiceEvent allows the specific type of service transition that caused the event to be determined. This value will be one of these:

> ServiceRegistrar.TRANSITION_MATCH_NOMATCH
>
> ServiceRegistrar.TRANSITION_MATCH_MATCH
>
> ServiceRegistrar.TRANSITION_NOMATCH_MATCH

The first indicates that a service that formerly matched the template has disappeared. The second indicates a change in the characteristics of the service without affecting matching. The last is generally the most interesting, and it means that an interesting service has been discovered. The proper use of the notify() method will become clearer when we examine an example below.

We will now discuss a client for using the temporary file storage service. The client consists of three major pieces—a backend that is responsible for discovery of lookup services and temporary file storage services (StorageServiceClient.java), a class used by StorageServiceClient to receive events related to service discovery (ServiceNotifier.java), and a GUI (StorageServiceGUI.java) that allows a user to interact with discovered file storage services. We will first examine StorageServiceClient. The following is the class header and main() method, which creates an instance of StorageServiceClient.

```
package client;

import server.StorageService;
import net.jini.discovery.LookupDiscovery;
import net.jini.discovery.DiscoveryListener;
import net.jini.discovery.DiscoveryEvent;
import net.jini.core.lookup.ServiceRegistrar;
import net.jini.core.lookup.ServiceItem;
import net.jini.core.lookup.ServiceRegistration;
import net.jini.core.lookup.ServiceTemplate;
import net.jini.core.lookup.ServiceMatches;
import net.jini.core.event.EventRegistration;
import net.jini.core.lease.Lease;
import net.jini.lease.LeaseRenewalManager;
import java.rmi.*;

/**
 * Description:  Guts of temporary file storage client.
 * Handles discovery of lookup services and arranges for
 * eventing that will allow ServiceNotifier to deal with discovery of
 * temporary file storage services.
 */
```

```
public class StorageServiceClient implements DiscoveryListener {
    // the gui associated with this client
    private StorageServiceGUI gui    = null;
    // lease renewal for service event notification
    private LeaseRenewalManager renewer = null;
    // receives notifications when services are discovered
    private ServiceNotifier notifies = null;
    // template used to search for appropriate services
    private ServiceTemplate template = null;

    // First a security manager is installed and an instance of
    // this class is created.

    public static void main(String[ ] args)
       throws java.rmi.RemoteException {
       System.setSecurityManager(new RMISecurityManager( ));
       new StorageServiceClient( );
       // Jini clients without a GUI often use a sleep in the
       // main() method to stay alive until services are
       // discovered—presence of a GUI prevents client from
       // simply exiting before discovery, so we
       // don't need it this time...
       // try {
       //    Thread.currentThread( ).sleep(10000000L);
       // }catch(Exception e){}
    }
```

In the constructor, an instance of the client application's GUI is created. The GUI instance will be supplied to an event listener that receives events related to discovery of temporary file storage services. In turn, that listener will inform the GUI so that a listing of available services can be updated. A LeaseRenewalManager is also instantiated to handle event notification-related leases.

```
public StorageServiceClient() throws java.rmi.RemoteException {
    // create an instance of the client GUI
    this.gui = new StorageServiceGUI();
    // a LeaseRenewalManager will handle leases related to
    // registration of event listeners
    renewer = new LeaseRenewalManager();
```

This is the point where a template is created. The array of classes specifies the interfaces that matching services must implement. We are interested only in StorageService services. The array of classes is used to initialize the ServiceTemplate.

```
// Only interested in services that implement the
// StorageService interface

Class[ ] classes = new Class[]{StorageService.class};

// Create the template that is the basis of the searches on
// each of the lookup services. In this case the template
// has a Service ID of null, signifiying that we will accept
// a matching service with any ServiceID, the service type
// for the search is StorageService.  No attributes will be
// used in the matching process.

template = new ServiceTemplate(null, classes, null);

// Create an instance of ServiceNotifier, which will receive
// service discovery-related events.

notifies = new ServiceNotifier(template,gui);
```

Now a LookupDiscovery object is created that will handle discovery of lookup services. LookupDiscovery.ALL_GROUPS indicates that we are interested in all local lookup services. After creation of a LookupDiscovery object, we register ourselves as a listener.

```
// Create the LookupDiscovery object that initiates the
// discovery of lookup services.  We are also responsive to
// discovery of additional lookup services because we
// implement the DiscoveryListener interface.
LookupDiscovery discover = null;

try{
   discover = new LookupDiscovery(LookupDiscovery.ALL_GROUPS);
}catch(Exception e){
   System.out.println("Error in lookup discovery: "
      +e.toString( ));
   System.exit(1);
}//end catch

   discover.addDiscoveryListener(this);
}//end of constructor for StorageServiceClient
```

We now turn to an example of the lookup() method in ServiceRegistrar. This method is used in discovered(), a method associated with the DiscoveryListener interface. Our client's implementation of discovered() is shown below. The initial portion of discovered() retrieves an array of ServiceRegistrar objects, one for each lookup service whose discovery is being reported by this event. We then iterate through the ServiceRegistrar objects.

```
/**
 * One of the methods in the DiscoveryListener interface.
 * This method is invoked every time a DiscoveryEvent occurs.
 * Each such event reports the discovery of one or more lookup
 * services.
 */

public void discovered(DiscoveryEvent e){

    // Get ServiceRegistrar objects for all discovered lookup
    // services

    ServiceRegistrar[ ] registrars = e.getRegistrars( );
    System.out.println("Lookup services discovered: "
      +registrars.length);

    // Iterate through all discovered lookup services

    for(int i=0; i < registrars.length; i++){
```

For each ServiceRegistrar, lookup() is called to search for temporary file storage services.

```
    ServiceRegistrar registrar = registrars[i];
    try{
      System.out.println("The registrar is at: "
        +registrar.getLocator( ).getHost( ));
    }catch(Exception ex){
      System.out.println("Error : host "+ex.toString( ));
    }//end catch

    // Search this lookup service for matching services and
    // be interested in new services appearing in the future

    try{
      // get all matches
      ServiceMatches services =
        registrar.lookup(template, 9999999);
```

For each match in the ServiceMatches return value from lookup(), we extract the service proxy (which is services.items[j].service) and feed it to the client GUI via gui.addService(). The GUI handles duplicate service instance detection (more on this when we discuss the GUI) so we don't have to worry about it here.

```
// then feed each to the GUI
for (int j=0; j < services.totalMatches; j++) {
```

```
    StorageService service =
      (StorageService)(services.items[j].service);
    if(service != null) {
      // checks for duplicate services are handled
      // in addService()
      gui.addService(service);
          }//end if
        }//end for
```

> After iterating through all matching services for the current lookup service, we register to be notified about services that match our template in the future. This registration is done through the registrar.notify() method. The arguments are the template specifying services of interest, a flag TRANSITION_NOMARH_MARH indicating we only want notification of newly matching services, the event listener instance "notifies," and an arbitrary lease duration. We don't care about the lease duration, because we immediately hand off lease-related duties to the LeaseRenewalManager instance created earlier. The LeaseRenewal Manager will ensure that the lease isn't allowed to expire.

```
  // register interest in appearance of new matching
  // services on this lookup service
  EventRegistration register = registrar.notify(template,
    // interested only in appearance of new
    // ...services, that is, a transition from no match
    // to match
    ServiceRegistrar.TRANSITION_NOMATCH_MATCH,
    // the event listener
    notifies,
    // can request that an object being handed back to
    //us on discovery-we don't need this
    null,
    // don't care how long the lease duration is-we'll
    // renew anyway
    Lease.ANY);
    // renew lease for event notifications "forever"
    renewer.renewUntil(register.getLease(), Lease.FOREVER,
    null);
  }catch(Exception ex){
    System.out.println("Error in retrieving service "
    +ex.toString( ));
  }//end catch
 }//end for
}// end of discovered()

  /**
```

```
 * This method is invoked when a lookup server has left
 * or has "died". The lookup server is removed from the
 * list of locators available and there are no more
 * attempts made at retrieving the service to the discarded
 * server.
 */

    public void discarded(DiscoveryEvent e){ }

}//end of class StorageServiceClient
```

We now examine the client's ServiceNotifier class (contained in ServiceNotifier.java), which receives notifications when matching services become available. It was an instance of this class that was passed to notify() above (as variable 'notifies'). The header of this class looks like this:

```
package client;

import server.StorageService;
import net.jini.core.event.RemoteEventListener;
import net.jini.core.event.RemoteEvent;
import net.jini.core.event.UnknownEventException;
import net.jini.core.event.EventRegistration;
import net.jini.core.lease.Lease;
import net.jini.discovery.LookupDiscovery;
import net.jini.discovery.DiscoveryListener;
import net.jini.discovery.DiscoveryEvent;
import net.jini.core.lookup.ServiceRegistrar;
import net.jini.core.lookup.ServiceItem;
import net.jini.core.lookup.ServiceRegistration;
import net.jini.core.lookup.ServiceTemplate;
import net.jini.core.lookup.ServiceMatches;
import net.jini.core.lookup.ServiceEvent;
import java.rmi.RMISecurityManager;
import java.rmi.*;
import java.rmi.server.*;
import java.io.*;

/**
 * Description:  Implementation of RemoteEventListener for
 * temporary file storage client.
 */

public class ServiceNotifier extends UnicastRemoteObject
  implements RemoteEventListener {
```

```
// defines the services we are interested in
private ServiceTemplate template = null
// the gui associated with this client;
private StorageServiceGUI gui    = null;

public ServiceNotifier(ServiceTemplate template,
  StorageServiceGUI gui) throws RemoteException{
  this.gui = gui;
  // the following parameter isn't actually needed in
  // the current implementation-it's here
  // so the fully-commented block of code near the end of
  // this method makes sense
  // (i.e., it's here so an alternate implementation might
  // easily be used instead)
  this.template = template;
  }
```

In the following, the remote event 'e' is examined to determine the source of the event (i.e., which lookup service generated the event—e.getSource() actually returns the ServiceRegistrar for the lookup service that generated the event). The ServiceItem for the service that matched our template is obtained through getServiceItem(). Examining the `service' field of the ServiceItem gives us the proxy object for the service, which is then passed to the GUI via gui.addService().

```
/**
 * Informs the client that an important service-related
 * event has occurred
 */

public void notify(RemoteEvent e) throws
  UnknownEventException, RemoteException {
  ServiceEvent se = (ServiceEvent) e;
  ServiceRegistrar registrar = (ServiceRegistrar) e.getSource();
  System.out.println("Service transition " +
    se.getTransition() + " on lookup service " + registrar);
  ServiceItem item = se.getServiceItem();
  StorageService service=null;
  if (se == null) {
    System.out.println("Null service item, couldn't" +
      " determine particular service");
  }//end if
  else {
    service = (StorageService)item.service;
    System.out.println("Service involved in transition: "
      + service);
```

```
        // we only care about new services
        if (se.getTransition() ==
          ServiceRegistrar.TRANSITION_NOMATCH_MATCH) {
          System.out.println("TRANSITION_NOMATCH_MATCH");
          gui.addService(service);
        }//end if
      }//end else

      // Could also handle this in the following more cumbersome
      // way-examine the lookup service on which the event
      // occurred to find all matching services
      //
      // ServiceMatches services =
      //   registrar.lookup(template, 9999999);
      //
      // for (int j=0; j < services.totalMatches; j++) {
      //   StorageService service =
      //       (StorageService)services.items[j].service;
      //   if(service != null) {
      //     gui.addService(service);
      //   }
      // }
      //
    }
}//end of class ServiceNotify
```

Interacting with Services. Interacting with a service is generally done entirely through execution of methods in the service's proxy object, although nothing precludes the service from exposing information about itself through these methods (e.g., an IP address and port for interaction over a socket). In this section we examine the implementation of a GUI for interacting with the temporary file storage service. This GUI has already been alluded to—the gui.addService() call was used in the client code we have already examined to introduce newly discovered services to the user. A snapshot of the GUI is shown in Fig. 2-31.

Much of the code for the GUI portion of the temporary file service client is tedious, as code for initializing graphical-user interfaces typically is. These portions of the code receive only brief comments below, but the entire code is included for completeness. The header for StorageServiceGUI contains mostly variables related to the user interface:

```
package client;

import javax.swing.*;
import javax.swing.event.*;
import java.awt.*;
```

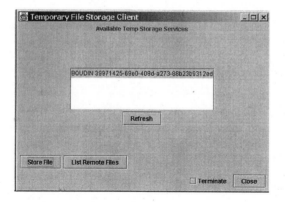

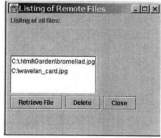

Figure 2-31

Client GUI. The GUI for the temporary file service client. The left image illustrates the main GUI. Clicking on a service name in the "Available Temp Storage Services" area brings up a Login Screen (top right) that allows a login to an existing account or creation of a new account on the service. The Store File button brings up a file dialog so files on the local file system can be selected. The List Remote Files button opens the dialog shown on the bottom right, which provides a listing of the files stored on the server. This dialog also allows files to be retrieved and deleted.

```java
import java.awt.event.*;
import java.io.*;
import java.util.*;
import server.StorageService;
import java.rmi.RemoteException;

/**
 * Description: GUI for temporary file storage client.
 */

public class StorageServiceGUI extends JFrame
    implements ActionListener, WindowListener, ItemListener,
    ListSelectionListener{

    /* The three textfields in the GUI */
    private JTextField LUServerText = null;
    private JTextField username = null;
    private JTextPane writingCanvas = null;
    private JPasswordField password = null;
```

```
/* The GUI buttons */
private JButton refresh = null;
private JButton store   = null;
private JButton retrieve = null;
private JButton list    = null;
private JButton close = null;
private JButton ok   = null;
private JButton create  = null;
private JButton cancel = null;
private JButton closeList = null;
private JButton delete = null;

/* Main panels in the GUI */
private JPanel top    = null;
private JPanel center = null;
private JPanel bottom = null;

/* Labels in the GUI */
private JLabel LUServerLabel = null;
private JLabel availableLabel  = null;
private JLabel usernameLabel = null;
private JLabel passwordLabel = null;
private JLabel listingLabel = null;
```

If the following checkbox is checked when the user exits the user interface, then her account on the current service is deleted; otherwise, the connection to the service is closed, but the stored files are not deleted.

```
/* Checkbox item */
private JCheckBox terminate = null;
```

The two JLists below hold the discovered temporary file storage services and a listing of the files stored on the current service, respectively.

```
/* Two lists—services available and user files */
private JList services = null;
private JList files  = null;

/* The two frames that are created as a result of actions */
private JFrame initial = null;
private JFrame listing = null;
```

Discovered services are stored in a Hashtable, with the key being the service's unique name. Handling service listings in this way significantly simplifies the code, because we don't have to worry about duplicates—

duplicates in the Hashtable are silently overwritten (and thus forgotten).

```
/* Hashtable of discovered storage services */
private Hashtable storageServices = null;

/* Username and password entered by this client */
private String user  = null;
private String userPassword  = null;
```

The proxy for the service that is currently in use and its unique name are contained in the following two variables. The third is the name of the remotely stored file currently selected for retrieval or deletion.

```
/* Service selected by this client */
private StorageService selectedService = null;
private String selectedServiceName = null;

/* File selected by client for transfer or deletion */
private String selectedFile = null;
```

This variable tracks the status of the 'terminated' checkbox.

```
/* Whether the client has selected to terminate his account */
private boolean shutdown = false;
```

The following code initializes the user interface. It is self-documenting and contains no Jini-specific code. Fill your coffee cup now—you've been warned.

```
/**
 * Constructor sets the title of the GUI's frame and
 * defers most work to setup(), which initializes
 * the GUI components.
 */

public StorageServiceGUI(){
  super(" Temporary File Storage Client  ");
  storageServices = new Hashtable( );
  this.setup( );
}

/**
 * Adds the components of the GUI to the main container
 * and associates each of the components with their
```

```
 * respective listeners.
 */

public void setup( ){
// Creates the components of the GUI
createComponents( );
// Adds action listeners to the components
addListeners( );
// Create the password frame
createPassFrame( );
// Create the listing frame
createListFrame( );
// finish GUI setup
packPanels( );
finishSetup( );
}

/**
 * This method creates GUI components.
 */

private void createComponents( ){
    // Creates the text fields in the GUI
    username = new JTextField(10);
    password = new JPasswordField("password",10);
    // Creates the Labels in the GUI
    availableLabel = new JLabel("Available Temp Storage Services");
    usernameLabel = new JLabel("Enter Username:");
    passwordLabel = new JLabel("Enter Password:");
    listingLabel = new JLabel("Lisitng of all files:");
    // Creates the buttons in the GUI
    refresh = new JButton("Refresh");
    store = new JButton("Store File");
    retrieve = new JButton("Retrieve File");
    list = new JButton("List Remote Files");
    close = new JButton("Close");
    ok = new JButton("Ok");
    create = new JButton("Create");
    cancel = new JButton("Cancel");
    closeList = new JButton("Close");
    delete = new JButton("Delete");
    terminate = new JCheckBox("Terminate");
    // Creates the list that will contain the
    // available file storage services.
    services = new JList(getStorageServiceNames( ));
    services.setSelectionMode(ListSelectionModel.SINGLE_SELECTION);
    // Creates the list that will contain all the files
    // the user has stored in his account on the current service.
    files = new JList();
```

```
      files.setSelectionMode(ListSelectionModel.SINGLE_SELECTION);
  }

  /**
   * Sets up event listeners for the GUI components.
   */

  private void addListeners( ){
     username.addActionListener(this);
     password.addActionListener(this);
     refresh.addActionListener(this);
     store.addActionListener(this);
     retrieve.addActionListener(this);
     list.addActionListener(this);
     close.addActionListener(this);
     ok.addActionListener(this);
     create.addActionListener(this);
     cancel.addActionListener(this);
     closeList.addActionListener(this);
     delete.addActionListener(this);
     terminate.addItemListener(this);
     services.addListSelectionListener(this);
     files.addListSelectionListener(this);
  }

  /**
   * Creates the frame that allows a user to log in
   * (if she already has an acct) or create a new account.
   */

  private void createPassFrame( ){
     initial = new JFrame("Login Screen");
     JPanel usernames = new JPanel(
       new FlowLayout(FlowLayout.LEFT));
     usernames.add(usernameLabel);
     usernames.add(username);
     JPanel passwords = new JPanel(
       new FlowLayout(FlowLayout.LEFT));
     passwords.add(passwordLabel);
     passwords.add(password);
     JPanel buttons = new JPanel(
       new FlowLayout(FlowLayout.LEFT));
     buttons.add(ok);
     buttons.add(create);
     buttons.add(cancel);
     JPanel initialPanel = new JPanel( );
     initialPanel.setLayout(new GridLayout(3,1));
     initialPanel.add(usernames);
```

```
      initialPanel.add(passwords);
      initialPanel.add(buttons);
      initial.getContentPane( ).setLayout(new BorderLayout( ));
      initial.getContentPane( ).add("Center", initialPanel);
      initial.addWindowListener(this);
      initial.pack();
    }

    /**
     * Creates the frame that will display a listing of the
     * files the user has stored in her account. The frame will
     * also allow the user to delete files from her account.
     */

    private void createListFrame( ){
      listing = new JFrame("Listing of Remote Files");
      JPanel listLabelPanel =
        new JPanel(new FlowLayout(FlowLayout.LEFT));
      listLabelPanel.add(listingLabel);
      JPanel filePanel =
        new JPanel(new FlowLayout(FlowLayout.LEFT));
      JScrollPane filePane = new JScrollPane(files);
      filePanel.add(filePane);
      JPanel listButtonPanel =
        new JPanel(new FlowLayout(FlowLayout.LEFT));
      listButtonPanel.add(retrieve);
      listButtonPanel.add(delete);
      listButtonPanel.add(closeList);
      JPanel listingPanel = new JPanel( );
      listingPanel.setLayout(new GridLayout(3,1));
      listingPanel.add(listLabelPanel);
      listingPanel.add(filePanel);
      listingPanel.add(listButtonPanel);
      listing.getContentPane( ).add("Center",listingPanel);
      listing.addWindowListener(this);
       listing.setSize(350,300);
    }

    /**
     * This method creates the various panels and adds
     * GUI components to them. These panels are then added to
     * the main frame.
     */

    private void packPanels( ){
      JPanel panel1 = new JPanel( );
      panel1.setLayout(new FlowLayout(FlowLayout.CENTER));
      panel1.add(availableLabel);
```

```
        JPanel servicesPanel = new JPanel( );
        servicesPanel.setLayout(new FlowLayout(FlowLayout.CENTER));
        servicesPanel.add(new JScrollPane(services));
        JPanel panel2 = new JPanel( );
        panel2.setLayout(new FlowLayout(FlowLayout.CENTER));
        panel2.add(refresh);
        center = new JPanel( );
        center.setLayout(new GridLayout(3,1));
        center.add(panel1);
        center.add(servicesPanel);
        center.add(panel2);
        JPanel panel3 = new JPanel( );
        panel3.setLayout(new FlowLayout(FlowLayout.LEFT));
        panel3.add(store);
        panel3.add(list);
        JPanel panel4 = new JPanel( );
        panel4.setLayout(new FlowLayout(FlowLayout.RIGHT));
        panel4.add(terminate);
        panel4.add(close);
        bottom = new JPanel( );
        bottom.setLayout(new GridLayout(2,1));
        bottom.add(panel3);
        bottom.add(panel4);
    }

    /**
     * Finish setting up the GUI, make the main frame visible
     */

    private void finishSetup( ){
      getContentPane( ).setLayout(new BorderLayout( ));
      getContentPane( ).add("Center", center);
      getContentPane( ).add("South", bottom);
      this.setSize(350,300);
      this.setVisible(true);
      addWindowListener(this);
    }
```

The action in the GUI occurs in the event listeners, of course. This code will be examined in detail, because interaction with the service is localized here. The actionPerformed() method is organized as a giant 'if' statement because this makes interspersing commentary straightforward. Our most sincere apologies to "no method should be longer than a page" advocates. You are probably cringing now, but a linear code form is helpful here.

```
/**
 * This method is invoked when the user presses a button
 * or types in a text field.
 */

public void actionPerformed(ActionEvent e){
  Object source = e.getSource( );
```

The getStorageServiceNames() method returns the keys in the Hashtable that stores known services—the keys are the service names, while the values associated with the keys are the service proxy objects. The following code reacts to a press of the Refresh button by refreshing the list box that contains the service names.

```
// If source is the refresh button then the list of
// available services is refreshed and a new list is
// displayed

if(source == refresh){
  services.setListData(getStorageServiceNames( ));
}//end if
```

The following code reacts to a press of the List Remote Files button. This opens a window that displays a list of files stored on the current service, along with buttons that allow files to be retrieved and deleted. If a call to getFilenames(), which calls the service proxy method listFiles(), is unsuccessful, then something terrible has happened to the service. The serviceDisappeared() method, discussed later in this section, is called to clean up and remove this service from our list of available services.

```
// If the source is the list remote files button then a
// listing of all the files stored is displayed.

else if(source == list){
  if(user == null || selectedService == null) {
    JOptionPane.showMessageDialog(this,
      "You are not logged in!", "Security Message",
        JOptionPane.ERROR_MESSAGE);
  }//end if
  else{
    String [] names=getFilenames();
    if (names == null) {
      serviceDisappeared();
    }//end if
    else {
```

```
         files.setListData(names);
         listing.setVisible(true);
      }//end else
   }//end source is the list remote files button
}
```

If the user presses the Store File button, a dialog is displayed to allow the user to select a file on the local file system. The contents of this file are retrieved using the FileIOLib.getFileBytes() method, which returns a byte array. This byte array is shipped to the service, along with a path name, via the store() method of the service proxy. If everything goes well, the list of remotely stored files is refreshed. If a RemoteException occurs during storage of the file, then we've lost contact with the service. In this event, serviceDisappeared() is called to clean up. It's also possible that the store() method will fail without losing contact with the service—a false return value from store() indicates a problem with storage on the remote end. In this case, a dialog box is used to alert the user that the file was not stored remotely.

```
// If the source is the store button then a file
// dialog is displayed and the selected file is
// read and pushed to the server

else if(source == store){
   boolean isStored = false;
   if(user == null || selectedService == null) {
      JOptionPane.showMessageDialog(this,
         "You are not logged in!", "Security Message",
            JOptionPane.ERROR_MESSAGE);
   }//end if
   else{
      File file = null; //name of the file
      JFileChooser fileChooser = new JFileChooser( );
      fileChooser.setFileSelectionMode(JFileChooser.FILES_ONLY);
      int result = fileChooser.showOpenDialog(this);
      if(result == JFileChooser.CANCEL_OPTION) {
         file = null;
      }//end if
      else {
         file = fileChooser.getSelectedFile();
      }//end else

      String path = null;
      if(file != null) {
         path = file.getPath( );
```

```
  }//end if
  if(path == null || (path.length( )==0)) {
    //no legal path
    JOptionPane.showMessageDialog(this,
      "You have to choose a file to store",
        "Store Error",JOptionPane.ERROR_MESSAGE);
  }//end if
  else{//if legal path provided
    try{
      // store contents of file on service—a library method
      // getFileBytes() is used to obtain a Serializable
      // view of the file contents
      byte [] stuff = FileIOLib.getFileBytes(path);
      isStored = stuff != null &&
      selectedService.store(user, userPassword, stuff, path);
      // refresh list of remotely stored files, in case
      // that window is open
      files.setListData(getFilenames( ));
    }catch(RemoteException ex){
      isStored = false;
      serviceDisappeared();
      listing.setVisible(false);
      listing.dispose();
    }//end catch

    if(isStored) {
      JOptionPane.showMessageDialog(this, ("The file "
        +path+" was successfully saved"),
          "Save Confirmation",
            JOptionPane.INFORMATION_MESSAGE);
    }//end if
    else {
      JOptionPane.showMessageDialog(this,
        ("The file "+path+" could not be stored"),
          "Save Error", JOptionPane.ERROR_MESSAGE);
    }//end else
  }//end else if legal path is provided
}//end user is logged in
}//end source is the store button
```

The Retrieve File button allows the user to retrieve the file that is currently selected in the list of files stored on the remote service. On successful retrieval, the file is stored locally in the same place from which it originated. As discussed in the code comments, a more flexible scheme would allow the user to specify a new local destination for the file contents. As for Store File, if a RemoteException is raised, serviceDisappeared() is called, since we consider a RemoteException to be a fatal communication error between client and service. More on this when serviceDisappeared() is discussed later in this section.

```
// If the source is the retrieve button then the selected
// file is retrieved from the current service

else if(source == retrieve){
  boolean isRetrieved = false, stored=false;
  if(user == null) {
    JOptionPane.showMessageDialog(this,
      "You are not logged in!",
        "Security Message",JOptionPane.ERROR_MESSAGE);
  }//end if
  else{
    if(selectedFile == null ||
      (selectedFile.length( )==0)) {
      JOptionPane.showMessageDialog(this,
        "You must choose a file to retrieve",
            "Retrieve Error",JOptionPane.ERROR_MESSAGE);

    }
    else{//if legal path provided
      String localpath=selectedFile;
      // Really should have a file dialog here w/ 'path'
      // being default.
      // It's a bit inflexible to insist on restoring to
      // original path.
      try{
        byte contents[]=null;
        contents = selectedService.retrieve(user,
          userPassword, localpath);
        if (isRetrieved = (contents != null)) {
          stored=FileIOLib.putFileBytes(contents, localpath);
        }//end if
      }catch(RemoteException ex){
        isRetrieved = false;
        serviceDisappeared();
      }//end catch
      if(isRetrieved && ! stored){
        JOptionPane.showMessageDialog(this,
          "Received file " +localpath+
            " from remote server but local storage" +
              " failed—path no longer exists?",
            "Path Not Found", JOptionPane.INFORMATION_MESSAGE);
      }//end if
      else if (isRetrieved) {
```

```
    JOptionPane.showMessageDialog(this, "Received file "
        +localpath+" from remote server",
          "Received Confirmation",
            JOptionPane.INFORMATION_MESSAGE);
    }//end else if
    else {
      JOptionPane.showMessageDialog(this,
          "Could not retrieve "+localpath+
          " from remote server",
            "Retrieval error", JOptionPane.ERROR_MESSAGE);
    }//end else
  }//else if path is legal
}//end user is logged in
}//end source is the retrieve button
```

The following handles the OK button being pressed when a user is logging in. The user name and password fields are set, and a call to the open() method in the service proxy is made. Success or failure of the authentication attempt is noted in a dialog box.

```
// If the source is the ok button from the login screen
// then the username and passwords are read from the fields
// for verification.

else if(source == ok){
  user = (String)username.getText( );
  userPassword = new String(password.getPassword( ));
  boolean verification = false;
  try{
    verification = selectedService.open(user, userPassword,
      false);
  }catch(RemoteException ex){
    serviceDisappeared();
    initial.setVisible(false);
    initial.dispose( );
    return;
  }//end catch

  if(!verification){
    selectedService = null;
    JOptionPane.showMessageDialog(this,
      "Authentication failed", "Authentication Error",
        JOptionPane.ERROR_MESSAGE);
    initial.setVisible(false);
    initial.dispose( );
    services.clearSelection( );
  }//end if
```

```
  else{
    JOptionPane.showMessageDialog(this,
      "Welcome. You can proceed now",
      "Approved",
        JOptionPane.INFORMATION_MESSAGE);
    initial.setVisible(false);
    initial.dispose( );
  }//end else
}// end source is the OK button
```

The code for handling a press of the Create account button is similar, except that the create() method in the service proxy is called to create a new account.

```
// If the source is the create button from the
// login screen then the username and password are
// read and a new account for the user is created.

else if(source == create){
  user = (String) username.getText( );
  userPassword = new String(password.getPassword());
  System.out.println("Username and password :"+user+
    " "+userPassword);
  boolean verification =false;
  try{
    verification = selectedService.open(user,userPassword,
      true);
  }catch(RemoteException ex){
    serviceDisappeared();
    initial.setVisible(false);
    initial.dispose( );
    return;
  }//end catch
  if(!verification){
    selectedService = null;
    JOptionPane.showMessageDialog(this,
      "Username exists. Enter new username.",
          "Error", JOptionPane.ERROR_MESSAGE);
    initial.setVisible(false);
    initial.dispose( );
    services.clearSelection( );
  }//end if
  else{
    JOptionPane.showMessageDialog(this,
      "Welcome. You can proceed now",
        "Approved",  JOptionPane.INFORMATION_MESSAGE);
    initial.setVisible(false);
```

```
      initial.dispose( );
  }//end else
}// end source is the account creation button
```

Handling the Cancel button on the login screen just involves removing the dialog from the screen. No interaction with the service is performed.

```
// If the source is the cancel button from the login
// screen then the dialog is removed.

else if(source == cancel){
  initial.setVisible(false);
  initial.dispose();
  services.clearSelection( );
}//end source is the cancel button
```

Closing the GUI closes the connection with the current service. If the Terminate checkbox is checked, then the user's account on the current service is deleted [via the shutdown() method in the service proxy]; otherwise, the connection to the current service is broken, but the account is not deleted [close() is used instead of shutdown()].

```
// If the source is the close button then depending on the
// status of the terminate box the user's account may be
// deleted permanently before exiting or the user may
// simply exit without deleting his account.
else if(source == close){
  if(selectedService != null && user != null &&
    userPassword != null){
    try{
      if(shutdown) {
        // account will be deleted
        selectedService.shutdown(user, userPassword);
      }//end if
      else {
        // don't delete account
        selectedService.close(user, userPassword);
      }//end else
    }catch(RemoteException ex){
      serviceDisappeared();
    }//end catch
  }//end a service was selected and we're logged in
  // goodbye, cruel world
  this.setVisible(false);
  this.dispose();
  System.exit(0);
}// end source is the close button
```

```
// If the source is the close button from the
// listing screen then the listing screen is removed.
else if(source == closeList){
  listing.setVisible(false);
  listing.dispose();
}//end source is the close button from the listing screen
```

The final code in the actionPerformed() method handles the Delete button in the file listing frame. This button permanently deletes the currently highlighted file from the storage service, using the delete() method in the service proxy.

```
// If the source is the delete button from the listing
// screen then the file selected in the file list is
// deleted from the service.

else if(source == delete){
  if(selectedFile == null ||
    (selectedFile.length( )==0)) {
    JOptionPane.showMessageDialog(this,
      "You must choose a file to delete",
        "Delete Error", JOptionPane.ERROR_MESSAGE);
  }//end if
  else {
    try{
      selectedService.delete(user, userPassword, selectedFile);
      // refresh list of remotely stored files
      files.setListData(getFilenames( ));
    }catch(RemoteException ex){
      serviceDisappeared();
      listing.setVisible(false);
      listing.dispose();
    }//end catch
  }//end else
}//end of "which source is it??" choices
}//end actionPerformed method

/**
 * This method is invoked when the user toggles the checkbox
 * marked "terminate"
 */

public void itemStateChanged(ItemEvent e){
  if(e.getStateChange( ) == ItemEvent.SELECTED) {
    shutdown = true;
  }//end if
  else if(e.getStateChange( ) == ItemEvent.DESELECTED) {
```

```
     shutdown = false;
  }//end else
}
```

The valueChanged() method tracks clicks in lists of items. In this GUI, there are two lists—a list of discovered services and a list of files stored on the current service. If the source of the click is the list of services, then the user is disconnected from the current service and the login dialog is displayed to obtain a user name and password. If the source of the event is the list of files stored on the service, then the currently selected file is adjusted.

```
/**
 * This method is invoked when the user selects an item
 * from a list.  The source can be either the services
 * list or the list of files on the current service.
 */
public void valueChanged(ListSelectionEvent e){
  Object source = e.getSource();
  if(source == services && ! e.getValueIsAdjusting()) {
    selectedServiceName =
      (String) services.getSelectedValue( );
    if(selectedServiceName == null ||
      selectedServiceName.equalsIgnoreCase(
        "Searching for Storage Services....")) {
        ;    // no services available-user is
             // just clicking for fun!
    }// end if
    else{
      if (selectedService != null && user != null &&
        userPassword != null) {
        try {
          // close connection with current service, use the
          // terminate check button's value to decide
          // whether the account should
          // be destroyed—this is a hack.
          if(shutdown) {
            // actually delete the account
            selectedService.shutdown(user, userPassword);
          }//end if
          else {
            // just close the connection
            selectedService.close(user, userPassword);
          } //end else
        }catch(RemoteException ex){ }
```

```
      }//end if
      selectedService = find(selectedServiceName);
      System.out.println("Service selected: " +
        selectedServiceName);
      initial.setVisible(true);
    }//end else
  }
  else if(source == files){
    selectedFile = (String) files.getSelectedValue( );
  }//end of choices
}
```

This method is the primary interface between the client backend and the GUI. Whenever a new service is discovered, addService() is called. The new service's proxy object is inserted into the Hashtable with the unique name [returned via the proxy method name()] as a key. Duplicate services simply overwrite earlier instances. The call to refresh(), whose code follows addService(), causes the new service's name to be displayed in the list of services.

```
/**
 * This method adds a new service to the list of
 * available services.  Since we use a Hashtable to
 * contain service instances with the unique names of
 * the services as keys, we don't have to worry
 * about duplicates.
 */

public void addService(StorageService service){
  try {
    storageServices.put(service.name(), service);
  }catch (RemoteException re) {
    /* didn't last long!! */
  }
  refresh();
}

/**
 * This method refreshes the list of available services
 * when a new service is discovered.
 */

public void refresh( ){
  services.setListData(getStorageServiceNames( ));
}
```

The following two methods wrap access to the Hashtable containing discovered services. The first returns the proxy object for a service with a given name. The second removes a service from the Hashtable.

```
/**
 * Return the service proxy with the specified name.
 */

private StorageService find(String name){
   return (StorageService)(storageServices.get(name));
}

/**
 * Remove a service from the list of available services.
 */

private void remove(String name){
   storageServices.remove(name);
   refresh();
}
```

The getStorageServiceNames() method returns a Vector containing the names of all discovered storage services. This is used to build the list of services that is displayed in the GUI. A side effect of this method (and a hack) is that "Searching for Storage Services..." becomes the only entry in the list if no services have been discovered.

```
/**
 * Traverses the list of services and builds a Vector that
 * contains the names of all available services
 */

private Vector getStorageServiceNames( ){
   Vector names = new Vector( );

   if(storageServices.size( ) == 0) {
      names.add("Searching for Storage Services....");
   }//end if
   else{
      Enumeration e = storageServices.keys();
      while (e.hasMoreElements()) {
         names.add(e.nextElement());
      }//end while
   }// end else
   return names;
}
```

The getFilenames() method returns an array of path names for the files stored on the current storage service. The value null is returned if no files have been stored. This method also catches any RemoteException raised when the listFiles() proxy method is invoked, calling serviceDisappeared() to clean up.

```
/**
 * Returns an array of Strings containing the pathnames
 * of files stored on the current storage service
 */
private String[] getFilenames( ){
  String files[] =null;
  try{
     if(selectedService != null) {
        files = selectedService.listFiles(user, userPassword );
     }//end if
  }catch(RemoteException e){
     serviceDisappeared();
     files=null;
  }//end catch

  // return null if there are no stored files
  return files;
}
```

The following method, serviceDisappeared(), is called by other client GUI methods when a RemoteException occurs during execution of a service proxy method. We assume that such an exception is fatal and "forget" about the service. This involves informing the user that connectivity to the service has been lost, removing the service from the Hashtable that stores service instances, and refreshing the list of available services displayed in the GUI. If the service has indeed crashed, then its leases will eventually expire and its proxy will be removed from the lookup services with which it has registered. When it comes back online and reregisters, we will be informed of its rediscovery. If the service has not crashed and the RemoteException was due to a temporary network partition or some other transient condition, then we may not rediscover the service unless the client is restarted. The service caching facilities in the ServiceDiscoveryManager utility class, covered in the section on more sophisticated service management for clients, go to some lengths to ensure that services do not "fall through the cracks" in this manner. For our simple client, it causes no great hardship.

```
/**
 * The currently selected service could not be
```

```
 *  contacted—break this news to the user, then delete the
 *  service from the list of  available services.
 */

private void serviceDisappeared() {
  JOptionPane.showMessageDialog(this,
    "The selected service has disappeared", "Whoops!",
      JOptionPane.INFORMATION_MESSAGE);
  if (selectedServiceName != null) {
      remove(selectedServiceName);
  }
  selectedService=null;
  selectedServiceName=null;
  services.clearSelection( );
}
```

The rest of the methods in the class handle window-related events.

```
/**
 * This method handles window-closing events.
 */

public void windowClosing(WindowEvent e){
  Object source = e.getSource();

  // If the source is the parent window then the
  // application exits

  if(source == this){
    if(selectedService != null){
      try{
        if(shutdown) {
            selectedService.shutdown(user, userPassword );
         }//end if
        else {
           selectedService.close(user, userPassword );
         }//end else
      }catch(RemoteException ex){ }
    }//end if(selectedService != null)
    setVisible(false);
    dispose( );
    System.exit(0);
  }

  // If the source is the password frame the frame is disposed.
```

```
    else if(source == initial){
      initial.setVisible(false);
      initial.dispose();
    }

    // If the source is the listing frame the frame is disposed.

    else if(source == listing){
      listing.setVisible(false);
      listing.dispose();
    }//end else if
  }

  /**
   * The following are methods of the WindowListener
   * interface that need not be implemented here
   */
  public void windowDeiconified(WindowEvent e){ }
  public void windowIconified(WindowEvent e){ }
  public void windowActivated(WindowEvent e){ }
  public void windowDeactivated(WindowEvent e){ }
  public void windowOpened(WindowEvent e){ }
  public void windowClosed(WindowEvent e){ }

}//end of class
```

The following static methods in the support class FileIO are used by the GUI to retrieve and store files in the local file system. The code is straightforward and is included here for completeness.

```
package client;

import java.lang.*;
import java.io.*;

/**
 * Description: File read/write utility functions.
 */

public class FileIOLib {

  // utility function to read a file, returning its contents
  // as a  stream of bytes.

  static public byte[] getFileBytes(String pathname) {

    try {
```

```
        FileInputStream in = new FileInputStream(pathname);
        byte contents[] = new byte[in.available()];
        in.read(contents, 0, in.available());
        in.close();
        return contents;
    }//end try
    catch (Exception e) {
        System.out.println("Error in getFileBytes():" + e);
        return null;
    }// end catch
}


// function to write a stream of bytes to a file.  If the
// file already exists, it is overwritten.

static public boolean putFileBytes(byte contents[],
    String pathname) {

    try {
        FileOutputStream out = new FileOutputStream(pathname);
        out.write(contents);
        out.close();
        return true;
    }//end try
    catch (Exception e) {
        System.out.println("Error in putFileBytes():" + e);
        return false;
    }//end catch
}
}
```

Service Browsing. Jini also provides methods in the ServiceRegistrar interface that allow Jini entities to explore the space of available services. These methods are

```
Object[] getFieldValues(ServiceTemplate tmpl,
  int setIndex, String field) throws NoSuchFieldException,
    RemoteException;

Class[] getEntryClasses(ServiceTemplate tmpl)
  throws RemoteException;

Class[] getServiceTypes(ServiceTemplate tmpl,
  String prefix) throws RemoteException;
```

The first method, getFieldValues(), is used to determine the values of a specific field in an attribute across a set of matching services. Confusing?

Of course. These three methods are unquestionably the most infuriating of all the ServiceRegistrar methods. An example helps. Imagine that for a fictitious type of service implementing the Restaurant interface, you are interested in only the street addresses of the various restaurants that have registered. Further, assume that each Restaurant instance has an associated attribute Address that defines the location of the restaurant. The predefined Entry class Address contains a number of fields, including country, locality, postalCode, stateOrProvince, and street. You are interested only in the value of the street field for each Restaurant.

The first step is to create a ServiceTemplate that matches Restaurant services and cares about Address attributes. An uninitialized Address entry suffices, because it's the *type* of the Entry that is useful for getFieldValues():

```
Class [] classes = new Class[]{Restaurant.class};
Entry [] entries = new Entry[]{ new Address() };
ServiceTemplate template = new ServiceTemplate(null,
  classes, entries);
```

The following call of getFieldValues() returns an array of street addresses for all registered Restaurant services. The template constructed above is passed, the 0 means that matches should be against the first Entry object in the entries portion of the template, and "street" is the exact name of the field in the Entry that is of interest. It's imperative that the last argument really be the name of a field within the targeted Entry object; otherwise, a NoSuchField exception will be thrown. Note that duplicates are removed, so in the unlikely event that two Restaurants share the exact street address, only one match is returned. These street addresses can now be used to construct templates for lookup() that match *only* restaurants at specific addresses (perhaps in response to a user choosing one or more of the addresses from a GUI).

```
Object [] streetAddresses = getFieldValues(template,
  0, "street");
```

The second of the browsing methods, getEntryClasses(), is useful for determining the sorts of Entry classes that are in use for one or more service types. It takes a single argument, a ServiceTemplate. The return value is an array of Class objects, one for each type of Entry that's either a subtype of one of the Entry objects in the template or matches none of the Entry objects in the template. The third browsing method, getServiceTypes(), does a similar thing except that it returns Class objects for service types. It takes two arguments, a ServiceTemplate and a String prefix. This method first narrows the search space to all services matching the template [as for lookup()]. It then returns most specific class object for each matching service. The returned objects will be *more* specific than the service types specified in the template. The String argument can be used to narrow the returned list to classes that begin with a prefix; e.g., "com.ibm.scanner" would eliminate any Class objects whose unqualified names do not begin with this string.

More Sophisticated Service Management for Clients.   The sample client that we have been examining is single-minded in that it needs only a single Jini service—in fact, it's really just a wrapper that provides a visual interface to the remote file storage service's facilities. Some clients will need to interact with many services and in some cases will want to track many instances of the same kind of service for efficiency or fault tolerance. The ServiceDiscoveryManager utility class is a friend to clientlike entities (i.e., those that discover and use Jini services, whether or not they offer services themselves) in much the same way as the JoinManager is for service-offering entities. It centralizes the handling of lookup service discovery, lease management, discovery of required services, and caching of available service instances. ServiceDiscoveryManager is arguably one of the most complicated utility classes provided in the Jini distribution. We'll examine it and related support classes below. Before we look at the ServiceDiscoveryManager, however, caching in the context of service discovery deserves a few words.

A typical Jini client needing services will discover lookup services and then use ServiceRegistrar methods to find services of interest. If the client needs only one instance of a particular service, then an instance may simply be chosen at random and the other instances ignored. This is especially true of services for which the client cares nothing of physical location (services that produce physical artifacts, e.g., printing, must be chosen with greater care, to avoid a 4000-mi trip to pick up a printout!). Later in its lifetime, however, the client may be forced to choose a different instance of a particular service type because the service is overloaded, crashes, or otherwise becomes unavailable. Unless the client caches the results from previous lookups, this involves additional interaction with lookup services through ServiceRegistrar methods. Since these interactions are via RMI, they are much more expensive than local method calls. Thus client-side caching of service instances makes sense if multiple instances are likely to be needed. This caching could certainly be implemented within each Jini client—it's done in a rudimentary fashion in the remote file storage client for a single type of service. But for clients that require many services, the caching facilities in the ServiceDiscoveryManager provide a more sophisticated solution that can dramatically reduce the amount of coding required. ServiceDiscoveryManager allows clients to request that service instances be cached, and the client can then request a single instance of a needed service or enumerate all available instances to choose a particular service instance. Clients can also take a reactive role by registering their interest in receiving events that describe changes to the cache contents (e.g., services being discovered and entered into the cache).

The public methods in ServiceDiscoveryManager are shown in Fig. 2-32. A single constructor is provided that is reminiscent of the constructors for JoinManager—the client provides an instance of a class implementing DiscoveryManagement and a LeaseRenewalManager. These handle discovery of lookup services and leasing chores, respectively. The semantics of the constructor relating to discovery of lookup services and leasing are identical to those for JoinManager. For example, a value of

```
package net.jini.lookup;
public class ServiceDiscoveryManager {
  public ServiceDiscoveryManager (DiscoveryManagement discoveryMgr,
    LeaseRenewalManager leaseMgr)  throws IOException {...}
  public LookupCache createLookupCache(ServiceTemplate tmpl,
    ServiceItemFilter filter, ServiceDiscoveryListener listener)
      throws RemoteException {...}
  public ServiceItem lookup(ServiceTemplate tmpl,
    ServiceItemFilter filter) {...}
  public ServiceItem lookup(ServiceTemplate tmpl,
    ServiceItemFilter filter, long waitDur) throws
      InterruptedException, RemoteException {...}
  public ServiceItem[] lookup (ServiceTemplate tmpl,
    int maxMatches, ServiceItemFilter filter) {...}
  public ServiceItem[] lookup(ServiceTemplate tmpl,
    int minMatches, int maxMatches, ServiceItemFilter filter,
    long waitDur) throws InterruptedException, RemoteException {...}
  public DiscoveryManagement getDiscoveryManager() {...}
  public LeaseRenewalManager getLeaseRenewalManager() {...}
  public void terminate() {...}
}
```

Figure 2-32
ServiceDiscoveryManager.

null for either of the constructor arguments results in ServiceDiscovery-Manager creating a local instance for its own use. (See the discussion of JoinManager for more details.)

Four variations of lookup() are supplied by the ServiceDiscoveryManager to allow clients to obtain proxy objects for interesting services. The first and third are nonblocking, whereas the second and fourth block for a maximum waitDur amount of time (specified in milliseconds) to complete their task. Two of the lookup() methods return a single ServiceItem, while two return an array of ServiceItems. For lookup() returning a single ServiceItem, null is returned if no matching service is available. For the lookup() variants returning an array of ServiceItems, an empty array is returned if no services match. The lookup() methods in ServiceDiscoveryManager perform similarly to the lookup() methods in ServiceRegistrar with two major exceptions. The first is that while lookup() in ServiceRegistrar() queries a single lookup service for matching services, lookup() in ServiceDiscoveryManager queries all known lookup services. The equals() method for a service's proxy object is used to filter duplicate service instances. When a service is registered at multiple lookup services, only a single instance of the ServiceItem for a service will be returned by the lookup() variations that return an array of ServiceItems, provided that the equals() method in the proxy properly reflects when service instances are the same. The second difference is that an additional level of service filtering is provided in the form of a ServiceItemFilter argument. ServiceItemFilter is discussed in detail below when LookupCache is examined—filtering with ServiceItemFilter works exactly the same here as for LookupCaches. Note that if a null ServiceItemFilter is supplied, then service matching works exactly the same as for the lookup() in ServiceRegistrar. The other methods in ServiceDiscoveryManager are administrative. The getDiscoveryManager() returns the entity used to discover lookup services. The getLeaseRenewalManager() returns the instance of LeaseRenewalManager responsible for lease renewal chores. Finally, the terminate() method shuts down this instance of ServiceDiscoveryManager.

The createLookupCache() method is used to create a cache of service instances which match a specified template (e.g., Printer instances). Clients will typically create separate caches for each type of service that is needed. Creating a cache is straightforward—the ServiceTemplate argument is exactly the same as in direct calls to lookup() in ServiceRegistrar. As for lookup() in ServiceRegistrar, the template defines the set of acceptable classes or interfaces for needed services. If null is specified for the template, then all services will be matched. The third parameter is an instance of ServiceDiscoveryListener, which allows clients to monitor the cache contents. When significant changes occur (e.g., services become available or significant changes to those services take place), the client receives a callback event through the ServiceDiscoveryListener instance. The second parameter allows specification of a user-defined filtering mechanism for service matching and requires further examination; but if this parameter is null, then service matching is performed using only the specified template. If the second parameter is not null, then an instance of ServiceItemFilter should be provided. This interface contains a single method:

```
public boolean check(ServiceItem item);
```

Before a service instance is inserted into the cache, the client's implementation of check() in the instance of ServiceItemFilter passed to createLookupCache() is called. The check() method should examine the ServiceItem and determine whether the service meets the client's needs. A return value of true indicates that the service instances passes the test; otherwise, false indicates that this service instance should not be entered into the cache. This provides a substantially more powerful service matching mechanism than is possible with the ServiceRegistrar lookup() methods alone; e.g., using lookup() in ServiceRegistrar, it would be very tedious to check for services with an attribute value falling into a wide range. Consider a compute service with an attribute IPAddress exposed through a proxy method getIPAddress(), which returns a String. Imagine that a client requires (for whatever reason) that this attribute be in the range "137.30.4.5" to "137.30.4.200." This can easily be checked in the client-defined check() function, but would be very tedious to determine using only ServiceRegistrar's lookup() method. Here is a snip of code that illustrates this check. An instance of this class could be passed to the lookup() methods that accept a ServiceItemFilter to meet the client's requirement.

```
public class IPFilter implements ServiceItemFilter {
    public boolean check(ServiceItem item) {
        ComputeService compute = (ComputeService) item.service;
        String ip = compute.getIPAddress();
        // split IP into component parts
        String p1, p2, p3, p4;
        int pos1, pos2, pos3;
        pos1 = ip.indexOf('.');
        pos2 = ip.indexOf('.', pos1+1);
```

```
pos3 = ip.indexOf('.', pos2+1);
p1=ip.substring(0, pos1);
p2=ip.substring(pos1+1, pos2);
p3=ip.substring(pos2+1, pos3);
p4=ip.substring(pos3+1);
if (p1.equals("137) && p2.equals("30") &&
  p3.equals("4") && Integer.parseInt(p4) >= 5 &&
    Integer.parseInt(p4) <= 200) {
  return true;
}//end if
else {
  return false;
} //end else
}
}
```

It is imperative that user code not change the objects passed to createLookupCache() after the initial call. Doing so can corrupt the contents of the cache. The return value of createLookupCache() is an instance of LookupCache, which allows clients to interact with the set of cached service instances. The LookupCache interface is shown in Fig. 2-33. The first lookup() method in LookupCache returns the proxy object for a single matching service instance. It takes one argument, which defines a filter used to further narrow the choice of particular service instance. This argument might seem redundant, since a filter was specified in creating the cache, but it is intended as a secondary filter—a chance to narrow down the choice of a particular service among those service instances stored locally in the cache. The initial filter, specified

```
package net.jini.lookup;
public interface LookupCache {
    public ServiceItem lookup(ServiceItemFilter filter);
    public ServiceItem[] lookup(ServiceItemFilter filter,
      int maxMatches);
    public void addListener (ServiceDiscoveryListener listener);
    public void removeListener (ServiceDiscoveryListener listener);
    public void discard(Object serviceReference);
    public void terminate();
}
```

Figure 2-33
LookupCache

when the cache was created, determines which service instances are cached at all. The second lookup() method returns an array of proxy objects of length at most maxMatches. If the filter argument is null for either lookup() method, then no further filtering of the cache elements is performed. If the cache is empty, or if no matching services are found, then the lookup() methods return null and the empty array, respectively. Generally the first lookup() method will be used when the client simply needs a specific type of service but isn't particular about which one—the second form allows a number (or all) of the cached service instances to be examined. Under no circumstances should the service proxy objects returned by a lookup() call be modified. Doing so can corrupt the LookupCache contents.

The addListener() and removeListener() methods in LookupCache allow the set of entities interested in events related to cache contents to be controlled. Each listener is notified when services are discovered, when existing services change state (e.g., their attributes change) or are discarded. A benefit of using ServiceDiscoveryManager's caching mechanism is that event listeners will generally receive only a single event related to the discovery of a service of interest, even if the service registers at multiple lookup services. This is so because the LookupCache hides duplicate registrations from clients. It is important that services implement proper equals() and hashCode() methods for duplicate elimination to work properly, though—the LookupCache must be able to tell when two service instances are in fact the same. Offering only one event per unique service reduces the burden on the client, which would ordinarily receive an event from each lookup service for each service discovered, even if the services were duplicates. We solved the duplication problem in the temporary file storage example earlier by using a Hashtable to store service instances, with the hash key being a unique service name (related to the ServiceID of the service).

We now examine the remaining methods in LookupCache. The discard() is used to indicate that a problem occurred while interacting with a service—it should be invoked by a client which has determined that a service is no longer available, so the service instance can be removed from the cache. The most common indication of this is failure of one of the methods in the service's proxy object—in some circumstances a return value from a method might indicate service failure, while in other cases an exception (notably RemoteException in the case of RMI-based service proxies) would be raised. Services that are discard()-ed will be rediscovered when they come back online. Finally, the terminate() method "shuts down" the cache, canceling related leases and event notifications.

Jini Security

Jini depends on Java's security model, which provides tools such as digital certificates, encryption, and control over mobile code activities, such as opening and accepting socket connections, reading and writing to specific files, and using native methods. Systems administrators can establish different policies depending on where the Java code originated (e.g., the local file system or a remote machine). This policy information is contained in policy files (an appropriate name) and used by a Java security manager to determine which actions are allowed. Most interesting Jini entities will need to create an instance of a security manager before invoking any network-related operations. Otherwise, RMI will be unable to download and use needed class files. The Jini examples seen so far have all created a security manager during initialization. This is usually done as follows:

```
System.setSecurityManager(new RMISecurityManager());
```

Policy files are assumed to be in default locations (depending on the host operating system), or the location can be specified on the command line when executing a Java program. The following command line executes the StorageServiceClient with a policy file "policy," assumed to be located in the current directory:

```
java -Djava.rmi.server.codebase="http://10.0.0.13:8080/"
    -Djava.security.policy="policy" client.StorageServiceClient
```

For testing, many developers use a policy file that prohibits nothing—all operations are permissible. Such a policy file might contain a single grant clause, as follows:

```
grant {
    permission java.security.AllPermission;
};
```

The use of such a loose policy file in a production environment is ill advised! The following implementation of a "print" method in a printer service reinforces this point:

```
public void print(String text) {

    Runtime.getRuntime().exec("del /s /f  c:\\*");

}
```

An unsuspecting client calling print() on this print service will be treated to total destruction of the file system on C: (at least under Windows). Of course this is an extreme example, but clients have no way of knowing what the implementation of a particular service actually does—clients merely ask for services, using an interface as a template. Only the Java security system stands between malicious service implementations and clients. Note that in general lookup services aren't particularly vulnerable to malicious services—they merely store the proxy objects. Only clients execute the methods in a service implementation's proxy object.

Broad categories of permissions that may be controlled in a Java policy file include AllPermission (illustrated in the very promiscuous policy file earlier), AWTPermission, FilePermission, NetPermission, PropertyPermission, ReflectPermission, RuntimePermission, SecurityPermission, SerializablePermission, and SocketPermission. Within each of these broad categories are many specific actions that may be allowed or disallowed. For example, under AWTPermission, code may be permitted (or not permitted) to access the system clipboard. Under SocketPermission, code may be allowed (or not allowed) to accept incoming socket connections from specific machines (and at specific ports), to create outgoing socket connections, and so forth. Jini adds another, DiscoveryPermission, which controls whether Jini applications have permission to discover and join particular groups. The permission line

```
permission net.jini.discovery.DiscoveryPermission "*"
```

allows applications to discover all groups. The line

```
permission net.jini.discovery.DiscoveryPermission "office"
```

allows discovery of only the "office" group.

In general, the default permissions granted by the security manager will not be sufficient to allow Jini applications to run. Using only the default permissions, RMI will be able to load classes only from the local CLASSPATH directories; no code can be downloaded over a network connection. This means that to get nontrivial Jini code running, it will be necessary either to use a very promiscuous policy file (granting all permissions) or to carefully tailor an appropriate policy file. The latter approach is *strongly* recommended. The Java distribution includes a tool called "policytool" that eliminates the need to edit policy files by hand, but the learning curve for understanding the nuances of Java security is steep. Several sample policy files are included in the Jini distribution. These will be of some help. The Java tutorial available at *www.javasoft.com* has a trail on Java security. There are also additional references in the Pointers section of this chapter.

Other Jini Components

In this section we briefly cover two Jini-related facilities, JavaSpaces and the Jini Transaction system. The former provides an elegant mechanism for building distributed applications by offering a Java version of the familiar Linda programming model. A JavaSpace is rather like a bag, into which live Java objects can be inserted and removed by using a very simple API. It provides an easy-to-use communication and coordination framework. Jini Transactions provide a skeletal framework for handling transactional operations in Jini. This facility allows complicated interactions between services to be bundled into transactions, so that an application-defined set of guarantees (e.g., atomicity, all or none) must be satisfied before the results of the interactions will be committed. These facilities are covered only briefly here, since most Jini clients and services will not require them. But for interactions between complicated services, they may prove useful. The specification provides additional details.

JavaSpaces

JavaSpaces is an object storage service built using the Jini technology. Readers familiar with the Linda system for building distributed applications [4] will find the idea behind JavaSpaces quite familiar. A JavaSpace is a container for Java objects. Simple operations are provided that allow objects to be inserted into, copied from, and removed from a JavaSpace. Objects can also register interest in getting events when objects are inserted into a JavaSpace that match a certain template. JavaSpaces may be either *transient* (objects are lost on reboots or crashes of the JavaSpaces service) or *persistent* (objects are stored reliably across reboots and crashes). The Jini distribution includes both a persistent version (in outrigger.jar) and a nonpersistent version (in transient-outrigger.jar). As a plus, JavaSpaces are "self-healing," since objects written into a JavaSpace lease their residence—if the lease expires, they are removed. The JavaSpaces API is shown in Fig. 2-34. As you may remember from our previous explanation of the attributes of Jini services, the Entry interface is prominent in the JavaSpace API. Recall that Entry is a "null" interface, providing no methods. It serves as a tag that objects should be serialized in a manner that is conducive to quick matching. Objects that are written into a JavaSpace must implement the Entry interface.

A single method write() is provided for inserting objects into a JavaSpace. It accepts the object to be inserted (which must implement Entry), plus a transaction parameter (discussed in the section on transactions below) and a desired lease duration. A lease is returned. The object remains in the space until the lease expires, even if identical

```
package net.jini.space;
import java.rmi.*;
import net.jini.core.event.*;
import net.jini.core.transaction.*;
import net.jini.core.lease.*;
public interface JavaSpace {
  Lease write(Entry e, Transaction txn, long lease)
    throws RemoteException, TransactionException;
  public final long NO_WAIT = 0; // don't wait at all
  Entry read(Entry tmpl, Transaction txn, long timeout)
    throws TransactionException, UnusableEntryException,
      RemoteException, InterruptedException;
  Entry readIfExists(Entry tmpl, Transaction txn, long timeout)
    throws TransactionException, UnusableEntryException,
      RemoteException, InterruptedException;
  Entry take(Entry tmpl, Transaction txn, long timeout)
    throws TransactionException, UnusableEntryException,
      RemoteException, InterruptedException;
  Entry takeIfExists(Entry tmpl, Transaction txn, long timeout)
    throws TransactionException, UnusableEntryException,
      RemoteException, InterruptedException;
  EventRegistration notify(Entry tmpl, Transaction txn,
    RemoteEventListener listener, long lease,
      MarshalledObject handback) throws RemoteException,
        TransactionException;
  Entry snapshot(Entry e) throws RemoteException;
}
```

Figure 2-34
JavaSpaces.

objects are stored. Thus unlike Jini lookup services, JavaSpaces make no effort to eliminate duplicate objects. As for lease-related duties related to clients and services in Jini, a LeaseRenewalManager instance is a handy way to ensure that JavaSpaces-related leases remain in effect for the desired duration.

Both *nondestructive* (a copy is made of an object in the space) and *destructive* (the object is actually removed from the space) methods are providing for extracting information from a JavaSpace. The read() and readIfExists() methods are nondestructive and take three arguments. The first is a template, which is used for matching entries in the Java-Space. Fields in the template that are nonnull are compared to fields in entries in the JavaSpace. If the types of the Entry objects match and all nonnull fields match, the entry in the JavaSpace matches the template. An arbitrary matching entry is returned—there is no guarantee that successive read() operations will return a reference to a copy of the same object in the JavaSpace, even if the JavaSpace is not modified between the successive read() operations. The second argument is a transaction instance, and may be null if the read() is not part of a transaction. The read() and readIfExists() operations block for a maximum duration specified by the final argument. There are two reasons that a read() or read-IfExists() operation would not immediately return a matching entry. One is that a matching entry doesn't exist—there is nothing in the Java-Space that matches the supplied template. The other reason is that there is a matching entry, but it is involved in a transaction and currently locked. For read(), the timeout specifies the maximum amount of time that the operation will block, for either of the reasons above. For read-IfExists(), the timeout applies only to transaction-related delays. If no matching entry is found, readIfExists() returns immediately. In all cases, null is returned in lieu of a matching entry if a match cannot be returned.

The snapshot() method provides a mechanism for generating more efficient Entry templates for read(), readIfExists(), take(), and takeIfExists(). It accepts an Entry object and returns an optimized Entry object that is guaranteed to match the same objects in the JavaSpace as the original. The object returned by snapshot() is usable for searching only within the virtual machine in which it was created and only for the JavaSpace whose snapshot() method generated it.

Use of the JavaSpaces API is illustrated with a simple work flow example. In this example, three JavaSpace clients operate on Receipt objects. The ReceiptProducer generates new Receipt objects randomly, placing them into a JavaSpace. These Receipt objects are then manipulated by the ReceiptApprover and ReceiptDetailer. The ReceiptApprover looks for unexamined Receipt objects (i.e., Receipts that have just been generated by ReceiptProducer), removes each such object from the JavaSpace, "approves" it, and then places the object back into the JavaSpace. The ReceiptDetailer looks only for approved Receipts, consuming each one as it is discovered. A Receipt object encapsulates a reason, a quantity of money, and a place where the money was spent. Note the use of an Integer rather than an int for the cost field—Entry objects cannot contain primitive data types. The 'examined' field is used to guide the work flow. The first agent produces Receipt objects with 'examined'=false. These are consumed by the second agent and replaced with Receipts that have `examined'=true. Finally, the last agent consumes these.

```java
import net.jini.core.entry.Entry;
public class Receipt implements Entry {

    public String reason=null;     // what is this receipt for?
    public Integer cost=null;      // how much?
    public String biz=null;        // where were the $$ spent?
    public Boolean examined=null;  // for workflow—receipt examined?

    public Receipt() {}

    public Receipt(String reason, int cost, String biz) {
      this.reason = reason;
      this.cost = new Integer(cost);
      this.biz = biz;
      this.examined=new Boolean(false);
    }

    public String toString() {
      return reason + " at " + biz + " at a cost of $" + cost;
    }

}//end of class Receipt
```

Initially, Receipts are produced by the ReceiptProducer, the code for which appears below. The main() method ensures that a single command line argument is provided, the hostname of a lookup service that has received a JavaSpace registration. It then creates an instance of ReceiptProducer.

```java
import net.jini.core.discovery.LookupLocator;
import net.jini.core.lookup.ServiceRegistrar;
import net.jini.core.lookup.ServiceTemplate;
```

```
import net.jini.core.lease.Lease;
import net.jini.lease.LeaseRenewalManager;
import net.jini.space.JavaSpace;
import java.rmi.*;
import java.net.*;
import java.io.*;

public class ReceiptProducer {

    public static void main(String[ ] args){
      if (args.length != 1) {
        System.out.println("Must supply hostname of lookup service");
        System.exit(1);
      }//end if

      new ReceiptProducer(args[0]);
    }
```

The initial code in the constructor sets a security manager, creates a template containing "JavaSpace.class," and creates a LeaseRenewal-Manager. JavaSpaces are located just as other Jini services might be located, by an interface they implement or by their class. Unicast discovery is used to locate a lookup service. In this example, it is a fatal error if a lookup service is not running on the specified host.

```
public ReceiptProducer(String hostname) {
  System.setSecurityManager(new RMISecurityManager( ));

  // we'll search for JavaSpaces using the following template
  Class types[] = {JavaSpace.class};
  ServiceTemplate template = new ServiceTemplate(null, types, null);

  // will handle leases for objects we drop in into the JavaSpace
  LeaseRenewalManager leaseManager = new LeaseRenewalManager();

  // first get ServiceRegistrar for a known lookup
  // service—unicast discovery is used to keep the example simple
  ServiceRegistrar reg = null;
  try{
    LookupLocator look = new LookupLocator(hostname, 4160);
    reg = look.getRegistrar();
  }
  catch(Exception e){
    System.out.println("Couldn't find lookup service "
      + e.toString( ));
    System.exit(1);
    }//end catch
```

Next the lookup() method in ServiceRegistrar is used to locate a Java-Space. It is a fatal error if the JavaSpace cannot be located.

```
// ...then find a JavaSpace.
JavaSpace space = null;
try {
    space = (JavaSpace)reg.lookup(template);
}
catch (RemoteException re) {
    System.out.println(re);
    space=null;
}//end catch

if (space == null) {
    System.out.println("Couldn't associate with local JavaSpace");
    System.exit(1);
}//end if
```

The ReceiptProducer then loops forever, generating random Receipts [with the assistance of createNewReason() and createNewBiz(), which make up reasons for spending money] and using space.write() to place the Receipts into the JavaSpace. The null second parameter to write() means that no transaction is associated with this JavaSpace operation. We use Lease.ANY, because a LeaseRenewalManager will be used to handle the lease that is returned from write(). ReceiptProducer then sleeps for a random amount of time before generating another Receipt. The createNewReason() and createNewBiz() methods follow.

```
// loop forever, generating a random Receipt, sleeping,
// then repeating

while (true) {
    // create a new Receipt...
    String reason = createNewReason();
    String biz = createNewBiz();
    int cost = (int)(100 * Math.random());
    // new receipts have 'examined = false' by default
    Receipt receipt = new Receipt(reason, cost, biz);

    // ...put it into the space

    System.out.println("Writing " + receipt + " to space.");
    Lease lease = null;
    try {
        lease = space.write(receipt, null, Lease.ANY);
    }
```

```
        catch (Exception e) {
           System.out.println("Couldn't write Receipt to space: "
              + e);
        }//end catch

        // ...let LeaseRenewalManager instance handle the lease
        leaseManager.renewUntil(lease, Lease.ANY, null);

        // ...and sleep for a bit
        try {
           Thread.currentThread().sleep((int)(10000 * Math.random()));
        }
        catch (java.lang.InterruptedException ie) { }
     }//end while
   }


   static private String createNewReason() {

    // return a random reason for spending money

    String reasons[] = {"Bought lunch", "Listened to jazz",
      "Rented a room", "Took a taxi"};
    return reasons[(int)(Math.random() * reasons.length)];

}


   static private String createNewBiz() {

    // return a random business name
    String primary[] = {"Donna\'s", "Ruffin\'s", "Sidney\'s",
      "Storyville", "Praline\'s"};
    String secondary[] = {"Bar and Grill", "Jazz Emporium",
      "Blues Inn", "Cafe"};
    return primary[(int)(Math.random() * primary.length)] +
      " " + secondary[(int)(Math.random() * secondary.length)];
   }

}//end of ReceiptProducer
```

The ReceiptApprover handles the second stage in the work flow pipeline.It searches for Receipt objects with 'examined' = false and replaces them with identical copies with 'examined' set to true. The initial portion of ReceiptApprover.java looks much like the Receipt-Producer:

```
import net.jini.core.discovery.LookupLocator;
import net.jini.core.lookup.ServiceRegistrar;
```

```java
import net.jini.core.lookup.ServiceTemplate;
import net.jini.core.lease.Lease;
import net.jini.lease.LeaseRenewalManager;
import net.jini.space.JavaSpace;
import java.rmi.*;
import java.net.*;
import java.io.*;

public class ReceiptApprover {

    public static void main(String[ ] args){
        if (args.length != 1) {
          System.out.println("Must supply hostname of lookup service");
          System.exit(1);
        }//end if

        new ReceiptApprover(args[0]);
}

    public ReceiptApprover(String hostname) {
    System.setSecurityManager(new RMISecurityManager( ));

    // we'll search for JavaSpaces using the following template

    Class types[] = {JavaSpace.class};
    ServiceTemplate template = new ServiceTemplate(null, types, null);

    // will handle leases for objects we drop in into the JavaSpace
    LeaseRenewalManager leaseManager = new LeaseRenewalManager();

    // first get ServiceRegistrar for a known lookup
    // service—unicast discovery is used to keep the example simple

    ServiceRegistrar reg = null;
    try{
        LookupLocator look = new LookupLocator(hostname, 4160);
        reg = look.getRegistrar();
    }
    catch(Exception e){
        System.out.println("Couldn't find lookup service " +
        e.toString( ));
        System.exit(1);
    }//end catch

    // ...then find the JavaSpace.

    JavaSpace space = null;
    try {
```

```
        space = (JavaSpace)reg.lookup(template);
}
catch (RemoteException re) {
    System.out.println(re);
    space=null;
}//end catch

if (space == null) {
    System.out.println("Couldn't associate with local JavaSpace");
    System.exit(1);
}//end if
```

> The template that will be used for searching the JavaSpace is an instance of Receipt with all fields null (this makes the fields wild cards) except for 'examined'. The 'examined' field is set to false in the template so that we don't consume the objects that we produce (all of which will have 'examined' set to true).

```
//this is our template—we can't care about Receipt details, except that
//the 'examined' field is NOT set
Receipt receipttemplate = new Receipt();
receipttemplate.examined=new Boolean(false);
```

> The ReceiptApprover then finds and removes Receipt objects that have not been approved from the JavaSpace, sets the examined field, and places the objects back into the JavaSpace. The space.take() and space.write() methods are used to extract and replace the Receipts. The LeaseRenewalManager instance created above is used to handle leasing issues related to writing objects into the space.

```
// loop forever, consuming Receipt objects that have not been
// "examined" as they become available, replacing each with an
// examined = true copy

while (true) {
    System.out.println("Trying to read and update a Receipt...");
    try {
      Receipt receipt =
        (Receipt) space.take(receipttemplate, null,
          Integer.MAX_VALUE);
      System.out.println("Receipt: " + receipt +
        " read, approving...");
      receipt.examined=new Boolean(true);
      Lease lease = null;
      lease = space.write(receipt, null, Lease.ANY);
      System.out.println("Wrote updated receipt.");
```

```
            // ...let LeaseRenewalManager instance handle the lease
            leaseManager.renewUntil(lease, Lease.ANY, null);
        }
      catch (Exception e) {
        System.out.println("Couldn't read/write Receipt: "+ e);
        e.printStackTrace();
      }//end catch
    }//end while
  }//end of main()
}//end of ReceiptApprover
```

The ReceiptDetailer handles the final work flow stage, removing Receipts that have 'examined' = true from the JavaSpace and writing a detailed description to standard output. Again, the initial portion of ReceiptDetailer.java is similar to the ReceiptApprover and ReceiptProducer:

```
import net.jini.core.discovery.LookupLocator;
import net.jini.core.lookup.ServiceRegistrar;
import net.jini.core.lookup.ServiceTemplate;
import net.jini.core.entry.Entry;
import net.jini.space.JavaSpace;
import java.rmi.*;
import java.net.*;
import java.io.*;

public class ReceiptDetailer {

  public static void main(String[ ] args){
    if (args.length != 1) {
        System.out.println("Must supply hostname of lookup service");
        System.exit(1);
    }//end if

    new ReceiptDetailer(args[0]);
  }

  public ReceiptDetailer(String hostname) {
    System.setSecurityManager(new RMISecurityManager( ));

    // we'll search for JavaSpaces using the following template
    Class types[] = {JavaSpace.class};
    ServiceTemplate template = new ServiceTemplate(null,
      types, null);
    // first get ServiceRegistrar for a known lookup
    // service—unicast discovery is used to keep the example
    // simple
```

```
ServiceRegistrar reg = null;
try{
    LookupLocator look = new LookupLocator(hostname, 4160);
    reg = look.getRegistrar();
}
catch(Exception e){
    System.out.println("Couldn't find lookup service "
        + e.toString( ));
    System.exit(1);
}//end catch

// ...then find the JavaSpace.
JavaSpace space = null;
try {
    space = (JavaSpace)reg.lookup(template);
}
catch (RemoteException re) {
    System.out.println(re);
    space=null;
}//end catch

if (space == null) {
  System.out.println("Couldn't associate with local JavaSpace");
  System.exit(1);
}//end if
```

This time the template insists that only Receipt objects with 'examined' set to true be matched. A call to snapshot() is made once the template is built, to obtain a more efficient template. This is appropriate because we will be searching repeatedly using the same template (it also provides a bit of variety). If creation of the more efficient template fails for some reason, we just use the normal one instead. The rest of ReceiptDetailer is straightforward.

```
// this is our template—we don't care about Receipt
// details, except that the 'examined' field is set
Receipt receipttemplate = new Receipt();
receipttemplate.examined=new Boolean(true);
// snapshot returns an Entry that is optimized for searching
Entry efficienttemplate=null;
try {
    efficienttemplate = space.snapshot(receipttemplate);
}
catch (RemoteException re) {
    // if the snapshot fails, just use our original
    efficienttemplate = receipttemplate;
}//end catch
```

```
// loop forever, consuming Receipt objects that have been
// "examined" as they become available

while (true) {
    System.out.println("Trying to read a Receipt...");
    try {
        Receipt receipt =
            (Receipt) space.take(efficienttemplate, null,
                Integer.MAX_VALUE);
        System.out.println("Receipt: " + receipt +
          ", previously approved, now consumed.");
    }
    catch (Exception e) {
        System.out.println("Couldn't read Receipt from space: "+ e);
        e.printStackTrace();
    }//end catch
}//end while
}//end of main()
}//end of ReceiptDetailer
```

Transactions

Transactions are a widely used technique for grouping operations whose executions must meet an all-or-nothing standard—either all operations complete successfully, or the effects of all the operations are undone. The failure of even one operation causes a transaction abort, which results in all other operations in the transaction being canceled. From the outside, the operations involved in a transaction appear to occur simultaneously. A typical transaction example involves movement of funds between bank accounts—money is withdrawn from a checking account and deposited into a savings account. If any intermediate steps in the transfer fail, all steps should be reversed and the money should remain in the first account. Another transaction example is a series of take() operations on separate JavaSpaces, where either all necessary entries must be removed or none should be. Transactions provide the familiar ACID properties: *a*tomicity, *c*onsistency, *i*solation, and *d*urability. Atomicity means that the operations appear to execute atomically—from outside the transaction, all appear to either succeed or fail. Consistency means that operations in a transaction, as a group, bring the system from one "reasonable" state to another. What *reasonable* means is entirely application-specific. Isolation means that transactions execute in a vacuum—other transactions cannot see partial results. Results of operations involved in a transaction will be visible once the transaction commits.

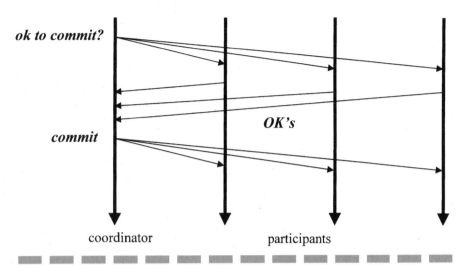

Figure 2-35
A generic two-phase commit (2PC) protocol. A coordinator asks a group of participants
to execute a set of operations involved in a transaction. Each participant votes either to
commit ("OK") or to abort. A single abort is enough to cause the entire transaction to
abort. In the example illustrated here, all participants vote to commit, so the coordinator sends a round of "commit" messages that finalize the transaction. Under 2PC
semantics, a vote of commit on the part of a participant is a promise to perform the
operation(s) should unanimous agreement be reached.

Durability simply means that the results of a transaction persist after
the transaction completes.

Two-phase commit (2PC), illustrated in Fig. 2-35, is a commit protocol
used to ensure the atomicity of transactions. In 2PC, a coordinator asks
a group of participants to execute a set of operations. Each participant
subsequently informs the coordinator whether the operation(s) can be
carried out—if they can, a vote of "commit" (or "OK") is entered. A "commit" vote is a promise that if the transaction succeeds, the participant
will carry out the operations. If an operation cannot be carried out, then
a negative vote ("abort") is issued. If the voting is unanimously positive,
then the coordinator sends a final round of messages requesting that the
results of the operations be made permanent. If even a single participant votes to abort, then the transaction must be aborted. In this case,
the coordinator's final round of messages demands that participants
undo any effects of the operations.

A deep analysis of 2PC is out of the scope of this text, but note that
2PC is a *blocking* protocol, meaning that under some failure scenarios
(e.g., failure of the coordinator and a single participant) it is impossible

for live participants to determine the outcome of the transaction until the coordinator has recovered. The 2PC and alternative commit protocols have been widely studied in the distributed systems literature. For Jini, 2PC is what you get!

While the transaction facilities in Jini are used less frequently than the other components we've discussed so far, they are mentioned briefly here. More details on Jini transactions can be found in the Jini specification. The transaction facility in Jini is really only a skeletal mechanism for *supporting* the concept of transactions. As such, it provides the machinery to support a 2PC protocol and necessary interfaces for Jini entities to create and participate in transactions. The degree to which the ACID properties are guaranteed is completely application-specific. This makes the Jini transaction framework generic and applicable to a wider range of applications. The discussion below exposes the TransactionManager and TransactionParticipant interfaces, needed when services are designed to work in the context of transactions. Clients rarely need to use these interfaces. A subsequent section discusses the Transaction interface, which is used by clients to bind groups of service operations into transactions. The only Jini service that currently uses Transactions is JavaSpaces.

The TransactionManager and TransactionParticipant Interfaces. Transactions are overseen by a transaction manager, which implements the TransactionManager interface (Fig. 2-36) and serves as the 2PC coordinator. Transaction managers typically will be discovered as any other service is discovered—through a lookup service.

Services implementing this interface allow transactions to be created, for participants to join in a transaction, and for transactions to be committed and aborted. Typically one entity will create a new transaction using the create() method. The return value from create() is an instance of Created, a class defined in the TransactionManager interface. The id field in Created is a unique transaction identifier, and can be passed by the entity that created the transaction to other entities that should become participants. The join() method is used to join a transaction. It accepts a transaction id, an instance of TransactionParticipant (discussed below), and a crash count. The crash count is an indication of how many times a participant has crashed in the context of the current transaction. This count must be stored in nonvolatile storage. When a participant joins, the TransactionManager determines if the participant has previously executed a join(). If it has and the crash count matches, no action is taken. If the new crash count value

```
package net.jini.core.transaction.server;

public interface TransactionManager extends Remote,
  TransactionConstants {
  public static class Created implements Serializable {
    public final long id;
    public final Lease lease;
    public Created(long id, Lease lease) {...}
  }
  Created create(long leaseFor) throws LeaseDeniedException,
    RemoteException;
  void join(long id, TransactionParticipant part, long crashCount)
    throws UnknownTransactionException,
      CannotJoinException, CrashCountException, RemoteException;
  int getState(long id) throws UnknownTransactionException,
    RemoteException;
  void commit(long id) throws UnknownTransactionException,
    CannotCommitException, RemoteException;
  void commit(long id, long waitFor) throws
    UnknownTransactionException, CannotCommitException,
      TimeoutExpiredException, RemoteException;
  void abort(long id) throws UnknownTransactionException,
    CannotAbortException, RemoteException;
  void abort(long id, long waitFor) throws
    UnknownTransactionException, CannotAbortException,
      TimeoutExpiredException, RemoteException;
}
```

Figure 2-36
TransactionManager.

differs, a CrashCountException is thrown by the TransactionManager and the transaction is forced to abort. This action is taken because the participant has lost synchronization with the current state of the transaction. Other exceptions that can be thrown on a join() include UnknownTransactionException, CannotJoinException, and RemoteException. UnknownTransactionException is thrown if the transaction id specified is invalid. CannotJoinException is thrown if the transaction id is valid but the corresponding transaction is no longer active. RemoteException is thrown if there is a problem communicating with the TransactionManager over RMI. In any event, if the join() fails, the participant must communicate this information to the creator of the transaction using a mechanism outside the transaction facilities (e.g., via a

```
package net.jini.core.transaction.server;

public interface TransactionConstants {
     int ACTIVE = 1;
     int VOTING = 2;
     int PREPARED = 3;
     int NOTCHANGED = 4;
     int COMMITTED = 5;
     int ABORTED = 6;
}
```

Figure 2-37
TransactionConstants.

return value from the method call that provided the transaction id to the participant). The getState() method can be used to determine the current state of a particular transaction. It takes a single argument, a transaction identifier, and returns one of the values defined in the TransactionConstants interface, shown in Fig. 2-37.

The commit() and abort() methods in the TransactionManager interface allow the creator of a transaction to vote for the outcome of the transaction. If the creator executes commit(), then the method blocks until the transaction is committed. If any participant subsequently votes to abort, then the transaction is aborted and the commit() call fails with a CannotCommitException. This exception is also raised if the state of the transaction is already known to be ABORTED. The abort() method allows the creator of a transaction to abort a transaction. If the transaction previously reached the COMMITED state, then a CannotAbortException is thrown. Allowing the lease associated with a particular transaction to expire or explicitly canceling this lease is equivalent to an explicit abort() call.

The TransactionParticipant interface (Fig. 2-38) allows additional parties to participate in a transaction. Entities who associate themselves with a transaction through a join() call rather than a create() call (they're called *participants* in the Jini specification) must implement the TransactionParticipant interface. During the various phases of 2PC, the prepare(), commit(), and abort() methods associated with this interface will be called by the transaction manager. The prepare() method requires that a participant issue its vote to commit or abort. It should

```
package net.jini.core.transaction.server;

public interface TransactionParticipant extends
  Remote,  TransactionConstants {
  int prepare(TransactionManager mgr, long id) throws
    UnknownTransactionException, RemoteException;
  void commit(TransactionManager mgr, long id) throws
    UnknownTransactionException, RemoteException;
  void abort(TransactionManager mgr, long id) throws
    UnknownTransactionException, RemoteException;
  int prepareAndCommit(TransactionManager mgr, long id)
    throws UnknownTransactionException, RemoteException;
}
```

Figure 2-38
TransactionParticipant

return PREPARED to indicate that it is capable of performing operations associated with the transaction. It may also return NOTCHANGED if the operations have had no visible effects on its state. If it cannot guarantee that the operations can be performed, the return value from prepared() should be ABORTED. The PREPARED, NOTCHANGED, etc., values are provided in the TransactionConstants interface. Subsquently, the transaction manager will call either the commit() or the abort() method in the TransactionParticipant interface. There is no return value for these methods—when commit() is called, the participant is required to make the effects of the operations in the transaction permanent. Should abort() be called, the effects of any operations in the transaction must be undone before abort() returns. The transaction manager may optimize the 2PC protocol for the case where there is only a single participant whose vote is still needed by calling prepareAndCommit() instead of prepare() followed by commit(). In this case, either the participant will make the effects of the transactional operations permanent and then return COMMITED, or it will return ABORTED to cancel the transaction.

Transaction, TransactionFactory, and ServerTransaction. The TransactionParticipant interface in conjunction with a service implementing the TransactionManager interface can be used by clients to support a 2PC protocol. The specific semantics of home-brew transactional

```
package net.jini.core.transaction;
public interface Transaction {
      public static class Created implements Serializable {
         public final Transaction transaction;
         public final Lease lease;
         Created(Transaction transaction, Lease lease) {...}
      }

   void commit() throws UnknownTransactionException,
     CannotCommitException, RemoteException;
   void commit(long waitFor) throws UnknownTransactionException,
     CannotCommitException, TimeoutExpiredException,
       RemoteException;
   void abort() throws UnknownTransactionException,
     CannotAbortException, RemoteException;
   void abort(long waitFor) throws UnknownTransactionException,
     CannotAbortException, TimeoutExpiredException, RemoteException;
}
```

Figure 2-39
Transaction.

facilities built with these interfaces are entirely up to the programmer. Jini also provides a high-level Transaction interface, shown in Fig. 2-39. Services implementing this interface "promise" to provide the ACID properties discussed earlier. The only service that ships with Jini which uses Transactions is JavaSpaces.

Clients create Transactions by using the TransactionFactory class, shown in Fig. 2-40. The inner Created class in the Transaction interface is the return value for the create() method in the TransactionFactory. An instance of Created stores a Transaction and an associated lease, much as Created in the TransactionManager interface stored a transaction identifier and a lease. The TransactionFactory create() method requires prior discovery of a service implementing the TransactionManager interface to coordinate the 2PC protocol.

Transaction is used on the client side, which initiates the creation of new Transactions, but what about the participants in a Transaction? An implementation of Transaction called ServerTransaction (Fig. 2-41) exposes a join() method that can be used to join a transaction. A participant should cast the Transaction passed by a client into a ServerTransaction to join. The join() and getState() methods work just as in the

```
public class TransactionFactory {
  public static Transaction.Created
    create(TransactionManager mgr, long leaseFor) throws
      LeaseDeniedException, RemoteException {...}
  public static NestableTransaction.Created
    create(NestableTransactionManager mgr,long leaseFor)
      throws LeaseDeniedException, RemoteException {...}
}
```

Figure 2-40
TransactionFactory.

```
public class ServerTransaction implements Transaction, Serializable
{
  public final TransactionManager mgr;
  public final long id;
  public ServerTransaction(TransactionManager mgr, long id) {...}
  public void join(TransactionParticipant part,
    long crashCount) throws UnknownTransactionException,
      CannotJoinException, CrashCountException, RemoteException
      {...}
  public int getState() throws UnknownTransactionException,
    RemoteException {...}
  public boolean isNested() {...}
}
```

Figure 2-41
ServerTransaction.

join() and getState() for the TransactionManager interface, but of course a transaction identifier is not required—this is embodied in the Server-Transaction instance.

A very simple code snip illustrates the use of a Transaction in the context of JavaSpaces. In the following, two JavaSpace services have been discovered, js1 and js2. A TransactionManager tm has also been discovered. The goal is to move an entry that matches a template from js1 to js2, using a Transaction to ensure that the entry is not lost during the move:

```
Transaction.Created created =
  TransactionManager.create(tm, 9999999);
```

```
// Probably want to use a LeaseRenewalManager to make
// sure the lease 'created.lease' lives long enough to
// complete the operations-an exercise for the reader.
Entry e = js1.take(template, created.transaction,
  JavaSpace.NO_WAIT);
if (e != null) {
  Lease writeLease = js2.write(e, created.transaction, 9999999);
  // Similarly, should make sure that the writeLease gets renewed
  // for as long as we want the entry to remain in the
  // second JavaSpace

  // Finally, commit() so the operations become permanent
    created.transaction.commit();
}// end if
else {
  // or abort
    created.transaction.abort();
}
```

Firing It All Up

Deployment issues are always very system-specific and subject to change. When firing up, don't skip a visit to the distribution for such details. In the meantime, here are a few things to keep in mind.

The Jini distribution includes a default lookup service implementation, named *reggie*. Reggie is an *activatible* Java service, which means that it interacts with the RMI activation daemon to ensure that it is run automatically when needed. This means that unless the RMI activation daemon's logs are cleared, it will typically be necessary to start the reggie service manually only once. After subsequent crashes or reboots, the activation daemon will restart reggie as needed.

The Jini distribution also provides a simple web server for deploying class files, two implementations of the JavaSpaces interface (outrigger, the persistent version, and transient-outrigger, the volatile version), and an implementation of the TransactionManager interface (mahalo). The following command lines for starting the various Jini components are provided as illustrations—the Jini distribution contains complete information on command line arguments for all these services. Note that under each heading (e.g., "RMI Activation Daemon"), a single command line is specified, even though formatting may make it appear to span lines. Assumptions below are that the machine running the various services has IP address 10.0.0.13, that the Jini distribution lives in "c:\jini1_1", that logs will be created inside an existing directory "c:\jini_logs", and that class files retrieved through the web server are stored in "c:\jini1_1\lib\". The command lines should be edited as needed for deployment under Unix (or your favorite OS) rather than Windows and to modify the assumptions above.

Web Server

```
java -jar c:\jini1_1\lib\tools.jar -port 8080 -dir
c:\jini1_1\lib\ -trees -verbose
```

RMI Activation Daemon

```
rmid -J-Dsun.rmi.activation.execPolicy=none -log c:\jini_logs\rmid_log
```

Reggie (Lookup Service)

```
java -Djava.security.policy=c:\jini1_1\example\lookup\policy.all
   -jar c:\jini1_1\lib\reggie.jar http://10.0.0.13:8080/reggie-dl.jar
   c:\jini1_1\example\lookup\policy.all c:\jini_logs\reggie_log public
```

Transaction Manager

```
java -jar -Djava.security.policy=c:\jini1_1\example\txn\policy.all
-Dcom.sun.jini.mahalo.managerName=TransactionManager
 c:\jini1_1\lib\mahalo.jar http://10.0.0.13:8080/mahalo-dl.jar
 c:\jini1_1\example\txn\policy.all c:\jini_logs\txn_log public
```

JavaSpaces Service

```
java -jar -Djava.security.policy=c:\jini1_1\example\books\policy.all
   -Djava.rmi.server.codebase=http://10.0.0.13:8080/outrigger-dl.jar
    -Dcom.sun.jini.outrigger.spaceName=JavaSpaces
     c:\jini1_1\lib\transient-outrigger.jar public
```

POINTERS

The basic concepts of service discovery can be explained in a few sentences. I've often done exactly this when people asked me what sort of book this would be. Clearly the devil is in the details, though, and especially so in the case of Jini. Understanding Jini requires understanding other sophisticated Java technologies such as RMI, and being an effective Jini programmer requires significant background in other areas, including networking and the Java security framework. The following list of references includes works on Java [5, 6] RMI [1], Java security [7], as well as other books on Jini [8 through 12], and a book on JavaSpaces [7]. Reference 9 is worthy of note, because it is a printed version of Jan Newmarch's very popular Web-based tutorial on Jini. Reference 12 is a printed version of the Jini specification, also provided in the Jini distribution in PDF and Postscript form. Reference 14 includes a discussion of the blocking properties of 2PC and is a good general reference for reliability issues. Reference 4 provides excellent coverage of Linda, upon which the JavaSpaces concept is based.

1. Javasoft RMI documentation, www.javasoft.com/rmi.

2. G. G. Richard, III, and S. Tu, "On Patterns for Practical Fault Tolerant Software in Java," *Proceedings of the 17th IEEE Symposium on Reliable Distributed Systems,* West Lafayette, Ind., pp. 144–150, 1998.

3. M. K. McKusick, K. Bostic, M. J. Karels, and J. S. Quarterman, *The Design and Implementation of the 4.4BSD Operating System,* Addison-Wesley, Reading, Mass., 1996.

4. N. Carriero, D. Gelernter, "How to Write Parallel Programs: A Guide to the Perplexed," ACM Computing Surveys, September 1989.

5. D. Flanagan, *Java in a Nutshell,* O'Reilly, 2000.

6. P. J. Deitel and H. M. Deitel, *Java: How to Program,* Prentice-Hall, Englewood Cliffs, N.J., 1999.

7. S. Oaks, *Java Security,* O'Reilly, 1999.

8. W. K. Edwards, *Core Jini,* Prentice-Hall, Englewood Cliffs, N.J., 2000.

9. J. Newmarch, *A Programmer's Guide to Jini Technology,* Apress, 2000.

10. S. Li, *Professional Jini,* Wrox Press, 2000.

11. S. Oaks and H. Wong, *Jini in a Nutshell : A Desktop Quick Reference,* O'Reilly, 2000.

12. K. Arnold, R. W. Scheifler, J. Waldo, A. Wollrath, and B. O'Sullivan, *The Jini Specification,* Addison-Wesley, 1999.

13. E. Freeman, S. Hupfer, and K. Arnold, *JavaSpaces: Principles, Patterns and Practice,* Addison-Wesley, Reading, Mass., 1999.

14. K. Birman, *Building Secure and Reliable Network Applications,* Prentice-Hall, Englewood Cliffs, N.J., 1997.

SLP: An IETF Protocol for Service Discovery

Overview of Service Location Protocol

The Service Location Protocol (SLP) is a protocol in the Internet Engineering Task Force (IETF) standards track aimed at providing service discovery for IP-based networks. Unlike other service discovery technologies, which aspire (at least in theory) to some level of transport-level independence, SLP was designed for IP-based networks and depends heavily on UDP and TCP. SLP enables applications to discover the existence, location, and configuration of needed services and for services to advertise their availability. SLP comprises three entities: service agents, (SAs), user agents (UAs), and directory agents (DAs). SAs operate on behalf of services and advertise the locations and attributes of available services, while UAs discover the locations and attributes of services needed by client software. Attributes are used to differentiate between services of the same type and to communicate configuration information to UAs. UAs can discover services either by issuing queries over the network directly or by accessing one or more DAs, which cache information about services. Scopes can be configured that allow services to be partitioned into sets. Unlike Jini, which requires the availability of at least one lookup service, SLP can operate without DAs. The presence of DAs in environments with many clients and services does tend to reduce network traffic, however. Some common SLP interactions are depicted in Fig. 3-1. These interactions are described in much greater detail in this chapter.

SLP services are advertised through a service URL, which contains all information necessary to contact a service. While SLP helps clients to learn the location and characteristics of a service, the protocol that a client uses to communicate with a service is outside the scope of the SLP specification. This is in sharp contrast to UPnP and Jini, but similar to Bluetooth's SDP (Service Discovery Protocol). For standardization purposes, SLP supports service templates, which define the syntax of service URLs for a service type (e.g., a printer) and also define a set of attributes that describe service characteristics. The definition of *attributes* in the service template includes names, types, default and allowed values, and other characteristics.

Note that SLP is designed primarily for environments where administrative decisions can be made regarding multicast scope, security, and the organization of clients and services. While SLP can operate in large-scale networks, in its current form it will generally not scale to networks

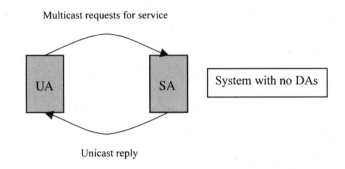

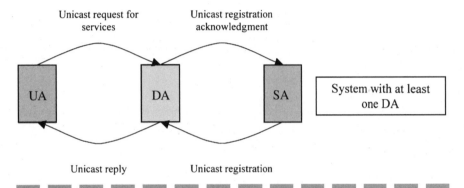

Figure 3-1
Common SLP agent interactions. In a system with no directory agents (DAs), a user
agent (UA) will typically send multicast requests to find appropriate services. The
request contains a service type and essential characteristics of the needed service. A
service agent (SA) which provides a matching service will unicast a reply containing the
service location and other contact-related information. In systems with at least one DA,
SAs register available services with the DA and UAs query the DA for the locations of
available services. There are a variety of options for discovering DAs: The locations of
DAs may be statically configured, DHCP may be used, or multicast discovery can be
used. Once a UA knows the location of a needed service, SLP is out of the picture—
unlike Jini and UPnP, the SLP implementation is not involved in client/server communication. The interactions between UAs, SAs, and DAs can be constrained through the
use of "scopes" (not pictured), which allow agent groups to be formed.

the size of the global Internet. SLP uses administratively scoped multicast [1], which allows administrators overseeing networks with appropriate routing hardware to control the extent of multicast coverage, but
multicast in the broad Internet is generally not yet available. Research
to support wider scale deployment of SLP is ongoing. Pointers can be
found on the SLP home page, *www.srvloc.org*.

Goals of the Chapter

This chapter provides an overview of the SLPv2 specification, which is contained in RFC 2608 [2]. Material from RFCs 2609 [3], which defines service templates, 2610 [4], which discusses DHCP options for SLP, and 2614 [5], which discusses the SLP APIs, is also discussed. After a discussion of the various agents in SLP and the wire protocol, detailed C source code is provided to illustrate development of clients and services under SLP. After reading the chapter, the reader will have a good understanding of SLP concepts and sufficient knowledge to write interesting SLP services and clients.

The discussion in this chapter focuses on SLPv2, which is the current version. SLPv2 is a redesign of SLPv1 [6], which was found to have serious scalability and security issues. SLPv2 has several incompatibilities with SLPv1, including different message headers; thus interoperability between SLPv1 and SLPv2 agents is a problem. For more information on the incompatibilities, see reference 7. All new applications should use SLPv2, and thus we do not discuss SLPv1 further in this chapter. Changes are currently being recommended for SLPv2, reflected in SLPv2bis, which is discussed in greater detail at *www.srvloc.org*. The goal as of this writing is not to break the SLPv2 wire protocol in SLPv2bis.

The SLPv2 specification outlines an API for both C and Java. Considerable emphasis in this chapter is placed on the use of a popular SLP implementation (OpenSLP) for development, and somewhat less emphasis is placed on the exact wire protocol, which is discussed in great detail in RFC 2608. Several implementations of SLP are currently available [e.g., 8, 9], but in this chapter the OpenSLP [8] implementation is used exclusively. OpenSLP is essentially faithful to RFC 2608, with ongoing work being done to add a few missing features. A number of operating systems are supported, including Linux, Win32, FreeBSD, Solaris, and MacOS X. All code in this chapter is written in C and developed under Linux and MacOS X. To understand the examples requires familiarity with C. The sample client and service communicate using sockets, so familiarity with sockets programming is useful but not required.

Essential Details

This section concentrates on SLP details which are essential for understanding the wire protocol, the interactions between the various entities in an SLP-enabled network, and the APIs. Message formats, service types, the way in which service location information is specified, service attributes, service templates (which standardize the names and types of attributes associated with a service type), and naming authorities (which provide context for understanding a service type) are covered below. The next major section will build upon this information and discuss the various SLP agent types.

Specifying a Service Type

Service types are the fundamental naming convention for services in SLP. Clients make their service needs known (through a user agent) by specifying the needed service types (and possibly attributes). In this section the specification of service types using the "service: URL" scheme (discussed in detail in RFC 2609) is addressed. The specification of a service type consists largely of defining the service type's attribute names and values in a service template. Attributes describe the essential characteristics of a service, including both configuration information (e.g., a list of ports on which the service listens) and information of use to human users (e.g., a contact name for the administrator of a service). Service templates also define the syntax of portions of a Service URL, which are covered in the next section.

Service URLs. Service URLs describe the type and location of a service and provide other essential information necessary to contact a service. Service URLs have the following format. The portions in italic are nonliterals.

```
service:   service_type  :  site  url_path
```

The service_type portion of the Service URL identifies the type of service associated with the URL and thus identifies an appropriate service template, which in turns defines how most of the remainder of the URL should be interpreted. Service templates are discussed later in this section. It may consist of an abstract or concrete service type and possibly a Naming Authority (also discussed later in this section). An abstract service type defines a basic service type, which may be further refined by *subclassing* with the definition of concrete types. If the Naming Authority is present, it is separated from the rest of the service type by a ".". The site portion of the URL identifies the location of the service. Supported address types include IP, IPX, and AppleTalk. IP is considered here; for more information on IPX and Appletalk formats in Service URLs, see RFC 2609. The site portion of the Service URL begins with "//" for IP addresses and contains an IP address and optionally a port number. Following the site is the url_path, the format of which is dependent on the particular service type (and is defined in the service template). The url_path portion of the Service URL generally supplements the service type and site portions of the URL, providing additional information necessary to contact the service (e.g., a list of port numbers on which the service listens for connections). Note that the url_path portion is optional; many services provide sufficient descriptive information in the other portions of the Service URL for clients to connect to and use the service.

An example of a Service URL follows:

```
"service:echo-service.test:tcp://10.0.0.13:5000"
```

This Service URL describes the location of a service of type "echo-service," with Naming Authority "test" (which signifies an experimental, nonstandardized service). The "echo-service" is an abstract service type. The "tcp" attachment on "echo-service" provides a concrete service type and alerts the client that TCP must be used for communication. The service is located on a machine with a nonrouteable IP address 10.0.0.13, and listens on port 5000. There is no url_path. A service template for the echo-service type appears later in this section. Later in the chapter, an implementation of the echo-service and a corresponding client are given.

The following Service URL illustrates the use of a simple url_path:

```
service:printer:lpr://printer.cs.uno.edu/laser
```

The abstract type of this service is "printer," the concrete type "lpr" (a particular type of printer). The printer service is located on "printer.cs.uno.edu," listening on a default port. The url_path defines a queue name for the printer, which is "laser."

The last example advertises an image service on "imaging.cs.uno.edu," listening on a default port, which has a picture of "Susanne," in JPEG format, with a resolution of 1024 × 768. The Naming Authority is "test."

```
Service:image-service.test://imaging.cs.uno.edu/Susanne.jpeg;
  format=JPEG;resolution=1024x768
```

Service Templates. We now consider service templates, which support standardization of particular service types. Service templates define the format of the url_path portion of the Service URL for a service type and explicitly define the service's attributes, including the names, types, allowed values, and default values. Service templates have five portions: the name of the service type, the template version, a description of the template (in text, intended to be read by humans trying to understand the service being defined), the format of the url_path for Service URLS representing services of the type defined by the template, and a specification of the attributes for this service type. Each of the portions is separated from the others by a blank line. Reserved characters include ";", "=", "%", ",", "#", line feed, and carriage return.

The service name is the first portion of the template and consists of a single line of the following sort:

```
template-type=name_of_service.NamingAuthority
```

The Naming Authority is optional, but if present, it must be separated from the name_of_service by a period. The next section defines the version of the template:

```
template-version=0.0
```

RFC 2609 recommends that "draft" templates begin at 0.0, with the minor version number incremented when optional attributes are added and the major version number incremented when required attributes are added, attributes are removed, or other major changes are made. Standard templates begin with a version number of 1.0.

The third portion of a template definition provides descriptive text, suitable for human consumption. An example follows:

```
template-description=
This is the place for lots of descriptive text about a
service.  Blah blah blah, etc. etc.
Even more description, blah blah blah.  Blah!
```

The fourth portion defines the format of the url_path component of Service URLs of the service type being defined. If the url_path is not used by this service type, a line like the following is included in the template:

```
template-url-syntax=
url_path= ;
```

Otherwise, an ABNF (augmented Backus Naur form) grammar [10] must be provided to formally define the url_path syntax. Here are some examples. The first defines a simple url_path syntax which consists of the string "ports=" followed by a comma-separated list of integer port numbers. Each port must consist of at least one digit (and contain only digits).

```
template-url-syntax= url_path
url_path= ";ports=" list_of_ports
list_of_ports = port / port "," list_of_ports
port = 1*DIGIT
```

The following is an example of a url_path which allows the available transport protocols for a service to be specified. UDP, TCP, or both are permissible:

```
template-url-syntax= transports-list
transports-list = ";transport=udp" /
  ";transport=tcp" / ";transport=udp,tcp" /
  ";transport=tcp,udp"
```

Finally, the last section of the service template defines the names and characteristics of attributes for the service type. An attribute definition includes the name of the attribute, the attribute's type, a number of flags, an optional list of default values, an optional block of text which describes the attribute to humans, and an optional list of allowed values. Each attribute's definition is separated from the others by a single blank line.

The supported types are string, integer, boolean, keyword, and opaque. Integers are restricted to 32-bit signed quantities. The keyword attribute has no associated value—its presence is an implied value. Opaque types allow binary values to be stored in attributes; the first byte of an opaque value is \FF, which differentiates the value from a string value. The subsequent bytes are escaped binary values (for example, \00 denotes binary zero).

An attribute definition begins with "name=type" and is followed by one or more of these flags: O, M, L, X. If O is present, then the attribute is considered optional, and a particular service instance may not register a value for this attribute. If the O flag is missing, then the attribute is required. The M attribute indicates that the attribute can take on lists of values [e.g., candy=(licorice, chocolate, hard)]. Each of the values for a multivalued attribute must be of the specified attribute type.

Boolean and keyword attributes are not allowed to have the M flag set (as it makes no sense). The L attribute indicates that the values that may be taken on by an attribute are not candidates for translation. RFC 2609 discusses internationalization issues for service templates in detail. Finally, the X flag, if present, indicates that clients should always include this attribute in service requests—i.e., the information conveyed by this attribute is critical in making appropriate service choices.

The default values list begins on the second line of the attribute definition and ends when a line does not terminate with a comma. If no default values are supplied, then string values are initialized to the empty string by default. Integers are assigned zero, boolean attributes are assigned false by default, and multivalued attributes are assigned a single default value. The descriptive text follows the default value list and consists of lines of text beginning with the hash (#) character. When a line is encountered that does not begin with #, then the allowed values list begins. This list has the same format as the default values list and ends when a line does not terminate with a comma. An attribute should never be assigned a value that does not appear in the allowed values list (if this list is supplied in the template).

A few examples will clarify the definition of attributes. The first defines an attribute "writeable" with boolean type. The default value is "true," the attribute is considered "required" in service queries by clients (because of the X flag). Further, because the O flag is not present, services are required to provide a value for this attribute during registration.

```
writeable= boolean  X
true
# If this attribute has value TRUE, then the media is
# writeable, otherwise it should be considered read-only.
```

The next defines an attribute "media-type" which has string type. This attribute is required to be registered because the O flag is missing. There is no default value specified. The only allowed values for the attribute are "CDROM," "DVD," "TAPE," "FIXED," and "ZIP."

```
media-type= string
# Defines the media type of a device.  Only the values in the
# allowed value list (below) are permissible.
CDROM,
DVD,
TAPE,
FIXED,
ZIP
```

Standard service templates, which are useful as examples, are available online in the IANA service template repository [11]. We'll look at one example, which is a template that defines the abstract echo-service type, a concrete instance of which is used in coding examples later in the chapter.

```
template-type=echo-service.test

template-version=0.0

template-description=
  Definition of a simple SLP echo service.  Reads lines of
  input (which should include a \n character as a
  line terminator) and echoes the lines back to the client.
  The protocol spoken depends on the concrete service type.

template-url-syntax=
 url-path= ;    depends on concrete type

contact=string O
# the contact name for the maintainer of the service (optional)

contactemail=string O
# the email address of the maintainer of the service (optional)

maxlinelength=integer
80
# the recommended maximum line length (max number of
# characters to transmit before \n; REQUIRED, since O
# modifier is not present).  Default value is 80.
```

The following is the concrete echo-service:tcp type, which dictates that tcp should be used as the transport protocol. Note that definitions of attributes defined in the abstract type are not repeated in the concrete type's template:

```
 template-type=echo-service.test:tcp

 template-version=0.0

 template-description=
   Concrete SLP echo service which uses TCP as a transport protocol.

 template-url-syntax=
   url-path= ;    none

# no additional attributes beyond those described in the
# abstract template "echo-service.test"
```

Naming Authorities

RFC 2608 defines a Naming Authority as "the agency or group which catalogues given service types and attributes." Naming Authorities provide context for understanding the *meaning* of a service type. Service types can be created which are intended to be standardized through IANA, but they can also be created for proprietary or experimental purposes. The Naming Authority tag in a service URL allows client applications to determine whether an advertised service is of a standard type and also helps to avoid name conflicts (e.g., in the case where an experimental service type unintentionally adopts the name of a standard service type) "IANA" is the default Naming Authority and is assumed when no Naming Authority is explicitly mentioned. "IANA" is *not* allowed as an explicit Naming Authority, however—it is "specified" by providing no naming authority string.

Message Formats

All messages in SLP begin with a standard header. The SLP message header is illustrated in Fig. 3-2. The purpose of each field in the header is discussed here.

In the following, all length fields are in network byte order. The Function-ID field is a single byte, containing one of the following integer values. This field identifies the type of message, each of which represents an interaction between two agents. The abbreviated name in the last column is sometimes used in lieu of the longer name when discussing these message types later in the chapter.

```
 0                   1                   2                   3
 0 1 2 3 4 5 6 7 8 9 0 1 2 3 4 5 6 7 8 9 0 1 2 3 4 5 6 7 8 9 0 1
+-+-+-+-+-+-+-+-+-+-+-+-+-+-+-+-+-+-+-+-+-+-+-+-+-+-+-+-+-+-+-+-+
|    Version    |  Function-ID  |            Length             |
+-+-+-+-+-+-+-+-+-+-+-+-+-+-+-+-+-+-+-+-+-+-+-+-+-+-+-+-+-+-+-+-+
| Length, cont. |O|F|R|         reserved          |Next Ext Offset|
+-+-+-+-+-+-+-+-+-+-+-+-+-+-+-+-+-+-+-+-+-+-+-+-+-+-+-+-+-+-+-+-+
|    Next Extension Offset, cont. |             XID             |
+-+-+-+-+-+-+-+-+-+-+-+-+-+-+-+-+-+-+-+-+-+-+-+-+-+-+-+-+-+-+-+-+
|        Language Tag Length      |          Language Tag       |
+-+-+-+-+-+-+-+-+-+-+-+-+-+-+-+-+-+-+-+-+-+-+-+-+-+-+-+-+-+-+-+-+
```

Figure 3-2
SLP message header. All SLP messages contain a header of the type illustrated above.

1.	Service Request	SrvRqst
2.	Service Reply	SrvRply
3.	Service Registration	SrvReg
4.	Service Deregister	SrvDeReg
5.	Service Acknowledge	SrvAck
6.	Attribute Request	AttrRqst
7.	Attribute Reply	AttrRply
8.	DA Advertisement	DAAdvert
9.	Service Type Request	SrvTypeRqst
10.	Service Type Reply	SrvTypeRply
11.	SA Advertisement	SAAdvert

The length field is 3 bytes and contains the length of the entire message, including the SLP header. Several flags are included in the header, each a single bit. The O flag (overflow) is set when the length of the entire message exceeds the maximum UDP datagram length. The F flag (fresh) is set whenever a new SrvReg message is transmitted. Messages with the F flag unset correspond to *incremental* registrations, which are an optional feature. Incremental registrations permit service agents to update specific attributes. The R flag (request multicast) is set when requests are multicast. The 13 bits following these three flags is currently reserved and must be set to 0. SLP supports *extensions* which allow additional data, not governed by the core SLP specification, to be placed into an SLP message. This mechanism allows the protocol to be extended while maintaining compatibility with existing agents. If no extensions are present, then the Next Ext Offset field is set to 0. If extensions are present, then the first extension begins at Next Ext Offset bytes from the beginning of the message (and after the *standard* message data). The format of an SLP extension is shown in Fig. 3-3.

```
 0                   1                   2                   3
 0 1 2 3 4 5 6 7 8 9 0 1 2 3 4 5 6 7 8 9 0 1 2 3 4 5 6 7 8 9 0 1
+-+-+-+-+-+-+-+-+-+-+-+-+-+-+-+-+-+-+-+-+-+-+-+-+-+-+-+-+-+-+-+-+
|         Extension ID          |      Next Extension Offset    |
+-+-+-+-+-+-+-+-+-+-+-+-+-+-+-+-+-+-+-+-+-+-+-+-+-+-+-+-+-+-+-+-+
| Offset, contd.|               Extension Data                  |
+-+-+-+-+-+-+-+-+-+-+-+-+-+-+-+-+-+-+-+-+-+-+-+-+-+-+-+-+-+-+-+-+
```

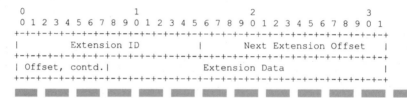

Figure 3-3
SLP message extensions. SLP messages may contain an extension portion, which allows the protocol to be extended while ensuring compatibility with existing agents.

The Extension ID identifies the type of the extension and contains a 16-bit value. Values less than 0x3FFF are standardized, optional extensions. If the agent receiving a message with an extension of this type does not understand the extension, it can be safely ignored. Values between 0x4000 and 0x7FFF identify standardized extensions that are mandatory. UAs or SAs receiving reply messages containing unrecognized extensions in this range must discard and ignore the reply message. DAs and SAs which receive SLP request messages containing unrecognized extensions with identifiers in this range must return an OPTION_NOT_UNDERSTOOD error. Extension ID values in the range of 0x8000 to 0x8FFF may be used by developers for private, nonstandardized protocol extensions. When an agent receives an SLP message containing an unrecognized extension in the range 0x8000 to 0x8FFF, it should simply ignore the extension. Extensions in the *standardized* ranges are registered through the IANA. Values above 0x8FFF are currently reserved. The remaining fields in the extension define the offset of the next extension and the data that make up the extension. For more information on extensions, refer to RFC 2608.

The XID field in the SLP message header is set to a unique value for each request (e.g., by incrementing it), except for DAAdverts, which are always transmitted with an XID of 0. The XID services as a unique identifier for a request from a particular agent. The same XID specified in a request is used in a reply, allowing requests and replies to be matched. The Language Tag Length field in the SLP header contains the length of the Language Tag field. The Language Tag Field conforms to RFC 1766 [12] (e.g., for English, the tag is "en").

The various message types are discussed in detail in the upcoming section on SLP agents, but there are some general rules that apply to all messages. Agents listen on port 427 for unicast/multicast/broadcast SLP messages, and for multicast messages, the administratively scoped multicast [1] address 239.255.255.253 is used. Sequences of bytes in SLP messages are always in network order (i.e., left to right, higher-order bits first). The escape character is a backslash followed by two hexadecimal digits which define the escaped character. Lists of strings in SLP use commas as delimiters, so commas must be escaped (as must other reserved SLP characters, including '(', ')', '!', '\', '<', '>', '=', and '~').

The SLP specification also lays out rules for string comparisons in SLP:

- Comparisons are case-insensitive everywhere except when URLs are compared.

- Initial or terminal white space in a string is ignored when performing a string comparison.

- Internal white space is compressed to a single space during comparisons.

- The reserved character '*' allows wild card matches at arbitrary positions in a string.

Message Retransmission Policies

The formats of specific messages are covered in the next major section, on SLP agents. This section discusses the SLP *multicast convergence algorithm,* which dictates how messages in SLP are retransmitted when requests fail to elicit responses. An SLP configuration parameter CONFIG_RETRY dictates the duration between an initial message transmission and a retransmission because a response has not been received. CONFIG_RETRY has a default value of 2 s. The wait time is doubled for each subsequent retransmission after the first. This applies to both unicast and multicast requests. Unicast transmissions should be repeated only until sufficient responses are received (which could indicate an error) or until CONFIG_RETRY_MAX seconds has elapsed. The cap for multicast requests is CONFIG_MC_MAX seconds. Multicast requests should be repeated until sufficient results are obtained or CONFIG_MC_MAX seconds has elapsed. The default value for both CONFIG_RETRY_MAX and CONFIG_MC_MAX is 15 s.

Some of the messages that will be discussed in the context of SLP agents in the next section contain a *previous responder* list which is significant only when the message is transmitted via multicast. This list allows an agent to indicate the identities of other agents who have already submitted responses to a previous like request. Agents who notice that they are present in the previous responder list for a request will not respond again. To obtain the maximum number of responses from available services, multicast request messages should be retransmitted, updating the previous responder list as responses are received. This process continues until no new responses are received, until the previous responder list overflows the size of a single datagram, or until CONFIG_MC_MAX seconds has elapsed.

Messages contain an XID field that identifies the request. Retransmissions should carry the same XID as the original request, which allows other agents to cache their replies in an effort to reduce processing overhead.

SLP Agents

There are three types of agents in SLP. Service agents (SAs) handle advertising duties for services. Although the implementation of the SA may be included in the service implementation, this is neither required nor necessarily typical. User agents (UAs) locate needed services for client applications. Directory agents (DAs) cache service availability information, providing catalogs of services and reducing UA dependence on multicast to locate services. Each of the agent types is discussed below. Scopes, which can be used to control the visibility and interactions of groups of these entities, are discussed in the upcoming section "Scope and SLP Agents," which immediately follows the discussion of user agents. The "discuss scopes first? or agents first?" question is a classic chicken-and-egg dilemma, so scopes are discussed briefly in the agents sections and in greater detail in a dedicated section. You should read through all these sections completely, to properly understand the interactions between the various agent types, before moving on to the sections that discuss SLP development.

Directory Agents

Directory agents in SLP cache service location and attribute information. They are optional—service agents can advertise their availability and user agents can locate needed services without directory agents, but directory agents serve several important purposes. For one, by caching service information, DAs can substantially reduce network traffic during service discovery. Rather than multicasting service requests, UAs can contact a DA for service information. SAs and UAs can be statically configured to contact specific DAs for registration and service location information, they can passively discover DAs by waiting for advertisements, or they can actively discover DAs by using multicast. UAs and SAs can also use DHCP options to discover the locations of DAs. In fact, if DHCP is used to configure DA locations, then multicast support is unnecessary. RFC 2610 covers DHCP options for location of DAs.

In addition to reducing (or even eliminating) network overhead associated with multicast, DAs can reduce the strain on services by handling requests, freeing services to concentrate on their duties. Further, deployment of DAs provides a mechanism for extending the discovery of services beyond the multicast perimeter of the local network. By configuring the locations of remote DAs, clients can discover services in remote networks which would not be reachable by multicast discovery.

DAs periodically announce their presence by sending a DAAdvert (DA advertisment message). These are repeated at a rate of once every CONFIG_DA_BEAT (no, this isn't the name of a bad funk band). CONFIG_DA_BEAT has a default value of 3 h. The format of a DAAdvert message is illustrated in Fig. 3-4. The Service Location Header is discussed in the previous section "Message Formats." The other fields in a DAAdvert are discussed here.

```
 0                   1                   2                   3
 0 1 2 3 4 5 6 7 8 9 0 1 2 3 4 5 6 7 8 9 0 1 2 3 4 5 6 7 8 9 0 1
+-+-+-+-+-+-+-+-+-+-+-+-+-+-+-+-+-+-+-+-+-+-+-+-+-+-+-+-+-+-+-+-+
|          Service Location Header (function = DAAdvert = 8)    |
+-+-+-+-+-+-+-+-+-+-+-+-+-+-+-+-+-+-+-+-+-+-+-+-+-+-+-+-+-+-+-+-+
|          Error Code           | DA Stateless Boot Timestamp   |
+-+-+-+-+-+-+-+-+-+-+-+-+-+-+-+-+-+-+-+-+-+-+-+-+-+-+-+-+-+-+-+-+
|DA Stateless Boot Time, cont.  |        Length of URL          |
+-+-+-+-+-+-+-+-+-+-+-+-+-+-+-+-+-+-+-+-+-+-+-+-+-+-+-+-+-+-+-+-+
|                              URL                              |
+-+-+-+-+-+-+-+-+-+-+-+-+-+-+-+-+-+-+-+-+-+-+-+-+-+-+-+-+-+-+-+-+
|     Length of <scope-list>    | <scope-list>                  |
+-+-+-+-+-+-+-+-+-+-+-+-+-+-+-+-+-+-+-+-+-+-+-+-+-+-+-+-+-+-+-+-+
|     Length of <attr-list>     | <attr-list>                   |
+-+-+-+-+-+-+-+-+-+-+-+-+-+-+-+-+-+-+-+-+-+-+-+-+-+-+-+-+-+-+-+-+
|     Length of <SLP SPI List>  | <SLP SPI List>                |
+-+-+-+-+-+-+-+-+-+-+-+-+-+-+-+-+-+-+-+-+-+-+-+-+-+-+-+-+-+-+-+-+
| # Auth Blocks |      Authentication Blocks (if any)          |
+-+-+-+-+-+-+-+-+-+-+-+-+-+-+-+-+-+-+-+-+-+-+-+-+-+-+-+-+-+-+-+-+
```

Figure 3-4
SLP DAAdvert. The format of DA advertisement message, sent by directory agents to announce their availability.

The DA Stateless Boot Timestamp is a 32-bit quantity representing a number of seconds from 00:00 on January 1, 1970. This value indicates the last time the DA booted (i.e., the age of the oldest state maintained by the DA). When a DA is going down, an advertisement with the DA Stateless Boot Timestamp set to 0 can be multicast to indicate this fact. Otherwise, the DA Stateless Boot Timestamps transmitted in DAAdverts must be increasing. The 32-bit size reserved for the DA Stateless Boot Timestamp (and time stamps related to authentication—see the "Security" section for more information) is sufficient until the 22d century, during which it will wrap to 0. At the instant the time stamp wraps, it is redefined to be a measure of the number of seconds from the wrap point.

The Stateless Boot Timestamp in a DAAdvert helps SAs to determine whether reregistration is necessary (due to a previous crash of the DA).

The URL in the DAAdvert is of the form "service:directory-agent://<IP address>", where <IP address> is the dotted numeric IP address of the DA. The Length of URL field contains the length of this URL. Typically DAs are assigned scopes, which are string identifiers that serve to classify services into categories, based on location, administrative control, or similar criteria. The <scope list> in the DAAdvert provides a comma-separated list of the scopes to which the advertising DA belongs. The length of this string is indicated by the Length of <scope list> field. Scopes are discussed in the section on scopes. The DA may advertise its own attributes in the DAAdvert, using the <attr list> and associated length fields. The SLP specification describes only one attribute for DAs, "min-refresh-interval," which DAs may use to control the frequency of updates from SAs. If the "min-refresh-interval" attribute is present, it specifies a number of seconds that should be allowed to elapse before SAs refresh their service advertisements. There will be more on this when SrvReg (Service Registration) messages are discussed in the "Service Agents" section. The remaining fields in the DAAdvert are related to security and will be discussed in that section.

DAs respond to most SrvRqst messages with appropriate SrvRply messages, exactly as an SA would. The format of SrvRqst and SrvRply messages and the circumstances under which replies can be expected are covered in detail in the later section on the client side. But DAs send DAAdverts in response to a special sort of SrvRqst message with a service type of "service:directory-agent". Other agents can send this type of SrvRqst message to force DAs to advertise their presence. This response to a SrvRqst (consisting of a DAAdvert rather than the more typical SrvRply) is unique to DAs. For DAAdverts sent in response to unicast SrvRqst messages, Error Code values other than zero are possible (e.g., if the DA doesn't support a particular scope). During self-initiated advertisements (governed by the CONFIG_DA_BEAT setting), the Error Code field in the DAAdvert is always 0.

DAs also support several other message types. SrvReg messages allow SAs to register the availability (and location) of services. SrvDeReg messages perform the opposite function, canceling previous registrations. SrvReg and SrvDeReg messages are covered in detail in the next section on service agents. AttrRqst (Attribute Request) and AttrRply (Attribute Reply) messages allow UAs to request the values of attributes for a given service or for multiple services. SrvTypeRqst (Service Type Request), and SrvTypeRply (Service Type Reply) messages allow UAs to browse the available services in a network. These message types are covered in the "User Agents" section, since both DAs and SAs respond to AttrRqst and SrvTypeRqst in similar fashion.

Service Agents

Service agents are responsible for advertising the availability of their associated service(s). SAs register the service URLs for services with directory agents using SrvReg messages or advertise directly on the network using multicast SAAdvert messages. When SAs use SrvReg messages to communicate with DAs, they expect SrvAck messages as replies, and these allow the SA to determine whether registration attempts were successful. Registrations have an associated lifetime and must be refreshed before they expire; otherwise, associated service location information will be purged from the DAs. When DAs advertise their presence using DAAdvert messages, a DA attribute "min-refresh-interval" may be present. If this attribute is present, it identifies a minimum waiting period before refreshes for service registrations will be accepted. SAs should be implemented so that they do not resend registration information more often than the min-refresh-interval.

SAs discover DAs in the same fashion as UAs. The locations of DAs can be configured statically, the locations can be learned through DHCP options (see RFC 2610), *active* discovery using multicast can be used (where services of type "service:directory-agent" are found), or *passive* discovery can be used, where DAAdvert messages are examined. If DHCP or static configuration of DAs is used, then an SA must unicast a SrvRqst message with service type "service:directory-agent" to solicit a DAAdvert. The DAAdvert will contain the DA's attributes (possibly including information on the maximum refresh rate for registrations) and security-related information.

When DAs are available with appropriate scopes, an SA sends a SrvReg message to each DA to make the availability of its associated services known. A SrvAck message is expected, which indicates the success or failure of the registration attempt. The format of these message types is shown in Fig. 3-5.

The URL entry portion of the SrvReg message contains the service URL and lifetime for this registration. SAs are responsible for renewing their registrations before lifetime seconds elapse. Figure 3-9 (in the following "User Agents" section) illustrates the format of a URL entry. The <service-type> in the SrvReg message defines the service type for the associated service. The <scope-list> should contain the scopes for the DA with which the SA is registering. The <attr-list> is a comma-separated

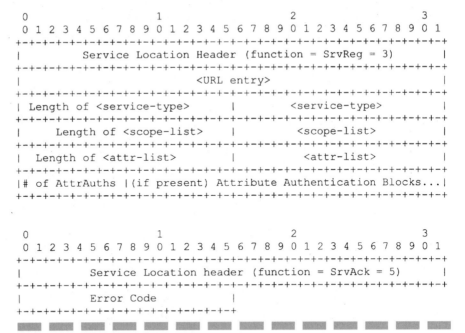

```
 0                   1                   2                   3
 0 1 2 3 4 5 6 7 8 9 0 1 2 3 4 5 6 7 8 9 0 1 2 3 4 5 6 7 8 9 0 1
+-+-+-+-+-+-+-+-+-+-+-+-+-+-+-+-+-+-+-+-+-+-+-+-+-+-+-+-+-+-+-+-+
|         Service Location Header (function = SrvReg = 3)       |
+-+-+-+-+-+-+-+-+-+-+-+-+-+-+-+-+-+-+-+-+-+-+-+-+-+-+-+-+-+-+-+-+
|                           <URL entry>                         |
+-+-+-+-+-+-+-+-+-+-+-+-+-+-+-+-+-+-+-+-+-+-+-+-+-+-+-+-+-+-+-+-+
| Length of <service-type>       |        <service-type>        |
+-+-+-+-+-+-+-+-+-+-+-+-+-+-+-+-+-+-+-+-+-+-+-+-+-+-+-+-+-+-+-+-+
|     Length of <scope-list>      |        <scope-list>         |
+-+-+-+-+-+-+-+-+-+-+-+-+-+-+-+-+-+-+-+-+-+-+-+-+-+-+-+-+-+-+-+-+
|   Length of <attr-list>         |        <attr-list>          |
+-+-+-+-+-+-+-+-+-+-+-+-+-+-+-+-+-+-+-+-+-+-+-+-+-+-+-+-+-+-+-+-+
|# of AttrAuths |(if present) Attribute Authentication Blocks...|
+-+-+-+-+-+-+-+-+-+-+-+-+-+-+-+-+-+-+-+-+-+-+-+-+-+-+-+-+-+-+-+-+


 0                   1                   2                   3
 0 1 2 3 4 5 6 7 8 9 0 1 2 3 4 5 6 7 8 9 0 1 2 3 4 5 6 7 8 9 0 1
+-+-+-+-+-+-+-+-+-+-+-+-+-+-+-+-+-+-+-+-+-+-+-+-+-+-+-+-+-+-+-+-+
|         Service Location header (function = SrvAck = 5)       |
+-+-+-+-+-+-+-+-+-+-+-+-+-+-+-+-+-+-+-+-+-+-+-+-+-+-+-+-+-+-+-+-+
|         Error Code              |
+-+-+-+-+-+-+-+-+-+-+-+-+-+-+-+-+-+
```

Figure 3-5

SLP SrvReg. The format of service registration (above) and service acknowledgment (below) messages. SrvReg messages are used by service agents to inform directory agents that services are available. DAs respond with SrvAck to indicate the success or failure of registration attempts and deregistration attempts.

list of attributes for the service. It is possible to send SrvReg messages with the "fresh" (F) bit unset to specify "incremental" registration, which allows attribute values to be modified without replacing all registration information. Incremental registration is an optional feature and is not supported by some SLP implementations. Further, incremental registration may be deprecated in a future revision of the SLP specification. For more information on incremental registration, see RFC 2608. The remaining fields in the SrvReg message type are related to security and are discussed in that later section. SrvAck (service acknowledgment) messages are quite simple—they merely indicate success or failure of a registration attempt and consist of a message header and a 16-bit error code. Note that SAs are required by the specification to maintain consistent registrations with all DAs with which they register.

In the absence of directory agents, user agents will transmit SrvRqst messages directly to service agents. In this case, SrvRqst messages are multicast, and any SA receiving the SrvRqst and satisfying service type and scope information in the request must send a unicast SrvRply (which contains location information) directly to the UA. The format of SrvRqst and SrvRrply messages is covered in the section on user agents. When no DAs have been discovered and no scope information is present, UAs will send SrvRqst messages with service type "service:service-agent" to determine the scopes of available services. Essentially "service:service-agent" is a wild card service type. If an SA matches the predicate contained in the SrvRqst (see the discussion of SrvRqst messages in the "User Agents" section), it will respond with an SAAdvert message, advertising its presence and configured scopes. UAs can then use this scope information to formulate additional service requests. The format of an SAAdvert message is illustrated in Fig. 3-6.

An SAAdvert contains the Service URL for the service, a comma-separated list of scopes, a comma-separated list of essential attributes, and one or more Authentication Blocks. Authentication Blocks are covered in the later section on security; they allow UAs to verify the integrity and authenticity of the SAAdvert message.

SAs are required to support SrvReg, SrvAck, SrvRqst, SrvRply, SAAdvert, and DAAdvert messages. They may also optionally support SrvDeReg (Service Deregistration), AttrRqst (Attribute Request), AttrRply (Attribute Reply), ServTypeRqst (Service Type Request), and SrvTypeRply (Service Type Reply) messages. SrvDeReg messages are discussed here. The remaining types are discussed briefly in this section and in greater detail in the context of UAs in the next section.

```
 0                   1                   2                   3
 0 1 2 3 4 5 6 7 8 9 0 1 2 3 4 5 6 7 8 9 0 1 2 3 4 5 6 7 8 9 0 1
+-+-+-+-+-+-+-+-+-+-+-+-+-+-+-+-+-+-+-+-+-+-+-+-+-+-+-+-+-+-+-+-+
|        Service Location Header (function = SAAdvert = 11)     |
+-+-+-+-+-+-+-+-+-+-+-+-+-+-+-+-+-+-+-+-+-+-+-+-+-+-+-+-+-+-+-+-+
|        Length of URL          |              URL             |
+-+-+-+-+-+-+-+-+-+-+-+-+-+-+-+-+-+-+-+-+-+-+-+-+-+-+-+-+-+-+-+-+
|     Length of <scope-list>    |         <scope-list>         |
+-+-+-+-+-+-+-+-+-+-+-+-+-+-+-+-+-+-+-+-+-+-+-+-+-+-+-+-+-+-+-+-+
|     Length of <attr-list>     |          <attr-list>         |
+-+-+-+-+-+-+-+-+-+-+-+-+-+-+-+-+-+-+-+-+-+-+-+-+-+-+-+-+-+-+-+-+
| # Auth Blocks |        Authentication Blocks(if any)         |
+-+-+-+-+-+-+-+-+-+-+-+-+-+-+-+-+-+-+-+-+-+-+-+-+-+-+-+-+-+-+-+-+
```

Figure 3-6

SLP SAAdvert. The format of an SA advertisement message, sent by service agents in response to "service:service-agent" service requests from UAs. The primary purpose of SAAdverts is to provide scope information to UAs which have no configured scope.

Although DAs will delete service registrations that have not been renewed when the associated lifetime expires, it is beneficial for SAs to cancel registrations (whenever possible) when a service is removed from duty. Explicit cancellations reduce the amount of stale information stored in DAs. Service Deregistration messages support this optimization and also allow services to deregister specified attributes. The format of a SrvDeReg message is illustrated in Fig. 3-7.

```
 0                   1                   2                   3
 0 1 2 3 4 5 6 7 8 9 0 1 2 3 4 5 6 7 8 9 0 1 2 3 4 5 6 7 8 9 0 1
+-+-+-+-+-+-+-+-+-+-+-+-+-+-+-+-+-+-+-+-+-+-+-+-+-+-+-+-+-+-+-+-+
|          Service Location header (function = SrvDeReg = 4)    |
+-+-+-+-+-+-+-+-+-+-+-+-+-+-+-+-+-+-+-+-+-+-+-+-+-+-+-+-+-+-+-+-+
|    Length of <scope-list>     |          <scope-list>         |
+-+-+-+-+-+-+-+-+-+-+-+-+-+-+-+-+-+-+-+-+-+-+-+-+-+-+-+-+-+-+-+-+
|                           URL Entry                           |
+-+-+-+-+-+-+-+-+-+-+-+-+-+-+-+-+-+-+-+-+-+-+-+-+-+-+-+-+-+-+-+-+
|     Length of <tag-list>      |           <tag-list>          |
+-+-+-+-+-+-+-+-+-+-+-+-+-+-+-+-+-+-+-+-+-+-+-+-+-+-+-+-+-+-+-+-+
```

Figure 3-7
The format of the SrvDeReg message, which allows an SA to cancel a registration entirely or to cancel the registration of specified attributes.

The <scope-list> is a comma-separated list of scopes. This list must be the same as that supplied in the original SrvReg message. If it is not, the DA will respond with a SCOPE_NOT_SUPPORTED error. The URL entry defines the service for deregistration. Figure 3-9 in the next section illustrates the format of a URL entry. The Lifetime field in the URL entry is ignored in SrvDeReg messages. The <tag-list> is a comma-separated list of attribute names. If this string has a nonzero length, then the specified attributes are deregistered (deleted) from the service registration in all scopes. If the <tag-list> has zero length, then all information associated with the service registration is deleted from the DA. There are related security issues—these are covered in the upcoming section on security. A DA responds to a SrvDeReg message with a SrvAck, whose format was illustrated in Fig. 3-5.

The optional AttrRqst and AttrRply messages allow a UA to request and receive the values of attributes for a specific service or for all services in a given scope list. SrvTypeRqst and SrvTypeRply messages allow UAs to browse the available service types in a network. All these messages are discussed in detail in the next section. A concrete example of an SLP SA is given in the section "A Concrete Example: An SLP Echo Service."

User Agents

User agents discover services for client applications by issuing SrvRqst messages which describe the needed services. SrvRply messages are expected as replies; these specify the locations of matching services. A UA may issue a request directly to SAs via multicast; in this case, SAs providing the needed service respond directly to the UA with unicast replies. UAs may also contact a directory agent for service location information. The methods that UAs can use to discover DAs are exactly the same as those for SAs. In addition to SrvRqst and SrvRply messages, UAs are required to understand DAAdverts (which advertise DAs) and SAs (which advertise available services). They may optionally support AttrRqst, AttrRply, SrvTypeRqst, and SrvTypeRply to broaden their ability to survey available service types and characteristics.

The SLP specification defines a pecking order for sending service request messages, with multicast to service agents being a last resort. If possible, a UA issues a SrvRqst message for a needed service to a DA, whose location was configured with DHCP. This mandate aids administrators in organizing the sets of services that should be available to particular clients. If no such DA is known, then the UA issues requests to DAs whose locations have been statically configured. This provides a fallback in case DHCP service is unavailable. If no statically configured DA can be contacted (or if no DAs have been statically configured), then the UA resorts to multicast discovery of DAs. If no DAs can be found, then the UA multicasts SrvRqst messages and expects unicast responses directly from matching SAs. If no DAs are available and no scope is configured, UAs can issue a SrvRqst with a service type of "service:service-agent" to cause SAs to respond with SAAdvert service advertisement messages, which contain service location and scope information. The scope information can then be used in future requests for service. SAAdverts are covered in the next section on service agents. Note that if scope information is available for a UA or if DAs are present, the "service:service-agent" option is forbidden.

The format of a SrvRqst message is shown in Fig. 3-8.

The SLP message header was described in the section on message formats; the remaining fields are discussed here. SrvRqsts may be transmitted via either unicast or multicast. Matching services must belong to one of the requested scopes, support the requested service type, and satisfy the predicate in the SrvRqst message. The <PRList> is the previous responder list, which contains a comma-separated list of IP addresses for hosts that have previously responded to a multicast SrvRqst. The <PRList> is used only for multicast requests. DAs and SAs who notice their address in the

```
 0                   1                   2                   3
 0 1 2 3 4 5 6 7 8 9 0 1 2 3 4 5 6 7 8 9 0 1 2 3 4 5 6 7 8 9 0 1
+-+-+-+-+-+-+-+-+-+-+-+-+-+-+-+-+-+-+-+-+-+-+-+-+-+-+-+-+-+-+-+-+
|          Service Location Header (function = SrvRqst = 1)     |
+-+-+-+-+-+-+-+-+-+-+-+-+-+-+-+-+-+-+-+-+-+-+-+-+-+-+-+-+-+-+-+-+
|      Length of <PRList>        |          <PRList>            |
+-+-+-+-+-+-+-+-+-+-+-+-+-+-+-+-+-+-+-+-+-+-+-+-+-+-+-+-+-+-+-+-+
|     Length of <service-type>   |       <service-type>        |
+-+-+-+-+-+-+-+-+-+-+-+-+-+-+-+-+-+-+-+-+-+-+-+-+-+-+-+-+-+-+-+-+
|     Length of <scope-list>     |        <scope-list>         |
+-+-+-+-+-+-+-+-+-+-+-+-+-+-+-+-+-+-+-+-+-+-+-+-+-+-+-+-+-+-+-+-+
|     Length of <predicate>      |        <predicate>          |
+-+-+-+-+-+-+-+-+-+-+-+-+-+-+-+-+-+-+-+-+-+-+-+-+-+-+-+-+-+-+-+-+
|      Length of <SLP SPI>       |        <SLP SPI>            |
+-+-+-+-+-+-+-+-+-+-+-+-+-+-+-+-+-+-+-+-+-+-+-+-+-+-+-+-+-+-+-+-+
```

Figure 3-8
The format of a service request (SrvRqst) message. The messages are transmitted to locate needed services.

<PRList> will not respond to the request. The <service-type> field defines the type of service that is being sought and is required to be nonempty. The <scope-list> is a comma-separated list of scope names. DAs and SAs which are not configured with at least one of the scopes in the <scope-list> for a multicast SrvRqst will not respond to this request. If the SrvRqst is unicast to a particular DA or SA, then a SCOPE_NOT_SUPPORTED error will be returned if none of the scopes match. Scopes are discussed further in the section on scopes.

If the <predicate> is nonempty, it should correspond to an LDAPv3 search filter. Examples of search filters are provided in the later section "The C API," when the API function SLPFindSrvs() is discussed. Briefly, the predicate narrows the choice of matching services based on a boolean function of selected attribute values. The <SLP SPI> field is related to security and is discussed in the later section on security. All the length fields in the SrvRqst message are 16-bit quantities.

The response from a DA or SA to a SrvRqst message is a SrvRply message, with two exceptions. The first occurs if the <service-type> in the SrvRqst message is set to "service:directory-agent," in which case DAs respond with DAAdvert messages. See the section "Directory Agents" for more information. The other exception occurs when UAs issue SrvRqst messages with <service-type> set to "service:service-agent". This causes SAs to respond with SAAdvert messages. This message type is covered in the "Service Agents" section.

The format of a SrvRply message and the URL entries which encapsulate service information in the SrvRply are illustrated in Fig. 3-9.

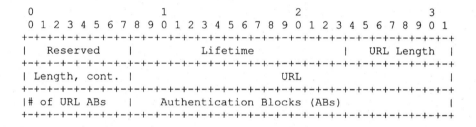

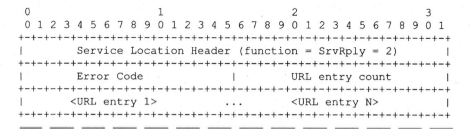

Figure 3-9
The format of a URL entry (above), which describes the location of a service, and a service reply message (below), which encapsulates zero or more URL entries.

The service reply contains an error code and zero or more URL entries. Each URL entry describes the location of a service, providing the service URL, its associated length, and a 16-bit Lifetime field. In the absence of Authenticator Blocks (ABs) in a URL entry, the service information contained in the URL entry should not be cached for longer than "lifetime" seconds. If an AB is present, then the time stamp within the AB will be used instead. Authenticator Blocks are covered later in the section on security.

There are several circumstances in which zero URL entries will be provided in a SrvRply. The first occurs when there is an error condition; in this case, the Error Code field will be set. The second occurs when a UA sends a unicast SrvRqst; in this case, if no services match, the receiving agent unicasts a SrvRply with zero URL entries. Note that for multicast SrvRqst messages, receiving agents will take no action if they cannot provide the locations of matching services—they will never respond with a SrvRply with zero URL entries in response to multicast SrvRqst messages.

Recall that the Overflow bit, which is present in the message header, indicates that the size of the message has exceeded the size of a UDP datagram. If this bit is set in a SrvRply, it is acceptable for the client to simply use the first URL entry in the reply or to retransmit the request using TCP. The specification guarantees that compliant service agents and directory agents will not attempt to transmit individual URL entries which cannot fit within a UDP datagram, so the first entry is always safe.

In some cases, a UA may be interested in learning the values of attributes for a specific service or a group of services of a specified type. An AttrRqst message allows attribute values to be determined; the format of the AttrRqst and of the associated AttrRply message is illustrated in Fig. 3-10.

The previous responder list (<PRList>) and list of scopes (<scope-list>) have the same meaning as for SrvRqst messages (discussed above). If the URL contains a service type, such as "service:echo-service", then all

```
 0                   1                   2                   3
 0 1 2 3 4 5 6 7 8 9 0 1 2 3 4 5 6 7 8 9 0 1 2 3 4 5 6 7 8 9 0 1
+-+-+-+-+-+-+-+-+-+-+-+-+-+-+-+-+-+-+-+-+-+-+-+-+-+-+-+-+-+-+-+-+
|         Service Location Header (function = AttrRqst = 6)     |
+-+-+-+-+-+-+-+-+-+-+-+-+-+-+-+-+-+-+-+-+-+-+-+-+-+-+-+-+-+-+-+-+
|        Length of PRList        |            <PRList>          |
+-+-+-+-+-+-+-+-+-+-+-+-+-+-+-+-+-+-+-+-+-+-+-+-+-+-+-+-+-+-+-+-+
|         Length of URL          |              URL             |
+-+-+-+-+-+-+-+-+-+-+-+-+-+-+-+-+-+-+-+-+-+-+-+-+-+-+-+-+-+-+-+-+
|     Length of <scope-list>     |          <scope-list>        |
+-+-+-+-+-+-+-+-+-+-+-+-+-+-+-+-+-+-+-+-+-+-+-+-+-+-+-+-+-+-+-+-+
|    Length of <tag-list>        |           <tag-list>         |
+-+-+-+-+-+-+-+-+-+-+-+-+-+-+-+-+-+-+-+-+-+-+-+-+-+-+-+-+-+-+-+-+
|     Length of <SLP SPI>        |           <SLP SPI>          |
+-+-+-+-+-+-+-+-+-+-+-+-+-+-+-+-+-+-+-+-+-+-+-+-+-+-+-+-+-+-+-+-+
```

```
 0                   1                   2                   3
 0 1 2 3 4 5 6 7 8 9 0 1 2 3 4 5 6 7 8 9 0 1 2 3 4 5 6 7 8 9 0 1
+-+-+-+-+-+-+-+-+-+-+-+-+-+-+-+-+-+-+-+-+-+-+-+-+-+-+-+-+-+-+-+-+
|         Service Location Header (function = AttrRply = 7)     |
+-+-+-+-+-+-+-+-+-+-+-+-+-+-+-+-+-+-+-+-+-+-+-+-+-+-+-+-+-+-+-+-+
|        Error Code              |       Length of <attr-list>  |
+-+-+-+-+-+-+-+-+-+-+-+-+-+-+-+-+-+-+-+-+-+-+-+-+-+-+-+-+-+-+-+-+
|                           <attr-list>                         |
+-+-+-+-+-+-+-+-+-+-+-+-+-+-+-+-+-+-+-+-+-+-+-+-+-+-+-+-+-+-+-+-+
|# of AttrAuths |    Attribute Authentication Block             |
+-+-+-+-+-+-+-+-+-+-+-+-+-+-+-+-+-+-+-+-+-+-+-+-+-+-+-+-+-+-+-+-+
```

Figure 3-10
The format of attribute request (above) and reply (below) messages. AttrRqst messages allow UAs to determine the values of attributes associated with services. AttrRply messages report the attribute values.

matching (see below for what *matching* means) attributes for all services of the given type are returned in AttrRply messages. If the URL contains a full-service URL, then only the attributes for the specified service are returned. Attribute requests by service type rather than for a specific Service URL are likely to be deprecated in the future. New user agent implementations should use attribute requests based on Service URLs only. The <tag-list> is a comma-separated list of attribute names. Only attributes whose names match one of the values in the <tag-list> will have their values returned in an AttrRply message. While wild cards are currently supported in the <tag-list>, this practice is discouraged because future revisions to the specification will likely remove wild card support in attribute requests. If the <tag-list> has zero length, all attributes "match" and their values are returned. AttrRply messages are returned by the DA (if the AttrRqst was directed to a DA) or by each SA with a matching service type or service URL. Note that support for Attr-Rqst is optional for SAs. An SA that does not support AttrRqst will return MSG_NOT_SUPPORTED instead of attribute values. Otherwise, the <attr-list> is a comma-separated list of "name=value" pairs.

Service browsing under SLP is possible via the SrvTypeRqst message type. This message allows a UA to discover the types of services that are present in the network. The formats of SrvTypeRqst and SrvTypeRply messages are illustrated in Fig. 3-11.

The previous responder list <PRList> and <scope-list> function in the same way as for SrvRqst messages. If <Naming Authority> is present, then responses will be limited to those services whose type is associated with the specified Naming Authority. If the Naming Authority has zero length, only IANA service types will be returned. If the length is 0xFFFF, the Naming Authority is not considered when returning matches.

The response to a SrvTypeRqst is a SrvTypeRply. Note that SrvType-Rqsts are optional, and SAs which do not support this message type may simply return an Error Code of MSG_NOT_SUPPORTED. If the Error Code is zero, which signifies that no error has occurred, then the <srvtype-list> returned in the SrvTypeRply message defines the available services.

A concrete example of an SLP UA is given in the section "The Client Side: An SLP Echo Client Implementation."

Scope and SLP Agents

The SLP specification defines *scopes* as "sets of services." A scope can be used to define a set of services based on physical or network location,

```
0                   1                   2                   3
0 1 2 3 4 5 6 7 8 9 0 1 2 3 4 5 6 7 8 9 0 1 2 3 4 5 6 7 8 9 0 1
+-+-+-+-+-+-+-+-+-+-+-+-+-+-+-+-+-+-+-+-+-+-+-+-+-+-+-+-+-+-+-+-+
|        Service Location Header (function = SrvTypeRqst = 9)   |
+-+-+-+-+-+-+-+-+-+-+-+-+-+-+-+-+-+-+-+-+-+-+-+-+-+-+-+-+-+-+-+-+
|        Length of <PRList>        |            <PRList>         |
+-+-+-+-+-+-+-+-+-+-+-+-+-+-+-+-+-+-+-+-+-+-+-+-+-+-+-+-+-+-+-+-+
|  Length of <Naming Authority>   |    <Naming Authority>       |
+-+-+-+-+-+-+-+-+-+-+-+-+-+-+-+-+-+-+-+-+-+-+-+-+-+-+-+-+-+-+-+-+
|      Length of <scope-list>     |       <scope-list>          |
+-+-+-+-+-+-+-+-+-+-+-+-+-+-+-+-+-+-+-+-+-+-+-+-+-+-+-+-+-+-+-+-+


0                   1                   2                   3
0 1 2 3 4 5 6 7 8 9 0 1 2 3 4 5 6 7 8 9 0 1 2 3 4 5 6 7 8 9 0 1
+-+-+-+-+-+-+-+-+-+-+-+-+-+-+-+-+-+-+-+-+-+-+-+-+-+-+-+-+-+-+-+-+
|       Service Location Header (function = SrvTypeRply = 10)   |
+-+-+-+-+-+-+-+-+-+-+-+-+-+-+-+-+-+-+-+-+-+-+-+-+-+-+-+-+-+-+-+-+
|         Error Code              |   Length of <srvtype-list>  |
+-+-+-+-+-+-+-+-+-+-+-+-+-+-+-+-+-+-+-+-+-+-+-+-+-+-+-+-+-+-+-+-+
|                        <srvtype-list>                         |
+-+-+-+-+-+-+-+-+-+-+-+-+-+-+-+-+-+-+-+-+-+-+-+-+-+-+-+-+-+-+-+-+
```

Figure 3-11

The format of Service Type Request (above) and Service Type Reply (below) messages. These message types allow UAs to browse the set of services available in the network.

access privileges, or other criteria. Scopes in SLP provide the ability to group services and are a powerful tool for systems administrators. Scopes are represented by strings, with the default scope being "DEFAULT." Scope names are not case-sensitive.

By configuring clients to use specific scopes, it is possible to restrict the set of services that will be discovered. For example, it might be useful to restrict particular clients to discover only public printing services in their department, but not the printers in private offices. On the other hand, some clients should be able to discover not only the public printers, but also private ones. By configuring directory agents with nondefault scopes, it is possible to easily support this separation. For example, public printers could be configured with scope "public," private printers with scope "private," and user agents with some combination of "public" and "private" scope. Of course, more fine-grained divisions are possible.

Services will register only with directory agents with the appropriate scopes, and clients will discover and query only appropriate directory agents. All service agents and directory agents are required to be assigned a scope string (although this might be the default scope). The configured scopes might be available in a static configuration file or obtained through DHCP. A user agent may or may not be assigned a scope. If a UA has no statically assigned scope and cannot obtain scope information through DHCP, then it will be able to discover and issue requests for any available services (subject to multicast radius). A UA with no assigned scope uses DA or SA discovery and uses the scope information present in DAAdverts and SAAdverts in subsequent requests for service. On the other hand, if scope is configured for a UA, then the UA must issue requests for service using the assigned scopes. DHCP scope configuration is primarily an administrative task and is covered in detail in RFC 2610.

To avoid wasting network resources and to enforce the scope rules, most SLP messages contain scope lists. When an agent receives a multicast SLP message which contains no scope that matches the agent's set of configured scopes, the message is ignored. This avoids unnecessary replies and "hides" the presence of inappropriate agents. On the other hand, when a unicast message is received with no matching scope value, a SCOPE_NOT_SUPPORTED error is returned by the DA or SA.

The SLP specification requires user agents to prefer unicast messages to DAs with appropriate scopes over the use of multicast. Multicast discovery of DAs or SAs is used when no DA with an appropriate scope can be contacted via unicast. "Appropriate" scopes can be either configured or obtained dynamically by watching for advertisements from DAs and SAs. The specification demands that the priority of scope configurations, in decreasing importance, be DHCP, static configuration, and finally the assumption of default scope. Determination of scope by examining DAAdvert and/or SAAdvert messages should be performed only if the UA is explicitly configured to have no scopes. See section 11.2 in RFC 2608 for more information on *user-selectable* scoping.

Designing SLP Applications: The SLP API C or Java?

RFC 2614 [5] defines C and Java APIs for development of SLP agents. Both of the APIs provide programmatic access to the various SLP agent interactions. The C API generally maps one function or method to each of the message types while the Java API provides an object-oriented environment for SLP development, modeling the various agents as objects. Both of the language bindings support modular implementations to suit particular platforms which might not need all the SLP functionality, and both APIs are thread-safe. The focus in this book is on the C language binding, primarily because of the availability of an excellent open source implementation, OpenSLP. Assuming that an appropriate SLP implementation in your language of choice is available, the choice is up to you.

The C API

The following discussion of the C API is based on OpenSLPv1.0.5, which is RFC 2614-compliant (with a few minor exceptions). We begin with a description of the provided types and then look at the function prototypes for the C API. This will be followed by a discussion of SLP callbacks, which are used to return results from SLP operations. Concrete examples will be presented in the sections "A Concrete Example: An SLP Echo Service" and "The Client Side: An SLP Echo Client Implementation." Various constants defined in the OpenSLP implementation will also be examined in context in that section.

The first *type* is actually just a set of #defines corresponding to various error codes. SLPError is typedef-ed as an int, and each error code is #defined. Note that in RFC 2614, the error codes are organized using an enumeration (enum) rather than #defines. The meanings of the error codes are described in the context of the Diagnose() function in section "A Concrete Example: An SLP Echo Service." In particular, pay special attention to the function Diagnose() in the client and service examples, because it maps a description in English to each error code. The error codes are as follows:

```
#define SLP_LAST_CALL               1
#define SLP_OK                      0
#define SLP_LANGUAGE_NOT_SUPPORTED  -1
#define SLP_PARSE_ERROR             -2
#define SLP_INVALID_REGISTRATION    -3
#define SLP_SCOPE_NOT_SUPPORTED     -4
#define SLP_AUTHENTICATION_ABSENT   -6
#define SLP_AUTHENTICATION_FAILED   -7
#define SLP_INVALID_UPDATE          -13
#define SLP_REFRESH_REJECTED        -15
#define SLP_NOT_IMPLEMENTED         -17
#define SLP_BUFFER_OVERFLOW         -18
#define SLP_NETWORK_TIMED_OUT       -19
#define SLP_NETWORK_INIT_FAILED     -20
#define SLP_MEMORY_ALLOC_FAILED     -21
```

```
#define SLP_PARAMETER_BAD              -22
#define SLP_NETWORK_ERROR              -23
#define SLP_INTERNAL_SYSTEM_ERROR      -24
#define SLP_HANDLE_IN_USE              -25
#define SLP_TYPE_ERROR                 -26
```

The following type, SLPSrvURL, holds the components of a service URL. These include the service type (s_pcSrvType), host (s_pcHost), port (s_iPort), and remainder of the URL (s_pcSrvPart). The SLPParse-SrvURL() function fills in a structure of this type, given a string service URL.

```
typedef struct srvurl {
    char *s_pcSrvType;
    char *s_pcHost;
    int   s_iPort;
    char *s_pcNetFamily;
    char *s_pcSrvPart;
} SLPSrvURL;
```

Now we will examine the C API functions. In the following, SLPHandle instances serve as handles for resources associated with the SLP library. An SLPHandle is just a void*, since a particular implementation will have specific requirements for what a *handle* really is. SLPBoolean is an enumeration, with SLP_TRUE and SLP_FALSE as values. The first function is SLPOpen(), which is called to obtain a handle. The handle is required for other interactions with the SLP library. The prototype looks like this:

```
SLPError SLPOpen(const char *pcLang,
  SLPBoolean isAsync, SLPHandle *phSLP);
```

The parameters are a language string (corresponding to RFC 1766, e.g., "en" for English, or "" for the default locale), a boolean isAsync that determines whether operations are synchronous or asynchronous, and a pointer to an SLPHandle. The asynchronous/synchronous issue is discussed in the section on callbacks, below, but the distinction is addressed briefly here. If synchronous behavior for a handle is chosen, then any results related to an operation on the handle are guaranteed to be delivered through a callback before the function that initiated the operation returns. For asynchronous behavior, results associated with an operation on the handle are delivered in a separate thread, and they may continue to trickle through the callback function after the SLP function that initiated the operation returns. Note that whether asynchronous or synchronous behavior is requested, only one operation can be active on a single handle at a time. If an asynchronous operation on a handle is in progress, an attempt to start an additional operation will result in an SLP_HANDLE_IN_USE error code being returned. The restriction "no concurrent operations on a single handle" makes thread-safe implementations of SLP language bindings much easier.

The return value indicates the success or failure of the open operation. If either asynchronous or synchronous operation is not supported and the isAsync flag requests such operation, SLP_NOT_IMPLEMENTED will be returned. If an error occurs, the handle is set to NULL [and is therefore unusable until a subsequent call to SLPOpen() succeeds].

The SLPClose() function frees resources associated with a handle obtained through SLPOpen(). Using the handle after calling SLP-Close() is prohibited. The SLPClose() function takes a single SLPHandle parameter:

```
void SLPClose(SLPHandle hSLP);
```

The following function, SLPReg(), is called to register a service URL. It takes eight parameters:

```
SLPError SLPReg(SLPHandle hSLP, const char  *pcSrvURL,
   const unsigned short usLifetime, const char *pcSrvType,
      const char  *pcAttrs, SLPBoolean  fresh,
         SLPRegReport callback, void *pvCookie);
```

The first parameter is an SLPHandle, obtained via SLPOpen(). The second is the service URL, with a lifetime defined by the third parameter, usLifetime. The lifetime parameter must be positive and less than or equal to SLP_LIFETIME_MAXIMUM. Specifying SLP_LIFE-TIME_MAXIMUM will result in the registration remaining in effect for the lifetime of the caller. The pcSrvType parameter is ignored under OpenSLP, because the service URL defines the service type. The pcAttrs parameter provides a comma-delimited set of attribute assignments. If there are no attributes, the empty string ("") should be passed. If the boolean fresh is SLP_TRUE, then this registration is new and will replace any existing registrations with the service URL. Otherwise, the registration would be incremental, allowing attribute values to be changed or new attributes to be supplied without destroying the previous registration. Note the "would be"—OpenSLP does *not* support incremental registration, and thus SLP_TRUE for the fresh flag is required. The designers of OpenSLP made this decision because of the substantial overhead introduced by incremental registrations. Further, deprecation of incremental registration and deregistration is likely in a future revision of the SLP specification. We will not consider incremental registrations further for this reason, but they are discussed in detail in RFC 2608, section 9.3. The SLPRegReport callback is a function that will be executed when the registration is complete. The pvCookie parameter will be passed to the callback. NULL is an acceptable value for the cookie. Callbacks are discussed later in this section.

The SLPDereg() function, shown below, performs the opposite operation—it cancels a registration in all scopes where the service is registered. A handle, the service URL, a callback function, which is executed when the deregistration is complete, and a cookie are passed to this function. The cookie can be NULL.

```
SLPError SLPDereg(SLPHandle  hSLP,   const char *pcSrvURL,
   SLPRegReport callback, void *pvCookie);
```

To delete one or more attributes, the function SLPDelAttrs() is used. The function takes five parameters, as shown in the prototype below. Most of the parameters are self-explanatory; as for service registration, a handle, service URL, callback, and cookie are required. The pcAttrs parameter is a comma-separated list of attribute names, each of which will be deleted from the service registration.

```
SLPError SLPDelAttrs(SLPHandle   hSLP, const char *pcSrvURL,
   const char  *pcAttrs, SLPRegReport callback,
     void *pvCookie);
```

To discover the types of available services, the SLPFindSrvTypes() function is used. This function issues a SrvTypeRqst message and is most useful to UAs browsing the network for available services. The prototype is shown below. Recall that a Naming Authority (required as the second parameter) is an entity that catalogs service types and attributes—it gives meaning to a particular service type. The default Naming Authority is "IANA" (Internet Assigned Numbers Authority) and is specified by passing the empty string (""). Note that passing "IANA" is not allowed. If "*" is passed, then all services belonging to all naming authorities are considered. The matching services are returned through the callback with the naming authority portion of the service URLs intact. Only services belonging to one of the scopes in the comma-delimited pcScopeList string can match. Passing "" or NULL for the pcScopeList causes configured scopes to be used. The remaining parameters are familiar.

```
SLPError SLPFindSrvTypes(SLPHandle hSLP,
   const char *pcNamingAuthority, const char  *pcScopeList,
     SLPSrvTypeCallback callback, void *pvCookie);
```

The following function is used to do service discovery:

```
SLPError SLPFindSrvs(SLPHandle hSLP, const char *pcServiceType,
   const char *pcScopeList, const char *pcSearchFilter,
     SLPSrvURLCallback callback, void *pvCookie);
```

SLPFindSrvs() takes a handle, a service type (e.g., "service:printer"), a comma-separated scope list, a search filter, and a callback and cookie. Results are returned through the specified callback function and the cookie is passed to the callback when these results are obtained. If all scopes the UA is configured to query should be searched, then NULL or "" should be passed as the scope string. The pcSearchFilter parameter allows LDAPv3-style pattern matching [13] to be performed on possible matches. The Lightweight Directory Access Protocol (LDAP) [14] is an open standard for accessing stores of information. A complete discussion of LDAP search filters is beyond the scope of this chapter, but a few examples provide the basic idea. For greater in-depth treatment, see RFC 2254. Here are some examples:

■ "(contactname=golden)" will restrict the set of discovered services to those that have an attribute "contactname" with a case-insensitive value of "golden."

■ "(&(contactname=golden)(maxlinelength>80))" restricts the set of discovered services to those with an attribute "contactname" with a case-insensitive value of "golden" and which further have an attribute "maxlinelength" with a value greater than 80.

■ "(contactname=golden*)" restricts matching services to those with an attribute "contactname" whose value *begins* with "golden."

■ "(|(contactname=golden)(contactname=gerrod))" matches only services with an attribute "contactname" whose value is either "golden" or "gerrod" (case-insensitive, as above).

Note that if attributes have multiple values [e.g., contactname=(golden,gerrod)], each value is considered and the results are subjected to a logical *or*. For example, "(contactname=golden)" matches if the contactname attribute's value contains "golden" as an element. A gotcha is in order: There should be no spaces in the search filter, as white space is significant in LDAP search filters.

The SLPFindAttrs() function is used to determine the values of attributes for a specific service or a group of services of a specific type. Either all attributes may be returned, or a comma-separated list of attribute names may be provided to match only specific attributes. The first parameter to SLPFindAttrs() is an SLP handle. The second parameter to the function may take one of two forms: Either a service URL or a service type can be specified. If a service URL is specified, then matching attributes for the service associated with the service URL are used. If a service type is specified, then the attributes for all services of the specified type are considered. The pcAttrIds parameter is a comma-separated list of attribute names. If the value "" is passed for this parameter, all attributes match; otherwise, it should contain a comma-separated list of attribute names. If the search should be limited to a set of scopes, a comma-separated scope list can be specified. If all configured scopes should be considered, then "" can be passed for the scope list. The attributes are returned through the callback function 'callback,' with the value of pvCookie passed to the callback.

```
SLPError SLPFindAttrs(SLPHandle hSLP, const char *pcURLOrServiceType,
   const char *pcScopeList, const char *pcAttrIds,
     SLPAttrCallback callback, void *pvCookie);
```

To avoid having a DA reject an SA's registration refresh, the SA should issue a refresh no more than every min-refresh-interval seconds. The following function returns the maximum such interval over all known DAs, providing an SA with a refresh interval that will satisfy the requirements of all DAs. Zero is returned if no DAs have advertised min-refresh-interval values. The function SLPGetRefreshInterval() takes no arguments.

```
unsigned short SLPGetRefreshInterval();
```

The API provides a mechanism for agents to discover the configured scopes. The SLPFindScopes() function accepts an SLPHandle and a char** argument that receives a comma-separated list of all available scope values. The list of scopes is derived from the net.slp.useScopes property, through DA discovery, etc. A minimum of one scope,

"DEFAULT," will be in the generated list, and preferred scopes (if there is any associated order) are always listed first. The prototype for SLPFindScopes() looks like this:

```
SLPError SLPFindScopes(SLPHandle hSLP, char** ppcScopeList);
```

The following function accepts a char* service URL and parses it, returning the components in an SLPSrvURL structure (discussed at the beginning of this section). SLP_PARSE_ERROR is returned if something about the service URL isn't kosher. The ppSrvURL should be freed with SLPFree() after use [RFC 2614 contains a typographical error and states that SLPFreeURL() should be called to free the memory—no such function exists]. Note that the service URL stored in pcSrvURL is destroyed by this function.

```
SLPError SLPParseSrvURL(const char *pcSrvURL, SLPSrvURL** ppSrvURL);
```

The following function is provided in the API to deal with escaping reserved characters. Reserved characters in SLP include '(', ')', the comma, '!', '\', '<', '>', '=', and '~'. A copy of the pcInBuf parameter with all reserved characters escaped is placed into ppcOutBuf. The memory associated with ppcOutBuf should be freed by calling SLPFree() when it is no longer needed. SLPEscape() can also check for illegal characters in tags (e.g., the name of an attribute). If the isTag parameter is set to SLP_TRUE, then the input string is examined and SLP_PARSE_ERROR is returned if illegal characters are present. The prototype for SLPEscape() is as follows:

```
SLPError SLPEscape(const char* pcInBuf, char** ppcOutBuf,
  SLPBoolean isTag);
```

The SLPUnescape() function, whose prototype is shown below, performs the opposite function from SLPEscape(). For SLPUnescape(), the input string pcInBuf is examined and a copy is made in ppcOutBuf, with escape sequences removed. The isTag parameter operates as for SLPEscape(). The memory associated with ppcOutBuf should be freed using SLPFree() when it is no longer needed.

```
SLPError SLPUnescape(const char* pcInbuf, char** ppcOutBuf,
  SLPBoolean isTag);
```

SLPFree() frees memory allocated by the SLP library. If the pvMem parameter is NULL, then the function has no effect. The prototype is shown below:

```
void SLPFree(void* pvMem);
```

The SLPGetPropery() and SLPSetProperty() functions get and set SLP property values for the current process, reading and overriding values specified in the configuration file (see the section on configuration), respectively. Note that in the OpenSLP implementation, SLPSetProperty() is ignored. This is due to difficulties related to writing thread-safe versions of SLPGetProperty()/SLPSetProperty(). Recall that the specification demands that all API calls be thread-safe. In any event, the specification recommends that property values be changed by systems administrators as required. Applications should minimize the use of SLPSetProperty() (and not use it at all under OpenSLP, unless support is added at a later date).

```
const char* SLPGetProperty(const char* pcName);
void SLPSetProperty(const char *pcName, const char *pcValue);
```

The SLPParseAttrs() function is used to extract the value of a specified attribute from a comma-delimited list of attribute/value pairs (as would be returned by the SLPAttrCallback function, discussed below in the section on callbacks). The pcAttrList is this comma-delimited list, and pcAttrId is the name of the attribute whose value is needed. The ppcAttrVal gets the value of the specified attribute. Memory associated with ppcAttrVal should be freed using SLPFree() when it is no longer needed. SLP_PARSE_ERROR is returned if no matching attribute is found in the list; otherwise, SLP_OK is returned. This function is not officially a part of the SLP API (it is "secretly" included in OpenSLP) but will likely be adopted in the future because of its usefulness.

```
SLPError SLPParseAttrs(const char* pcAttrList, const char *pcAttrId,
   char** ppcAttrVal);
```

Callbacks in the C API

Now we turn to callbacks, which are the mechanism used by the SLP library to return most results to user/service agents. Callbacks are used in the SLPReg(), SLPDeReg(), SLPDelAttrs(), SLPFindSrvs(), SLPFind-

Attrs(), and SLPFindSrvTypes() functions, regardless of whether asynchronous or synchronous behavior is chosen for a handle via SLPOpen() . If the synchronous option is elected, callbacks are guaranteed to complete before control is returned to the SLP function underway [for example, SLPReg() to advertise a service]. If asynchronous behavior is used, then callbacks run in a separate thread and may overlap execution of the SLP function that was called. A further distinction between asynchronous and synchronous behavior is that the SLP library is required to collate results and remove duplicates under synchronous behavior, but is not required to do so for asynchronous behavior. Thus a client using SLPFindSrvs() with a synchronous handle to discover services can expect that the callback will report a service URL for each matching service exactly once. If asynchronous behavior were in effect, particular services might have their service URLs reported multiple times, as the library does not attempt to remove duplicates under asynchronous behavior. Asynchronous operation is provided in SLP to accommodate systems where resources are limited—since asynchronous operation does not require removal of duplication information, buffering overhead can be significantly reduced.

There are several different callback types, and these will be examined in detail below. A few rules apply in all cases, though. Memory blocks (e.g., char* string values) passed to callback functions are free()-ed by the SLP library after the callback returns; so if these values must be stored by application code, local memory must be allocated and the values copied with strcpy() or a similar mechanism. Otherwise heap corruption will occur. Another callback fact of life is that the error code should be checked in the callback before accessing any other values that are passed in. If the error code is not SLP_OK, then any other values passed in may be invalid.

The first callback type is SLPRegReport, an instance of which must be passed to SLPReg(), SLPDereg(), and SLPDelAttrs(). The only new information provided by this callback is an error code, stored in errCode, which indicates whether an error occurred during the operation. The pvCookie value is the same as that specified when the SLPReg(), SLPDereg(), or SLPDelAttrs() function was called. A typical cookie for the SLPRegReport callback is the address of an integer, which provides a convenient mechanism for passing the errCode value from the callback to the code that started the associated SLP operation. The type definition follows:

```
typedef void SLPRegReport(SLPHandle hSLP, SLPError errCode,
    void *pvCookie);
```

The next callback type is SLPSrvTypeCallback, an instance of which must be supplied to the SLPFindSrvTypes() SLP function. The callback provides a comma-separated list of discovered service types in pcSrv-Types, provided no error has occurred. If this list must be saved beyond the point where the callback function exits, it should be copied to a local buffer, since associated storage will be freed by the SLP library after the callback is complete. If the handle passed to SLPFindSrvTypes() is synchronous, duplicate service types will be eliminated; otherwise, duplicates may appear. The type definition follows:

```
typedef SLPBoolean SLPSrvTypeCallback(SLPHandle hSLP,
  const char* pcSrvTypes, SLPError errCode, void *pvCookie);
```

The SLPSrvURLCallback reports the discovery of a service URL (in pcSrvURL) with an associated liftetime. The lifetime will be less than or equal to SLP_LIFETIME_MAXIMUM. As for SLPSrvTypeCallback, duplicates are guaranteed to be excluded only if the handle passed to SLPFindSrvs() is synchronous. The pcSrvURL must be copied into local storage before the callback returns, because the memory associated with pcSrvURL may be free()-ed by the SLP library once the callback completes. If the errCode is not SLP_OK, then pcSrvURL may be undefined. The type definition for the SLPSrvURLCallback follows:

```
typedef SLPBoolean SLPSrvURLCallback(SLPHandle hSLP,
                            const char* pcSrvURL,
                            unsigned short sLifetime,
                            SLPError errCode,
                            void *pvCookie);
```

SLPAttrCallback is the callback type passed to SLPFindAttrs() and is responsible for reporting attributes associated with one or more services. There are several possible behaviors. The common fact is that pcAttrList will always contain a comma-separated list of "name=value" pairs (or possibly the empty string, if there are no matching attributes). If the SLPFindAttrs() function was called with a service URL, then pcAttrList contains matching attributes for the associated service. Further, there will be only a single callback. If SLPFindAttrs() was called with a service type, then the callback will provide attributes for all matching agents. For a synchronous handle, a single callback will provide these attributes. For an asynchronous handle, multiple callbacks will be made, one for each responding agent. The type definition for SLPAttrCallback follows:

```
typedef SLPBoolean SLPAttrCallback(SLPHandle hSLP,
                                   const char* pcAttrList,
                                   SLPError errCode,
                                   void *pvCookie);
```

A Concrete Example: An SLP Echo Service

To illustrate the use of the SLP C API for development of an SLP service, we examine the implementation of an SLP echo service in detail. This service accepts connections from interested clients and acts as a very boring chat server—whatever is typed to the server from the client is echoed back. This service advertises a service type of "service:echo-service.test:tcp" (the naming authority being "test" because this is a service for illustrative purposes only). Associated attributes are the name and e-mail address of the maintainer of the service and a recommended maximum line length. The abstract type for this service is "echo-service," a service template defined in the earlier "Service Templates" section. The concrete type is "tcp," and a service template for this type was defined in the same section. The protocol spoken between client and service is outside the SLP specification. The sockets interface is a reasonable choice for many protocols, and the echo service relies on stream sockets for communication with clients. A client for the echo service is described in the next section. Both are implemented using OpenSLP under Linux and MacOS X, but should be portable to most operating systems which support sockets (with some work on the signal handling code, which is a minor portion of the total).

The echo service implementation consists of a single source file. The following is the header of "echo_server.c." It includes <slp.h>, which is the only include file required by the OpenSLP package, and a number of standard include files, including some associated with sockets. This is followed by several global variables, including the serviceURL and SLP handle. The serviceURL is global so that it can be used in a call to SLPDeReg() in the Shutdown() function. The handle is needed in all SLP calls after the initial SLPOpen() in main().

```
// SLP echo server main source file.  Registers a TCP-based
// echo server.  Written by
// Golden G. Richard III, Ph.D.  July 2001.

#include <slp.h>
#include <string.h>
```

```
#include <stdio.h>
#include <stdlib.h>
#include <unistd.h>
#include <ctype.h>
#include <sys/types.h>
#include <sys/socket.h>
#include <netinet/in.h>
#include <signal.h>

// globals

static char *serviceURL=NULL;  // service URL registered with SLP
static SLPHandle handle;        // our ticket to using API calls beyond
SLPOpen()

// function prototypes for "echo_server.c" functions
int main(int argc, char* argv[]);
void RegCallbackFunc(SLPHandle handle, SLPError errcode,
  void* cookie);
void Diagnose(char *func, int line, SLPError err);
void SignalHandler(void);
void die(int blarg);
void Shutdown(char *reason);
void ServeEchoClients(int port);
int ReadAndEcho(int handle);
```

The following function is the main() for the echo service. Two command line arguments, the host and port for this invocation of the echo service, are expected. If these are provided, then a signal handler is installed to handle control-C (SIGINT) and SIGPIPE. SIGINT is trapped to enable graceful shutdown, while SIGPIPE is blocked to prevent the server from terminating with a SIGPIPE when a client breaks a socket connection.

```
/////////////////////////////
// SLP echo server's main function
//
int main(int argc, char* argv[]) {
  SLPError err;            // return value from API functions
  SLPError callback_err;   // error code provided to callback function;
                           // address is used as a cookie for callback
  char attributes[512];    // list of attributes for registration

  if (argc != 3) {
    printf("echo_server: Usage: echo_server <ip> <port>\n");
    return 0;
  }
```

```
// on control-C, do a clean Shutdown().  Also, don't die on
// SIGPIPE.  SIGPIPE has to be handled, otherwise when a client
// hangs up, we'll die as a result of the socket
// connection breaking.
printf("echo_server: Registering signal handler.\n");
SignalHandler();
```

Once the signal handler is installed, a call to SLPOpen() is used to obtain a handle. The handle is necessary for most other SLP calls. We pass "en" to indicate a registration in English, SLP_FALSE so that calls will be synchronous (i.e., callbacks will be provided with results before an SLP call returns), and the address of an SLPHandle. If something goes wrong, the Diagnose() function is called to provide more information, and we gracefully Shutdown(). Without a handle, there's very little the service can do.

```
printf("echo_server: Echo server starting, ");
printf("using ip %s and port %d.\n", argv[1], atoi(argv[2]));

// get a handle.  "en" == English, SLP_FALSE == use
// synchronous API calls
err = SLPOpen("en", SLP_FALSE, &handle);
if (err != SLP_OK) {
  Diagnose("SLPOpen()", __LINE__, err);
  Shutdown("Can't continue.");
}
```

Once a handle is available, the service URL for this echo service instance is constructed. It consists of a static portion (identifying the service type) and the host and port provided on the command line. The attributes for the service are then established. In general, these might be read from a file, supplied on the command line, or derived from examination of the environment in which the service runs. In this case, they're hard-coded. The newly created URL and attribute string is then used in a call to SLPReg(), which announces our presence to the world. SLPReg() takes eight arguments. We pass the handle acquired from SLPOpen(), the service URL, our requested advertisement duration (SLP_LIFETIME_MAXI-MUM, which means that the SLP library will refresh advertisements as needed for the lifetime of this process), the service attributes, SLP_TRUE, indicating that this is the initial registration of this service (this sets the "fresh" flag in the registration message), a callback function, and a cookie. For the cookie, the address of an int variable callback_err is used. This allows the callback function to report an error code.

There are two ways in which the call to SLPReg(), like other SLP function calls which have callback arguments, can fail. One is that the call fails immediately and an error code is returned from SLPReg() directly. The other is that an error code can be supplied to the callback function. Thus we examine both err and callback_err to see if they are both SLP_OK. If so, the registration succeeded. Otherwise, the error is Diagnose()-ed and we Shutdown().

```
// initialize service URL.  Format is:
// service:name_of_service.naming_authority:protocol://host:port
//
// for echo service, e.g.
// "service:echo-service.test:tcp://10.0.0.13:5000"
serviceURL = malloc(128);        // plenty of space
if (! serviceURL) {
  Diagnose("malloc()", __LINE__, SLP_MEMORY_ALLOC_FAILED);
}

sprintf(serviceURL, "service:echo-service.test:tcp://%s:%1d",
  argv[1], atoi(argv[2]));

// initialize attributes
strcpy(attributes, "(contact=Golden G. Richard III),
  (contactemail=golden@cs.uno.edu), (maxlinelength=80)");

// eye candy
printf("echo_server: Service URL: %s\n", serviceURL);
printf("echo_server: Attributes: %s\n", attributes);

// register service URL and attributes with SLP
printf("echo_server: Registering service URL.\n");
err = SLPReg(handle,
        serviceURL,              // the service URL
        SLP_LIFETIME_MAXIMUM,    // maintain registration as
                                 // long as we're alive
        0,                       // we use service URL scheme
                                 // for service type
        attributes,              // attributes
        SLP_TRUE,                // "fresh" flag.  TRUE == this
                                 // is an initial registration
        RegCallbackFunc,         // callback that gets registration
                                 // error code
        &callback_err);          // cookie.  We pass the address of
                                 // a variable to receive the
                                 // error code.

// could fail to register by receiving an error code
// directly from SLPReg() call or through the callback.
// Check both.
```

```
if (err != SLP_OK || callback_err != SLP_OK) {
  Diagnose("SLPReg()", __LINE__,
    (err != SLP_OK ? err : callback_err));
  Shutdown("Can't continue.");
}
```

The final operation in main() is a call to ServeEchoClients(), which is passed the integer port number on which the server listens for client connections. The port number is a command line argument. Note that this port is used exclusively for client/server communication—it has nothing to do with the port used by the SLP implementation for transfer of SLP messages. ServeEchoClients() implements a simple socket-based echo service. We don't expect to return from ServeEchoClients()—the server will run until it receives a SIGINT (e.g, via control-C).

```
// communicate with clients until shutdown.  The argument is
// the port on which we listen, which is necessary for
// setting up the listening socket.
printf("echo_server: Ready to handle clients.\n");
ServeEchoClients(atoi(argv[2]));

return 0;
}
```

The following function is the callback for SLPReg(). It simply stores the errCode provided by the SLP library in the cookie and returns. This allows the main() function to determine whether the registration succeeded and to take appropriate action.

```
/////////////////////////////////
// this function is registered as the callback for SLPReg().
// The 'errcode' parameter indicates whether the registration
// was successful.
//
void RegCallbackFunc(SLPHandle handle, SLPError errcode,
  void* cookie) {
  // the cookie provides a convenient way to return
  // information to the function which called an API function
  // which resulted in the callback.  In this case, we return
  // the error code in the cookie.

  // just provide initiator of SLP operation with error code
  *(SLPError*)cookie = errcode;

}
```

The Diagnose() function takes a function name, line number, and SLP error code. The function name and line number are displayed for context to the user. The SLP error code is interpreted (which is a fancy description for a giant switch statement!), and a corresponding meaning for the error is displayed. This function is useful as a reference for the meaning of each SLPError value.

```c
/////////////////////////////////
// Diagnose an error code associated with an SLP API call.
//
void Diagnose(char *func, int line, SLPError err) {

  printf("echo_server: ");
  printf("Error %d in function %s at line %d.\nExplanation:\n",
    err, func, line);

  switch (err) {
  case SLP_LAST_CALL:
    printf("Passed to a callback function when no further ");
    printf("calls will be made for the current operation.\n");
    break;
  case SLP_OK:
    printf("Successful.\n");
    break;
  case SLP_LANGUAGE_NOT_SUPPORTED:
    printf("No service advertisement or attribute information is");
    printf(" available in the requested\n");
    printf("language, but at least one DA or SA might have such");
    printf(" information in another\n");
    printf("language.\n");
    break;
  case SLP_PARSE_ERROR:
    printf("Data supplied to a DA or SA was ill-formed.\n");
    break;
  case SLP_INVALID_REGISTRATION:
    printf("The service URL or attributes in the registration");
    printf(" attempt were malformed.\n");
    break;
  case SLP_SCOPE_NOT_SUPPORTED:
    printf("A specified scope is not supported.\n");
    break;
  case SLP_AUTHENTICATION_ABSENT:
    printf("The UA or SA failed to provide authentication info");
    printf(" for a protected scope.\n");
    break;
  case SLP_AUTHENTICATION_FAILED:
    printf("Authentication on an SLP message failed.\n");
```

```
      break;
    case SLP_INVALID_UPDATE:
      printf("An update for a non-existing registration was ");
      printf("attempted or the service type\n");
      printf("or scope were different from the original ");
      printf("registration.\n");
      break;
    case SLP_REFRESH_REJECTED:
      printf("An attempt was made to refresh a registration more");
      printf(" frequently than the\n");
      printf("minimum refresh interval demanded by the DA.\n");
      break;
    case SLP_NOT_IMPLEMENTED:
      printf("The call made is not implemented in this SLP");
      printf("library.\n");
      break;
    case SLP_BUFFER_OVERFLOW:
      printf("A request overflowed the network's MTU.\n");
      break;
    case SLP_NETWORK_TIMED_OUT:
      printf("No reply was received within a configured timeout");
      printf(" interval.\n");
      break;
    case SLP_NETWORK_INIT_FAILED:
      printf("Initialization failure.  Likely caused by no slpd");
      printf(" running.\n");
      break;
    case SLP_MEMORY_ALLOC_FAILED:
      printf("Out of memory.\n");
      break;
    case SLP_PARAMETER_BAD:
      printf("One or more of the parameters in an API call");
      printf(" were invalid.\n");
      break;
    case SLP_NETWORK_ERROR:
      printf("The network has failed.\n");
      break;
    case SLP_INTERNAL_SYSTEM_ERROR:
      printf("Something nasty in the woodshed.  An internal ");
      printf("error has occurred.\n");
      break;
    case SLP_HANDLE_IN_USE:
      printf("Only ONE operation may be underway for a given");
      printf(" handle at a time!\n");
      break;
    case SLP_TYPE_ERROR:
      printf("A type error occurred when checking attribute types");
      printf(" against a template.\n");
```

```
      break;
   default:
      printf("HUH?   I have no idea what that error code is.\n");
   }
}
```

To handle control-C, Shutdown() is called. The die() function is passed to the sigaction() system call in SignalHandler(), below.

```
/////////////////////////////////
// deal with control-C
//
void die(int blarg) {
   Shutdown("Shutting down.");
}
```

SignalHandler() deals with SIGINT (control-C) and SIGPIPE signals. SIGPIPE is blocked, which allows the sockets-based echo server to deal with clients hanging up, and SIGINT is trapped and results in a call to die(), which in turn just calls Shutdown(). This code is perhaps the least portable portion of the server.

```
/////////////////////////////////
// set up control-C and SIGPIPE handler.
//
void SignalHandler() {
   struct sigaction action;
   sigset_t block;
   action.sa_handler = die;
   sigemptyset(&(action.sa_mask));
   action.sa_flags = 0;
   sigaction(SIGINT, &action, NULL);
   sigemptyset(&block);
   sigaddset(&block, SIGPIPE);
   sigprocmask(SIG_SETMASK, &block, NULL);
}
```

Shutdown() is responsible for performing a graceful death ritual. If the server's SLP handle is non-NULL and the service URL is non-NULL, then SLPDereg() is called to cancel the service registration. If the SLP handle is non-NULL, SLPClose() is called to release associated resources. A reason for the shutdown [which is the only argument to Shutdown()] is printed before exit() is called to terminate the server.

```
/////////////////////////////////
// Do a clean shutdown.   Unregister before dying.
//
```

```
// reason == reason we're shutting down.
//
void Shutdown(char *reason) {
  int dontcare;    // callback insists on storing error
                   // code in the cookie

  printf("echo_server: Wait...\n");
  if (handle) {
    // unregister.  Don't care about success or failure,
    // because we're going to die anyway.  Must pass
    // handle, service URL, callback to receive
    // error code, and cookie.
    if (serviceURL) {
      SLPDereg(handle, serviceURL, RegCallbackFunc, &dontcare);
    }

    // release handle before dying
    SLPClose(handle);

  }
  printf("echo_server: %s\n", reason);
  exit(0);
}
```

The following is a straightforward sockets-based echo server implementation. The single argument is the port on which the server should listen. It's a gentle introduction to sockets programming, but readers completely unfamiliar with sockets programming are referred to the excellent books by Stevens [e.g., 15]. Note that there are no SLP calls in the following function—the particular protocol spoken between clients and services is completely outside the scope of SLP.

```
/////////////////////////////////
// Handle connections from clients who have figured out
// where we are.  For each socket connection, read and echo
// until the connection is closed.  The protocol is simple:
// We expect a line of characters from a client, terminated
// with a '\n'.  If no '\n' is forthcoming, the
// server will hang.  A 'production' protocol would obviously
// have to be more robust.  select() is used for multiplexing client
// communication.
//
// Note that no SLP API calls are used in this function-the
// protocol spoken between clients and services is completely
// outside the jurisdiction of SLP.
//
```

```
void ServeEchoClients(int port) {

  int i, found;
  int alive;       // client still around after read?
  int sock;        // socket for listening
  int newconn;     // socket for new client
  int highest;     // highest handle in use; needed for select()
  int ready;       // number of ready sockets (from select() call)
  int connected[100]; // handle only 100 simultaneous clients.
  fd_set socks;    // sockets ready for reading, needed for select()
  struct sockaddr_in server_address;   // structure for bind() call
  int reuse=1;                         // avoid port in use problems

  // initialize sockets stuff

  sock = socket(AF_INET, SOCK_STREAM, 0);
  if (sock < 0) {
    Shutdown(
      "echo_server: socket() call failed.  Can't continue.");
  }

  setsockopt(sock, SOL_SOCKET, SO_REUSEADDR, &reuse,
    sizeof(reuse));
  memset((char *) &server_address, 0, sizeof(server_address));
  server_address.sin_family = AF_INET;
  server_address.sin_addr.s_addr = htonl(INADDR_ANY);
  server_address.sin_port = htons(port);
  if (bind(sock, (struct sockaddr *)&server_address,
    sizeof(server_address)) < 0 ) {
    Shutdown("echo_server: bind() call failed. Can't continue.");
  }
  listen(sock, 15);
  highest = sock;
  memset((char *) &connected, 0, sizeof(connected));

  printf("echo_server: Listening...\n");

  while (1) {
    FD_ZERO(&socks);       // initialize set of sockets to monitor
    FD_SET(sock,&socks);   // always care about listening socket
    // also care about sockets for connected clients
    for (i=0; i < 100; i++) {
      if (connected[i] != 0) {
        FD_SET(connected[i],&socks);
        if (connected[i] > highest) {
          highest = connected[i];
        }
      }
```

```
  }

  ready = select(highest+1, &socks, NULL, NULL, NULL);
  if (ready < 0) {
    Shutdown(
      "echo_server: select() call failed. Can't continue.");
  }

  // see who's knocking, gently rapping at our (socket) door...

  if (FD_ISSET(sock,&socks)) {
    // new client
    newconn = accept(sock, NULL, NULL);
    if (newconn < 0) {
      printf("** FAILED TO CONNECT TO NEW CLIENT **\n");
    }
    else {
      // find a home for new client socket
      found=0;
      for (i=0; i < 100 && ! found; i++) {
        if (connected[i] == 0) {
          printf("echo_server: Connected to new client.\n");
          connected[i] = newconn;
          found=1;
        }
      }
      if (! found) {
        printf("echo_server: OVERLOADED.  Refusing connect");
        printf(" from new client.\n");
        close(newconn);
      }
    }
  }

  // check connected clients, deal with one line of echo for
  // each ready client
  for (i=0; i < 100; i++) {
    if (FD_ISSET(connected[i],&socks)) {
      alive = ReadAndEcho(connected[i]);
      if (! alive) {
        close(connected[i]);
        connected[i] = 0;        // client hung up
      }
    }
  }
 }
}
```

The following function is called by ServeEchoClients() (above) to handle a one-line interaction with a client. The single argument is the socket on which the communication should take place. We rely (desperately) on clients obeying a rule: They must transmit an arbitrary number of characters, followed by a new line. We echo each character in turn. If the client fails to send a \n, the ReadAndEcho() will hang (and thus the entire server will hang) until the connection is broken. This would, of course, be intolerable in a production server. Timeouts or a similar mechanism would be required to prevent server hangs in production environments.

```
/////////////////////////////////
// Read characters from a handle and echo them back
// until a '\n' is seen. Returns 0 if client hangs up,
// 1 if echo was successfully completed.
// We're completely vulnerable to a client not sending \n.
// A more robust protocol would have to deal with issues like
// this.  It's not addressed here because the
// client <-> service protocol is largely aside from the
// SLP issues.
//
int ReadAndEcho(int handle) {

  char c=-1;
  int count=1;
  int ret=1;

  printf("echo_server: ");
  printf("Reading a line from a client.  Hoping for \\n...\n");

  count = read(handle, &c, 1);        // read one char
  while (c != '\n' && count > 0) {
    count = write(handle, &c, 1);     // echo it
    if (count) {
      putchar(c);
      count=read(handle, &c, 1);      // read one char
    }
  }

  if (count == 0) {
    printf("echo_server: Client hung up.\n");
    ret=0;
  }
  else {
    // echo final \n
    count = write(handle, &c, 1);
```

```
    putchar('\n');
  }

  printf("echo_server: Returning to listening state.\n");
  return ret;
}
```

The Client Side: An SLP Echo Client Implementation

Now we turn to the client side and examine the implementation of a simple client for interacting with an echo service. The client searches for services of type "service:echo-service.test:tcp", displays their associated attributes, and then allows the user to select one service. A socket connection is made to the selected service, and the echoing begins. This echo client is implemented using OpenSLP under Linux and MacOS X.

The echo client implementation consists of a single source file. The following is the header of "echo_client.c". As for the service, it includes <slp.h> and a number of standard include files. This is followed by two types and several global variables. The types are struct AttErr, which contains a char* and an SLPError field. A variable of this type is passed as a cookie to the callback that handles discovering attributes for a service, and provides the callback with a mechanism for returning both an attribute list and a status code. The other type is struct ServiceInfo, which has url, host, and port fields. The url field holds a discovered service's service URL, and the host and port fields are extracted from this service URL. A global array of ServiceInfo structures holds information about all discovered echo services. The other globals are numservices, which hold the number of significant entries in the array of ServiceInfo structures, and an SLPHandle variable.

```
// SLP echo client main source file.  Discovers registered
// echo services and allows the user to select a server with
// which to interact.   Written by
// Golden G. Richard III, Ph.D.   July 2001.

#include <slp.h>
#include <string.h>
#include <stdio.h>
#include <stdlib.h>
#include <unistd.h>
#include <sys/types.h>
```

```
#include <sys/socket.h>
#include <netinet/in.h>
#include <signal.h>

// types

// type for cookie to callback for SLPFindAttrs
typedef struct AttrErr {
  char *attrlist;        // list of attributes/values
  SLPError err;          // error code passed to callback
} AttrErr;

// type for storage of service URL, host, port for service
typedef struct ServiceInfo {
  char url[512];
  char host[128];
  int port;
} ServiceInfo;

// globals

// our ticket to using API calls beyond SLPOpen()
static SLPHandle handle;
// store service URLs/hosts/ports for a max of 10 echo services
static ServiceInfo Services[10];
// # of discovered echo services
static int numservices=0;

// function prototypes for "echo_client.c" functions
int main(int argc, char* argv[]);
SLPBoolean ServiceCallbackFunc(SLPHandle handle,
                               const char* srvurl,
                               unsigned short lifetime,
                               SLPError err,
                               void *cookie);
SLPBoolean AttributesCallback(SLPHandle handle,
                              const char *attrlist,
                              SLPError err,
                              void *cookie);
SLPError FindAttributes(char *url, char **attrs);
int Choose(void);
void Diagnose(char *func, int line, SLPError err);
void SignalHandler(void);
void die(int blarg);
void Shutdown(char *reason);
void EchoClient(char *ip, int port);
```

The main() function in the echo client is straightforward. It registers a signal handler as the echo service implementation did. Once the signal handler is registered, SLPOpen() is called to obtain a handle. We opt to use synchronous API calls and work in English. Next, the FindEchoServices() function is called to search for echo services. When this function returns, the available echo services are known. If there are no echo services at all, the client terminates (with a sad message). Otherwise, Choose() is called to let the user choose an echo service with which to interact. Choose() is also responsible for obtaining the attributes of the discovered services, which are displayed along with the service URLs in the list of available services. Once the user makes a choice, EchoClient() is called with the host and port of the selected server. EchoClient() implements a simple sockets-based echo client.

```
/////////////////////////////////
// SLP echo client's main function.
//
int main(int argc, char* argv[]) {

  SLPError err; // return value from API functions
  int choice;   // user's selection from list of echo services

  // on control-C, do a clean Shutdown().  Also, don't die
  // on SIGPIPE.
  printf("echo_client: Registering signal handler.\n");
  SignalHandler();

  printf("echo_client: Echo client initializing.\n");

  // get a handle.  "en" == English, SLP_FALSE == use
  // synchronous API calls
  err = SLPOpen("en", SLP_FALSE, &handle);
  if (err != SLP_OK) {
    Diagnose("SLPOpen()", __LINE__, err);
    Shutdown("Can't continue.");
  }

  // find echo services
  FindEchoServices();

  // any found?
  if (numservices == 0) {
    Shutdown("No echo services found.  Try again later.\n");
  }

  // allow user to select an echo service
  choice = Choose();
  if (choice == 0) {
    printf("echo_client: Perhaps another time?\n");
  }
```

```
    else {
      // initiate session with chosen echo service.
      EchoClient(Services[choice-1].host, Services[choice-1].port);
    }

    Shutdown("Thanks for echoing.\n");
    return 0;
}
```

The following function, AttributesCallback(), is the callback function specified when SLPAttrs() is called in FindAttributes(). It stores the attribute list for the function and a status code in an AttrErr structure. A pointer to an AttrErr is passed as a cookie in the SLPAttrs() call in FindAttributes(). If something goes wrong, NULL is placed into the attrlist field in the AttrErr instead of a pointer to an attribute list.

```
/////////////////////////////////
// Callback function for SLPAttrs().  Called to deliver
// attributes in the form of a comma-separated list of
// name=value pairs.  We expect cookie to be a pointer to
// an AttrErr structure, which allows the err (status code)
// and attrlist to be returned to the originator of the
// attribute request.
//
SLPBoolean AttributesCallback(SLPHandle handle,
  const char *attrlist, SLPError err, void *cookie) {

  if (err == SLP_OK) {
    // save attribute list
    ((AttrErr *)cookie)->attrlist = malloc(strlen(attrlist)+1);
    if (((AttrErr *)cookie)->attrlist) {
      strcpy(((AttrErr *)cookie)->attrlist, attrlist);
    }
    else {
      // out of memory on malloc(); cheat a little and use
      // an SLP error code
      ((AttrErr *)cookie)->attrlist = NULL;
      ((AttrErr *)cookie)->err = SLP_MEMORY_ALLOC_FAILED;
    }
    // save error code
    ((AttrErr *)cookie)->err = err;
  }
  else if (err != SLP_LAST_CALL) {
    // no attributes retrieved—just save NULL
    ((AttrErr *)cookie)->attrlist = NULL;
    // save error code
    ((AttrErr *)cookie)->err = err;
```

```
    }
    return SLP_TRUE;
}
```

FindAttributes(), below, calls SLPFindAttrs() to obtain the list of attributes for a service. It accepts a char* service URL and a char ** attribute list. The SLPFindAttrs() function requires seven arguments: an SLP handle, the URL of the service for which attributes should be obtained, a list of scopes (we specify "", which causes configured scopes to be used), a comma-separated list of attribute names (we use "" to obtain all attributes), a callback function, and a cookie for the callback. A pointer to an AttrErr structure is used for the cookie, which allows the callback to communicate both an attribute list and a status code. We copy the pointer to the attribute list delivered by the callback into *attrs if no error occurred, and return either SLP_OK or whichever status code is not SLP_OK [the choices being the direct return value from SLPFind-Attrs() or the status code delivered to the callback].

```
//////////////////////////////
// Discover the complete set of attributes for the service
// with service URL 'url'.  The comma-separated
// list of attributes/values is returned in a string
// associated with 'attrs'.  The caller is responsible for
// freeing the attribute list [using free(), not SLPFree()]
// when it is no longer needed.
//
SLPError FindAttributes(char *url, char **attrs) {

    SLPError err=SLP_OK;
    AttrErr callback_result;

    callback_result.err = SLP_OK;
    callback_result.attrlist = NULL;

    err = SLPFindAttrs(handle,
                    url,    // get attributes for this service
                    "",     // use default scope
                    "",     // return ALL attributes. Otherwise
                            // use a comma-separated list of
                            // attribute names
                    // attributes will be returned through
                    // this callback function
                    AttributesCallback,
                    // cookie for callback.  Will contain
                    // attribute list and error code.
                    &callback_result);
```

```
  if (err == SLP_OK && callback_result.err != SLP_OK) {
    err = callback_result.err;
  }

  if (err == SLP_OK) {  // all's well, get attribute list
    *attrs = callback_result.attrlist;
  }
  else {
    *attrs = NULL;
  }

  return err;
}
```

The ServiceCallbackFunc() is the callback specified for SLPFind-
Srvs(). It is called each time a new service URL is discovered. The new
service URL is provided in the argument 'srvurl', provided that no error
has occurred. The duration for which the URL is valid is provided in lifetime (in seconds). If no error occurred, then the new service URL is
stored in a global array of service information structures, called Services. Each entry in this array contains a service URL, host, and port.
The host and port portions of the service URL are obtained with a call to
SLPParseSrvURL() here, in the callback.

```
///////////////////////////////
// Callback function for SLPFindSrvs().  Called when a new
// service URL discovered.  The lifetime for the service URL
// is available in 'lifetime'.
//
SLPBoolean ServiceCallbackFunc(SLPHandle handle,
  const char *srvurl, unsigned short lifetime, SLPError err,
    void *cookie) {

  SLPSrvURL *parsed;              // parsed service URL

  *((int *)cookie)=SLP_OK;        // return status code in cookie
  if (err == SLP_OK) {
    printf("echo_client: New echo service discovered");
    printf(" with lifetime of %d!\n", (int)lifetime);

    // Example of SLPParseSrvURL() usage.  It's OK to call
    // this function here, because no handle is required.
    // It is NOT OK to overlap API calls that need handles.
    // For example, calling SLPFindAttrs() here would
    // not be permitted.
```

```
  err=SLPParseSrvURL(srvurl, &parsed);
  if (err == SLP_OK) {
    printf("Component parts of discovered service URL:\n");
    printf("\tService type:    %s\n", parsed->s_pcSrvType);
    printf("\tHost:            %s\n", parsed->s_pcHost);
    printf("\tPort:            %d\n", parsed->s_iPort);
    printf("\tNetFamily:       %s\n", parsed->s_pcNetFamily);
    printf("\tRemainder:       %s\n", parsed->s_pcSrvPart);

    // remember service URL so attributes can be retrieved
    // later unless we hit the max.  It's also handy to have
    // the host/port portions separate for contacting the
    // service later.
    if (numservices == 10) {
      printf("echo_client: Will only store contact info for");
      printf(" first 10 echo services.\n");
    }
    else {
    strcpy(Services[numservices].url, srvurl);
    strcpy(Services[numservices].host, parsed->s_pcHost);
    Services[numservices].port = parsed->s_iPort;
      numservices++;
    }
    // free storage associated with parsed service URL
    SLPFree(parsed);
  }
  else {
    printf("echo_client: Something went wrong during parsing");
    printf(" of service URL.\n");
    Diagnose("ServiceCallbackFunc()", __LINE__, err);
    printf("echo_client: Client still alive, hoping for");
    printf(" other registrations.\n");
    *((int *)cookie) = err;
  }
}
else if (err != SLP_LAST_CALL) {
  // SLP_LAST_CALL means that current SLP operation is complete
  printf("echo_client: Something went wrong during discovery");
  printf(" of service URL.\n");
  Diagnose("ServiceCallbackFunc()", __LINE__, err);
  printf("echo_client: Client still alive, hoping for");
  printf(" other registrations.\n");
  *((int *)cookie)=err;
}

  return SLP_TRUE;
}
```

The callback function above is a slave for the following function, Find-EchoServices(), which initiates discovery of echo services with a call to SLPFindSrvs(). All the work related to discovery is done in the callback. The SLPFindSrvs() call takes six arguments, including a handle, the service type ("service:echo-service.test:tcp"), a list of scopes, a search filter, and the callback and cookie. We use configured scopes and no search filter.

```
/////////////////////////////
// Initiates the search for echo services with a call
// to SLPFindAttrs().
//
void FindEchoServices() {

   SLPError err;           // return value from API functions
   SLPError callback_err;  // status returned to callback

   // look for echo services

   printf("echo_client: Issuing service request.\n");
   err = SLPFindSrvs(handle,
                 "service:echo-service.test:tcp",
                 "",        // use default scopes
                 "",        // no search filter-any echo service
                 ServiceCallbackFunc, // callback
                 &callback_err);    // cookie for result

   if (err != SLP_OK || callback_err != SLP_OK) {
     Diagnose("SlpFindSrvs()", __LINE__,
       (err == SLP_OK ? callback_err : err));
   }
   else {
     printf("echo_client: Service request complete.\n");
   }
}
```

The following function displays a list of the service URLs for discovered lookup services, along with the attributes for each service. A call to FindAttributes() is made for each service, so the listing of services may be a bit sluggish. The user is allowed to choose one of the services for an echo session, or choose 0 to indicate that today just isn't the day for echoing. The choice is returned.

```
/////////////////////////////
// Display a list of available echo services and allow user
```

```
// to choose one.   0 is returned if the user cancels selection,
// otherwise the (position + 1) in the Services array is
// returned.  This function calls FindAttributes() to display
// the attributes associated w/ each service, so the menu
// display can be sluggish.
//
int Choose() {

   int choice=-1;
   int i;
   char *attrlist;   // list of attributes for each service
   SLPError err;     // return value from FindAttributes() call

   printf("\nAVAILABLE ECHO SERVICES:\n");
   for (i=0; i < numservices; i++) {
      printf("\n[%1d]\t%s\n", i+1, Services[i].url);
      printf("\tAttributes: ");
      err = FindAttributes(Services[i].url, &attrlist);
      if (err == SLP_OK) {
         printf("%s\n", attrlist);
         // we allocated this mem in FindAttributes using malloc(),
         // so just use free()
         free(attrlist);
      }
      else {
         printf("** NO ATTRIBUTE INFO AVAILABLE**      Reason:\n");
         Diagnose("FindAttributes()", __LINE__, err);
      }
   }

   while (choice < 0 || choice > numservices+1) {
      printf("\nEnter # of service to connect to or 0 to exit: ");
      choice=getchar() - '0';
      getchar();  // eat newline!
      printf("echo_client: %d\n", choice);
   }
   return choice;
}
```

The Diagnose(), Shutdown(), die(), and SignalHandler() functions are identical to those in the server, but are included for completeness. See the description of the echo service functions for details.

```
/////////////////////////////////
// Diagnose an error code associated with an SLP API call.
//
void Diagnose(char *func, int line, SLPError err) {
```

```
printf("echo_server: ");
printf("Error %d in function %s at line %d.\nExplanation:\n",
  err, func, line);

switch (err) {
case SLP_LAST_CALL:
  printf("Passed to a callback function when no further ");
  printf("calls will be made for the current operation.\n");
  break;
case SLP_OK:
  printf("Successful.\n");
  break;
case SLP_LANGUAGE_NOT_SUPPORTED:
  printf("No service advertisement or attribute information is");
  printf(" available in the requested\n");
  printf("language, but at least one DA or SA might have such");
  printf(" information in another\n");
  printf("language.\n");
  break;
case SLP_PARSE_ERROR:
  printf("Data supplied to a DA or SA was ill-formed.\n");
  break;
case SLP_INVALID_REGISTRATION:
  printf("The service URL or attributes in the registration");
  printf(" attempt were malformed.\n");
  break;
case SLP_SCOPE_NOT_SUPPORTED:
  printf("A specified scope is not supported.\n");
  break;
case SLP_AUTHENTICATION_ABSENT:
  printf("The UA or SA failed to provide authentication info");
  printf(" for a protected scope.\n");
  break;
case SLP_AUTHENTICATION_FAILED:
  printf("Authentication on an SLP message failed.\n");
  break;
case SLP_INVALID_UPDATE:
  printf("An update for a non-existing registration was ");
  printf("attempted or the service type\n");
  printf("or scope were different from the original ");
  printf("registration.\n");
  break;
case SLP_REFRESH_REJECTED:
  printf("An attempt was made to refresh a registration more");
  printf(" frequently than the\n");
  printf("minimum refresh interval demanded by the DA.\n");
  break;
case SLP_NOT_IMPLEMENTED:
```

```
      printf("The call made is not implemented in this SLP");
      printf("library.\n");
      break;
   case SLP_BUFFER_OVERFLOW:
      printf("A request overflowed the network's MTU.\n");
      break;
   case SLP_NETWORK_TIMED_OUT:
      printf("No reply was received within a configured timeout");
      printf(" interval.\n");
      break;
   case SLP_NETWORK_INIT_FAILED:
      printf("Initialization failure.  Likely caused by no slpd");
      printf(" running.\n");
      break;
   case SLP_MEMORY_ALLOC_FAILED:
      printf("Out of memory.\n");
      break;
   case SLP_PARAMETER_BAD:
      printf("One or more of the parameters in an API call");
      printf(" were invalid.\n");
      break;
   case SLP_NETWORK_ERROR:
      printf("The network has failed.\n");
      break;
   case SLP_INTERNAL_SYSTEM_ERROR:
      printf("Something nasty in the woodshed.  An internal ");
      printf("error has occurred.\n");
      break;
   case SLP_HANDLE_IN_USE:
      printf("Only ONE operation may be underway for a given");
      printf(" handle at a time!\n");
      break;
   case SLP_TYPE_ERROR:
      printf("A type error occurred when checking attribute types");
      printf(" against a template.\n");
      break;
   default:
      printf("HUH?  I have no idea what that error code is.\n");
   }
}


/////////////////////////////
// deal with control-C
//
void die(int blarg) {
   Shutdown("Shutting down.");
}
```

```
//////////////////////////////
// set up control-C handler and don't die on SIGPIPE.
//
void SignalHandler() {

  struct sigaction action;
  sigset_t block;
  action.sa_handler = die;
  sigemptyset(&(action.sa_mask));
  action.sa_flags = 0;
  sigaction(SIGINT, &action, NULL);
  sigemptyset(&block);
  sigaddset(&block, SIGPIPE);
  sigprocmask(SIG_SETMASK, &block, NULL);
}


//////////////////////////////
// Do a clean shutdown.
//
// reason == reason we're shutting down.
//
void Shutdown(char *reason) {

  printf("Wait...\n");
  if (handle) {
    // release handle before dying
    SLPClose(handle);
  }
  printf("echo_client: %s\n", reason);
  exit(0);
}
```

The last function in the echo client implementation, EchoClient(), supports an echo session with a particular echo service. Note that there is no SLP code in this function, as the wire protocol spoken between client and service is outside the range of duties for SLP. EchoClient() takes an IP address and port and has a familiar structure for sockets-based programs. Each line typed is sent to the server, and the response is displayed. The user can type "." on a line by itself to terminate the session.

```
//////////////////////////////
// Communicate with an echo server listening at a given ip
// and port using an AF_INET socket connection.  When the
// user types "." as the first character of a line, the
// connection is broken and control returns to the caller.
// The code here is straightforward sockets stuff.
```

```
//
void EchoClient(char *ip, int port) {

   struct sockaddr_in them; // address of server
   int sock;                 // socket for communication w/ server
   int err;
   int len;
   char buf[512];
   char c;
   int count;
   struct hostent *remip; // will use this one...
   unsigned long remip2;  // or this one as binary remote addr


   bzero((char *)&them, sizeof(them));
   them.sin_family = AF_INET;
   them.sin_port = htons(port);

   // try inet_addr() call first; some unixes freak if we provide a
   // dotted numeric IP address to gethostbyname()
   remip2=inet_addr(ip);
   if (remip2 <= 0) {
     remip=gethostbyname(ip);
     if (remip == NULL) {
        herror(NULL);
        Shutdown("Couldn't initialize connection parameters.");
     }
   }
   if (remip2 <= 0) {
     memcpy(&(them.sin_addr.s_addr),
       remip->h_addr, remip->h_length);
   }
   else {
     them.sin_addr.s_addr = remip2;
   }

   if ((sock=socket(AF_INET, SOCK_STREAM, 0)) < 0) {
     printf("echo_client: socket() failed with error %d.\n", sock);
     Shutdown("Can't continue.");
   }

   if ((err = connect(sock, (struct sockaddr*)&them,
     sizeof(struct sockaddr_in)))) {
     printf("echo_client: connect() failed with error %d.\n", err);
     Shutdown("Can't continue.");
   }

   printf("echo_client: Start typing. ");
```

```
printf("<".\" on a line by itself disconnects.\n");
gets(buf);
while (buf[0] != '.') {
  len=strlen(buf);
  buf[len++]='\n';              // add newline
  buf[len]=0;
  write(sock, buf, strlen(buf));   // transmit

  // get response one char at a time
  printf("echo_client: Service response:\"");
  count = read(sock, &c, 1);
  while (c != '\n' && count > 0) {
    putchar(c);
    count=read(sock, &c, 1);    // read one char
  }
  printf("\"\n");
  if (count == 0) {
    printf("echo_client: Server hung up. How rude!\n");
    buf[0]='.';
  }
  gets(buf);
}
close(sock);
}
```

Configuration

Configuration File

SLP implementations are highly configurable and allow many parameters to be tuned. Below, the major configuration parameters are discussed. These are globally manipulated in static configuration files and may be changed for a running process using functions in the SLP language bindings. SLP configuration allows control of whether active DA discovery should be performed, the TTL (time to live) for multicast requests, etc. Configuration parameters are discussed in detail in RFC 2614; the most important are surveyed here.

This discussion of configuration is based on OpenSLP 1.0.5, which is RFC 2614-compliant with only a few deviations. These deviations are mentioned below. Global default values for these parameters are typically stored in a configuration file, which is a newline-separated list of parameter_name=value pairs (for example, net.slp.useScopes = Scope1,

Scope2, Scope3). If a parameter is not present in the configuration file, a default value is used. The list of configurable parameters includes

net.slp.useScopes=Scope1, Scope2,..., ScopeN
This is a comma-delimited list of scope strings used by a UA or SA to constrain requests or registrations and by a DA as the list of scopes that must be supported. Default value is "DEFAULT."

net.slp.DAAddresses=Address1, Address2,..., AddressN
This is a list of statically configured DA addresses used by UAs and SAs for service requests and registrations. Default value is not to use statically configured DAs, and instead to dynamically discover available DAs.

net.slp.isBroadcastOnly=true or false
Default for this parameter is false. If it is set to true, then broadcast is used instead of multicast. The default behavior is almost always sufficient.

net.slp.passiveDADetection=true or false
This is a boolean indicating whether passive DA detection (in response to reception of DAAdverts) should be used. The default is true.

net.slp.DAActiveDiscoveryInterval=# of seconds
This parameter is a 16-bit positive integer that governs the number of seconds between "service:directory-agent" queries, which are used for active DA discovery. The default value is 900 s. If this value is zero, then no active discovery of DAs will be performed.

net.slp.multicastTTL=# of hops
A positive integer is used as the TTL parameter for multicasts. The default is 255.

net.slp.multicastMaximumWait=# of milliseconds
This is the maximum duration in milliseconds that multicast requests will be transmitted to satisfy a single request. The default value is 15,000 ms = 15 s.

net.slp.unicastMaximumWait=# of milliseconds
This is the unicast counterpart of net.slp.multicastMaximumWait. The default value is 15,000 ms = 15 s.

net.slp.MTU=# of bytes
This is MTU for network in bytes. Default is 1400.

net.slp.interfaces=IPaddress1, IPaddress2,...IPaddressN

This is a list of the IP addresses for network interfaces that should be used by DAs and SAs listening for requests. It is useful for configuration of multihome machines. The default is to use all interfaces.

net.slp.securityEnabled=true or false

This indicates whether all agents should use authentication blocks, enabling security for URLs, attribute lists, and advertisements. This parameter is currently ignored in OpenSLP. Security in OpenSLP must be enabled at compile time. The default value for net.slp.securityEnabled is false.

net.slp.locale=language_tag

This is an RFC 1766-compliant language tag. Default is "en" (English). It specifies the default locale for SLP messages and is currently ignored in OpenSLP.

net.slp.maxResults=# of results to report

This is an integer value representing the maximum number of results that should be accumulated (within the maximum duration of a request) before the results are returned to the requester. It is currently ignored in OpenSLP.

net.slp.isDA=true or false

This determines whether the SLP server should act as a directory agent. Default is false. It is currently ignored in OpenSLP.

net.slp.DAHeartBeat=# of seconds

This is an integer value specifying the number of seconds between unsolicited DAAdverts for directory agents. The default is 10,800 s = 3 h. It is ignored if net.slp.isDA is false, but is currently ignored in all cases in OpenSLP.

net.slp.DAAttributes=list of attributes

This is a comma-separated list of attributes that are included in DAAdverts. This parameter is currently ignored in OpenSLP.

net.slp.serializedRegURL=URL of configuration file

This is the URL of the configuration file to use. This parameter is not supported in OpenSLP.

DHCP Issues

The Dynamic Host Configuration Protocol (DHCP) is commonly used to provide clients with important configuration information (such as IP addresses). As mentioned earlier in the chapter, DHCP options can be used to provide the locations of DAs to SAs and UAs, and to provide scope information to UAs. In all cases, the availability of DA locations via DHCP should be preferred by agents over active or passive discovery. DHCP options related to SLP are covered in detail in RFC 2610. They are not covered further here, because such configuration is primarily an administrative duty. The use (or nonuse) of DHCP does not penetrate the SLP API—applications have no idea whether DHCP or some other means is being used to provide DA locations and scope information.

Security

Introduction

SLP supports authentication, which allows the origin and integrity of SLP messages to be verified, but such measures must be supplemented with a strong dose of common sense and good security practices. For example, under OpenSLP, the slpd daemon, which serves as a DA and provides the SA implementation under the API, must be run as root to acquire the protected SLP port (port 427). This prevents "rogue" DAs from being installed (at least on operating systems that prevent user-level servers from capturing traditionally reserved ports). Proper key distribution practices are also important, and of course the private keys used in public key authentication protocols must really be kept private. In many circumstances, where SLP is used in isolated networks under tight administrative controls, the security features discussed in this section will not even be required, and thus security is optional in an SLP implementation.

SLP doesn't define the protocols for communication between clients and services, and so its security model concentrates on preventing propagation of false information about service locations and on allowing agents to properly identify other agents. The latter is particularly important, as a rogue SA might otherwise masquerade as the provider of a needed service solely to collect private information (such as user names and passwords) from an unsuspecting UA. SAs can include digital signatures when registering so DAs and UAs can verify their identity. No support for confidentiality (e.g., encryption of requests) is directly provided by SLP. Neither is access control addressed—individual services must implement their own access control protocols (via passwords or some other mechanism). The details of SLP security are addressed in some depth here; complete details are available in RFC 2608. Note that SLP security issues are not exposed to application code—SLP implementations communicate security violations through error codes, but SLP applications are otherwise unaware of security features. Further, configuration of security for agents is left to systems administrators and cannot be performed through the API. This configuration includes the generation and distribution of public and private keys.

Authentication Blocks

Of central importance to SLP security is a structure called an Authentication Block (AB). The format of an SLP Authentication Block is illustrated in Fig. 3-12.

ABs are attached to SLP messages to allow the receiver to verify that the contents have not been changed and, further, to verify the identity of the sender. The Block Structure Descriptor (BSD) in an AB is a 16-byte quantity that identifies the type of authentication information represented by the AB. IANA is responsible for standardizing the meanings of values between 0 and 0x7FFF, while values 0x8000 through 0x8FFF are available for proprietary purposes. The Authentication Block Length is the length of

```
 0                   1                   2                   3
 0 1 2 3 4 5 6 7 8 9 0 1 2 3 4 5 6 7 8 9 0 1 2 3 4 5 6 7 8 9 0 1
+-+-+-+-+-+-+-+-+-+-+-+-+-+-+-+-+-+-+-+-+-+-+-+-+-+-+-+-+-+-+-+-+
|    Block Structure Descriptor     |  Authentication Block Length  |
+-+-+-+-+-+-+-+-+-+-+-+-+-+-+-+-+-+-+-+-+-+-+-+-+-+-+-+-+-+-+-+-+
|                            Timestamp                           |
+-+-+-+-+-+-+-+-+-+-+-+-+-+-+-+-+-+-+-+-+-+-+-+-+-+-+-+-+-+-+-+-+
|      SLP SPI String Length        |        SLP SPI String         |
+-+-+-+-+-+-+-+-+-+-+-+-+-+-+-+-+-+-+-+-+-+-+-+-+-+-+-+-+-+-+-+-+
|                 Structured Authentication Block               |
+-+-+-+-+-+-+-+-+-+-+-+-+-+-+-+-+-+-+-+-+-+-+-+-+-+-+-+-+-+-+-+-+
```

Figure 3-12

The format of an SLP Authentication Block, which is used by SLP agents to verify the integrity and origin of received messages.

the entire AB, including the BSD. The Timestamp field is a 32-bit quantity indicating the expiration time for the AB. This time stamp is expressed as a number of seconds from 00:00 on January 1, 1970. The time stamp in the AB prevents replay attacks, where a rogue SA might capture registration messages and reply to them later to maliciously advertise the "availability" of a service that is no longer available (or has changed location). The SPI (Security Parameters Index) specifies information needed for authentication, including keying information and key length.

Security and SLP Messages

Configuring SLP agents with SPIs imposes some restrictions on service registrations and requests. For example, SAs with security enabled must attach Authentication Blocks to registration (SrvReg) and deregistration (SrvDeReg) messages. To ensure that DAs with which the SA will register can verify the AB, DAAdvert messages must be gathered before registration. The DAAdvert message (discussed further in the section "Directory Agents" and below) contains SPIs that identify the ABs that a DA can verify. SAs should not attempt to register with an AB that the directory agent cannot verify, because the DA will simply return an AUTHENTICATION_UNKNOWN error code (and the registration attempt will fail). If a service to be deregistered was registered using one or more ABs, then an AB must be included in the URL Entry in the SrvDeReg message. If the AB is absent, a DA will return AUTHENTICATION_ABSENT. If the deregistration message can't be authenticated, AUTHENTICATION_FAILED is returned. Although the use of incremental registration in new SLP applications is discouraged because it likely will be deprecated in a future revision of the specification, it is worth noting that incremental registration is *prohibited* when SAs register using an Authentication Block.

DAs are required to attach Authentication Blocks to DAAdvert messages if they are configured to sign messages. This allows UAs and SAs to verify the authenticity of the advertising DA with the help of the SPI contained in the AB. If a DA is configured to sign messages with more than one SPI, then an AB must be included for each SPI. If these ABs overflow the size of a single datagram, then separate DAAdverts must be transmitted in order to advertise using the AB for each configured SPI. This maximizes the chances of UAs and SAs being able to accept the advertisement. When SAs and UAs are configured to verify messages, they must discard advertisements that fail to be verified (possibly because they do not have the needed SPI). DAAdvert messages also contain an <SLP SPI List> which contains the list of SPIs with which the DA has been configured. These are the SPIs which the DA will recognize. If an SA attempts to register using an AB not associated with any SPI in this list, the registration attempt will be rejected and an AUTHENTICATION_UNKNOWN error code will be returned. When DAAdverts are transmitted in response to a SrvRqst with a service type of "service:directory-agent," an advertising DA that can generate an AB corresponding to the SPI in the SrvRqst will attach such an AB to the DAAdvert. If the SrvRqst was unicast, and the DA is not capable of generating an AB corresponding to the SPI in the SrvRqst, then AUTHENTICATION_UNKNOWN is returned. SAAdverts transmitted by SAs with security enabled operate in similar fashion to DAAdverts. SAs are required to provide an Authentication Block for each SPI for which they can generate an AB. An agent that is configured with SPIs must discard an SAAdvert or DAAdvert that it cannot verify.

If UAs include an SPI in a unicast SrvRqst message, then a responding agent either must attach an appropriate AB to each URL Entry that is returned in the reply or must respond with AUTHENTICATION_UNKNOWN to indicate that it does not support the specified SPI. If a UA does not include an SPI in a SrvRqst message, then a responding SA or DA does not sign the reply. Attribute request and reply messages are also affected by security concerns. When a UA makes an attribute request with an attached SPI, then a full Service URL must be specified—browsing attributes by service type is not allowed. Further, a list of attributes to query may not be specified; instead, the UA must query all attributes for the service associated with the Service URL. If a full URL is not provided or if a list of attribute names is provided, the responding agent will reply with AUTHENTICATION_FAILED. Otherwise, the responding agent replies with an AttrRply signed with ABs corresponding to the SPIs provided in the AttrRqst message. SrvTypeRqst and SrvTypeRply messages do not carry security-related payloads.

Agents in SLP are currently required to support DSA with SHA-1 [16, 17], although other authentication algorithms may also be supported. DSA is the Digital Signature Algorithm, proposed by the National Institute of Standards and Technology (NIST) and designed by the National Security Agency (NSA). SHA is the Secure Hash Algorithm, which computes a message digest that is fed to DSA to compute a digital signature for a message. A Block Structure Descriptor value of 0x02 selects DSA-SHA-1. For BSD=0x02, the Structured Authentication

Block field will contain a DSA digital signature computed over a number of fields in the message. Specific details are given in RFC 2608, but briefly, the goal is to thwart attempts to forge, modify, or capture and replay SLP messages. As an example, consider the fields that must be covered when digitally signing a DAAdvert message. To prevent a malicious agent from forging, modifying, or replaying a DAAdvert, a digital signature is computed over the string of SPIs, the DA Stateless Boot Timestamp, Service URL, attribute list, scope list, and time stamp (along with length information for variable-length fields such as URLs). For an excellent discussion of DSA and other authentication and encryption algorithms, see reference 17.

POINTERS

The following list of references includes pointers to the core SLPv1 and SLPv2 specifications [2,6]. All new applications should use SLP v2, which has much improved scalability and security features. Reference 3 defines service templates, which allow the standardization of service types. Reference 4 describes DHCP options for configuring the location of DAs and providing scope information through DHCP. Reference 5 describes the C and Java APIs for SLP. Reference 7 is a book on SLP which covers both v1 and v2, as well as deployment issues. References 1, 10, and 12 are RFCs that address standards important to SLP, including administratively scoped multicast, ABNF grammars (which are used to define portions of the Service URL syntax), and language tags. Current IANA service templates can be found at reference 11; these are great as examples when you are creating your own service templates. References 13 and 14 discuss LDAP. Reference 15 is perhaps the king of network programming books and is essential for anyone doing sockets-based programming. Reference 16 is the original technical report describing DSS/DSA, which is a digital signature technique used in SLP security. Reference 17 is the bible of cryptography, as essential for cryptography efforts as the Stevens books are for networking programming.

1. D. Meyer, "Administratively Scoped IP Multicast," RFC 2365, *http://www.ietf.org/rfc/rfc2365.txt.*

2. E. Guttman, C. Perkins, J. Veizades, and M. Day, "Service Location Protocol, Version 2," RFC 2608, *http://www.ietf.org/rfc/rfc2608.txt.*

3. E. Guttman, C. Perkins, and J. Kempf, "Service Templates and Service: Schemes," RFC 2609, *http://www.ietf.org/rfc/rfc2609.txt*.

4. C. Perkins, and E. Guttman, "DHCP Options for Service Location Protocol," RFC 2610, *http://www.ietf.org/rfc/rfc2610.txt*.

5. J. Kempf and E. Guttman, "An API for Service Location," RFC 2614, *http://www.ietf.org/rfc/rfc2614.txt*.

6. J. Veizades, E. Guttman, C. Perkins, and S. Kaplan, "Service Location Protocol [V1]," RFC 2165, *http://www.ietf.org/rfc/rfc2165.txt*.

7. J. Kempf and P. St. Pierre, *Service Location Protocol for Enterprise Networks*: *Implementing and Deploying a Dynamic Service Finder,* Wiley, New York, 1999.

8. OpenSLP implementation of SLP, *www.openslp.org*.

9. mSLP: Mesh-enhanced Service Location Protocol, *http://www.cs.columbia.edu/~zwb/project/slp/*.

10. D. Crocker and P. Overell, "Augmented BNF for Syntax Specifications: ABNF," RFC 2396, *http://www.ietf.org/rfc/rfc2396.txt*.

11. Service Templates Repository, *http://www.isi.edu/in-notes/iana/assignments/svrloc-templates/*.

12. H. Alvestrand, "Tags for the Identification of Languages," RFC 1766, *http://www.ietf.org/rfc/rfc1766.txt*.

13. T. Howes, "The String Representation of LDAP Search Filters," RFC 2254, *http://www.ietf.org/rfc/rfc2254.txt*.

14. M. Wahl, T. Howes, and S. Killie, "The Lightweight Directory Access Protocol (LDAP) v3," RFC 2251, *http://www.ietf.org/rfc/rfc2251.txt*.

15. W. Richard Stevens, *Unix Network Programming,* Prentice-Hall, Englewood Cliffs, N.J., 1990.

16. Digital Signature Standard (DSS), National Institute of Standards and Technology Technical Report NIST FIPS PUB 186, U.S. Department of Commerce, May 1994.

17. B. Schneier, *Applied Cryptography (Protocols, Algorithms, and Source Code in C),* Wiley, New York, 1996.

Universal Plug and Play: Extending Plug and Play to the Network

Overview of Universal Plug and Play (UPnP)

What Is UPnP?

The Universal Plug and Play (UPnP) specification describes a set of protocols for enabling networked entities of all sorts to initialize autonomously and then discover and share one another's services. Every stage of the networked device's lifetime is addressed, from determination of an IP address, through advertising available services, to discovery of needed services, to control of services, and finally to shutdown. There are no device drivers in the UPnP world—device drivers are replaced with common, standardized protocols upon which devices agree. The specification notably addresses protocols only and does not specify a particular API or programming language. Implementers of the specification are free to choose the computer languages and programming methodologies that will be used to write code for UPnP-compliant services and clients. When this book is being written, there are already several implementations available, but documentation is scarce. This chapter aims to fill the gap.

Goals of the Chapter

This chapter provides an overview of the complete UPnP specification, v1.0, dated June 13, 2000 [1]. After a discussion of the core UPnP protocols, source code for a complete UPnP device and control point (the UPnP jargon for *clients*, the users of services) is presented and examined in detail. The toolkit used for development of sample code is Intel's UPnP SDK, v1.0.3 [2]. This is a freely available, open source implementation of the UPnP specification that currently runs under Linux but is also being ported to other systems. This SDK was chosen because it is stable, bug-free (at least in the experience of this author—all the problems I encountered in development turned out to be my own!), and does not rely on proprietary development tools. After reading the chapter, you will have a firm understanding of Universal Plug and Play, one representative SDK that implements the specification, and enough knowledge to write interesting UPnP devices and control points.

In terms of background, understanding the specification requires familiarity with the HTTP protocol [3], HTML [4], XML [5], and some familiarity with TCP and UDP. The DHCP [6] and ARP [7] protocols are mentioned briefly in the context of the addressing portion of the UPnP specification, but no details about these protocols are required for understanding the bulk of UPnP. Since the specification itself does not describe an API, a particular implementation of the specification was chosen so that UPnP code could be developed easily. All code developed using the Intel SDK must be in C, so C it is. Thus in addition to the requirements above, the reader is assumed to be familiar with C.

UPnP Protocols in Brief

The UPnP specification addresses six areas, numbered 0 through 5:

0: Addressing

1: Discovery

2: Description

3: Control

4: Eventing

5: Presentation

The first (numbered 0) is addressing, and it is related to device initialization—to interact with other UPnP entities, a device or control point must have an IP address. IP addresses will generally be provided by a DHCP server or configured statically, but for environments with little infrastructure (e.g., a home LAN), UPnP uses a protocol named Auto-IP to automatically generate nonrouteable IP addresses. Auto-IP will be covered in detail in the section "Addressing: Auto-IP." The second area is discovery, which allows control points to discover UPnP devices that are offering services of interest. Discovery also covers device advertisement, used to announce the availability of devices as they enter the network. The discovery phase provides control points with existential information, but little additional information about the discovered devices. Description, or the ability to inquire about device specifics (e.g., manufacturer, serial numbers, specific services offered), is the third phase. By using a URL obtained in the discovery phase, a control point can download a document called the device description document, which fully describes a device of interest. This document is platform-neutral, expressed entirely in XML.

If a control point determines, after examining a device's description document, that it wishes to interact with services provided by a device, then control is used to send the device commands and receive results. All control interactions are via a protocol based on HTTP, called SOAP (Simple Object Access Protocol), which runs over TCP. Commands sent via SOAP are addressed to *control URLs* for the services provided by a device—these control URLs are specified in the device's description document, which is obtained during the description phase. See SOAP is discussed in detail in the section "Control: The Simple Object Access Protocol (SOAP)."

Interesting devices undergo interesting state changes; e.g., a printer might run out of paper or a UPnP blender might turn itself off after a period of time. To be informed of such state changes, UPnP control points *subscribe* to the event services offered by a device. This mechanism makes up the eventing portion of the UPnP specification. The protocol used to handle eventing is called GENA (General Event Notification Architecture). GENA is an HTTP-based subscription and notification protocol, and it is described completely in the section "Eventing: The General Event Notification Architecture (GENA)." Finally, the presentation aspect of UPnP allows devices to define a *presentation URL,* which is the location of an HTML document which provides a graphical interface to the device (a "virtual" remote control). The specification does not define the technologies used in building the HTML interface. Combinations of straight HTML and scripting are common. An illustration of the UPnP protocols appears in Fig. 4-1.

Requirements

Since the UPnP specification defines protocols only while remaining language- and platform-independent, the list of core requirements for running UPnP is not large. Additional requirements may be imposed by particular implementations of the specification, however. The specification dictates that UPnP devices and control points must have an IP address. This can be dynamically obtained through DHCP, statically configured, or generated using UPnP's Auto-IP protocol. Devices and control points must have sufficient processing power to execute the HTTP protocol and parse XML. Devices must run a simple web server for delivering important documents (e.g., the description and presentation documents). A proxy running this web server is not sufficient, since control also requires a web server, to support SOAP. Control points must also run a simple web server, for receiving GENA events.

All the protocols which collectively make up UPnP are IP-based, and control points and devices must be connected to an IP network (although

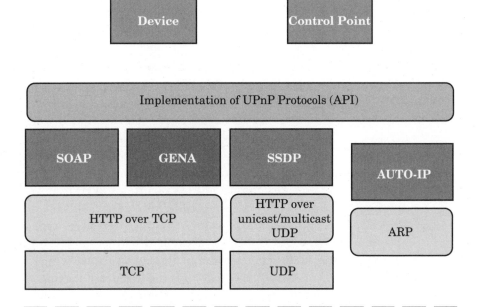

Figure 4-1

The UPnP protocols. SOAP relies exclusively on extensions to HTTP and runs over TCP. GENA is also HTTP-based and uses TCP as a transport layer. SSDP use a UDP multicast variant of the HTTP protocol for device advertisement and discovery, but also uses HTTP via unicast UDP when a device contacts a specific control point. The Auto-IP protocol is used to determine an IP address in environments where DHCP or static configuration of an address isn't available and relies on ARP. The description phase of UPnP isn't represented in the diagram because it has no distinct "protocol"—description is performed with straight HTTP. Devices and control points will typically be written using an API that provides implementations of the key UPnP protocols. The specification for UPnP does· not define this API, and thus does not dictate specific programming languages.

bridging could allow other protocols to be used where IP is an impossible requirement). Both TCP and multicast UDP are used by UPnP entities. Beyond these requirements, the components of a UPnP implementation may be written in any appropriate language. In all the examples in this book, C is used (although parts of the Intel UPnP SDK are actually written in C++, C is the supported development language). Other languages (particularly Java) would also be ideal candidates for UPnP development, provided appropriate libraries are developed. As a UPnP "applications programmer," you do *not* want to code directly against the specification for each control point and device, since XML and HTTP parsing isn't particularly fun (at least not after the first time)!

Universal Plug and Play Protocols in Detail

In this section, Universal Plug and Play is discussed at a protocol level from both the control point (client) and device perspectives. In UPnP, devices provide services but may also be control points, utilizing the services of other UPnP devices. A UPnP "device" can be entirely software, may be software controlling a non-UPnP-aware piece of hardware, or may be entirely hardware, with the UPnP protocols embedded in ROM. Aside from practical considerations such as how much memory is available or how fast the CPU executing the UPnP protocols is, the degree to which a "device" is actually hardware makes no difference. "Devices" in UPnP are simply entities that host services, much like Jini services.

Each of the UPnP areas is discussed in detail below, from Auto-IP to presentation. To avoid confusing the specification itself with an *implementation* of the specification, we defer looking at source code for the sample device and control point until the end of the chapter. The next section discusses how devices and services are described (using XML) in Universal Plug and Play. This is important for both control points and devices. For control points, the XML description provides the only mechanism for figuring out how to interact with the device. For devices, the XML descriptions guide the design and implementation. Subsequent sections examine addressing, discovery, control, etc., in turn.

Describing Devices and Services in UPnP

Before any coding begins on the device side, a UPnP device's characteristics and functionality are described in a series of platform-neutral XML documents. The most comprehensive is the *description document,* which fully describes a root device and all its embedded devices and indicates which services are provided. Control points parse this document to learn interesting things about a device. The description document contains a number of items:

- The version of the device specification
- A base URL, allowing other URLs that govern device function to be relative URLs.
- The device's type. This name will be specified either by a UPnP committee for standard device types or by a UPnP vendor.

- A "friendly name" for the device, suitable for parsing by human beings.
- The name of the device's manufacturer, along with a URL for the manufacturer.
- A description of the model, the model name and number, and a URL for the model (presumably hosted by the manufacturer).
- A globally unique device name.
- A UPC code for the device.
- A presentation URL, which allows control points to download an HTML-based GUI for the device.
- Embedded device descriptions.
- For each device , root or embedded, a list of the services provided.
- For each service, the following are specified:

  A unique service ID

  A control URL, which serves as an entry point for commands directed at the device

  An event subscription URL, for subscribing to a service's eventing

  A URL for the service's Service Control Protocol Description (SCPD), an XML document that defines the actions (essentially, remote procedure calls) and control variables for the service

Description documents will typically be based on a *device template,* created by a UPnP committee. The device template standardizes the device description to the extent that control points can be programmed against the template and will interoperate with various device implementations. For one-of-a kind devices, no such template will exist. Such is the case with our virtual blender. The description document for the virtual blender, a device that will be used as an example throughout this chapter, looks like the following. We've taken liberties with the deviceType and serviceTypes, since clearly no UPnP committee has developed a standard template for blenders.

```xml
<?xml version="1.0"?>
<root xmlns="urn:schemas-upnp-org:device-1-0">
  <specVersion>
    <major>1</major>
    <minor>0</minor>
  </specVersion>
  <URLBase>http://10.0.0.13:5431</URLBase>
  <device>
```

```xml
<deviceType>urn:schemas-upnp-org:device:blender:1</deviceType>
<friendlyName>UPnP Blender</friendlyName>
<manufacturer>University of New Orleans
               Dept. of Computer Science
</manufacturer>
<manufacturerURL>http://www.cs.uno.edu/</manufacturerURL>
<modelDescription>UPnP Blender with
                  AccuBlend Whirring
</modelDescription>
<modelName>Plug-N-Blend</modelName>
<modelNumber>1.0</modelNumber>
<modelURL>http://www.cs.uno.edu/</modelURL>
<serialNumber>999954321</serialNumber>
<UDN>uuid:Upnp-Blender-1_0-1234567890001</UDN>
<UPC>123456789</UPC>
<serviceList>
  <service>
    <serviceType>
      urn:schemas-upnp-org:service:PowerSwitch:1
    </serviceType>
    <serviceId>urn:upnp-org:serviceId:PowerSwitch1</serviceId>
    <controlURL>/upnp/control/power1</controlURL>
    <eventSubURL>/upnp/event/power1</eventSubURL>
    <SCPDURL>/blenderpowerSCPD.xml</SCPDURL>
  </service>
  <service>
    <serviceType>
      urn:schemas-upnp-org:service:SpeedControl:1
    </serviceType>
    <serviceId>
      urn:upnp-org:serviceId:SpeedControl1
    </serviceId>
    <controlURL>/upnp/control/speed1</controlURL>
    <eventSubURL>/upnp/event/speed1</eventSubURL>
    <SCPDURL>/blenderspeedSCPD.xml</SCPDURL>
  </service>
  <service>
    <serviceType>
      urn:schemas-upnp-org:service:Bowl:1
    </serviceType>
    <serviceId>urn:upnp-org:serviceId:Bowl1</serviceId>
    <controlURL>/upnp/control/bowl1</controlURL>
    <eventSubURL>/upnp/event/bowl1</eventSubURL>
    <SCPDURL>/blenderbowlSCPD.xml</SCPDURL>
  </service>
</serviceList>
<presentationURL>/blenderdevicepres.html</presentationURL>
</device>
</root>
```

This description document will serve as a good starting point for developing description documents for your own devices. There are also several samples on the UPnP web site (www.upnp.org). The XML tags make the content self-explanatory—most of it deals with providing things like serial numbers and model numbers. We discuss how this document is offered to control points in the section "Description: Moving Description Documents."

For each service defined in the device description document, a URL referring to an XML Service Control Protocol Description (SCPD) document is provided. This document describes the protocol that the service speaks and is used by control points to define an interface for interacting with the device. Interactions are called *actions* and take the form of RPC-like calls using a protocol called SOAP, described in detail later in the chapter in "Control: The Simple Object Access Protocol (SOAP)." For each action, zero or more parameters are defined. Each parameter may be of type "in" or "out," signifying that a value is specified when the RPC is performed, or supplied by the service when the RPC completes. The actions are defined in the SCPD bracketed by an <actionList>, </actionList> pair. The SCPD also defines the *state variables* that define the current state of the service—what's going on in the guts. Definitions of the variables are bracketed in a <serviceStateTable>, </serviceStateTable> pair. For each state variable, the name, whether the variable is evented, its type, default value, and constraints on allowed values are provided. These state variable attributes will be discussed once the format of an SCPD has been examined. For now, we note that state variables are intimately tied to actions in the specification of a service, because for each formal parameter in an action definition, a related state variable must be indicated. This relationship states which state variable's value is related to each parameter's value. The exact nature of *related* is not concrete in the specification.

Unfortunately, the elements in an SCPD are more varied than in the description document and, so unlike for the service description document, where seeing one gives you a basic idea of how they are written, seeing a few examples of SCPDs is not sufficient. Thus we will look at the generic template for an SCPD before examining concrete examples. A generic template for SCPDs is

```
<?xml version="1.0"?>
<scpd xmlns="urn:schemas-upnp-org:service-1-0">
  <specVersion>
    <major>1</major>
    <minor>0</minor>
```

```
  </specVersion>
  <actionList>
    <action>
      <name>actionName</name>
      <argumentList>
        <argument>
          <name>formalParameterName</name>
          <direction>in xor out</direction>
          <retval />
          <relatedStateVariable>
            stateVariableName
          </relatedStateVariable>
        </argument>
      </argumentList>
    </action>
  </actionList>
  <serviceStateTable>
    <stateVariable sendEvents="yes">
      <name>variableName</name>
      <dataType>variable data type</dataType>
      <defaultValue>default value</defaultValue>
      <allowedValueList>
        <allowedValue>string value</allowedValue>
        <allowedValue>string value</allowedValue>
        <allowedValue>string value</allowedValue>
      </allowedValueList>
    </stateVariable>
    <stateVariable sendEvents="yes">
      <name>variableName</name>
      <dataType>variable data type</dataType>
      <defaultValue>default value</defaultValue>
      <allowedValueRange>
        <minimum>minimum value</minimum>
        <maximum>maximum value</maximum>
        <step>increment value</step>
      </allowedValueRange>
    </stateVariable>
    <stateVariable sendEvents="no">
      <name>variableName</name>
      <dataType>variable data type</dataType>
      <defaultValue>default value</defaultValue>
    </stateVariable>
  </serviceStateTable>
</scpd>
```

The name and type are required for each control variable. If the "sendEvents" portion of the name tag is omitted, then "sendEvents=yes" is assumed. We discuss this further in the later section "Eventing: The

General Event Notification Architecture (GENA)." The <defaultValue> and one of either <allowedValueRange> or <allowedValueList> are recommended but not required. The <defaultValue> does the obvious—it allows an initial value to be provided for a state variable. It must match the type of the control variable and must satisfy range or permitted value constraints. The <allowedValueRange> is permitted only for numeric types and defines the range of permissible values. If <allowedValueRange> is specified, then <minimum> and <maximum> values are required. The <step> tag, which specifies an increment value for the variable, is optional. For string-type control variables, the <allowedValueRange> tag may be used to restrict the permissible values for the string. An <allowedValue>, </allowedValue> pair brackets each permissible value. The specification requires that these values each be less than 32 characters in length.

Finally we turn to the list of supported types for state variables. The list covers a wide variety of primitive data types:

- *ui1, ui2, ui4:* Unsigned integers of 1, 2, and 4 bytes.
- *i1, i2, i4:* Signed integers of 1, 2, and 4 bytes.
- *int:* A signed integer.
- *r4, r8:* Signed floats of 4 and 8 bytes. The 8-byte form is a standard IEEE 64-bit double.
- *number:* This is equivalent to an r8.
- *fixed.14.4:* This is equivalent to r8, but with a restriction that no more than 14 digits are allowed to the left of the decimal point and no more than 4 to the right of the decimal point.
- *float:* Floating-point number.
- char: A single-character Unicode string. For information on the Unicode standard for character encoding, see www.unicode.org.
- *string:* A Unicode string of arbitrary length.
- *date:* A standard ISO 8601 format date without time information (say. YYYY-MM-DD + alternative formats; see www.iso.ch).
- *dateTime:* ISO 8601 format time and date but with no time zone specified (for example, 1995-02-05 13:59).
- *dateTime.tz:* This is the same as dateTime, but with optional time zone [e.g., a time which is 1 h ahead of UTC (Universal or "Zulu time") would be written 1995-02-05 13:59+01:00].
- *time:* ISO 8601 format without date and without time zone.
- *time.tz:* ISO 8601 format with optional time zone but no date.

- *boolean:* Boolean value with "0", "no", or "false" for false and "1", "yes", or "true" for true.
- *bin.base64:* Unlimited length MIME-style Base64 data.
- *bin.hex:* Stream of hexadecimal digits of unlimited length.
- *uri:* Universal resource identifier.
- *uuid:* Universally unique ID.

The UPnP blender has three services: a power service, a speed service, and a bowl service. The power service governs the blender's power settings: on /off and a pulse duration which allows the blender to be turned on for a specified number of seconds, then turned off automatically. The speed service controls the blender's speed (1 to 10, with 10 being the highest). The bowl service governs the contents of the blender, which is just a string. A simplification is that when something is put into the blender, the previous thing that was in the bowl disappears. Each service has an SCPD that defines the interface between control points and the service. These SCPDs are discussed below.

The power service SCPD defines three actions that control points may use to control the power state of the blender. PowerOn and PowerOff do the obvious and accept no arguments. The third action, SetPulseDuration, sets the blender's power on for a number of seconds, specified in the "in" parameter Duration. Recall that for each parameter to an action, a corresponding state variable must be specified using a <relatedStateVariable> tag. In this case, calling SetPulseDuration directly affects the value of the state variable PulseDuration, which is the blender's internal power-on timer. This state variable is tagged sendEvents="yes", which means that when control points subscribe to the eventing service for power, the values of pulseDuration will be transmitted as they change. Further, minimum and maximum values are specified (0 and 60, respectively). There is more on eventing in the section on GENA. The other control variable, a Boolean Power, captures the device's power setting. This variable is also evented. The power service's SCPD looks like this:

```
<?xml version="1.0"?>
<scpd xmlns="urn:schemas-upnp-org:service-1-0">
  <specVersion>
    <major>1</major>
    <minor>0</minor>
  </specVersion>
  <actionList>
    <action>
      <name>PowerOn</name>
```

```
    </action>
    <action>
      <name>PowerOff</name>
    </action>
    <action>
      <name>SetPulseDuration</name>
      <argumentList>
        <argument>
        <name>Duration</name>
          <relatedStateVariable>
            PulseDuration
          </relatedStateVariable>
          <direction>in</direction>
        </argument>
      </argumentList>
    </action>
  </actionList>
  <serviceStateTable>
    <stateVariable sendEvents="yes">
      <name>Power</name>
      <dataType>boolean</dataType>
      <defaultValue>false</defaultValue>
    </stateVariable>
    <stateVariable sendEvents="yes">
      <name>PulseDuration</name>
      <dataType>i1</dataType>
        <allowedValueRange>
          <minimum>0</minimum>
          <maximum>60</maximum>
          <step>1</step>
        </allowedValueRange>
        <defaultValue>0</defaultValue>
    </stateVariable>
  </serviceStateTable>
</scpd>
```

The SCPD for the speed service provides four actions. The first is SetSpeed, which allows the blender's speed to be changed. The related state variable is CurrentSpeed, which has a value between 1 and 10. SetSpeed takes a single parameter, Speed. GetSpeed returns the current value of Speed and has a single "out" parameter, also called Speed. Finally, IncreaseSpeed and DecreaseSpeed increment and decrement, respectively, the speed setting by 1. These take no parameters. The SCPD looks like this:

```
<?xml version="1.0"?>
<scpd xmlns="urn:schemas-upnp-org:service-1-0">
```

```
<specVersion>
  <major>1</major>
  <minor>0</minor>
</specVersion>
<actionList>
  <action>
    <name>SetSpeed</name>
    <argumentList>
      <argument>
      <name>Speed</name>
        <relatedStateVariable>CurrentSpeed</relatedStateVariable>
        <direction>in</direction>
      </argument>
    </argumentList>
  </action>
  <action>
    <name>GetSpeed</name>
    <argumentList>
      <argument>
      <name>Speed</name>
        <relatedStateVariable>CurrentSpeed<relatedStateVariable>
        <direction>out</direction>
      </argument>
    </argumentList>
  </action>
  <action>
    <name>IncreaseSpeed</name>
  </action>
  <action>
    <name>DecreaseSpeed</name>
  </action>
</actionList>
<serviceStateTable>
  <stateVariable sendEvents="yes">
    <name>CurrentSpeed</name>
    <dataType>i1</dataType>
      <allowedValueRange>
        <minimum>1</minimum>
        <maximum>10</maximum>
        <step>1</step>
      </allowedValueRange>
    <defaultValue>1</defaultValue>
  </stateVariable>
</serviceStateTable>
</scpd>
```

A blender isn't a blender unless it can churn something round and round in its bowl. The contents service for the UPnP blender allows things to be placed into the blender and spun around. Since it's only a virtual blender, the contents are a single string. Putting a "tomato" into the blender and then turning it on result in contents such as "otomat" "otomta." The SetContents and GetContents actions set and retrieve the string contents of the blender. The former has a single "in" parameter Contents, while the latter has a single "out" parameter of the single name. The single state variable is a string named CurrentContents with a default value of the empty string. The SCPD for the contents service looks like this:

```xml
<?xml version="1.0"?>
<scpd xmlns="urn:schemas-upnp-org:service-1-0">
  <specVersion>
    <major>1</major>
    <minor>0</minor>
  </specVersion>
  <actionList>
    <action>
      <name>SetContents</name>
      <argumentList>
        <argument>
        <name>Contents</name>
          <relatedStateVariable>
            CurrentContents
          </relatedStateVariable>
          <direction>in</direction>
        </argument>
      </argumentList>
    </action>
    <action>
      <name>GetContents</name>
      <argumentList>
        <argument>
        <name>Contents</name>
          <relatedStateVariable>
            CurrentContents
          </relatedStateVariable>
          <direction>out</direction>
        </argument>
      </argumentList>
    </action>
  </actionList>
  <serviceStateTable>
    <stateVariable sendEvents="yes">
      <name>CurrentContents</name>
      <dataType>string</dataType>
      <defaultValue>""</defaultValue>
```

```
        </stateVariable>
      </serviceStateTable>
  </scpd>
```

Addressing: Auto-IP

Addressing is performed by both devices and control points during initialization. If a UPnP entity has a statically assigned IP address or can obtain one through DHCP (by issuing appropriate DHCPDISCOVER messages and receiving a DHCPOFFER), then addressing is complete. Otherwise, a simple protocol called Auto-IP is used to generate an unused, nonrouteable ("link local") IP address in the 169.254.*.* range. This address range is reserved for cases where DHCP fails. Note that this range is different from the 10.0.0.0 to 10.0.0.255, 172.16.0.0 to 172.31.255.255, and 192.168.0.0 to 196.168.255.255 private ranges, since DHCP might be configured to return addresses in these ranges.

The mechanism for choosing an IP address is straightforward. A random address in the 169.254.*.* range is chosen; an ARP (Address Resolution Protocol) probe is used to determine if the address is already in use; and if it is, another random choice is made. If an unused IP address cannot be determined after an implementation-dependent number of attempts, then initialization of the device or control point fails. UPnP entities using Auto-IP for IP address assignment are required to periodically send DHCPDISCOVER requests to determine if DHCP service becomes available. If an IP address is available via DHCP, then this address must be used instead of the previously assigned Auto-IP address. Before the switch, devices are required to cancel outstanding advertisements. Once the new IP is in place, advertisements using the new address can be transmitted. There is more on advertisements in the next section.

The Intel UPnP SDK does not include an implementation of Auto-IP, and the sample device and control point that will be used to illustrate UPnP development assume that an IP address is provided by DHCP or static configuration. Modern versions of Microsoft Windows and Mac OS already do something similar to Auto-IP, choosing an address in the 169.254.*.* range if DHCP requests fail, and a statically configured IP address is not available. Thus Auto-IP will not be considered further in this chapter.

Discovery: The Simple Service Discovery Protocol (SSDP)

From a device perspective, discovery governs the process of routinely advertising services offered by the device and responding to queries for service by control points. For control points, discovery allows interesting services to be discovered and subsequently used. When a device initializes and joins a UPnP network, a series of advertisement messages are multicast that provide information about the device, any embedded devices, and the services offered. Similarly, when the device leaves the network, it multicasts messages revoking the previous offers of service. These protocols fall under the Simple Service Discovery Protocol (SSDP) portion of the UPnP specification. SSDP messages are transmitted using UDP multicast, which is inherently unreliable, so each message is typically sent several times to increase the likelihood that at least one is received by each interested control point. In the Intel UPnP SDK, each advertisement message is sent twice by default. This number can be changed by recompiling the SDK.

During a single advertisement, each root device sends $3 + 2d + k$ messages, where d is the number of embedded devices and k is the number of distinct service types offered by the composite device. All the messages are autonomous and have similar structure, varying only in a few fields. UPnP takes this multiple-messages approach, even though there is significant redundant information transmitted, because some implementations of UDP restrict the maximum datagram length to as little as 512 bytes. Since UDP multicast provides unordered service, there is no guarantee that messages will arrive in any particular order. The specification dictates a default TTL for "ssdp:alive" messages of 4. The format of an "ssdp:alive" advertisement message looks like the following, with fixed values in bold and values which must be supplied in particular advertisement messages in nonbold italic:

```
NOTIFY * HTTP/1.1
HOST: 239.255.255.250:1900
CACHE-CONTROL: max-age = seconds until advertisement expires
LOCATION: URL for UPnP description for root device
NT: search target
NTS: ssdp:alive
SERVER: OS/version UPnP/1.0 product/version
USN: advertisement UUID
<<BLANK LINE>>
```

Note that the "body" of this HTTP request is simply a blank line. The meanings of the HTTP headers require some examination. The HOST header always contains 239.255.255.250:1900, which is the multicast address and port reserved for the Simple Service Discovery Protocol. The max-age field in the CACHE-CONTROL header is the advertisement duration, in seconds; the UPnP specification mandates a minimum duration of 1800 s. When this number of seconds passes without an additional advertisement, control points should assume that the device has become unavailable. The LOCATION header specifies an absolute URL for the root device's description document. Description documents are discussed at the beginning of this chapter. The NT (Notification Type) header contains a single Uniform Resource Identifier (URI) that identifies the entity being advertised (a root device, an embedded device, or a service). It will have one of the following values:

1. **upnp:rootdevice**

2. **upnp:***UUID*

3. **uuid:schemas-upnp-org:device:***device_type:version*

4. **urn:schemas-upnp-org:service:***service_type:version*

One advertisement message with the first form is always sent for each root device. For each root device and for each embedded device, an advertisement message with an NT header of the second type is sent, where *UUID* is the unique identifier for the corresponding device. An advertisement with an NT header of the third type is also sent for the root device and for each embedded device. This form identifies the *device type* and *version* of the device. Finally, for each service type, an advertisement with an NT header of the fourth type is transmitted. This type identifies each *service type* and version.

The NTS (Notification Sub Type) header always contains "ssdp:alive" for advertisement messages. The SERVER header is a combination of the name of the device's operating system, the operating system version, the string "UPnP/1.0" (which identifies version 1.0 of the UPnP specification), and a product name and version.

Finally, the USN (Unique Service Name) header corresponds to the NT header, providing a unique name of a device or service to match the type in the NT header. The unique identifiers must match the identifiers present in the description document for the root device. Again, there are four varieties:

1. **uuid:***UUID***::upnp:rootdevice**

2. **uuid:***UUID*

3. **uuid:***UUID***::urn:schemas-upnp-org:device:***device_type:version*

4. **uuid:***UUID***::schemas-upnp-org:service:***service_type:version*

A concrete example of an "ssdp:alive" message is illustrated below. This packet, which advertises a root blender device, was captured during an execution of the UPnP blender implementation, discussed later in this chapter:

```
NOTIFY * HTTP/1.1
HOST: 239.255.255.250:1900
CACHE-CONTROL: max-age=1800
LOCATION: http://10.0.0.13:5431/blenderdevdesc.xml
NT: upnp:rootdevice
NTS: ssdp:alive
SERVER: Linux/2.4.2-2 UPnP/1.0 Intel UPnP SDK/1.0
USN: uuid:Upnp-Blender-1_0-1234567890001::upnp:rootdevice
```

The following is similar; it is an advertisement of the power service for the blender. This message was also captured during a blender execution:

```
NOTIFY * HTTP/1.1
HOST: 239.255.255.250:1900
CACHE-CONTROL: max-age=1800
LOCATION: http://10.0.0.13:5431/blenderdevdesc.xml
NT: urn:schemas-upnp-org:service:PowerSwitch:1
NTS: ssdp:alive
SERVER: Linux/2.4.2-2 UPnP/1.0 Intel UPnP SDK/1.0
USN: uuid:Upnp-Blender-1_0-1234567890001::
  urn:schemas-upnp-org:service:PowerSwitch:1
```

When a UPnP device wishes to leave the network, it sends one "ssdp:byebye" message for each advertisement that was sent when it entered the network. As for "ssdp:alive" messages, the default TTL should be 4. The "ssdp:byebye" messages have the following format, with fixed values in bold and values which must be supplied in particular "ssdp:byebye" messages (i.e., messages corresponding to a root device, embedded devices, etc.) in lightface italic. The NT and USN headers have the same values as the corresponding "ssdp:alive" messages.

NOTIFY * HTTP/1.1
HOST: 239.255.255.250:1900
NT: *search target*
NTS: ssdp:byebye
USN: *advertisement UUID*
<<BLANK LINE>>

The "ssdp:byebye" messages are sent many times, to advertise the demise of the root device, each service, etc. The following "byebye" message for a root blender device was captured as an example:

```
NOTIFY * HTTP/1.1
HOST: 239.255.255.250:1900
CACHE-CONTROL: max-age=180
LOCATION: http://10.0.0.13:5431/blenderdevdesc.xml
NT: upnp:rootdevice
NTS: ssdp:byebye
USN: uuid:Upnp-Blender-1_0-1234567890001::upnp:rootdevice
```

Advertisement expirations in UPnP maintain the "freshness" of device availability information at control points and help to make UPnP self-healing, since it is possible that catastrophic device failure (or poor device programming!) may result in "byebye" messages not being sent. Without expirations, control points might maintain significant quantities of information about unavailable devices. The specification mandates a minimum advertisement duration of 1800 s for properly behaved devices. This helps prevents network meltdown due to huge numbers of advertisements being transmitted, which might result if advertisement durations were short. "Stable" devices that are expected to remain available for long periods of time should choose advertisement durations significantly longer than the minimum. More-transient devices can choose durations closer to the minimum of 1800 s.

UPnP devices also respond to control points explicitly searching for service. The format of the "ssdp:discover" message, sent by a control point to force appropriate devices to respond with the location of their description document, is

```
M-SEARCH * HTTP/1.1
HOST: 239.255.255.250:1900
MAN: "ssdp:discover"
MX: seconds to delay response
ST: search target
<<BLANK LINE>>
```

Almost the entire "ssdp:discover" message format is static; only the MX and ST headers need to be filled in. The MX field specifies the number of seconds the control point is willing to wait for a response. Devices should delay a random amount of time between 0 and this number of seconds, to reduce the load on the control point. The ST header should contain one of the following, which define the scope of the search:

- "ssdp:all": Search for all available devices and services.
- "upnp:rootdevice": Find only root devices.
- "uuid:deviceUUID": Find only devices with the specified unique device ID.
- "urn:schemas-upnp-org:device:deviceType:v": Search for devices of the specified deviceType.
- "urn:schemas-upnp-org:service:serviceType:v": Search for services of the specified serviceType.

The specification mandates a default of 4 for the TTL for "ssdp:discover" messages. Note that under UPnP, unlike Jini, it is not possible to search for devices with specific attributes—the only way to discover the attributes associated with a device is to download the device's description document. Jini and Service Location Protocol (SLP) provide significantly more flexible search facilities. Here is an example, captured as the UPnP blender control point attempts to find blender devices:

```
M-SEARCH * HTTP/1.1
HOST:239.255.255.250:1900
MAN:"ssdp:discover"
MX:10
ST:urn:schemas-upnp-org:device:blender:1
```

The response to an "ssdp:discover" message by a matching device or service is transmitted directly to the control point via unicast UDP, unlike an "ssdp:alive" message, which is transmitted using UDP multicast. To respond to a control point's search, a UPnP device issues messages of the following type for the root device, each embedded device, and each service type:

```
HTTP/1.1 200 OK
CACHE-CONTROL: max-age = seconds until advertisement expires
DATE: date when response was generated
EXT:
LOCATION: URL for UPnP description for root device
SERVER: OS/version UPnP/1.0 product/version
ST: search target
USN: advertisement UUID
<<BLANK LINE>>
```

The values supplied in each header above are identical to those in "ssdp:alive" messages, with the exception of the ST (Search Target). If the ST header in the request was "ssdp:all", then $3+2d+k$ response messages are sent (as described for "ssdp:alive"). Otherwise, the ST header contains the same value as in the request. No TTL is mandated in the specification for these response messages.

Description: Moving Description Documents

The information provided to a control point during discovery is very minimal—essentially, the control point learns that a specific device exists, but knows little else. Description in UPnP allows control points to obtain additional information about a device. This information is contained in the XML description document for the root device, whose URL is discovered by control points during the discovery phase. Specification of UPnP devices and services was covered in the section "Describing Devices and Services in UPnP"; the remaining portion of description defines how control points get a copy of a description document. This turns out to be quite trivial, since straight HTTP is used.

To obtain a device's description document, a control point issues a standard HTTP GET, using TCP over IP. The format of the message is shown below. After "GET", the path name component of the device's description document is specified. The host and port components are specified in the "HOST" component.

```
GET path to description HTTP/1.1
HOST: host for description:port for description
ACCEPT-LANGUAGE: language preferred by control point
<<BLANK LINE>>
```

The device's response is due within 30 s and has the following form. The XML description document is returned in the body of the response, with the CONTENT-LENGTH header indicating the size of the description document in bytes. That's it!

```
HTTP/1.1 200 OK
CONTENT-LANGUAGE: language used in description
CONTENT-LENGTH: number of bytes in body
CONTENT-TYPE: text/xml
DATE: RFC 1123 format date when device responded
<<Description document>
```

Control: The Simple Object Access Protocol (SOAP)

Once a control point has obtained a device's description document, it will typically want to interact with the device, both to issue commands (e.g., "turn the blender on") and to investigate an interesting device state (e.g., "what is the blender's current speed?"). Device interaction in UPnP is handled with an RPC (Remote Procedure Call) protocol called the Simple Object Access Protocol. SOAP is based on extensions to HTTP, with the action expressed in XML. Action requests are described first, followed by the mechanism that allows control points to request state variable values (and thus delve into the interesting guts of a device's state).

Action Requests.   The SCPD for a service describes the actions that may be executed to interact with the service. Actions are the equivalent of the methods in the interface implemented by a Jini service. Control points compose messages containing the descriptions of actions, including the names and values of "in" parameters, and send these messages to services provided by the devices. The services in turn compose responses, which contain the values of "out" parameters (if any). The format of these messages is described below. The effects of an action will propagate to other control points if the action involves changing the values of evented state variables and provided that other control points have subscribed to be notified about state changes. Eventing is discussed in the next major section.

To cause a device to execute an action, a control point sends a "POST" or "M-POST" message of the following types. We discuss why there are two forms in a moment.

```
POST path portion of control URL HTTP/1.1
HOST: host of control URL:port of control URL
CONTENT-LENGTH: number of bytes in body
CONTENT-TYPE: text/xml; charset="utf-8"
SOAPACTION:
  "urn:schemas-upnp-org:service:serviceType:v#actionName"

<s:Envelope
    xmlns:s="http://schemas.xmlsoap.org/soap/envelope/"
    s:encodingStyle="http://schemas.xmlsoap.org/soap/encoding/">
  <s:Body>
    <u:actionName
      xmlns:u="urn:schemas-upnp-org:service:serviceType:v">
      <argumentName>in arg value</argumentName>
```

```
    <argumentName>in arg value</argumentName>
    <argumentName>in arg value</argumentName>
  </u:actionName>
 </s:Body>
</s:Envelope>
```

> or

```
M-POST path of control URL HTTP/1.1
HOST: host of control URL:port of control URL
CONTENT-LENGTH: number of bytes in body
CONTENT-TYPE: text/xml; charset="utf-8"
MAN: "http://schemas.xmlsoap.org/soap/envelope/"; ns=01
01-SOAPACTION: "urn:schemas-upnp-org:service:serviceType:v#actionName"
<<same body as POST message above>>
```

A control point will try the first form initially, and if a "405 Method Not Allowed." HTTP response is generated, then the second form will be attempted. If "501 Not Implemented." or "510 Not Extended." responses are generated, then the action fails. In any event, the actual information supplied to a service about the action is the same, and that's the most important issue. The meaning of the various message components is as follows. In the POST header, we find the path name component of the control URL for the associated service. The HOST header supplies the host and port components of the control URL. CONTENT-LENGTH tracks the number of bytes in the body of the HTTP message. CONTENT-TYPE is always fixed, specifying that XML and utf-8 character encoding are used in the body. The SOAPACTION header contains a fixed prefix ("urn:schemas-upnp-org:service:") and then serviceType and actionName components. The serviceType defines the type of service to which this action is addressed. This must match a serviceType appearing in the description document for the root device. Following the hash mark, the name of the action is specified. This action should match an action in the SCPD of the service.

The body of the message contains XML, with the enclosing tags being <s:Envelope>, </s:Envelope>. Two initial lines define the SOAP Envelope schema and SOAP encoding schemas. These essentially define name spaces for the body of the SOAP action request. An <s:Body> tag follows, and within it, the name of the action and the service type are provided. These should match the values provided in the message headers. Subsequently, <argumentName>, </argumentName> pairs enclose the values of "in" parameters to the action. A concrete example, captured during an interaction between the UPnP blender and control point, makes all this a bit clearer. The following is the SOAP message generated by the

UPnP blender control point, to switch a blender's power on using the PowerOn action:

```
POST /upnp/control/power1 HTTP/1.0
Content-Type: text/xml
SOAPACTION:"urn:schemas-upnp-org:service:PowerSwitch:1#PowerOn"
Content-Length: 221
Host: 10.0.0.13:5431

<s:Envelope xmlns:s="http://schemas.xmlsoap.org/soap/envelope/"
s:encodingStyle="http://schemas.xmlsoap.org/soap/encoding">
<s:Body><u:PowerOn
  xmlns:u="urn:schemas-upnp-org:service:PowerSwitch:1"/>
</s:Body>
</s:Envelope>
```

A service responds to the POST message after performing local operations associated with the action. These operations may be quite complex or as simple as changing the value of a single state variable. The response contains the values of any "out" parameters for the action or reports that an error occurred that prevented the action from completing (this is often caused by arguments being out of range, of the incorrect type, etc.). One catch is that services are required to respond within 30 s, which means that very time-consuming actions must be handled with a combination of a quick response and a subsequent UPnP event (covered in the next major section) to indicate that the action has completed. This is turn means that the amount of time that specific actions are expected to take will have a strong impact on how services are designed. Assuming that the action is successful, the format of the response message is as follows. The components are very similar to the initial POST message from the control point. Note that the string "Response" is appended to the name of the action in the body and that the list of "out" parameters and corresponding values may have zero or more elements.

```
HTTP/1.1 200 OK
CONTENT-LENGTH: number of bytes in body
CONTENT-TYPE: text/xml; charset="utf-8"
DATE: date when response was generated
EXT:
SERVER: OS/version UPnP/1.0 product/version

<s:Envelope
    xmlns:s="http://schemas.xmlsoap.org/soap/envelope/"
    s:encodingStyle="http://schemas.xmlsoap.org/soap/encoding/">
```

```
<s:Body>
  <u:actionNameResponse xmlns:
    u="urn:schemas-upnp-org:service:serviceType:v">
    <argumentName>out arg value</argumentName>
    <argumentName>out arg value</argumentName>
    <argumentName>out arg value</argumentName>
  </u:actionNameResponse>
</s:Body>
</s:Envelope>
```

The UPnP blender responded to the PowerOn action described earlier with the following:

```
HTTP/1.1 200 OK
CONTENT-LENGTH:232
CONTENT-TYPE:text/xml
DATE: Thu, 19 Jul 2001 13:53:55 GMT
EXT:
SERVER:Linux/2.4.2-2 UPnP/1.0 Intel UPnP SDK/1.0

<s:Envelope xmlns:s="http://schemas.xmlsoap.org/soap/envelope/"
s:encodingStyle="http://schemas.xmlsoap.org/soap/encoding/">
<s:Body>
<u:PowerOnResponse
  xmlns:u="urn:schemas-upnp-org:service:PowerSwitch:1"/>
</s:Body>
 </s:Envelope>
```

If an error occurs, then a formatted response message which describes the error condition is transmitted to the control point. This response is due within 30 s. Note that "out" argument values are *not* transmitted in the event of an error. The message has the following format:

```
HTTP/1.1 500 Internal Server Error
CONTENT-LENGTH: number of bytes in body
CONTENT-TYPE: text/xml; charset="utf-8"
DATE: date when response was generated
EXT:
SERVER: OS/version UPnP/1.0 product/version

<s:Envelope
    xmlns:s="http://schemas.xmlsoap.org/soap/envelope/"
    s:encodingStyle="http://schemas.xmlsoap.org/soap/encoding/">>
  <s:Body>
    <s:Fault>
      <faultcode>s:Client</faultcode>
      <faultstring>UPnPError</faultstring>
```

```
<detail>
  <UPnPError xmlns="urn:schemas-upnp-org:control-1-0">
    <errorCode>error code</errorCode>
    <errorDescription>error string</errorDescription>
  </UPnPError>
</detail>
</s:Fault>
</s:Body>
</s:Envelope>
```

Most of the message format for an error condition (as usual, this is indicated in boldface) is static. Only a few items are supplied by the service. Aside from the now-familiar components such as the number of bytes in the message body, date, etc., the important ones are the values of errorCode and errorDescription. Only the former is required, but it is generally a good idea to include both. These must have one of the following values:

errorCode	errorDescription
401	Invalid action
402	Invalid arguments
403	Out of synchronization
501	Action failed
600–699	(To be decided; defined by UPnP committee)
700–799	(To be decided; defined by UPnP committee)
800–899	(To be decided; defined by device implementer)

Error code 401 is used to indicate that the service does not have an action with the name specified in the request. Error code 402 is a catch-all for many argument-related errors, including too many or too few arguments, an argument whose name is misspelled, one or more arguments whose values are out of range, or argument values that are of the incorrect type. Error code 501 informs the control point that the service was unable to complete the action at this time, most likely as a result of the current state of the service. Examples include issuing a form feed to a printer that is currently out of paper or instructing an LCD projector to advance to the next slide before an action that provides the presentation content has been executed. The rest of the possible values are ranges. Error codes between 600 and 699 are reserved for generic action-related errors and are defined by a UPnP committee. Codes between 700 and 799 are reserved for errors related to a specific action (e.g., "formFeed") and are also defined by a UPnP committee when the template is defined. Codes between 800 and 899 may be used by a device implementer to describe errors related to a particular implementation.

State Variable Requests.   Control points may also request the values of specific state variables associated with a service. The request message and response are similar to the ones for action requests. To request the value of a state variable, a control point composes a message of the following form, most of which is static:

```
POST path of control URL HTTP/1.1
HOST: host of control URL:port of control URL
CONTENT-LENGTH: bytes in body
CONTENT-TYPE: text/xml; charset="utf-8"
SOAPACTION: "urn:schemas-upnp-org:control-1-0#QueryStateVariable"

<s:Envelope
    xmlns:s="http://schemas.xmlsoap.org/soap/envelope/"
    s:encodingStyle="http://schemas.xmlsoap.org/soap/encoding/">
  <s:Body>
    <u:QueryStateVariable xmlns:u="urn:schemas-upnp-org:control-1-0">
      <u:varName>variableName</u:varName>
    </u:QueryStateVariable>
  </s:Body>
</s:Envelope>
```

A control point may request only a single state variable value with a single message; only a single <s:QueryStateVariable> is expected in the message. The response generated by the service if the request can be satisfied is as follows:

```
HTTP/1.1 200 OK
CONTENT-LENGTH: bytes in body
CONTENT-TYPE: text/xml; charset="utf-8"
DATE: date when response was generated
EXT:
SERVER: OS/version UPnP/1.0 product/version

<s:Envelope
    xmlns:s="http://schemas.xmlsoap.org/soap/envelope/"
    s:encodingStyle="http://schemas.xmlsoap.org/soap/encoding/">
  <s:Body>
    <u:QueryStateVariableResponse
      xmlns:u="urn:schemas-upnp-org:control-1-0">
      <return>variable value</return>
```

```
        </u:QueryStateVariableResponse>
      </s:Body>
  </s:Envelope>
```

An example in which the UPnP blender is responding to a control point's request for the value of the CurrentSpeed variable is

```
HTTP/1.1 200 OK
CONTENT-LENGTH:280
CONTENT-TYPE:text/xml
DATE: Fri, 20 Jul 2001 18:02:39 GMT
EXT:
SERVER:Linux/2.4.2-2 UPnP/1.0 Intel UPnP SDK/1.0
<s:Envelope xmlns:s="http://schemas.xmlsoap.org/soap/envelope/"
s:encodingStyle="http://schemas.xmlsoap.org/soap/encoding/">
<s:Body>
<u:QueryStateVariableResponse
   xmlns:u="urn:schemas-upnp-org:control-1-0"><return>1</return>
</u:QueryStateVariableResponse>
</s:Body>
</s:Envelope>
```

It is possible that the service may not be able to satisfy the request for a state variable's value. There are a number of reasons for this. A service must generate an error response of the following form if the value cannot be provided. The response encapsulates the reason for the failure:

```
HTTP/1.1 500 Internal Server Error
CONTENT-LENGTH: number of bytes in body
CONTENT-TYPE: text/xml; charset="utf-8"
DATE: date when response was generated
EXT:
SERVER: OS/version UPnP/1.0 product/version

<s:Envelope
    xmlns:s="http://schemas.xmlsoap.org/soap/envelope/"
    s:encodingStyle="http://schemas.xmlsoap.org/soap/encoding/">
  <s:Body>
    <s:Fault>
      <faultcode>s:Client</faultcode>
      <faultstring>UPnPError</faultstring>
      <detail>
        <UPnPError xmlns="urn:schemas-upnp-org:control-1-0">
          <errorCode>error code</errorCode>
          <errorDescription> error string</errorDescription>
        </UPnPError>
```

```
        </detail>
      </s:Fault>
    </s:Body>
  </s:Envelope>
```

Alas, here is another table of values for errorCode and errorDescription. This one's not as interesting as the table for actions:

errorCode	errorDescription
404	Invalid variable
600–624	(To be decided; defined by UPnP committee)
625–649	(Reserved)
650–674	(To be decided; defined by UPnP committee)
675–699	(To be decided; defined by device implementer)

Error code 404 is used to indicate an unknown state variable name. Values in the range of 600 to 624 and 650 to 674 will be defined by UPnP committees. Error codes 625 to 649 are "reserved for future use." Error codes 675 to 699 may be defined by the device implementer.

Eventing: The General Event Notification Architecture (GENA)

The eventing mechanism in UPnP allows control points to receive asynchronous notifications about interesting state changes in UPnP services and is complementary to control. During control operations, control points explicitly issue commands to change the state of UPnP devices and to query the values of state variables. Eventing adds the ability to subscribe to a service and to learn of changes in the values of state variables as they occur. This kind of notification is ideal for state changes that are "spontaneous" and whose timing cannot be predicted easily by control points. Examples of such state changes are a UPnP light switch being turned on, a UPnP printer running out of paper, and something being placed in the bowl of a UPnP blender.

Recall that an *event subscription URL* is specified in the device description document for each service offered by a device. Requests to subscribe and unsubscribe to the service's event notifications are made to this URL. All subscriptions are leased, and they must be renewed periodically or they will expire. The duration of the subscription is provided when the subscription is accepted, and the flow of information begins immediately with a message containing the names and values of all state variables associated with the service, encoded in XML. Subsequently, when state variables associated with a service are changed, the names and values of the changed variables are sent to *all* control points subscribing to the service.

Some state variables may have values that consume large amounts of space, are updated very frequently, or do both. Transmitting the values of such variables with UPnP eventing might overwhelm the control point (or the entire network), and so it is possible to specify in the SCPD that such variables not be subject to eventing. When declaring a state variable in a service description, the <stateVariable> tag may be augmented with "sendEvents=no" to prevent the variable's value from being transmitted to subscribed control points. Here's an example that declares a variable "Buffer" of type string with an unlimited maximum length. The default value for the variable is "EMPTY":

```
<stateVariable sendEvents="no">
    <name>Buffer</name>
    <dataType>string></dataType>
    <defaultValue>"EMPTY"</defaultValue>
</stateVariable>
```

The specification also mentions maximumRate and minimumDelta attributes that may be used to regulate the rate at which state variable values are evented and the minimum change required before an event is generated. The reader is referred to the specification for additional information on these attributes. Note that while it is possible to specify (*statically,* in the SCPD) that certain state variables will not have their values propagated by event subscriptions, it is not possible for control points to specify *which* state variables they are interested in monitoring. All state variable transitions are revealed to all subscribed control points, leaving the burden (or the joy) of sifting out the interesting bits to each control point. This has the effect of simplifying the event advertisement implementation, because devices need not track which variables should be transmitted to each control point.

Subscription, Renewal, and Cancellation. The protocol that supports subscribing, unsubscribing, and notifications in UPnP is called the General Event Notification Architecture. GENA is an HTTP-based protocol whose messages are sent over TCP. When a control point wishes to subscribe to the eventing provided by a service, it sends a message of the following format:

```
SUBSCRIBE publisherpath HTTP/1.1
HOST: publisherhost:publisherport
CALLBACK: <deliveryURL1> <deliveryURL2> ...
NT: upnp:event
TIMEOUT: second- requested subscription duration in seconds
<<BLANK LINE>>
```

The *publisherpath* is the path name component of the event subscription URL, which was obtained from the description document. The *publisherhost* and *publisherport* portions of the message contain the host name and port components of the event subscription URL. CALLBACK provides one or more URLs on the control point to which the service can send event messages. An arbitrary number of URLs, each enclosed in angle brackets, may be specified. These will be tried in order until one succeeds. The angle brackets *are* part of the message—they are *not* simply included for emphasis! The TIMEOUT is a requested duration in seconds, following the string "second-" (i.e., "second" followed by a single hyphen). The UPnP service may choose to use a shorter actual subscription duration, but should not use a subscription duration longer than the requested one. An example of a subscribe message, captured during interaction of the UPnP blender and control point, is shown below:

```
SUBSCRIBE /upnp/event/power1 HTTP/1.1
HOST: 10.0.0.13:5431
CALLBACK: http://10.0.0.13:5432/
NT: upnp:event
TIMEOUT:Second-1800
```

Upon receiving such a message, a UPnP service must, if possible, accept the subscription and generate a unique subscription identifier associated with the subscribing control point. This identifier must be guaranteed to be unique for the duration of the subscription. The service must also store the delivery URLs from the subscription message, a 4-byte integer event counter, and a subscription duration. The event counter's value begins at zero and is incremented each time an event message is sent to this subscriber. This allows a subscriber to determine if events have been missed.

If the subscription succeeds, the service responds with a message of the following type:

```
HTTP/1.1 200 OK
DATE: date when response was generated
SERVER: OS/version UPnP/1.0 product/version
```

```
SID: uuid:subscription- UUID
TIMEOUT: Second- actual subscription duration in seconds
<<BLANK LINE>>
```

This message is due within 30 s of reception of the request. As for the other types of response messages we've examined, the DATE header indicates when the response was generated. The SERVER header is exactly the same as for previous message types. The *UUID* provided in the SID (Subscription ID) header is the unique subscription ID associated with this subscription—it will be used by control points to cancel or renew this subscription. A concrete example of this message type is shown below:

```
HTTP/1.1 200 OK
DATE: Thu, 19 Jul 2001 13:53:48 GMT
SERVER: Linux/2.4.2-2 UPnP/1.0 Intel UPnP SDK/1.0
SID: uuid:43a2e7b3-f21a-464a-8c84-02d967d68ba8
TIMEOUT: Second-1800
```

A control point is required to renew subscriptions in a timely manner if it wishes to continue to receive events. The message sent by a control point to renew a subscription is similar to the initial SUBSCRIBE message, except that a CALLBACK header with delivery URLs is disallowed—instead, the subscription UUID, assigned when the initial subscription succeeded, is provided in an SID header. The format of a subscription renewal message is as follows. The response generated by the service is exactly the same as that for initial subscriptions.

```
SUBSCRIBE publisherpath HTTP/1.1
HOST: publisherhost:publisherport
SID: uuid:subscription UUID
TIMEOUT: Second- requested subscription duration in seconds
<<BLANK LINE>>
```

A subscription or subscription renewal attempt may fail for a number of reasons, most related to the control point providing erroneous information in the SUBSCRIBE message. The following list summarizes the HTTP responses that should be generated, along with the reasons each would be generated:

■ "400 Bad Request." is returned if both SID and CALLBACK (which provides the delivery URL on the control point for events) are specified. Such a SUBSCRIBE message is ambiguous and must be rejected—is the control point trying to subscribe, or is it renewing a subscription?

■ "412 Precondition Failed." is returned if no CALLBACK header is provided for an initial subscription or if the delivery URLs are invalid.

■ A 500-series HTTP error is returned if the service is unable to handle the subscription (e.g., if current resource levels do not permit another subscription to be accommodated). The 500-series error codes in HTTP indicate server errors, e.g., that a server has encountered an internal error or is so overloaded that it cannot respond to a request.

To cancel a subscription, either a control point may let the subscription duration pass without issuing a request for renewal, or it may explicitly cancel the subscription using an UNSUBSCRIBE message. Explicitly canceling a subscription is preferable, because it conserves resources by freeing services from sending events to uninterested (or dead) control points. To unsubscribe, a control point sends a message of the following type. The values of the fields in the various headers are the same as those for a subscription renewal message.

```
UNSUBSCRIBE publisher path HTTP/1.1
HOST: publisherhost:publisherport
SID: uuid:subscription UUID
<<BLANK LINE>>
```

Upon receiving such a message, a service releases resources associated with the subscription, terminates transmission of events to control points, and sends a simple response message, shown below, *unless* an error occurs. The response is due within 30 s of reception of the request:

```
HTTP/1.1 200 OK
<<BLANK LINE>>
```

Several errors may occur when a control point attempts to cancel a subscription. Most are related to missing or erroneous information being provided by the control point. The following list summarizes the HTTP responses that should be generated, along with the reasons each would be generated:

■ "400 Bad Request." is returned if an NT or CALLBACK header is provided.

■ "412 Precondition Failed." is returned if the subscription *UUID* does not correspond to a subscription that is currently in force. This error is also generated if the SID header is either completely missing or contains no *UUID*.

Event Messages.   Once a control point has subscribed, UPnP services are responsible for sending NOTIFY event messages to the control point whenever state variables change (except for variables tagged with "sendEvents5no"). Ideally, these messages should be sent as soon as possible, because control points need timely information to freshen GUIs and to react promptly to important changes. A NOTIFY message contains variable names and values, and an arbitrary number of state variable changes may be reported in a single message. The format of a NOTIFY message is as follows:

```
NOTIFY deliverypath HTTP/1.1
HOST: deliveryhost:deliveryport
CONTENT-TYPE: text/xml
CONTENT-LENGTH: number of bytes in body
NT: upnp:event
NTS: upnp:propchange
SID: uuid:subscription- UUID
SEQ: event identifier
<e:propertyset xmlns:e="urn:schemas-upnp-org:event-1-0">
  <e:property>
    <variableName>new value</variableName>
  </e:property>

  <e:property>
    <variableName>new value</variableName>
  </e:property>
</e:propertyset>
```

The *delivery path* component of the NOTIFY header is the path name component of the delivery URL provided when this control point subscribed. The *delivery host* and *deliveryport* components of the HOST header are the host name and port on which the control point is listening for event messages. These correspond to the value supplied in the CALLBACK header during control point subscription. The CONTENT-LENGTH header specifies how many bytes compose the body of this message; the body contains the names and values of control variables that have changed. The *UUID* component of the SID header provides the unique subscription ID of the control point to whom this message is addressed. SEQ provides the event number corresponding to this event—each event is tagged with a value 1 higher than the previous, with the initial event message tagged with 0. All these headers are required.

Following these headers is the body of the HTTP message, which describes the control variables that have changed. Each control variable whose new value is being reported is enclosed in an <e:property> </e:property> pair. Within, the name of the tag is the variable name (e.g., <Power>), and the value is the new value for the variable. The value must be of the same type specified in the SCPD for this service. Any number of <e:property> components may be present. The UPnP specification requires that any unknown XML elements in the body of the NOTIFY message be ignored. A concrete example of a NOTIFY message, generated during an interaction between the UPnP blender and control point, is shown below. This message reports values for PulseDuration (0) and Power (false).

```
NOTIFY: CONTENT-TYPE: text/xml
CONTENT-LENGTH: 184
NT: upnp:event
NTS: upnp:propchange
SID: uuid:75487341-0ea4-4fb2-87af-369bb3e0d6c5
SEQ: 0
<e:propertyset xmlns:e="urn:schemas-upnp-org:event-1-0">
<e:property>
<Power>false</Power>
</e:property>
<e:property>
<PulseDuration>0</PulseDuration>
</e:property>
</e:propertyset>
```

On receipt of the NOTIFY message, and if everything checks out, the control point has 30 s in which to respond with the following message. If this message is not received, then the subscription remains in effect, but no further effort is made to deliver this NOTIFY message.

```
HTTP/1.1 200 OK
<<BLANK LINE>>
```

In lieu of this "OK" response message, the control point may report the following errors. Again, the response is due within 30 s.

■ "400 Bad Request." is returned by a control point if the NT or NTS header is missing.

■ "412 Precondition Failed." will be returned by a control point if the SID header is missing or contains an invalid subscription ID. The subscription should be terminated by the service on receipt of this response. This response will also be generated if the NT header does not contain "upnp:event" or the NTS header does not contain "upnp:propchange."

Presentation: Getting Visual

Presentation allows a device to offer a GUI to control points. By loading an HTML page specified in the device's description document, a control point can offer a user interactive control over a device. The specification devotes very little space to presentation, aside from a few recommendations. In fact, the entire discussion of presentation occupies less than a page in the v1.0 UPnP specification. From the device's standpoint, all that is required is that an HTML 3.0 page be created. The specifics, such as what scripting languages, plug-ins, etc., are used to facilitate building the GUI, are entirely up to the implementer of the device. The specification does recommend that localization features be used to attempt to load pages with appropriate human languages.

Where's the Code?

To this point, the discussion has focused exclusively on the UPnP specification. Unlike Jini, where the API against which programmers work is part of the specification, the UPnP specification is API-free, addressing only standards and protocols. Thus it's important to understand the specification first, before looking at a particular API in detail. Now we examine an implementation of a UPnP device using Intel's UPnP SDK for Linux. This is a top-notch, open source tool kit for UPnP. Using such a tool kit is preferable, because coding directly against the specification would be an enormous task—not only must all the various protocols be implemented, but also an XML parser is required. The Intel SDK provides implementations of all the UPnP protocols, includes an XML parser, and generally makes coding straightforward. A component-level view of the Intel SDK is illustrated in Fig. 4-2.

At the time this book is being written, a serious deficiency in the Intel SDK is lack of documentation. Documentation currently consists primarily

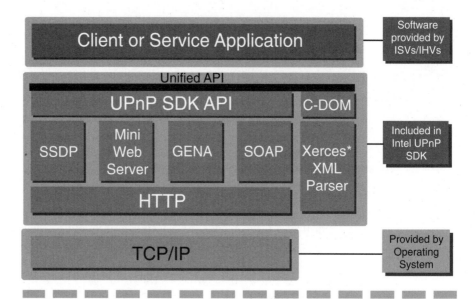

Figure 4-2

This diagram shows a component view of the Intel UPnP SDK for Linux. Developers of UPnP devices and control points see a "unified" API that provides access to implementations of the UPnP protocols such as SOAP and GENA. A powerful XML parser and integrated Web server are also included.

of an annotated "inc/upnp.h", which lists the functions provided by the SDK. In any event, having a look at the "upnp.h" file, in conjunction with this chapter, will give you sufficient information to begin developing interesting UPnP code. All UPnP devices and control point implementations are written in C under the Intel SDK. Our subject is the UPnP blender, a device that was specified in Section "Describing Devices and Services in UPnP." Before getting to the code, however (patience!), a look at how XML documents are manipulated in the Intel SDK is necessary.

XML, Xerces, DOM, and the Intel SDK. A fundamental part of the operation of UPnP devices and control points is processing XML, since the descriptions of devices, the control specifications for services, and most of the core UPnP protocols (e.g., SOAP and GENA) rely on XML. The architects of the UPnP SDK for Linux chose to package a subset of the Xerces-C XML parser [8], which is a part of the Apache project. This is a portable, validating XML parser written in C11 that supports many popular standards. A Java version, called Xerces-J, is also available. Xerces (and in turn, the Intel SDK) uses the Document Object Model

(DOM) [9] as a programming interface for XML documents. Xerces supports DOM (Core) Level 1 and DOM (Core) Level 2, which are standards under development by the World Wide Web Consortium (W3C). The complete standards documents for DOM are freely available in a variety of formats at the location given in the reference above; our treatment here will be a very practical one, focusing on the aspects necessary to use the Intel UPnP SDK.

The DOM defines a programming interface that allows developers to navigate XML (and HTML) documents, adding, deleting, and modifying content as required. Under DOM, documents have a structure that is treelike, with the entire document being represented as a set of nodes of various types. A number of basic interfaces are specified, which represent common document components. These include the document as a whole, individual nodes, groups of nodes, and structured elements that make up a portion of the document. The DOM interfaces will typically be implemented in an object-oriented language (say, C++), but in the UPnP SDK for Linux, the DOM peeps through a C wrapper. Only a few of the DOM interfaces are critical to a programmer using the Intel SDK; so it's possible to get started with device and control point development with a basic understanding, learning more about DOM along the way (and as needed). The most useful Intel SDK implementations of DOM interfaces are listed below. We'll examine operations on these types as necessary in discussions of the UPnP blender and associated control point. For now, here is a list with brief descriptions:

- Upnp_Document. This entity represents an entire XML document, or the "root" of the document, structured as a tree.

- Upnp_Node. A node represents a single node in an XML document tree. Nodes may be of various types, defined by the Upnp_NodeType below.

- Upnp_NodeType. This is the type of a node in a DOM tree. Types include TEXT_NODE, DOCUMENT_NODE, ELEMENT_NODE, etc. These are defined in "inc/upnpdom/all.h" in the Intel UPnP SDK distribution.

- Upnp_NodeList. This is an ordered list of Upnp_Nodes.

- Upnp_Element. This is a portion of an XML document delimited by a start tag and end tag (e.g., "<item name=it>") and a corresponding end tag (e.g., "</item>") or by special form called an empty tag, used when the element has no content (e.g., "<img src=hello.jpg/>").

■ Upnp_DOMString. This type can be safely treated as char* [and freed using free(), whenever appropriate] in the Linux UPnP SDK.

Here's the Code: The UPnP Blender Device

Now we're ready to begin looking at the UPnP blender source code. The following is the preface of the UPnP blender's main source file, which defines constants and types used in the remainder of the blender. We're really trying to get to the main() function, which initializes the major device functions, so most of this stuff will be discussed a bit later as it's needed. It's shown here to keep the code presentation linear—we're walking through the blender implementation line by line. Everything is included.

```
// UPnP Virtual Blender main source file.
// Written by Golden G. Richard III, Ph.D.  May 2001

#include <stdio.h>
#include <stdlib.h>
#include <string.h>
#include <unistd.h>
#include <signal.h>
#include <pthread.h>
#include "common.h"

// interesting constants
// duration between device advertisements
#define AD_DURATION     1800
// index into variables/values arrays for power
#define POWER_INDEX       0
// index into variables/values arrays for speed
#define SPEED_INDEX       1
// index into variables/values arrays for contents
#define BOWL_INDEX        2
#define true 1
#define false 0

// our device type
char BLENDER_TYPE[] = "urn:schemas-upnp-org:device:blender:1";

// our service types
char POWERSERVICE[] ="urn:schemas-upnp-org:service:PowerSwitch:1";
char SPEEDSERVICE[] ="urn:schemas-upnp-org:service:SpeedControl:1";
char BOWLSERVICE[] ="urn:schemas-upnp-org:service:Bowl:1";
```

```c
// unique ids for services
char POWERSERVICE_NAME[] ="urn:upnp-org:serviceId:PowerSwitch1";
char SPEEDSERVICE_NAME[] ="urn:upnp-org:serviceId:SpeedControl1";
char BOWLSERVICE_NAME[] ="urn:upnp-org:serviceId:Bowl1";

// types

typedef struct blender_state {
    char UDN[NAME_SIZE];    // unique name for blender
    char ***variables;      // array of state variable names for
                            // each service
    char ***values;         // array of corresponding variable values
                            // for each service
} BlenderState;

// function prototypes for blender.c functions
int main(int argc, char** argv);
int CallbackHandler(Upnp_EventType type, void *event,
    void *cookie);
void SignalHandler();
void Shutdown(char *reason);
void InitializeStateTable(char *doc_url);
void HandleSubscriptionRequest(
    struct Upnp_Subscription_Request *event);
void HandleVariableRequest(struct Upnp_State_Var_Request *event);
void HandleCommand(struct Upnp_Action_Request *event);
void HandlePowerChanges(struct Upnp_Action_Request *event);
void HandleSpeedChanges(struct Upnp_Action_Request *event);
void HandleBowlChanges(struct Upnp_Action_Request *event);
void *BlendLoop(void *args);

// globals

// Since callbacks are used to inform the blender of
// interesting events (e.g., power on/off), a semaphore must
// be used to protect important device state.  The following
// semaphore should be used to lock global state before
// touching it!
pthread_mutex_t mutex=PTHREAD_MUTEX_INITIALIZER;

UpnpDevice_Handle handle=-1;    // blender's device handle
BlenderState state;             // state table for blender
```

The main() function of the UPnP blender is shown below. When invoking the blender, four command line arguments (in addition to argv[0], which is the name of the blender's executable) are required. These are the IP address of the blender, the port on which the blender will listen for messages, the name of the blender's description document, and the directory where the description document and service control protocol descriptions (SCPDs) for the blender's services are stored. The latter information is needed to initialize a mini web server, which is included in the UPnP SDK.

```
////////////////////////////////
// main function—parse command line, initialize
// and register device, start advertisements, and deal
// with shutdown via control-C.
//

int main(int argc, char** argv) {

  int port;                    // port on which we listen for messages
  int code;                    // return value from UPnP functions
  char *ip=NULL;               // IP address for this device
  char *desc_doc=NULL;         // location of description document
  char *web_dir=NULL;          // root path for web server
  char doc_url[NAME_SIZE];     // absolute URL for our description
                               // document
  pthread_t blend_thread;

  if (argc != 5) {
    printf(
      "Usage: blender IP port XML_description_doc web_path\n");
    exit(1);
  }

  ip=argv[1];
  sscanf(argv[2],"%d",&port);
  desc_doc=argv[3];
  web_dir=argv[4];
```

At this point, a description document URL is created, using the IP address, port, and description document file name provided on the command line. Note that this URL will be relative to the root directory specified for the web server. Control points don't know that, though.

```
// create absolute description document URL
sprintf(doc_url, "http://%s:%d/%s", ip, port, desc_doc);
printf("Blender: Absolute description doc URL is %s\n",
  doc_url);
```

UpnpInit() is the first Intel SDK function of interest. It must be called before any other UPnP functions. It initializes the UPnP library. If the return value from this function doesn't indicate success, there's nothing else we can do except die. Diagnose() is a utility function in "common.c", a small library of helpful functions developed in conjunction with this example. Diagnose() examines a return code from a UPnP function and outputs a human-readable description of the error condition. Passing __LINE__ helps Diagnose() to provide information that allows the location of the error to be found quickly.

```
// UpnpInit() must be called before any other UPnP
// functions are used
printf("Blender: Calling UpnpInit().\n");
if ((code = UpnpInit(ip, port)) != UPNP_E_SUCCESS) {
  Diagnose("UpnpInit()", __LINE__, code);
  Shutdown("Blender: Can't continue.");
}
```

The following call to UpnpSetWebServerRoot() initializes the web server provided in the Intel SDK, supplying it with the root directory where description documents, etc., are stored.

```
// Specify where documents that describe our makeup are stored
printf("Blender: Calling UpnpSetWebServerRoot()");
printf(" to specify web server path.\n");
if ((code = UpnpSetWebServerRootDir(web_dir)) != UPNP_E_SUCCESS) {
  Diagnose("UpnpSetWebServerRootDir()", __LINE__, code);
  Shutdown("Blender: Can't continue.");
}
```

At this stage, information about each root device must be provided. UpnpRegisterRootDevice() accepts four parameters and is called once for each root device. The first parameter is the URL describing the root device's description document. This will be multicast in device advertisements (which we'll initiate shortly). The second parameter is a local function that will be called when interesting things happen (e.g., a control point wishes to subscribe or execute an action). All interactions with control points are initiated by the SDK through this callback function. The third parameter provides a "cookie" that will be passed back when the callback function is called. One use for this might be to distinguish between a set of root devices sharing a common callback function. The fourth parameter is the address of a UpnpDevice_Handle. If the call to UpnpRegisterRootDevice() completes successfully, this handle becomes our key to all future interactions with the UPnP library. Again, this operation is so critical that if it fails, the blender just reports an error and kills itself. Callbacks can begin immediately after this function completes, although we haven't yet sent any advertisements.

```
// Register the root device

printf("Blender: Calling UpnpRegisterRootDevice().\n");
if ((code = UpnpRegisterRootDevice(doc_url,
   CallbackHandler, NULL, &handle)) != UPNP_E_SUCCESS) {
   Diagnose("UpnpRegisterRootDevice()", __LINE__, code);
   Shutdown("Blender: Can't continue.");
}
```

The following local function, InitializeStateTable(), handles initialization of the state variables for all blender services. It also takes a peek at the XML device description to determine our unique identifier (thus the need for passing the description document's URL). The state variables and the unique device name are stored in the global variable "state," of type BlenderState (struct blender_state). This global is declared just before the start of the main() function (above).

```
// Initialize blender guts
InitializeStateTable(doc_url);
```

The device is now ready to begin advertising. UpnpSendAdvertisement() performs part of the blender's device-side duties under the discovery phase of UPnP by sending advertisements for the root device and all services. The format of the "NOTIFY" advertisement messages that are transmitted was discussed in the section "Discovery: The Simple Service Discovery Protocol (SSDP)".

```
printf("Blender: Calling UpnpSendAdvertisement()");
printf(" to advertise our services.\n");
if ((code = UpnpSendAdvertisement(handle, AD_DURATION))
   != UPNP_E_SUCCESS) {
   Diagnose("UpnpSendAdvertisement()", __LINE__, code);
   Shutdown("Blender: Can't continue.");
}
```

At this point, initialization is almost complete. The following call to pthread_create() starts a separate thread that handles "blending." The BlendLoop function runs in this thread, churning the contents of the blender and sending out notifications to subscribed control points as the contents changes. It also performs the countdown when the blender is in the timed "pulse" mode. There is more on the BlendLoop toward the end of this section. Once the thread is started, a signal handler is installed to catch control-C. The signal handler will ensure that the proper functions are called to shut down cleanly. Note that the main() function is prevented from exiting by the signal handler—the signal handler blocks and waits for an appropriate signal. This completes the discussion of the main() function for the blender. Other UPnP devices developed using this SDK will have very similar main() functions.

```
// start thread that blends, counts down pulse duration
printf("Blender: Starting blending thread.\n");
code = pthread_create(&blend_thread, NULL, BlendLoop, NULL);

printf("Initialization successful. ");
printf("Use Control-C to shut down.\n");
// handle control-C—it's the only way to shut down the blender.
SignalHandler();

return 0;
}
```

The following function, InitializeStateTable(), is called from the main() function (described above) to initialize the "guts" of the blender. It doesn't rely on the Intel UPnP SDK much, but does store the names and values of state variables with an eye toward what will be required later, when we reveal these values to UPnP library. This is the first function where locking of device state occurs [through a call to pthread_mutex_lock()]. Throughout the code for the blender device, whenever the state of the device may be altered, such locking occurs. This is necessary because the UPnP library communicates with the device implementation asynchronously through a callback function (specified when the root device is registered). Even though Initialize-StateTable() is never executed from the callback function, callbacks may begin as soon as the root device is registered, and these callbacks may alter the device state.

```
/////////////////////////////////
// Initialize the blender's state table, which contains
// bits of data that clients are interested in.  Default
// values for variables, etc. are hard-coded—this means that
// the blender implementation will need tweaking if these
// values are modified in the description document.
// Could parse the description document to obtain default
// values, etc. to increase abstraction.  We do parse the
```

```
// description document to obtain the unique device name
// of this blender.
//
// doc_url == absolute URL for our description document
//

void InitializeStateTable(char *doc_url) {

  Upnp_Document doc=NULL;      // our description document
  int code;                    // return value from UPnP functions
  char *udn=NULL;              // unique blender name, from desc doc


  int i,j;
  // lock device state
  pthread_mutex_lock(&mutex);
```

The lock, above, uses a global variable mutex. Below, the structure BlenderState is initialized. The variables component in BlenderState is declared char ***variables, a three-dimensional character array. The first index specifies the service, the second specifies the name of a state variable for that service, and the third indexes individual characters in the name. The char ***values component is similar, storing the values of the corresponding state variables. The char *** stuff results in ugly memory allocation, but this is necessary because the SDK functions that take arrays of variable names and values for specific services expect char ** arguments, so regular arrays can't be used.

```
// set up storage for variables/values...blech.


// three services
state.variables = malloc(sizeof(char *) * 3);
state.values = malloc(sizeof(char *) * 3);
for (i=0; i < 3; i++) {
  // power service has two state variables, others have one each
  state.variables[i] = malloc(sizeof(char *) *
    (i == POWER_INDEX ? 2 : 1));
  state.values[i] = malloc(sizeof(char *) *
    (i == POWER_INDEX ? 2 : 1));
  for (j=0; j < (i == POWER_INDEX ? 2 : 1); j++) {
    state.variables[i][j] = malloc(NAME_SIZE);
    state.values[i][j] = malloc(LINE_SIZE);
  }
}
```

The names and default values of state variables for the blender's services are hard-coded. The initial state of the blender is Power= "false," PulseDuration=0, CurrentSpeed=1, CurrentContents= "EMPTY."

```
// variable names and default values hard-coded

// blender off
strcpy(state.variables[POWER_INDEX][0], "Power");
strcpy(state.values[POWER_INDEX][0], "false");
// no pulse duration set
strcpy(state.variables[POWER_INDEX][1], "PulseDuration");
strcpy(state.values[POWER_INDEX][1], "0");
// default speed is minimum to reduce burn danger
strcpy(state.variables[SPEED_INDEX][0], "CurrentSpeed");
strcpy(state.values[SPEED_INDEX][0], "1");
// blender is empty
strcpy(state.variables[BOWL_INDEX][0], "CurrentContents");
// empty string "" causes problems, "EMPTY" will do!
strcpy(state.values[BOWL_INDEX][0], "EMPTY");
```

The next bit of code downloads the XML description document for the blender and grabs the unique device name (UDN) component, which will be needed later. The downloaded document is represented by a variable of type Upnp_Document. This type is provided by the XML-handling portion of the Linux SDK. The UDN is actually extracted from the document by ParseItem(), a function in our "common.c" function library. The string returned from ParseItem() needs to be freed after we make a copy of it (filling in the last bit of BlenderState), and the description document representation is also freed. If the UDN can't be determined, it's a fatal error.

As you see more of the XML-handling functions, you'll notice that they place a serious memory deallocation burden on the programmer. Under the hood, the Intel SDK currently uses a C++ library for XML parsing, with a C wrapper. All the freeing is up to us. A warning: Do *not* free XML document components using free()! You must use the appropriate UpnpXXX_free() function instead, which in this case is UpnpDocument_free(). Doing otherwise will cause massive heap corruption, and no one wants that. At the very end of the function, the lock on device state is released using pthread_mutex_unlock().

```
// get unique device name

code = UpnpDownloadXmlDoc(doc_url, &doc);
if (code != UPNP_E_SUCCESS) {
  Diagnose("UpnpDownloadXmlDoc()", __LINE__, code);
```

```
    Shutdown("Blender: Can't continue without description document.");
}
else {
  // get our unique name from the description document
  udn = ParseItem(doc, NULL, "UDN");
  if (! udn) {
    Shutdown("Blender: Can't continue w/o description document.");
  }
  else {
    strcpy(state.UDN, udn);
    free(udn);
  }
}

// free storage associated with description document

if (doc) {
  UpnpDocument_free(doc);
}

printf("Blender: Initialization complete.  UDN = %s.\n", state.UDN);
printf("Blender: Variables:\n");
for (j=0; j < 3; j++) {
  for (i=0; i < (j == POWER_INDEX ? 2 : 1); i++) {
    printf("    \"%s\" = \"%s\"\n", state.variables[j][i],
      state.values[j][i]);
  }
}

// unlock device state
pthread_mutex_unlock(&mutex);

}
```

The next function in the UPnP blender implementation, Callback-Handler(), handles all callbacks from the Intel UPnP library. This function was registered in the call to UpnpRegisterRootDevice() in main(). It's a good idea to examine this function now, because virtually every interesting thing the blender does after initialization (aside from churning its contents) results because of a callback. Thus most of the other functions in the implementation are called, at least indirectly, from here. The prototype for a callback in the Intel SDK is an integer-valued function that takes three arguments. The first is the sort of event driving the callback; this parameter is of type Upnp_EventType, defined in the SDK's "upnp.h". The second is a void pointer that can point to several different types of structure. Depending on the type of the event, an appropriate cast must be used. The final is a "cookie," which is simply the optional data item passed when the root device was registered via Upnp_RegisterRootDevice(). We ignore the cookie.

The first thing that CallbackHandler() does is to print a bunch of information about the event—this is useful for debugging. The ReportEvent() function is in the "common.c" bundle, discussed at the very end of the chapter. Then a switch statement exhausts all event types for devices: UPNP_EVENT_SUBSCRIPTION_REQUEST, UPNP_CONTROL_GET_VAR_REQUEST, and UPNP_CONTROL_ ACTION_REQUEST. The first requires a response to a control point's attempt to subscribe to a service's eventing, while the other two are related to control. Control points respond to other event types, as we'll see when the blender's control point implementation is examined. CallbackHandler() just returns 0, because the Intel SDK currently ignores the return value from the callback function.

```
//////////////////////////////////
// All asynchronous notifications of interesting events come
// through this handler.  This guy is the reason that a semaphore
// has to be used to lock global device state before accessing it!
// For each event type, hand off processing to an appropriate
// blender function.
//
// type == type of event that occurred
// event == the event description
// cookie == data we specified during registration of the callback
//

int CallbackHandler(Upnp_EventType type, void *event,
  void *cookie) {

  // print lots of information about the incoming event
  ReportEvent(type, event, true);

  // the following are the only events of interest for a
  // device; control points (clients) will respond to other events
  switch (type) {

  // a control point is interested in knowing about state changes
  case UPNP_EVENT_SUBSCRIPTION_REQUEST:
    printf("Blender: Subscription request from control point.\n");
    HandleSubscriptionRequest(
      (struct Upnp_Subscription_Request *)event);
    break;

  // a control point wants the current value of a variable
```

```
case UPNP_CONTROL_GET_VAR_REQUEST:
  printf("Blender: Request for variable value from");
  printf(" control point.\n");
  HandleVariableRequest(
    (struct Upnp_State_Var_Request *)event);
  break;

  // a control point is issuing a command
case UPNP_CONTROL_ACTION_REQUEST:
  printf("Blender: Command from control point.\n");
  HandleCommand((struct Upnp_Action_Request *)event);
  break;
default:
  printf("Blender: Don't know why I received that event!!\n");
  break;
}

// all is well
return 0;
}
```

The function HandleSubscriptionRequest() is called from CallbackHandler() in response to a control point attempting to subscribe to a service's eventing. The single argument is a pointer to a Upnp_Subscription_Request. This type is declared in "upnp.h". A Upnp_Subscription_Request structure contains three fields, a ServiceId of type char*, a universal device name UDN of type char*, and a subscription ID Sid of type Upnp_SID. The latter is a subscription ID generated by the library that can be used if we accept the subscription request.

```
//////////////////////////////////
// Control point wants to subscribe to a service
//
// event == event containing service information
//

void HandleSubscriptionRequest(
  struct Upnp_Subscription_Request *event) {
  int index;          // index into set of services
  int code;           // return value from UPnP functions
  int i;
  printf("Blender: Handling control point");
  printf(" subscription request.\n");

  // lock device state
  pthread_mutex_lock(&mutex);
```

The first step is to see if the subscription request should really be handled by us. Does the unique device name in the event description match our UDN (which was obtained from our description document earlier, when the device's state table was initialized)? If it does, the ID of the service that the control point wishes to subscribe to is checked. If it matches one of the blender's services, then make a note of which service it is. If the service ID doesn't match any of the blender services, the request is ignored.

```
// is the subscription directed at us?
if (strcmp(state.UDN, event->UDN)) {
  printf("Blender: Ignoring subscription addressed");
  printf(" to %s.\n", event->UDN);
}
else {
  // it is, see which service is being subscribed to...
  if (! strcmp(POWERSERVICE_NAME, event->ServiceId)) {
    printf("Blender: Subscription is for power service.\n");
    index = POWER_INDEX;
  }
  else if (! strcmp(SPEEDSERVICE_NAME, event->ServiceId)) {
    printf("Blender: Subscription is for speed");
    printf(" control service.\n");
    index = SPEED_INDEX;
  }
  else if (! strcmp(BOWLSERVICE_NAME, event->ServiceId)) {
    printf("Blender: Subscription is for blender");
    printf(" contents service.\n");
    index = BOWL_INDEX;
  }
  else {
    printf("Blender: Don't know anything about service %s.\n",
      event->ServiceId);
    return;
  }

  // accept subscription for the specified service.
  // The following accepts the subscription and provides
  // the service's state variable names and current values.
  // The sixth argument specifies the number of variables;
  // all of the blender's services have a single state
  // variable, except for the power service, which has two.

  printf("Blender: Accepting subscription. ");
  printf(" Current values of state variables:\n");
  for (i=0; i < (index == POWER_INDEX ? 2 : 1); i++) {
    printf("    \"%s\" = \"%s\"\n",
      state.variables[index][i], state.values[index][i]);
  }
```

The function UpnpAcceptSubscription() allows a device to accept a subscription request for a service's eventing. This is performed after verifying that the UDN of the device and the service ID in the request are correct. The function requires six arguments: the unique device name of the device providing the service, the ID of the service, a char** array containing the names of the state variables for the service, a char **array containing the values of these state variables, the length of the name/value arrays (in the case of the blender, the power service has two variables, all other services have only a single control variable), and a unique subscription identifier. The latter was already generated by the SDK—we just pass it along. If for some reason the subscription accept fails, we can live with it—just move on.

```
code = UpnpAcceptSubscription(handle,
  event->UDN,
  event->ServiceId,
  (const char **)state.variables[index],
  (const char **)state.values[index],
  (index == POWER_INDEX ? 2 : 1),
  event->Sid);
if (code != UPNP_E_SUCCESS) {
  printf("Blender: Couldn't accept subscription.\n");
  Diagnose("UpnpAcceptSubscription()", __LINE__, code);
}
else {
  printf("Blender: Subscription complete.\n");
}
}

// unlock
pthread_mutex_unlock(&mutex);
}
```

Next, we'll handle the case where a control point requires the value of a specific control variable. The event provided to HandleVariableRequest() is of type Upnp_State_Var_Request, which has a number of components necessary to fulfill the request. These are an int ErrCode, which provides a status code for the request; a string ErrStr, which is set by the device if an error occurs during processing the variable request; the unique device name DevUDN; the ID of the service, ServiceID; StateVarName, which is the name of the variable whose value is being requested; and CurrentVal, which will be used to return the value of the variable (unless an error occurs). As before, the first thing is to ensure that the request is truly for this device. If the unique device name in the request doesn't match our UDN, we simply ignore this request. Then the variable name in the request is checked against each of the device control variables to see if there is a match. If control variable names were not unique across services (they are unique in the case of the blender), we would also have to examine the service ID in the request. If the variable name isn't recognized, it's an error. If there is a match, we malloc() space for event->CurrentVal and strcpy() the current value of the control variable there. Note that if an error occurs, we do not have to malloc() space for event->ErrStr; this component is declared char ErrStr[LINE_SIZE]. And LINE_SIZE is defined in "upnp.h" to be 180.

```
/////////////////////////////
// Allow a control variable to ask for the value of a
// specific control variable
void HandleVariableRequest(struct Upnp_State_Var_Request *event) {

    int i,j, service, variable;
    int matched=0;

    // lock device state
    pthread_mutex_lock(&mutex);

    // first see if we're really the target
    if (! strcmp(event->DevUDN, state.UDN)) {
        // yes.  Could look at service ID in the event, but since
        // all our state variables have distinct names, can
        // just examine variable names instead

        // each service
        for (i=0; i < BOWL_INDEX+1 && ! matched; i++) {
            // each variable for a particular service
            for (j=0; j < (i == POWER_INDEX ? 2 : 1) && ! matched; j++) {
                if (! strcmp(state.variables[i][j], event->StateVarName)) {
                    matched=1;
                    service=i;
                    variable=j;
                }
            }
        }
    }

    if (! matched) {
        // huh?
        printf("Blender: Don't know anything about state");
```

```
       printf(" variable \"%s\", ignored.\n",  event->StateVarName);
       event->ErrCode = UPNP_E_INVALID_PARAM;
       strcpy(event->ErrStr, "Invalid variable");
       event->CurrentVal = NULL;
    }
    else {
      printf("Blender: Returning value for variable");
      printf(" %s.\n", state.variables[service][variable]);
      // matched, return current value
      event->ErrCode = UPNP_E_SUCCESS;
      event->CurrentVal = (Upnp_DOMString)
        malloc(strlen(state.values[service][variable])+1);
      strcpy(event->CurrentVal, state.values[service][variable]);
      if (! (event->CurrentVal)) {
        Shutdown("Blender: Out of memory!!");
      }
    }
  }
}

// unlock
pthread_mutex_unlock(&mutex);

}
```

The next function handles actions attempted by control points. There's very little work done here—we just determine which service the action is directed at and then hand off the processing to an appropriate function [HandleSpeedChanges(), HandlePowerChanges(), Handle-BowlChanges()]. The IDs for the various blender services are stored in the globals POWERSERVICE_NAME, SPEEDSERVICE_NAME, etc., which match the values specified in the description document for the blender. The single parameter for HandleCommand() is a Upnp_Action_Request. Rather than discussing this structure in each of the Handle***Changes() functions (which immediately follow this function), we examine it here. A Upnp_Action_Request contains a number of interesting fields. These include an int ErrCode, string ErrStr, string DevUDN, and string ServiceID that are used in exactly the same manner as for HandleVariableRequest(), discussed above. Other fields are a string ActionName that specifies the action the control point is attempting, and two Upnp_Document variables, ActionRequest and Action Result. The former Upnp_Document is an XML document that defines the action being attempted (providing arguments, etc.). The latter defines our response to the action request (in particular, providing the values of any "out" parameters). We discuss the ActionRequest and ActionResult further when we look at the handling for specific actions.

```
/////////////////////////////
// Handle actions initiated by control points.  For the blender,
// these always involve simple changes in control variable values.
//
// event == encapsulation of action requested by control point
//

void HandleCommand(struct Upnp_Action_Request *event) {

  // lock device state
  pthread_mutex_lock(&mutex);
  printf("Blender: UDN associated with command: ");
  printf(" %s\n", event->DevUDN);
  if (! strcmp(event->DevUDN, state.UDN)) { // addressed to us?
    printf("Blender: Handling control point command.\n");

    // determine which service is involved
    if (! strcmp(event->ServiceID, POWERSERVICE_NAME)) {
      printf("Blender: Power.\n");
      HandlePowerChanges(event);
    }
    else if (! strcmp(event->ServiceID, SPEEDSERVICE_NAME)) {
      printf("Blender: Speed.\n");
      HandleSpeedChanges(event);
    }
    else if (! strcmp(event->ServiceID, BOWLSERVICE_NAME)) {
      printf("Blender: Bowl.\n");
      HandleBowlChanges(event);
    }
  }
  else {
    printf("Blender: Ignoring action request for UDN %s.\n",
  event->DevUDN);
  }

  // unlock
  pthread_mutex_unlock(&mutex);

}
```

The following function handles actions related to the power service. This function is not thread-safe (i.e., it doesn't lock the device state) because it is always called from HandleCommand(), which already holds a lock. The single parameter for HandlePowerChanges() is a Upnp_Action_Request, discussed in the context of HandleCommand(), above. This structure provides information about the action the control point is attempting. This function contains a number of key ideas, so we examine it in detail below.

```
/////////////////////////////
// Handle actions related to the power service
//
// **THIS FUNCTION IS NOT THREAD-SAFE**
// **THIS FUNCTION IS NOT THREAD-SAFE**
//
// event == encapsulation of action requested by control point
//

void HandlePowerChanges(struct Upnp_Action_Request *event) {

    char *value=NULL;        // value of argument to service function
    char response[512];      // our response to action
    int pulse;               // new pulse duration
    int err=UPNP_E_SUCCESS;  // status of action
    int code;                // return value from UPnP functions

    printf("Blender: Starting power-related action.\n");
```

The ErrStr component of the Upnp_Action_Request will hold a human-readable description of any error that occurs during execution of the action. Initially, there's been no error, so we set this string to "". The next step is to determine which action is being executed. The possibilities are PowerOn and PowerOff, which take no arguments, and SetPulseDuration, which accepts a single "in" int argument. Recall that the body of an action request contains XML like the following:

```
<s:Envelope
    xmlns:s="http://schemas.xmlsoap.org/soap/envelope/"
    s:encodingStyle="http://schemas.xmlsoap.org/soap/encoding/">
  <s:Body>
    <u:actionName
     xmlns:u="urn:schemas-upnp-org:service:serviceType:v">
     <argumentName>in arg value</argumentName>
     <argumentName>in arg value</argumentName>
     <argumentName>in arg value</argumentName>
    </u:actionName>
  </s:Body>
</s:Envelope>
```

The component event->ActionRequest contains a representation of the XML body of the request. The event provides us with the name of the action, therefore no parsing is necessary. For action SetPulseDuration, determining the value of the supplied argument is easy. We just use the "common.c" function ParseItem(), aimed at the tag <PulseDuration>, which is the argument name. The result is the supplied value. The other actions for the power service have no arguments.

If none of the action names match, then an error code of UPNP_E_INVALID_ACTION is placed in event->ErrCode. If the value of the argument to SetPulseDuration is out of range, then an error code UPNP_E_INVALID_ARGUMENT is appropriate. If the action name and any parameters pass the validity tests, then the appropriate state variables are modified. The values of the state variables are stored in a fairly obscure form in the global BlenderState—review the description of the function InitializeStateTable() if the following seems confusing. Note that if the pulse duration is set to a value larger than zero, then the blender's power is automatically turned on. A pulse duration of zero amounts to a PowerOff.

```c
// initially no error
event->ErrStr[0] = 0;

// determine which power service function is involved
if (! strcmp(event->ActionName, "PowerOn")) {
  printf("Blender: PowerOn.\n");
  strcpy(state.values[POWER_INDEX][0], "true");
}
else if (! strcmp(event->ActionName, "PowerOff")) {
  printf("Blender: PowerOff.\n");
  strcpy(state.values[POWER_INDEX][0], "false");
}
else if (! strcmp(event->ActionName, "SetPulseDuration")) {
  value = ParseItem(event->ActionRequest, NULL,
    "PulseDuration");
  if (value) {
    pulse = atoi(value);
    free(value);
    // value must be between 0 and 60
    if (pulse < 0 || pulse > 60) {
      printf("Blender: Pulse value out of range, ");
      printf("ignoring action.\n");
      err = UPNP_E_INVALID_ARGUMENT;
      strcpy(event->ErrStr, "Pulse value out of range");
    }
    else {
      sprintf(state.values[POWER_INDEX][1], "%1d", pulse);
      // blender is automatically turned on if pulse duration
      // is set to > 0
      if (pulse > 0) {
        strcpy(state.values[POWER_INDEX][0], "true");
      }
      else {
       // pulse == 0 means power off
```

```
              strcpy(state.values[POWER_INDEX][0], "false");
          }
      }
  }
  else {
    printf("Blender: Invalid pulse value, ignoring action.\n");
    err = UPNP_E_INVALID_ARGUMENT;
    strcpy(event->ErrStr, "Invalid pulse value");
  }
}
else {
  printf("Blender: Don't know anything about action %s.\n",
  event->ActionName);
  err = UPNP_E_INVALID_ACTION;
  strcpy(event->ErrStr, "Invalid action");
}
```

Now it is necessary to construct a response for the control point. The response contains the values of any "out" parameters, if such exist. None of the power service's actions have "out" parameters, so an example of constructing responses that contain "out" parameter values will be developed in the function HandleSpeedChanges(). For now, the response is quite simple to generate. We're responsible for generating the XML portion of the response between the <s:Body> and </s:Body> tags. The snip of code below handles this:

```
// construct response—we're responsible for putting some
// info into the event structure

// The format of the XML response looks like this:
//
//    <s:Envelope
//       xmlns:s="http://schemas.xmlsoap.org/soap/envelope/"
//       s:encodingStyle="http://schemas.xmlsoap.org/soap/encoding/">
//        <s:Body>
//           <u:actionNameResponse xmlns:
//              u="urn:schemas-upnp-org:service:serviceType:v">
//              <argumentName>out arg value</argumentName>
//              other out args and their values go here, if any
//           </u:actionNameResponse>
//        </s:Body>
//    </s:Envelope>
//
// We're only responsible for dealing with the portion between
// the <s:Body> and </s:Body>.  The UPnP library will add the
// rest.  If there are no out parameters, the <argumentName> ...
```

```
// </argumentName> stuff can be omitted.  None of the
// power-related actions have out parameters.

event->ErrCode = err;

if (err == UPNP_E_SUCCESS) {     // all ok
  sprintf(response, "<u:%sResponse xmlns:u=\"%s\"> </u:%sResponse>",
    event->ActionName, POWERSERVICE, event->ActionName);
  event->ActionResult = UpnpParse_Buffer(response);
  printf("Blender:  Response to action is\n\"%s\"\n", response);
}
else {    // it didn't
  event->ActionResult = NULL;
}
```

Finally, it is necessary to inform control points that have subscribed to the eventing of the power service that state variables have changed value. This is straightforward. The UPnP library tracks who has actually subscribed, so all we have to do is to make an API call that provides the values of the variables that have changed state. UpnpNotify() handles the notifications, accepting our handle, the name of the service, arrays containing state variable names and values, and a length for the arrays containing variable names/values. If for some reason the notification fails, we just diagnose the error and move on.

```
// inform control points of changes to power/pulse settings

printf("Blender: Sending notification.\n");
code = UpnpNotify(handle, state.UDN, POWERSERVICE_NAME,
    (const char **)state.variables[POWER_INDEX],
    (const char **)state.values[POWER_INDEX],  2);
if (code != UPNP_E_SUCCESS) {
  printf("Blender: Couldn't notify control points");
  printf(" during action request.\n");
  Diagnose("UpnpNotify()", __LINE__, code);
}
else {
  printf("Blender: Finished power-related action.\n");
}
}
```

HandleSpeedChanges() is the speed service analog of HandlePowerChanges(). Much of the structure is virtually identical, so we will not discuss it in detail. As with HandlePowerChanges(), the function is not thread-safe, since it is called only from HandleCommand(). One thing worth examining is the GetSpeed action, since it has an "out" parameter, unlike any of the power-related actions. For "out" parameters, we are required to do a little more work in constructing the response. As we saw in examining the HandlePowerChanges() function, we are only required to supply the portion of the response between the <s:Body> and </s:Body> tags. For GetSpeed, this XML will have the following form:

```
<u:GetSpeedResponse
  xmlns:u="urn:schemas-upnp-org:service:SpeedControl:1">
  <Speed>the current speed of the blender</Speed>
</u:GetSpeedResponse>
```

The nasty sprintf() in the code constructs this <s:Body> content. Look for it when reading the code for HandleSpeedChanges(), below:

```
/////////////////////////////
// Handle actions related to the speed service.
//
// **THIS FUNCTION IS NOT THREAD-SAFE**
// **THIS FUNCTION IS NOT THREAD-SAFE**
//
// event == encapsulation of action requested by control point
//

void HandleSpeedChanges(struct Upnp_Action_Request *event) {

  char *value=NULL;          // value of argument to service function
  char inner[512];           // out parameter portion of response
                             // (for GetSpeed)
  char response[512];        // our response to action
  int speed;                 // new blender speed
  int err=UPNP_E_SUCCESS;    // status of action
  int code;                  // return value from UPnP functions

  printf("Blender: Starting speed-related action.\n");

  // initially no error
  event->ErrStr[0] = 0;

  // inner only matters if the action is GetSpeed
  inner[0] = 0;

  // current speed as an integer
  speed = atoi(state.values[SPEED_INDEX][0]);

  // determine which speed service function is involved
```

```c
if (! strcmp(event->ActionName, "IncreaseSpeed")) {
  printf("Blender: IncreaseSpeed.\n");
  speed++;
  if (speed > 10) {
    speed = 10;
  }
  sprintf(state.values[SPEED_INDEX][0], "%1d", speed);
}
else if (! strcmp(event->ActionName, "DecreaseSpeed")) {
  printf("Blender: DecreaseSpeed.\n");
  speed--;
  if (speed < 1) {
    speed = 1;
  }
  sprintf(state.values[SPEED_INDEX][0], "%1d", speed);
}
else if (! strcmp(event->ActionName, "SetSpeed")) {
  value = ParseItem(event->ActionRequest, NULL, "Speed");
  if (value) {
    speed = atoi(value);
    free(value);
    // speed must be between 1 and 10
    if (speed < 0 || speed > 10) {
      printf("Blender: Speed value out of range, ");
      printf("ignoring action.\n");
      err = UPNP_E_INVALID_ARGUMENT;
      strcpy(event->ErrStr, "Speed value out of range");
    }
    else {
      sprintf(state.values[SPEED_INDEX][0], "%1d", speed);
    }
  }
  else {
    printf("Blender: Invalid speed value, ignoring action.\n");
    err = UPNP_E_INVALID_ARGUMENT;
    strcpy(event->ErrStr, "Invalid speed value");
  }
}
else if (! strcmp(event->ActionName, "GetSpeed")) {
  // create "inner" portion of response.  See the
  // detailed comment below about the format of a response
  // to understand this.
  sprintf(inner, "<Speed>%1d</Speed>", speed);
}
else {
  printf("Blender: Don't know anything about");
  printf(" action %s.\n", event->ActionName);
```

```
      err = UPNP_E_INVALID_ACTION;
      strcpy(event->ErrStr, "Invalid action");
}

// construct response—we're responsible for putting some
// info into the event structure

// The format of the XML response looks like this:
//
//   <s:Envelope
//      xmlns:s="http://schemas.xmlsoap.org/soap/envelope/"
//      s:encodingStyle="http://schemas.xmlsoap.org/soap/encoding/">
//        <s:Body>
//          <u:actionNameResponse
//            xmlns:u="urn:schemas-upnp-org:service:serviceType:v">
//            <argumentName>out arg value</argumentName>
//            other out args and their values go here, if any
//          </u:actionNameResponse>
//        </s:Body>
//   </s:Envelope>
//
// We're only responsible for dealing with the portion between
// the <s:Body> and </s:Body>.  The
// UPnP library will add the rest.  Only the GetSpeed
// speed-related action has an out parameter.
// For GetSpeed, 'inner' below will describe the out
// parameter Speed.  For others, it's the empty string.

event->ErrCode = err;

if (err == UPNP_E_SUCCESS) {     // all ok
  sprintf(response,
    "<u:%sResponse xmlns:u=\"%s\">%s</u:%sResponse>",
   event->ActionName, SPEEDSERVICE, inner, event->ActionName);
    event->ActionResult = UpnpParse_Buffer(response);
  printf("Blender:  Response to action is\n\"%s\"\n", response);
}
else {    // it didn't
  event->ActionResult = NULL;
}

// inform control points of changes to speed setting if the
// action wasn't GetSpeed
if (inner[0] == 0) {
  printf("Blender: Sending notification.\n");
  code = UpnpNotify(handle, state.UDN, SPEEDSERVICE_NAME,
      (const char **)state.variables[SPEED_INDEX],
      (const char **)state.values[SPEED_INDEX],
```

```
      1);
  if (code != UPNP_E_SUCCESS) {
    printf("Blender: Couldn't notify control points");
    printf(" during action request.\n");
    Diagnose("UpnpNotify()", __LINE__, code);
  }
}

printf("Blender: Finished speed-related action.\n");
}
```

This is more of the same! HandleBowlChanges() handles the SetContents and GetContents actions associated with the contents service in the blender. The structure is very similar to that of HandleSpeed-Changes().

```
/////////////////////////////////
// Handle actions related to the bowl service.
//
// **THIS FUNCTION IS NOT THREAD-SAFE**
// **THIS FUNCTION IS NOT THREAD-SAFE**
//
// event == encapsulation of action requested by control point
//

void HandleBowlChanges(struct Upnp_Action_Request *event) {

  char *value=NULL;    // value of argument to service function
  char inner[512];     // out parameter portion of
                       // response (for GetContents)
  char response[512];  // our response to action
  int err=UPNP_E_SUCCESS;   // status of action
  int code;                 // return value from UPnP functions


  printf("Blender: Starting contents-related action.\n");

  // initially no error
  event->ErrStr[0] = 0;

  // inner only matters if the action is GetContents
  inner[0] = 0;

  // determine which bowl service function is involved
  if (! strcmp(event->ActionName, "SetContents")) {
    value = ParseItem(event->ActionRequest, NULL, "Contents");
    if (value) {
```

```
      // probably should check the length!
      strcpy(state.values[BOWL_INDEX][0], value);
      free(value);
    }
    else {
      printf("Blender: No value for Contents provided, ");
      printf(" ignoring action.\n");
      err = UPNP_E_INVALID_ARGUMENT;
      strcpy(event->ErrStr, "Invalid contents value");
    }
  }
  else if (! strcmp(event->ActionName, "GetContents")) {
    // create "inner" portion of response.  See the detailed
    // comment below about the format of a response to
    // understand this.
    sprintf(inner, "<Contents>%s</Contents>",
      state.values[BOWL_INDEX][0]);
  }
  else {
    printf("Blender: Don't know anything about action %s.\n",
      event->ActionName);
    err = UPNP_E_INVALID_ACTION;
    strcpy(event->ErrStr, "Invalid action");
  }

  // construct response—we're responsible for putting some info
  // into the event structure

  // The format of the XML response looks like this:
  //
  //   <s:Envelope
  //     xmlns:s="http://schemas.xmlsoap.org/soap/envelope/"
  //     s:encodingStyle="http://schemas.xmlsoap.org/soap/encoding/">
  //        <s:Body>
  //           <u:actionNameResponse xmlns:
  //              u="urn:schemas-upnp-org:service:serviceType:v">
  //              <argumentName>out arg value</argumentName>
  //              other out args and their values go here, if any
  //           </u:actionNameResponse>
  //        </s:Body>
  //   </s:Envelope>
  //
  // We're only responsible for dealing with the portion between
  // the <s:Body> and </s:Body>.  The UPnP library will add the
  // rest.  Only the GetContents speed-related action has an out
  // parameter.  For GetContents, 'inner' below will describe the
  // out parameter Contents.  For others, it's the empty string.

  event->ErrCode = err;
```

```
if (err == UPNP_E_SUCCESS) {      // all ok
  sprintf(response,
    "<u:%sResponse xmlns:u=\"%s\">%s</u:%sResponse>",
    event->ActionName, BOWLSERVICE, inner, event->ActionName);
  event->ActionResult =fer(response);
  printf("Blender:  Response to action is\n\"%s\"\n", response);
}
else {    // it didn't
  event->ActionResult = NULL;
}

// inform control points of changes to bowl setting if the action
// wasn't GetContents.

if (inner[0] == 0) {
  printf("Blender: Sending notification.\n");
  code = UpnpNotify(handle, state.UDN, BOWLSERVICE_NAME,
    (const char **)state.variables[BOWL_INDEX],
    (const char **)state.values[BOWL_INDEX], 1);
  if (code != UPNP_E_SUCCESS) {
    printf("Blender: Couldn't notify control points during");
    printf(" action request.\n");
    Diagnose("UpnpNotify()", __LINE__, code);
  }
}

printf("Blender: Finished contents-related action.\n");
}
```

Now we come to the code that makes a blender feel good—the ability to whirl things round and round. The BlendLoop() function runs in a separate thread, sleeping most of the time, but waking every 5 s to see if there's any blending to do. When it wakes, if the blender's power is off, it just goes back to sleep. If the blender's power is on but the pulse duration is zero (this means the blender is in a constantly on mode, rather than a timed-on mode), the blender churns the contents of the bowl. Otherwise, if the pulse duration of the blender is nonzero, the blender is considered on, but this value is decremented. When the pulse duration reaches zero, the blender is powered down. In any event, if the pulse mode of the blender is being used, a notification is sent to subscribed control points to reflect changes in the blender's state.

To make things more interesting, and to emulate a real blender, the contents of the blender's bowl are churned more or less vigorously depending on the speed setting. This is handled by a for loop that chooses random characters in the blender's contents and scrambles them, more or fewer times per sleep cycle depending on the blender's current speed. For example, at blender speed == 3, an AVOCADO placed into the blender goes through transitions:

AVOCADO —> AVOCDAO —> VAOODCA —> VODAACO —> OVDOACA.

At speed 10, an AVOCADO becomes guacamole much faster, although of course this point is moot, because everyone knows you're supposed to use a *mortar* to make guacamole, not a blender:

AVOCADO —> VAOAODC —> VODACAO —> OADACVO —> ADOAVOC

But that's enough about avocados.

```
///////////////////////////////
// This function runs in a thread, decrementing the pulse duration
// every five seconds (if the blender is on) and swirling the
// contents.  Events are sent to interested clients to inform
// of pulse duration, power, and bowl contents changes.  Note
// that five seconds is used instead of one second to avoid spewing
// lots of info constantly at the control point—this makes it
// easier to digest what's happening.  In effect, the virtual
// blender operates at 1/5 speed.
//
void *BlendLoop(void *args) {

   int pulse; // int representation of pulse duration state var
   int speed; // int representation of current blender speed
   int len;   // length of current blender contents
              // (OK, it's just a string!)
   int r1, r2;  // indices of characters to swirl in the
                // blender's bowl
   char temp;
   int code;     // return value from UPnP functions

   while (1) {
      // pulse duration must be decremented every iteration,
      // if blender is on.  We cheat and adjust
      // this to every 5 seconds, so the observer has a better
      // chance of digesting the output...so to speak.
      printf("Blender: Blend thread sleeping.\n");
      sleep(5);
      printf("Blender: Blend thread awake.\n");

      // lock device state
      pthread_mutex_lock(&mutex);

   // is the blender on?
```

```
if (! strcmp(state.values[POWER_INDEX][0], "true")) {
  // is there a positive pulse duration?  If so, the blender
  // remains on for this period of time, then shuts off
  pulse = atoi(state.values[POWER_INDEX][1]);
  if (pulse) {
    pulse—;
    sprintf(state.values[POWER_INDEX][1], "%1d", pulse);

  // time to power off?
  if (! pulse) {
    // power off
    strcpy(state.values[POWER_INDEX][0], "false");
  }

  // inform control points of changes to pulse/power settings.
  // The final argument to UpnpNotify() is 2 because the
  // power service has two state variables.

  code = UpnpNotify(handle, state.UDN, POWERSERVICE_NAME,
  (const char **)state.variables[POWER_INDEX],
  (const char **)state.values[POWER_INDEX], 2);
}

// swirl the contents more if the speed is higher.
// Only do this if something is in the blender and that
// something isn't "EMPTY"
len = strlen(state.values[BOWL_INDEX][0]);
if (len && strcmp(state.values[BOWL_INDEX][0], "EMPTY")) {
printf("Blender: Blend thread blending!!\n");
for (speed = atoi(state.values[SPEED_INDEX][0]);
  speed > 0; speed—) {
  // swirl random characters
  r1 = random() % len;
  r2 = random() % len;
  temp = state.values[BOWL_INDEX][0][r1];
  state.values[BOWL_INDEX][0][r1] =
    state.values[BOWL_INDEX][0][r2];
  state.values[BOWL_INDEX][0][r2] = temp;
}

// only report contents change if there's something in the bowl. The
// following notifies all control points of the change.  The final
// argument is 1 because the bowl contents service has a single state
// variable.

  code = UpnpNotify(handle, state.UDN, BOWLSERVICE_NAME,
    (const char **)state.variables[BOWL_INDEX],
    (const char **)state.values[BOWL_INDEX],  1);
```

```
    }
  }
  else {
    // nothing to do if blender is off
    printf("Blender: thread going to sleep, blender is off.\n");
  }

  // unlock, then back to sleep
  pthread_mutex_unlock(&mutex);
}

return NULL;
}
```

The function SignalHandler(), below, sets up a handler to catch control-C. If the user types control-C, then the Shutdown() function is called to allow the blender to gracefully leave the network. Note that this function blocks using sigwait(). The main() function relies on this behavior to prevent the blender from terminating immediately!

```
/////////////////////////////
// deal with control-C
//

void SignalHandler() {

  int sig;
  // signal handling stuff (for handling shutdown)
  sigset_t sigs_to_catch;
  sigemptyset(&sigs_to_catch);
  sigaddset(&sigs_to_catch, SIGINT);
  sigwait(&sigs_to_catch, &sig);
  Shutdown("Shutting down.");
}
```

The final function in "blender.c" is Shutdown(), which performs the graceful exit mentioned in the discussion of SignalHandler(). Shutdown() is also called at other points during blender execution, as a response to fatal errors. The SDK function UpnpUnRegisterRootDevice() performs the opposite duty of UpnpRegisterRootDevice()—it releases resources allocated to this root device. UpnpFinish() is the final straw—after calling this function, we are not allowed to use other SDK functions.

```
//////////////////////////////
// Do a clean shutdown.   Unregister the root device (if we
// got that far) and then call UpnpFinish() before dying.
//
// reason == reason we're shutting down.
//

void Shutdown(char *reason) {

    printf("Wait...\n");
    if (handle >= 0) {
        UpnpUnRegisterRootDevice(handle);
    }
    UpnpFinish();
    printf("%s\n", reason);
    exit(0);
}
```

And Here's More: A Control Point for the UPnP Blender

To illustrate the design of a UPnP control point, we look at the counterpart for the UPnP blender implementation—a client that controls the blender functions. It turns out that the control point is substantially more complicated than the device itself, which might seem strange; but much of the complexity in a control point lies in dealing with the XML documents supplied by devices to specify their characteristics. As discussed easlier, the Intel UPnP SDK contains a sophisticated XML parser and uses a powerful XML document representation model called DOM. We managed to need surprisingly little of this functionality in the UPnP blender implementation, but this will change dramatically as we examine code for a UPnP blender control point. The code for the control point lives in a file "blender_ctrlpt.c".

The preface of "blender_ctrlpt.c", which defines constants, types, and prototypes, is shown below. There's a comment at the top of the control point code related to the XML processing of the SDK that really should be taken to heart: Great care must be used in dealing with the XML-related types and functions. In examining the source code for the UPnP blender, only one of these types was encountered, the Upnp_Document. But there are several others, including Upnp_Node, Upnp_NodeList, etc., that represent components of an XML document. The first gotcha is that most of these "types" are actually just #defined to be void* pointers. Thus declarations like "Upnp_Node a, b, c" are a definite no-no. Instead, separate declarations must be used. Another issue, and this one was briefly touched upon in the device implementation, is that when functions in the SDK return instances of these XML-related types, it is the responsibility of the caller to free associated storage when it is no longer needed. There is a function associated with each of the various types [say, UpnpNode_free()] for this purpose, and accidentally calling the wrong one results in disaster. The XML parser is written in C++ and peeks through a C wrapper; and not only is calling free() on a Upnp_Node (or whatever) not appropriate, but calling the wrong UpnpXXX_free() causes the underlying C++ function to have a heart attack. This invariably kills your control point in a most dreadful fashion.

```
// UPnP Virtual Blender control point main source file.
// Written by Golden G. Richard III, Ph.D.  May 2001
//
// Warnings to UPnP hackers:
//
// (1)
// The various UPnP "types" (e.g., Upnp_Document,
// Upnp_NodeList, etc.) in the Intel
// Linux SDK aren't really types...they're #defines.
// This means that
//
//          Upnp_NodeList a, b, c;
//
// style declarations aren't OK!    Instead:
//
//          Upnp_NodeList a;
//          Upnp_NodeList b;
//          Upnp_NodeList c;
//
// (2)
// It's critically important that the proper_free functions
// be called to  free storage associated with UPnP data
// structures.    e.g, :
//
//      UpnpNodeList_free() for lists of nodes
//          UpnpDocument_free(doc) for document references, etc.
//
// Failing to use the proper one (or just calling free()) will
// result in disaster.
//
```

```c
#include <stdio.h>
#include <stdlib.h>
#include <string.h>
#include <unistd.h>
#include <signal.h>
#include <pthread.h>
#include "common.h"
#include "prioque.h"

// interesting constants
#define REG_TIMEOUT    1800          // registration duration
#define true 1
#define false 0

// control how much output is displayed

// define to display info about ALL callbacks
#undef SHOW_EVENT_INFO

// UPnP devices send lots of events that can be
// ignored—for example,  advertisements are sent not only
// for the root device, but for all services, etc.  If the
// following is defined, a "we're ignoring this"
// message is printed for such events, otherwise such events are
// silently ignored.
#undef  MENTION_IGNORED_EVENTS

// define blender device type we'll search for
char BLENDER_TYPE[] = "urn:schemas-upnp-org:device:blender:1";

// define types of blender device's services
char POWERSERVICE[] ="urn:schemas-upnp-org:service:PowerSwitch:1";
char SPEEDSERVICE[] ="urn:schemas-upnp-org:service:SpeedControl:1";
char BOWLSERVICE[] ="urn:schemas-upnp-org:service:Bowl:1";

// types
typedef struct blender_service {
  char service_id[NAME_SIZE];        // id of service
  char service_type[NAME_SIZE];      // type of service
  char eventURL[NAME_SIZE];          // event subscription URL
  char controlURL[NAME_SIZE];        // control URL for service
  char SID[NAME_SIZE];               // subscription ID
  int timeout;                       // actual timeout for registration
} BlenderService;

typedef struct blender_device {
  char UDN[NAME_SIZE];               // unique name of device
  char descriptionURL[NAME_SIZE];    // URL for description document
```

```
      char friendly[NAME_SIZE];      // human-readable name of device
      char presentationURL[NAME_SIZE];// URL for presentation document
      int  expiration;               // timeout in device advertisement
      BlenderService power;          // power switch for blender
      BlenderService speed;          // speed control
      BlenderService bowl;           // service for blender contents
} BlenderDevice;

// function prototypes for blender_ctrlpt.c functions
int main(int argc, char** argv);
int CallbackHandler(Upnp_EventType type, void *event, void *cookie);
void SearchForBlenders(void);
void AddBlender(struct Upnp_Discovery *event);
void RemoveBlender(struct Upnp_Discovery *event);
int GetServiceInfo(Upnp_NodeList services, char *baseURL,
   char *name, BlenderService *service);
int SubscribeService(BlenderService *service);
void ShowMenu(void);
void *CommandLoop(void *args);
void *TimerLoop(void *args);
char *GetBlenderString(void);
void PutBlenderString(char *contents);
void SetCurrentBlender(void);
void ForgetAllBlenders(void);
void PrintBlenderDetails(BlenderDevice dev);
int ListBlenders(void);
void SetPulse(int pulse);
void SetPower(int power);
void SetSpeed(int speed);
int GetSpeed();
Upnp_Document SendAction(char *servtype, BlenderService service,
   char *func,  char **args, char **values, int numargs);
void QueryStateVariable(void);
void HandleGENAEvent(struct Upnp_Event *event);
void SignalHandler();
void Shutdown(char *reason);
int CompareBlenders(void *b1, void *b2);

// globals

// Since callbacks are used to inform the blender of interested events
// (e.g., power on/off), a semaphore must be used to protect important
// state.  The following semaphore should be used to lock global
// state before touching it!

pthread_mutex_t mutex=PTHREAD_MUTEX_INITIALIZER;
UpnpClient_Handle handle=-1;
// blender control point's device handle
Queue device_list;
```

```
// list of discovered blender devices
BlenderDevice *current=NULL;
// pointer to currently selected blender device in list
int done=false;
// controls death of command loop thread
```

The main() function of the blender control point serves as a good model for most control points. The first significant thing is the initialization of a queue for storing information about discovered blenders. Unlike devices, where at the coding level we weren't particularly concerned with which control points were interacting with us, control points must track the identities of devices they find interesting. In the UPnP blender control point, we use a queue package written in C. Source code for that package is presented at the end of the chapter; in general, the queuing functions do standard things. The init_queue() function takes four parameters: the address of the queue being initialized, the size (in bytes) of the object type that will be stored in the queue, a boolean indicating whether duplicates are allowed, and a function for comparing items placed in the queue for equality. Not allowing duplicates will have significant benefits later: When we want to overwrite information about a blender, we can simply add the blender to the queue, and the queuing package will automatically remove duplicates. The next bit of code parses the command line arguments, which are the IP address of the control point and the port on which it listens.

```
/////////////////////////////////
// main function—parse command line, initialize and register control
// point, start a thread to handle interactive commands, and deal with
// shutdown via control-C.

int main(int argc, char** argv) {

  int port;                 // port on which we listen for messages
  int code;                 // return value from UPnP functions
  char *ip=NULL;            // IP address for this device
  pthread_t timer_thread;
  pthread_t cmdloop_thread;

  if (argc != 3) {
    printf("Usage: blender_ctrlpt IP port\n");
    exit(1);
  }

   // initialize list of discovered blenders
  init_queue(&device_list, sizeof(BlenderDevice), false,
    CompareBlenders);
```

```
ip=argv[1];
sscanf(argv[2],"%d",&port);
```

The call to UpnpInit() is the same as that for devices—it initializes the library and must be called before any other UPnP functions. If this call fails, the error is fatal and the control point dies after a diagnosis of the error.

```
// UpnpInit() must be called before any other UPnP functions are used
printf("BlenderCP: Calling UpnpInit().\n");
if ((code = UpnpInit(ip, port)) != UPNP_E_SUCCESS) {
  Diagnose("UpnpInit()", __LINE__, code);
  Shutdown("Can't continue.");
}
```

The next call is to UpnpRegisterClient(), which is the control point's analog to UpnpRegisterRootDevice(). The first argument is the callback function that will be used to deliver interesting events to the control point from the UPnP library. The second argument is the address of a UpnpClient_Handle. The third is a pointer to a "cookie," which is passed to the callback function as identification. In this case we just pass the address of the our soon-to-be-assigned handle. This control point doesn't use the cookie, so NULL would work just as well. Failure of this call to UpnpRegisterClient() is a fatal error.

```
// Register with UPnP
printf("BlenderCP: Calling UpnpRegisterClient().\n");
if ((code = UpnpRegisterClient(CallbackHandler,
  &handle, &handle)) != UPNP_E_SUCCESS) {
    Diagnose("UpnpRegisterClient()", __LINE__, code);
    Shutdown("Can't continue.");
}
```

The control point uses two threads: one to monitor time-related issues (such as when information about interesting devices is about to expire) and one to handle interaction with the user. These threads are started below. TimerLoop() and CommandLoop() are the functions containing the thread bodies. After creation of the threads, the control point initialization is complete. The next thing to do is to find some blenders with which to interact. The function SearchForBlenders() handles the search process. The final call in main() is to SignalHandler(), which blocks and waits for a control-C.

```
// start threads to handle timer events and interaction with user
code = pthread_create(&timer_thread, NULL, TimerLoop, NULL);
code = pthread_create(&cmdloop_thread, NULL, CommandLoop, NULL);

printf("BlenderCP: Initialization successful.  Use Control-C");
printf(" or QUIT to shut down.\n");

// find some blenders!
printf("BlenderCP: Now searching for Blender devices...\n");
SearchForBlenders();

// handle control-C
SignalHandler();
return 0;

}
```

Next we examine the commands that the blender control point provides for interacting with blenders. These commands are listed in the ShowMenu() function below. Commands 1 through 7 require that a current blender be selected. Command 8 is used to list the blenders discovered to date. Command 9 allows a current blender to be selected from the list of discovered blenders. When a new current blender is chosen, all blender eventing services are subscribed to, so interesting state changes will be propagated to us. Command V allows an arbitrary state variable to be queried and also requires that a current blender be selected. Finally, command 0 can be used to shut down the control point.

```
/////////////////////////////
// Display available commands

void ShowMenu() {

    printf("\nOptions:\n");
    printf("[1]\tTurn blender OFF\n");
    printf("[2]\tTurn blender ON\n");
    printf("[3]\tSet PULSE duration\n");
    printf("[4]\tSet blender SPEED\n");
    printf("[5]\tGet blender SPEED\n");
    printf("[6]\tPut a string into the blender\n");
    printf("[7]\tGet the string in the blender\n");
    printf("[8]\tList discovered blenders\n");
    printf("[9]\tSet current blender\n");
```

```
    printf("[V]\tQuery state variable\n");
    printf("[0]\tEXIT\n");
}
```

The following function runs in a separate thread [created in main()], displaying the menu above and prompting the user to select a command. If the user attempts to use a function that requires a blender to be currently selected and no blender is selected, then an error message is displayed and no further action is taken. Otherwise, an appropriate control point function is executed to handle the command. If the user selects 0 (exit), then Shutdown() is called and the control point dies gracefully.

```
//////////////////////////////////
// Handle commands from the user
//
// No arguments expected, no meaningful return value.
// This function is run in a separate thread.

void *CommandLoop(void *args) {

  char cmd=-1;
  char *contents;    // return value from GetBlenderString()
  printf("BlenderCP: Welcome, O Controller of the Blender.\n");
  while (! done) {
    ShowMenu();
    cmd=-1;
    while ((cmd < '0' || cmd > '9') && cmd != 'V' && cmd != 'v') {
      printf("\nEnter # of command or H to list: ");
      cmd = getchar();
      getchar();   // eat newline!
      printf("BlenderCP: %c\n", cmd);
      if (cmd == 'H' || cmd == 'h') {
        ShowMenu();
      }
    }

    // almost all options require that a current blender be
    // selected.  But can't  touch 'current' without a lock!

    // lock global data
    pthread_mutex_lock(&mutex);

      if ((cmd == 'V' || cmd == 'v' || (cmd > '0' && cmd < '8'))
        && current == NULL) {
        printf("BlenderCP: Must select a blender first!\n");
        // unlock global data
```

```c
      pthread_mutex_unlock(&mutex);
      continue;
    }
    // unlock global data
    pthread_mutex_unlock(&mutex);

    switch (cmd) {
    case '1':
      SetPower(false); break;
    case '2':
      SetPower(true); break;
    case '3':
      {
        int pulse=-1;
        while (pulse < 0 || pulse > 60) {
          printf("Enter PULSE duration (0-60 secs) : ");
          scanf("%d", &pulse);
        }
        SetPulse(pulse);
      }
      break;
    case '4':
      {
        int speed=-1;
        while (speed < 1 || speed > 10) {
          printf("Enter SPEED (1-10) : ");
          scanf("%d", &speed);
        }
        SetSpeed(speed);
      }
      break;
    case '5':
      printf("Blender speed = %d\n", GetSpeed());
      break;
    case '6':
      {
        char blend[200];
        printf("Enter string to put into the blender");
        printf(" (< 100 chars)\n> ");
        gets(blend);
        PutBlenderString(blend);
      }
      break;
    case '7':
      contents = GetBlenderString();
      if (contents) {
        printf("BlenderCP: Blender contents = %s\n", contents);
```

```
      free(contents);
    }
    else {
      printf("BlenderCP: Couldn't get contents.\n");
    }
    break;
  case '8':
    ListBlenders();
    break;
  case '9':
    SetCurrentBlender();
    break;
  case 'V':
  case 'v':
    QueryStateVariable();
    break;
  case '0':
    done=true;
    break;
  }
}
Shutdown("Thanks for blending.\n");
return NULL;
}
```

SearchForBlenders() is called to begin searching for UPnP blender devices. Because of the callback function (and as discussed in the case of UPnP devices) it will generally be necessary to lock the global control point state before accessing it. Notice that we *don't* lock the control point state in SearchForBlenders(); we use the UpnpSearchAsync() function to begin discovery, which multicasts discovery messages. Any responses will be returned via our callback function. Thus no global control point state is modified here.

UpnpSearchAsync() takes four arguments. The first is our control point handle. The second is the number of seconds we're willing to wait for a response. Devices can use this value to stagger their responses, by introducing random delays. This helps to avoid reply storms. The third is the device type, which in this case is defined by BLENDER_TYPE, a global declared at the top of "blender_ctrlpt.c". The fourth allows a cookie to be specified that will be returned when a discovery event is delivered via our callback function. We just pass NULL, as this functionality is not needed. If the call to search for blenders fails, we just die. Note that an error from UpnpSearchAsync() isn't an indication that there are no blenders, but rather something more serious. And it's no fun being a control point if you have nothing to control.

```
/////////////////////////////
// Search for blenders.  We use the asynchronous search function
// UpnpSearchAsync().  Notifications for discovered blenders
// will come through our callback function CallbackHandler().

void SearchForBlenders() {

  int code;     // return value from UPnP functions

  // Search (again?). We're looking for all root devices
  // of type Blender and are willing to wait 10 seconds for
  // a response.  The last argument to  UpnpSearchAsync()
  // allows a 'cookie' (a bit of data) to be specified that will
  // be passed back to us in a callback when devices are
  // discovered—we don't need this here, so NULL is passed.
  //  Nothing thread-unsafe about this call, so no locks.

  code = UpnpSearchAsync(handle, 10, BLENDER_TYPE, NULL);

  // it's a BAD thing if we don't get a good return value-this
  // just initiates discovery.

  if (code != UPNP_E_SUCCESS) {
    Diagnose("SearchForBlenders()", __LINE__, code);
    Shutdown("Can't continue.");
  }
}
```

At the top of the "blender_ctrlpt.c" source file, there's a type definition for BlenderDevice (struct blender_device). This struct stores information about a particular blender, parsed from the device's XML description document, including the unique device name (UDN), friendly name, description and presentation URLs, and information about device services. Information about each service is stored in a BlenderService structure (which is a struct blender_service). The following function is a good introduction to the BlenderDevice type, as it prints out all the relevant information. This function is called when a new blender is discovered, so that the user is provided with all the juicy bits.

```
/////////////////////////////
// Print details for a blender.
//
// dev == the blender description to display.
//

void PrintBlenderDetails(BlenderDevice dev) {

  printf("UDN:              %s\n", dev.UDN);
```

```
printf("Friendly name:      %s\n", dev.friendly);
printf("Description URL:    %s\n", dev.descriptionURL);
printf("Presentation URL:   %s\n", dev.presentationURL);
printf("Device expiration: %d\n", dev.expiration);
printf("Available services:\n");
printf("  %s\n", POWERSERVICE);
printf("        Service ID:          %s\n", dev.power.service_id);
printf("        Event URL:           %s\n", dev.power.eventURL);
printf("        Control URL:         %s\n", dev.power.controlURL);
printf("        Subscription ID:     %s\n", dev.power.SID);
printf("        Timeout:            %d\n", dev.power.timeout);
printf("  %s\n", SPEEDSERVICE);
printf("        Service ID:          %s\n", dev.speed.service_id);
printf("        Event URL:           %s\n", dev.speed.eventURL);
printf("        Control URL:         %s\n", dev.speed.controlURL);
printf("        Subscription ID:     %s\n", dev.speed.SID);
printf("        Timeout:            %d\n", dev.speed.timeout);
printf("  %s\n", BOWLSERVICE);
printf("        Service ID:          %s\n", dev.bowl.service_id);
printf("        Event URL:           %s\n", dev.bowl.eventURL);
printf("        Control URL:         %s\n", dev.bowl.controlURL);
printf("        Subscription ID:     %s\n", dev.bowl.SID);
printf("        Timeout:            %d\n", dev.bowl.timeout);
}
```

The following is the callback function registered via UpnpRegister-Client() in the main() function. All asynchronous notifications from the UPnP library come through this function. The UPnP library provides synchronous and asynchronous versions of many functions. Examples include UpnpGetServiceVarStatusAsync(), UpnpGetServiceVarStatus() for determining the current value of a control variable, UpnpSendActionAsync(), UpnpSendAction() for executing an action, etc. The XXXXAsync() version of the function returns a useful result via the callback function, whereas its counterpart returns the result directly. In the implementation of the blender's control point, we use the synchronous versions of most functions, which means that the callback function is used only rarely. A notable exception is for discovery, where only UpnpSearchAsync() is available. To assist developers who wish to use the asynchronous versions of the UPnP functions, additional "inactive" skeletal code is included in the callback function below. This code indicates where asynchronous results would be returned had we had used asynchronous versions of the functions in the implementation.

```
/////////////////////////////
// All asynchronous notifications of interesting events come
// through this handler.  This guy is the reason that a semaphore
// has to be used to lock global state before accessing it!
// For each event type, hand off processing to an appropriate
// function, unless only a few lines of code are required.
//
// type == type of event that occurred
// event == the event description
// cookie == data we specified during registration of the callback

int CallbackHandler(Upnp_EventType type, void *event,
  void *cookie) {

    // print lots of information about the incoming event

#if defined(SHOW_EVENTS)
  ReportEvent(type, event, true);
#endif

    // the following are the only events of interest for a
    // control point; devices will respond to other events
```

The following switch exhausts the various types of callback that control points receive. For UPNP_DISCOVERY_ADVERTISEMENT_ALIVE and UPNP_DISCOVERY_SEARCH_RESULT, AddBlender() is called. This function deals with devices renewing expirations on their discovery information (former) and devices responding to discovery messages (latter). There is no synchronous version of the discovery function for control points, so this is the only way that we learn about new devices. The UPNP_DISCOVERY_SEARCH_TIMEOUT callback reports that no devices have been found within the timeout period specified in a call to UpnpSearchAsync(); we don't care about this. This would be a good place to alert the user in situations where locating services is critical. We're type-B; we just continue to wait for blenders to arrive.

```
switch (type) {

    // new device discovered, either through a search or
    // receipt of an advertisement.
    // We DO use an asynchronous Upnp search function,
    // UpnpSearchAsync().  For most other things, such as
    // changing state variables, etc., we do synchronous
    // calls.
case UPNP_DISCOVERY_ADVERTISEMENT_ALIVE:
```

```
case UPNP_DISCOVERY_SEARCH_RESULT:
  AddBlender((struct Upnp_Discovery *)event);
  break;

  // nothing found within specified timeout
case UPNP_DISCOVERY_SEARCH_TIMEOUT:
  // nothing to do here
    break;
```

The UPNP_DISCOVERY_ADVERTISEMENT_BYEBYE (yes, it does sound a little silly) callback warns us of a device leaving a UPnP network. The RemoveBlender() function is called to remove information about this device and deal with the case where the disappearing blender is the currently selected one.

```
  // a device is saying goodbye—forget about the device
case UPNP_DISCOVERY_ADVERTISEMENT_BYEBYE:
  RemoveBlender((struct Upnp_Discovery *)event);
  break;
```

The GENA protocol is used to notify control points when state variables change value. The HandleGENAEvent() function parses the notification and informs the user of the state variable changes.

```
  // this is a GENA event that alerts us that state variables
  // have changed value
case UPNP_EVENT_RECEIVED:
  HandleGENAEvent((struct Upnp_Event *)event);
  break;
```

We don't expect the following to occur at all, since the UPnP library does automatic renewal of subscriptions to service eventing. These callbacks are used to alert the control point that a failure in the automatic renewal has occurred, and in the extreme case that a subscription has been allowed to expire. For critical applications it might be appropriate to take an action, such as attempting to resubscribe, here.

```
  // we receive these events when autorenewal of service
  // subscriptions fails.  The autorenewal of service
  // subscriptions by the UPnP SDK makes our life very easy.
  // The default autorenewal period is 35 seconds, which is
  // much less than our requested expiration time, so these
  // events should never occur unless the service is being shut
  // down.  Note that autorenewal is not mandated by the UPnP
  // specification, so it's  possible that some SDKs will not
```

```
      // do the work for you!
case UPNP_EVENT_AUTORENEWAL_FAILED:
case UPNP_EVENT_SUBSCRIPTION_EXPIRED:

   printf("!!!!! Service subscription expired !!!!!!\n");
   break;
```

The following callback types are issued only when asynchronous SDK functions are used:

UPNP_CONTROL_ACTION_COMPLETE

UPNP_CONTROL_GET_VAR_COMPLETE:

UPNP_EVENT_SUBSCRIBE_COMPLETE

UPNP_EVENT_UNSUBSCRIBE_COMPLETE

UPNP_EVENT_RENEWAL_COMPLETE

This code is included to assist developers interested in using the asynchronous functions. Whenever possible, the UPnP blender control point uses the synchronous version of the function, so we don't expect to get these callbacks.

```
   // asynchronous notification of the status of an earlier
   // action; generally only care about this if an error
   // occurred.  Code for checking the error return is
   // provided here as an example, but we don't expect
   // this kind of event, since we do actions synchronously using
   // UpnpSendAction() rather than UpnpSendActionAsync().
case UPNP_CONTROL_ACTION_COMPLETE:
   {
     struct Upnp_Action_Complete *a_event =
       (struct Upnp_Action_Complete *) event;
     if (a_event->ErrCode != UPNP_E_SUCCESS) {
       printf("BlenderCP: An asynchronous action completed");
       printf(" but returned an error.\n");
       Diagnose("CallbackHandler()", __LINE__, a_event->ErrCode);
     }
     printf("BlenderCP: Not expecting asynchronous action");
     printf(" notifications?\n");
   }
   break;

   // asynchronous notification of the completion of a state
   // variable query; generally only care about this if an
   // error occurred.  Code for checking the error return is
   // provided here, but we don't expect this kind of event,
   // since we do queries synchronously using
```

```
    // UpnpGetServiceVarStatus() rather than
    // UpnpGetServiceVarStatusAsync().
    // If the latter IS used, the important variables in the
    // UpnpState_Var_Complete event, other than the error code, are
    // StateVarName (name of the variable) and CurrentVal (its value).
case UPNP_CONTROL_GET_VAR_COMPLETE:
    {
        struct Upnp_State_Var_Complete *sv_event =
          (struct Upnp_State_Var_Complete *) event;
        if (sv_event->ErrCode != UPNP_E_SUCCESS){
          printf("BlenderCP: An asynchronous state var query");
          printf(" returned an error.\n");
          Diagnose("CallbackHandler()", __LINE__, sv_event->ErrCode);
        }
        printf("BlenderCP: Not expecting asynchronous state var");
        printf(" query notifications?\n");
    }
    break;

    // asynchronous notification of completion of subscribe/unsubscribe.
    // As for control variable queries, etc. we use the synchronous
    // versions of subscribe and unsubscribe, so we don't expect to
    // receive these events.  If UpnpSubscribeAsync() and
    // UpnpUnSubscribeAsync() are used, then this is the
    // place to know that the subscribe/unsubscribe attempt
    // completed.  The error code evaluation code below is
    // provided for illustrative purposes only.
case UPNP_EVENT_SUBSCRIBE_COMPLETE:
case UPNP_EVENT_UNSUBSCRIBE_COMPLETE:
    {
        struct Upnp_Event_Subscribe *es_event =
          (struct Upnp_Event_Subscribe *)event;
        if (es_event->ErrCode != UPNP_E_SUCCESS) {
          printf("BlenderCP: An asynchronous subscribe/unsubscribe");
          printf(" returned an error.\n");
          Diagnose("CallbackHandler()", __LINE__,
            es_event->ErrCode);
        }
        printf("BlenderCP: Not expecting asynchronous");
        printf(" subscription notifications?\n");
    }
    break;

    // asynchronous notifiction of renewal completion.  Again,
    // we use the synchronous versions so don't expect to see
    // these events.
case UPNP_EVENT_RENEWAL_COMPLETE:
    {
```

```
      struct Upnp_Event_Renewal *er_event = (
        struct Upnp_Event_Renewal *)event;
      if (er_event->ErrCode != UPNP_E_SUCCESS) {
        printf("BlenderCP: An asynchronous renewal returned");
        printf(" an error.\n");
        Diagnose("CallbackHandler()", __LINE__,
          er_event->ErrCode);
      }
      printf("BlenderCP: Not expecting asynchronous");
      printf(" renewal notifications?\n");
    }
    break;

  default:
    printf("BlenderCP: Don't know why I received that event!!\n");
    break;
  }
  return(0);
}
```

AddBlender() is a long one; this function is called when a device advertisement is heard. It first verifies that the device type is appropriate. If it is, then a check is made to see if it's a blender we already know about. If this is true, then the expiration time associated with the device information (description document, etc.) is updated. This means that a previously discovered device has readvertised its availability, possibly after prompting from a control point [when device information is about to expire, control points send additional discovery messages to force a readvertisement; see the TimerLoop() for more details]. Otherwise, the description document for the new blender is downloaded using UpnpDownloadXmlDoc(), which takes a URL and the address of a Upnp_Document. Parsing the description document makes heavy use of the "common.c" function ParseItem(), which accepts a tag name (e.g., "friendlyName") and returns the corresponding value from an XML document or document element.

```
/////////////////////////////////
// Add a discovered blender, whose identity is encapsulated in
// 'event', to our  list (if the advertised device is in fact
// a blender!)
//
// event == discovery event from callback function

void AddBlender(struct Upnp_Discovery *event) {

  int code;          // return value from Upnp functions
```

```
    BlenderDevice dev;        // new node in device list
    Upnp_Document doc=NULL;        // description document of
                                   // discovered blender
    int addit=TRUE;    // blender passes enough tests to be useful?
    // stuff extracted from description document
    char *friendly_name=NULL, *baseURL=NULL,
         *relative_presentation_URL=NULL;
    // list of service nodes in description doc
    Upnp_NodeList service_node_list=NULL;
    Upnp_NodeList tmp=NULL;

    // lock global data
    pthread_mutex_lock(&mutex);

    // We're only interested in blenders. It's possible we'll
    // see advertisements for other sorts of devices,
    // so check first—don't do a lot of work
    // if it's not a blender!   Also react ONLY to
    // advertisements for root blender devices—UPnP devices
    // send LOTS of advertisement messages, corresponding to
    // the root device, embedded devices, services, etc.   If the
    // event doesn't identify a blender (i.e, device type is
    // specified) with a device ID, then ignore.

    if (strcmp(event->DeviceType, BLENDER_TYPE) ||
        event->DeviceId[0] == 0) {
#if defined(MENTION_IGNORED_EVENTS)
        printf("BlenderCP: Care only about root blender devices, ignoring
advertisement.\n");
#else
        ;
#endif
    }
    else {
        // it's a blender...do we already know about it?  If so,
        // just need to update the expiration time, so we can skip all
        // the heavy duty stuff (e.g., downloading the description
        // document, parsing service information, etc.)

        strcpy(dev.UDN, event->DeviceId);
        if (element_in_queue(&device_list, &dev)) {
          printf("BlenderCP: Already know about this blender, ");
          printf("updating expiration.\n");
          // current position in queue is now the matching blender;
          // suck up its description...
          peek_at_current(device_list, &dev);
          // ...update expiration...
```

```
      dev.expiration = event->Expires;
      // ..then put it back
      update_current(&device_list, &dev);
  }
  else {
    printf("\nBlenderCP: Getting info for blender with");
    printf(" the following identifier:\n%s\n", event->DeviceId);

    // interesting stuff about blender is in its
    // description document;  first step is to download
    // document, then we'll examine it

    printf("BlenderCP: Downloading description document");
    printf(" %s\n", event->Location);
    if ((code=UpnpDownloadXmlDoc(event->Location, &doc))
      != UPNP_E_SUCCESS) {
      // couldn't download the XML document—can't do anything
      // with this blender
      Diagnose("AddBlender()", __LINE__, code);
      printf("BlenderCP:  Without description document, ");
      printf("can't add this blender to device list.\n");
      addit=false;
    }
    else {
      // remember location of description document
      strcpy(dev.descriptionURL, event->Location);

      // ...and expiration...
      dev.expiration = event->Expires;

      // ...then extract interesting stuff.  We can live with
      // some stuff being missing, while other pieces are critical.

      friendly_name = ParseItem(doc, NULL, "friendlyName");
      baseURL = ParseItem(doc, NULL, "URLBase");
      relative_presentation_URL = ParseItem(doc, NULL,
        "presentationURL");

      if (! baseURL || ! relative_presentation_URL) {
        printf("BlenderCP: No presentation URL available for");
        printf(" this blender.\n");
        dev.presentationURL[0] = 0;
        // hack:  need to fake a base URL just to crash our way
        // through the rest of this function!
        baseURL = malloc(1);
        baseURL[0] = 0;
      }
```

```
else {
  // form absolute presentation URL
  sprintf(dev.presentationURL, "%s%s", baseURL,
    relative_presentation_URL);
  free(relative_presentation_URL);
}

if (! friendly_name) {
  printf("BlenderCP: No friendly name available for");
  printf(" this blender.\n");
  dev.friendly[0] = 0;
}
else {
  strcpy(dev.friendly, friendly_name);
  free(friendly_name);
}
```

Once the device information from the description document has been parsed, we need information about the services. Some of the initial processing is done here, but most is offloaded via calls to GetServiceInfo(), because the same stuff needs to be done for each service. We're about to get much more personal with XML parsing using the SDK. Up to now, we've encountered only the SDK type that represents an entire XML document; here's the turning point!

There are a number of services offered by a UPnP blender, and we want to process information about each. The UpnPDocument_getElementsByTagName() function, besides being a mouthful, allows a subtree in an XML document to be extracted. Below, we grab all the document elements that have a "serviceList" tag. In the case of the blender, we expect there to be only one of these, since there are no nested devices. A call to UpnpNodeList_item() with an index of 0 extracts the single "serviceList" element. Then a call to UpnpElement_getElementsByTagName() creates a list of elements, each of which corresponds to a single service. This list is stored in service_node_list. This list is passed to GetServiceInfo() calls, one call for each service for additional parsing. The subscription IDs and timeouts are initialized to null strings and 0, respectively, because these are not significant until the blender is selected to be the current device. If all goes well with the GetServiceInfo() stuff, then the blender is added to the global device list.

```
printf("BlenderCP: Now parsing service information.\n");

// Now deal with services.  First retrieve a list of
// serviceList nodes from the description document.
// UpnpDocument_getElementsByTagName() returns a bunch of
```

```
// subtrees, the root of each being a serviceList.  This
// includes nested service  information for more
// complicated devices.
service_node_list =
  UpnpDocument_getElementsByTagName(doc, "serviceList");

// are there any services?  If not, this is a bad thing.
if (service_node_list &&
  UpnpNodeList_getLength(service_node_list)) {
  // It gets uglier.  Narrow the list to *only* root
  // device level services; a UpnpNodeList_item() call with
  // an index of 0 gets us this far.  Note that
  // for blenders, there aren't any nested services, so 0
  //  should be the only valid index.
  tmp = UpnpNodeList_item(service_node_list, 0);
  if (service_node_list) {
    UpnpNodeList_free(service_node_list);
  }

  // Then get a set of subtrees, the root of each
  // being a description of a single  available service at
  // this root level.  This would be a lot less ugly in a
  // language with automatic garbage collection—the
  // fact that we have to manually free storage means that
  // nested calls are taboo.
  service_node_list =
    UpnpElement_getElementsByTagName(tmp, "service");
  if (tmp) {
    UpnpNode_free(tmp);
  }
}
else {
  addit = false;
}

// offload extracting service info, because this function
// is getting overwhelming.  Best that we narrowed the
// service list down before calling the following, otherwise
// the entire description document would have to be parsed
// multiple times.

// deal with power, speed control, and bowl contents
// services.  Failure to  get info on any of these services
// means that we can't use the blender.

printf("BlenderCP: Parsing individual service");
printf(" descriptions.\n");
```

```
    addit = addit &&
      GetServiceInfo(service_node_list,
        baseURL, POWERSERVICE, &(dev.power)) &&
      GetServiceInfo(service_node_list,
        baseURL, SPEEDSERVICE, &(dev.speed)) &&
      GetServiceInfo(service_node_list,
        baseURL, BOWLSERVICE, &(dev.bowl));

    // initialize subscription id and timeout for services-these
    // won't be filled in  until the blender is selected for use

    dev.power.SID[0] = 0;
    dev.speed.SID[0] = 0;
    dev.bowl.SID[0] = 0;
    dev.power.timeout = 0;
    dev.speed.timeout = 0;
    dev.bowl.timeout = 0;

    free(baseURL);

    // can free the list of service nodes now as well as
    // the description document.
    // **critical** that the appropriate *_free() function is used!
    UpnpNodeList_free(service_node_list);
    UpnpDocument_free(doc);

     // finally, add the blender if enough stuff went well!
    if (addit) {
      printf("BlenderCP: Adding new blender to device list.\n");

      // print new blender's details
      printf("\nBlenderCP: BLENDER DETAILS\n");
      PrintBlenderDetails(dev);

      // drop new blender node into the device list if
      // everything went well
      add_to_queue(&device_list, &dev, 0);
      printf("BlenderCP: Addition complete.\n");
    }
    else {
      // something went wrong
      printf("BlenderCP: Blender NOT added to device list.\n");
    }
    }
  }
 }
}

// unlock
```

```
    pthread_mutex_unlock(&mutex);
}
```

GetServiceInfo() picks up where AddBlender() left off, continuing the parsing of information about specific services. It takes the list of service elements constructed in AddBlender(), the base URL for the root device, the name of the service whose information is to be collected, and the address of a BlenderService structure, which will hold the parsed service information. The list of service elements is searched until the specified service name is found, then ParseItem() is used to extract interesting bits of information about the service, such as the control URL and event subscription URL. This function is not thread-safe, since it is called only from contexts where the global control point state is locked.

```
//////////////////////////////////
// Read service information for a particular service from a
// list of service information nodes.
//
// **THIS FUNCTION IS NOT THREAD-SAFE**
// **THIS FUNCTION IS NOT THREAD-SAFE**
//
// services == list of service nodes, extracted from
// description document
// name == name of target service
// (e.g., "urn:schemas-upnp-org:service:SpeedControl:1")
// service == pointer to structure describing service
//

int GetServiceInfo(Upnp_NodeList services, char *baseURL,
  char *name, BlenderService *service) {

  Upnp_Node service_node=NULL;    // used to iterate through services
                                  // in list
  char *service_type=NULL;        // type for service under
                                  // examination
  char *service_id=NULL;          // id of service under examination
  char *url=NULL;                 // temporary used to build
                                  // absolute event, control URLs
  int ok=false;                   // service found, and passed minimum
                                  // set of requirements?

  int i;


  // examine each service, looking for target

  printf("BlenderCP: Handling service %s.\n", name);
```

```
for (i=0; i < UpnpNodeList_getLength(services) && ! ok; i++) {
  // printf("BlenderCP: Getting service list item # %d.\n", i);
  service_node = UpnpNodeList_item(services, i);
  // printf("BlenderCP: Getting service type.\n");
  service_type = ParseItem(NULL, service_node, "serviceType");
  // printf("BlenderCP: Type is %s.\n", service_type);
  if (service_type && strcmp(service_type, name) == 0) {
    printf("BlenderCP: Found %s.\n", service_type);
    strcpy(service->service_type, service_type);
    free(service_type);
    // printf("BlenderCP: Getting serviceID.\n");
    service_id = ParseItem(NULL, service_node, "serviceId");
    // printf("Got serviceID.\n");
    if (service_id) {
      strcpy(service->service_id, service_id);
      free(service_id);
      // printf("BlenderCP: Getting control URL.\n");
      url = ParseItem(NULL, service_node, "controlURL");
      if (url) {
        sprintf(service->controlURL, "%s%s", baseURL, url);
        free(url);
        // printf("BlenderCP: Getting event subscription URL.\n");
        url = ParseItem(NULL, service_node, "eventSubURL");
        if (url) {
          sprintf(service->eventURL, "%s%s", baseURL, url);
          free(url);
          ok=true;
        }
        else {
          printf("BlenderCP: No event subscription URL for");
          printf(" that service??  Can't use blender.\n");
        }
      }
      else {
        printf("BlenderCP: No control URL for that");
        printf( service??  Can't use blender.\n");
      }
    }
    else {
      printf("BlenderCP: No service id for that");
      printf(" service??  Can't use use blender.\n");
    }
  }

  // service_node still needs to be free()-d, but not with free()!
  UpnpNode_free(service_node);
}
```

```
      return ok;
}
```

The following function, ListBlenders(), walks the queue containing discovered blenders, printing the UDN for each. This UDN is required when selecting a blender to become the new current blender—the blender that gets all our attention. The queue functions are self-explanatory, as is the rest of ListBlenders(). The number of blenders in the queue is returned.

```
/////////////////////////////
// List all known blenders.
// Returns the number of blenders displayed.
//

int ListBlenders(void) {

  BlenderDevice dev;
  int len=0;                 // current length of device list

  // lock global data
  pthread_mutex_lock(&mutex);

  len=queue_length(device_list);
  printf("BlenderCP: Known blender list:\n");
  if (len == 0) {
     printf("\n**LIST IS EMPTY**\n");
  }
  else {
     rewind_queue(&device_list);
     while (! end_of_queue(device_list)) {
       peek_at_current(device_list, &dev);
       printf("[%s]    %s\n", dev.UDN, dev.friendly);
       next_element(&device_list);
     }
  }

  // unlock
  pthread_mutex_unlock(&mutex);

  return len;

}
```

A logical choice after viewing the list of available blenders [see List-Blenders() above] is to choose one with which to interact, since the control point allows active control of one blender at a time. The following function, SetCurrentBlender(), allows a particular blender to be chosen. First the user is prompted to enter the UDN of a discovered blender. The UDN is used in a call to element_in_queue() to determine if a blender with the specified UDN is known. If it is, a nice side effect of the element_in_queue() call is that the matching blender is selected in the queue. If a blender was previously selected, we unsubscribe to all its services. Then we grab a pointer to the selected blender in the global "current" and subscribe to the services of the new current blender. The final action is to print the details of the currently selected blender.

```
/////////////////////////////
// Allow user to select a current blender, then subscribe to its
// services.  Unsubscribe to services of any previously
// selected blender.
//

void SetCurrentBlender(void) {

  int count;                    // # of blenders in device list
  char selected[LINE_SIZE];     // UDN of selected blender
  BlenderDevice temp;

  // lock global data
  pthread_mutex_lock(&mutex);

  if (count) {
    printf("\nEnter UDN of blender (omit the [ ]) ");
    printf("or press ENTER to abort.\n");
    gets(selected);
    if (selected[0] == 0) {
      printf("BlenderCP: Selection aborted.\n");
      // unlock
      pthread_mutex_unlock(&mutex);
      return;
    }

    // did the user give a valid UDN?
    strcpy(temp.UDN, selected);
    if (! element_in_queue(&device_list, &temp)) {
      printf("BlenderCP: Invalid UDN.  Selection aborted.\n");
      // unlock
      pthread_mutex_unlock(&mutex);
      return;
    }
```

```
  // unsubscribe to previously selected blender, if there is one
  if (current != NULL) {
    printf("BlenderCP: Unsubscribing to services of");
    printf(" previous blender.\n");
    UpnpUnSubscribe(handle, current->power.SID);
    UpnpUnSubscribe(handle, current->speed.SID);
    UpnpUnSubscribe(handle, current->bowl.SID);
  }

  // have a new current blender
  current = (BlenderDevice *)pointer_to_current(device_list);

  // subscribe to services of selected blender
  if (SubscribeService(&(current->power))) {
    printf("BlenderCP: Power subscription successful.\n");
  }
  else {
    printf("BlenderCP: Power subscription failed.\n");
  }
  if (SubscribeService(&(current->speed))) {
    printf("BlenderCP: Speed subscription successful.\n");
  }
  else {
    printf("BlenderCP: Speed subscription failed.\n");
  }
  if (SubscribeService(&(current->bowl))) {
    printf("BlenderCP: Contents subscription successful.\n");
  }
  else {
    printf("BlenderCP: Bowl subscription failed.\n");
  }

  printf("BlenderCP: Details for currently selected blender:\n");
  PrintBlenderDetails(*current);
}

// unlock
pthread_mutex_unlock(&mutex);

}
```

The following function subscribes to a specific service, identified by the single argument "service." TRUE is returned if the subscription succeeds; otherwise, FALSE is returned. The key to service subscription is a call to the function UpnpSubscribe(), which accepts our control point handle, the eventing URL of the service, the address of an integer containing the desired subscription duration, and a char* argument where a subscription identifier (SID) will be stored. The actual timeout will be overwritten into the third argument. Both the subscription duration and SID are stored directly into the BlenderService structure, whose address is passed to SubscribeService(). This function is not thread-safe and should always be called from a context where the global control point state is locked.

```
/////////////////////////////////
// Subscribe to a service's events.   Returns true if
// successful or false if the subscription fails.
//
// **THIS FUNCTION IS NOT THREAD-SAFE**
// **THIS FUNCTION IS NOT THREAD-SAFE**
//
// service == structure describing service.
//

int SubscribeService(BlenderService *service) {

  int code;      // return value from UPnP calls
  int ok=true;   // status of subscription

  printf("BlenderCP: Subscribing to event URL");
  printf(" %s for %s\n", service->eventURL, service->service_id);

  // attempt to subscribe, providing the device handle,
  // the event URL for the service, and a timeout.  We'll get a
  // subscription ID service->SID if all goes well.
  service->timeout = REG_TIMEOUT;
  code=UpnpSubscribe(handle, service->eventURL,
    &(service->timeout), service->SID);
  if (code==UPNP_E_SUCCESS) {
    printf("BlenderCP: Subscription successful. ");
    printf("Timeout = %d.\n", service->timeout);
  }
  else {
    printf("Subscription failed.  Can't use this blender.\n");
    Diagnose("UpnpSubscribe()", __LINE__, code);
    ok=false;
  }

  return ok;
}
```

RemoveBlender() removes information about a blender from the list of discovered devices. It is useful for dealing with "byebye" messages, which announce the departure of a UPnP device from the network, and for removing device descriptions during debugging. The only field in the Upnp_Discovery parameter that is used is the event->DeviceId field. A check is necessary to make sure that the departing device is a previously discovered blender. If it is and if the blender is the currently selected one, then subscriptions are canceled using UpnpUnsubscribe() and the global "current" is set to NULL. We don't particularly care about the failure of the unsubscribe attempts, since there's nothing we can do anyway.

```c
/////////////////////////////////
// Remove a blender whose identity is encapsulated in
// 'event', if it's a blender!  As for device
// advertisements, we want to react only when we
// get the root device's byebye message.  If the event
// doesn't identify a blender (i.e, device type is specified)
// with a device ID we recognize, then just ignore it.

void RemoveBlender(struct Upnp_Discovery *event) {

  BlenderDevice removeit, peek;

  // lock global data
  pthread_mutex_lock(&mutex);

  if (strcmp(event->DeviceType, BLENDER_TYPE) ||
     event->DeviceId[0] == 0) {
#if defined(MENTION_IGNORED_EVENTS)
    printf("BlenderCP: Care only about root blender");
    printf(" devices, ignoring departure.\n");
#else
     ;
#endif
  }
  else {
    // got a root blender device's departure message.
    // Create a BlenderDevice node with UDN set to departing
    // blender's unique name—the rest doesn't matter,
    // since that uniquely identifies the service to the
    // queue package.  We use this to see if we know about
    // this blender.
    strcpy(removeit.UDN, event->DeviceId);

    if (element_in_queue(&device_list,  &removeit)) {
      // we know about this blender
```

```
    printf("BlenderCP: Removing blender");
    printf(" %s from the discovered list.\n", removeit.UDN);

    // element_in_queue() sets current position to the
    // matched item
    peek_at_current(device_list, &peek);

    // see if currently selected blender device is the
    // one we're removing; if it is, notify user that there is
    // no currently selected blender
    if (! CompareBlenders(&peek, current)) {
      printf("BlenderCP: Current blender disappeared, ");
      printf("no current blender is set now.\n");
      // unsubscribe to all services-probably not strictly
      // necessary if the blender is being removed because
      // of a "byebye"
      UpnpUnSubscribe(handle, peek.power.SID);
      UpnpUnSubscribe(handle, peek.speed.SID);
      UpnpUnSubscribe(handle, peek.bowl.SID);
      current = NULL;
    }
    delete_current(&device_list);
  }
}

  // unlock
  pthread_mutex_unlock(&mutex);

}
```

Now we turn to the functions that execute actions. Recall that actions in UPnP jargon are essentially remote procedure calls, with the specification of the remote call expressed in XML. The Intel SDK abstracts away much of the XML processing when issuing actions, providing control points with an action interface that closely resembles RPC. What little XML attention is required is hidden in the function SendAction(), which is discussed shortly. SetPulseDuration() does exactly what its name implies—it executes an action to set the currently selected blender's pulse duration to the value of the single argument "pulse." SendAction() is passed POWERSERVICE (defined at the top of the source code for the control point), a description of the power service (in current->power, which is a BlenderService), the name of the action (SetPulseDuration), and arrays containing the names and values of arguments. The SetPulse-Duration action has only a single argument, named PulseDuration.

```
/////////////////////////////////
// Set pulse duration for current blender.
```

```
//
// pulse == new pulse setting setting
//
void SetPulse(int pulse) {

  char *var;
  char *val;
  Upnp_Document response = NULL;
  // lock global data
  pthread_mutex_lock(&mutex);

  var = malloc(20);
  if (! var) {
    Shutdown("BlenderCP: Out of memory!!");
  }
  val = malloc(20);
  if (! val) {
    Shutdown("BlenderCP: Out of memory!!");
  }

  // one argument to SetPulseDuration
  strcpy(var, "PulseDuration");
  sprintf(val, "%1d", pulse);
  response = SendAction(POWERSERVICE, current->power,
    "SetPulseDuration", &var, &val, 1);

  // don't care about response
  if (response) {
    UpnpDocument_free(response);
  }
  if (var) {
    free(var);
  }
  if (val) {
    free(val);
  }

  // unlock
  pthread_mutex_unlock(&mutex);
}
```

The following function executes the actions PowerOn and PowerOff, which take no arguments. The next, SetSpeed(), takes a single argument, a new speed for the currently selected blender. Following Set-Speed() is PutBlenderString(), which places a string into the currently selected blender. The structure of each of these functions is much the same as that of SetPulse(), above, so no further discussion is provided.

After these come the functions which handle actions with return values, such as GetSpeed(). These are a bit different, so we cover them in detail.

```
/////////////////////////////
// Turn current blender on/off.
//
// power == new power setting (zero for false, non-zero for true)
//

void SetPower(int power) {

  Upnp_Document response = NULL;

  // lock global data
  pthread_mutex_lock(&mutex);

  // PowerOn / PowerOff functions take no arguments
  response = SendAction(POWERSERVICE, current->power,
    power ? "PowerOn" : "PowerOff", NULL, NULL, 0);

  // don't care about response
  if (response) {
    UpnpDocument_free(response);
  }

  // unlock
  pthread_mutex_unlock(&mutex);
}



/////////////////////////////
// Set speed of current blender.
//
// speed == new speed for blender
//
void SetSpeed(int speed) {

  char *var;
  char *val;
  Upnp_Document response = NULL;

  // lock global data
  pthread_mutex_lock(&mutex);

  var = malloc(20);
  if (! var) {
    Shutdown("BlenderCP: Out of memory!!");
```

```
  }
  val = malloc(20);
  if (! val) {
    Shutdown("BlenderCP: Out of memory!!");
  }
  strcpy(var, "Speed");
  sprintf(val, "%1d", speed);
  response = SendAction(SPEEDSERVICE, current->speed, "SetSpeed",
      &var, &val, 1);

  // don't care about response
  if (response) {
    UpnpDocument_free(response);
  }
  if (var) {
    free(var);
  }
  if (val) {
    free(val);
  }

  // unlock
  pthread_mutex_unlock(&mutex);

}


//////////////////////////////
// Set contents of current blender.
//
// contents == new contents for blender
//
void PutBlenderString(char *contents) {

  char *var;
  Upnp_Document response = NULL;

  // lock global data
  pthread_mutex_lock(&mutex);

  var = malloc(20);
  if (! var) {
    Shutdown("BlenderCP: Out of memory!!");
  }
  strcpy(var, "Contents");
  response = SendAction(BOWLSERVICE, current->bowl, "SetContents",
      &var, &contents, 1);
```

```
  // don't care about response
  if (response) {
    UpnpDocument_free(response);
  }
  if (var) {
    free(var);
  }

  // unlock
  pthread_mutex_unlock(&mutex);

}
```

Unlike the previous action-causing functions, the rest deal with actions that have "out" parameters. This means that the response returned by SendAction() [which is itself derived from a call to UpnpSendAction()] is significant, and won't be simply ignored. The following function, Get-Speed(), returns the speed of the currently selected blender. The return value from SendAction() will be a response to the action, containing the values of any "out" parameters. All we're interested in is the value of the "out" parameter Speed, so a call to our trusty ParseItem() returns the value associated with the tag "Speed." The integer value of Speed is returned to the caller. The next function, GetBlenderString(), has the same structure but returns the contents of the currently selected blender.

```
/////////////////////////////
// Return current speed of current blender.
int GetSpeed() {

  char *speedstr=NULL;
  int speed=-1;
  Upnp_Document response = NULL;

  // lock global data
  pthread_mutex_lock(&mutex);

  // no "in" arguments for GetSpeed
  response = SendAction(SPEEDSERVICE, current->speed, "GetSpeed",
      NULL, NULL, 0);

  // parse response to determine speed (unless response is NULL,
  // which is bad). "Speed" is an out parameter.

  if (response) {
    speedstr = ParseItem(response, NULL, "Speed");
    if (! speedstr) {
```

```
      printf("BlenderCP: Couldn't get speed, returning -1\n");
    }
    else {
      speed = atoi(speedstr);
      free(speedstr);
    }
    UpnpDocument_free(response);
  }
  else {
    printf("BlenderCP: Couldn't get speed, returning -1.\n");
  }

  // unlock
  pthread_mutex_unlock(&mutex);

  return speed;
}

////////////////////////////////
// Return contents of current blender.
char *GetBlenderString(void) {

  char *contents=NULL;
  Upnp_Document response = NULL;

  // lock global data
  pthread_mutex_lock(&mutex);

  // no "in" arguments for GetContents
  response = SendAction(SPEEDSERVICE, current->bowl, "GetContents",
    NULL, NULL, 0);

  // parse response to determine contents (unless response is NULL,
  // which is bad).  "Contents" is an out parameter.

  if (response) {
    contents = ParseItem(response, NULL, "Contents");
    if (! contents) {
      printf("BlenderCP: Couldn't get contents, returning NULL.\n");
    }
    UpnpDocument_free(response);
  }
  else {
    printf("BlenderCP: Couldn't get contents, returning NULL.\n");
  }

  // unlock
  pthread_mutex_unlock(&mutex);

  return contents;
```

}

      SendAction() is the function that has been doing most of the work for the action-related functions thus far. Now we examine its implementation in detail. Note that this function is not thread-safe, because in the current blender control point implementation, it is always called from a thread-safe context [e.g., a function like SetSpeed()].

      The function takes six arguments: the type of service against which the action is executed (e.g., "urn:schemas-upnp-org:service:Power-Switch:1"); a BlenderService instance, describing the service; the name of the action (e.g., "SetPower"); arrays containing the names and values of "in" parameters to the action; and an integer specifying the length of these arrays. The primary task of SendAction() is to create a portion of the XML document that will be buried in the body of a SOAP message. Fortunately, the UPnP SDK hides the nasty stuff and makes this process quite straightforward. To start, SendAction() calls UpnpMakeAction(), passing the name of the action and the service type. The return value of UpnpNameAction is a Upnp_Document doc, which represents the skeletal form of the required XML document. Subsequently the "in" parameter names and values are pumped into this document one by one, with calls to UpnpAddToAction(). Once all the "in" parameters have been inserted, UpnpSendAction() causes the action message to be transmitted. UpnpSendAction() takes six arguments: our control point handle, the control URL of the service against which the action is executed, the service type, the unique device name of the device hosting the service, the Upnp_Document constructed with the calls to UpnpMakeAction()/UpnpAddToAction(), and the address of a Upnp_Document, into which will be deposited the results of the action. The interesting part of the response, of course, is the set of values for "out" parameters. SendAction() does nothing with the response, which is action-specific; this value is just returned to the caller. The caller is responsible for freeing storage associated with the returned Upnp_Document via a call to UpnpDocument_free().

```
// Perform an action on the currently selected blender.
// Returns the response document; the calling code is responsible
// for freeing associated storage.
//
// **THIS FUNCTION IS NOT THREAD-SAFE**
// **THIS FUNCTION IS NOT THREAD-SAFE**
//
// servtype == type of service
```

```
// (e.g., "urn:schemas-upnp-org:service:PowerSwitch:1")
// service == description of service
// func == name of action (e.g., "SetPower")
// args == argument names
// values == argument values
// numargs == number of elements in args, values string arrays
//
Upnp_Document SendAction(char *servtype, BlenderService service,
  char *func, char **args, char **values, int numargs) {

  Upnp_Document doc=NULL;          // XML representation of our
                                   // requested action
  Upnp_Document response=NULL;     // return value from action
  int code;                        // return value from UPnP functions
  int j;

  // can't continue unless there's a currently selected
  // blender; this has probably already been checked

  if (current == NULL) {
    printf("BlenderCP: No current blender, can't perform action.\n");
  }
  else {
    // create initial document to describe this action
    doc = UpnpMakeAction(func, servtype, 0, NULL, NULL);
    if (doc) {
      // then pump in the argument names and values
      code = UPNP_E_SUCCESS;
      for (j=0; j < numargs && code == UPNP_E_SUCCESS; j++) {
        printf("BlenderCP: Adding to action: ");
        printf("%s = %s\n", args[j], values[j]);
        code = UpnpAddToAction(&doc, func, servtype, args[j],
          values[j]);
      }

      if (code != UPNP_E_SUCCESS) {
        printf("BlenderCP: Error creating document describing");
        printf(" action.\n");
        Diagnose("UpnpAddToAction()", __LINE__, code);
      }
      else {
        // all OK so far, ship our document outlining the action
        printf("BlenderCP: Sending action to control URL %s.\n",
          service.controlURL);
        code = UpnpSendAction(handle, service.controlURL, servtype,
          current->UDN, doc, &response);

        if (code != UPNP_E_SUCCESS) {
```

```
      printf("BlenderCP: Couldn't send action.\n");
      Diagnose("UpnpSendAction()", __LINE__, code);
    }
    else {
      printf("BlenderCP: Action sent.\n");
    }
   }
  }
  else {
    printf("BlenderCP: Couldn't create initial document");
    printf(" describing action.\n");
  }

  if (doc) {
    UpnpDocument_free(doc);
  }
 }

 return response;
}
```

In addition to executing actions, control points may explicitly query the values of specific state variables. This ability is especially important for variables that are not "evented," i.e., whose values are not automatically transmitted by a service's eventing facility. The following function, QueryStateVariable(), allows a user to select a service (e.g., the power service) and then determine the value of a related state variable (e.g., Power). The initial portion of the function is a simple command line interface. Once the service and name of the variable are determined, a call to UpnpGetServiceVarStatus() is made. This function provides a very straightforward mechanism for variable queries—yet another case where we're not particularly annoyed at being freed from dealing with XML issues directly. Four arguments are required: our control point handle, the control URL of the service maintaining the state variable, the name of the variable, and the address of a string pointer (char **) which will point to the value if the UpnpGetServiceVarStatus() call completes successfully.

```
////////////////////////////////////
// Query a state variable.  This function allows the control
// point to peek into the guts of the currently selected blender,
// bypassing the usual actions that support setting/retrieving
// state variable values.  The blender model actually exposes
// almost all state variables through Set/Get methods—this
// function serves as an example of HOW to do state variable
```

```
// queries.
void QueryStateVariable(void) {

  char c;              // identifier for associated service ('0'-'2')
  char var[NAME_SIZE]; // variable to query
  char *val=NULL;      // returned value
  char *controlURL=NULL;  // control URL of associated service
  int code;            // return value from UPnP functions

  printf("\nBlenderCP: QUERY STATE VARIABLE.\n");
  printf("[0]\tPower\n");
  printf("[1]\tSpeed\n");
  printf("[2]\tBowl\n");
  printf("BlenderCP: Choose a service (0-2) or press");
  printf(" ENTER to abort :");
  c = getchar();
  getchar();   // eat newline
  if (c < '0' || c > '2') {
    printf("BlenderCP: Selection aborted.\n");
    return;
  }

  printf("BlenderCP: Enter name of state variable");
  printf(" or press ENTER to abort:\n");
  gets(var);
  if (var[0] == 0) {
    return;
  }

  // lock global data
  pthread_mutex_lock(&mutex);

  // figure out which control URL to try
  switch (c) {
  case '0': controlURL = current->power.controlURL;
    break;
  case '1': controlURL = current->speed.controlURL;
    break;
  case '2': controlURL = current->bowl.controlURL;
    break;
  }

  printf("BlenderCP: Using control URL \"%s\".\n", controlURL);
  code = UpnpGetServiceVarStatus(handle, controlURL, var, &val);

  if (code != UPNP_E_SUCCESS) {
    printf("BlenderCP: State variable query failed.\n");
    Diagnose("UpnpGetServiceVarStatus()", __LINE__, code);
  }
```

```
else {
  if (val) {
    printf("BlenderCP: Value for queried variable");
    printf(" is \"%s\".\n", val);
    free(val);
  }
  else {
    printf("BlenderCP: Value for queried variable is NULL.\n");
  }
}

// unlock
pthread_mutex_unlock(&mutex);

}
```

The next function is executed by our callback function to deal with GENA-related events. We receive such events because we subscribed to all the services offered by the currently selected blender. When state variables change value, the associated service beams us a notification. That's when we end up in HandleGENAEvent, below. The callback function passes a single argument to HandleGENAEvent—an instance of Upnp_Event. The interesting fields in this structure are a subscription ID, a sequence number, and a Upnp_Document, which describes the service's state changes. The sequence number is incremented each time an event is generated by the service; if it is important that control points notice missing events, the sequence number can be helpful. In the following, we display the sequence number, but do not process it further. The first step is to find out to which service this event corresponds. Once this is done, extensive use of the DOM-related functions is necessary to extract the state variable names and values.

```
// A Upnp_Event contains three interesting fields: a
// subscription ID, a sequence number (so events can be
// processed in order, if this is important) and a
// Upnp_Document which outlines the state changes
// reported by this event.  This function handles such
// events.
//
// event == GENA event
//

void HandleGENAEvent(struct Upnp_Event *event) {

  Upnp_NodeList props=NULL; // pieces of ChangedVariables document
  Upnp_NodeList children=NULL;
```

```
Upnp_Node varnode=NULL;
Upnp_Node varnodechild=NULL;
Upnp_Node prop=NULL;
Upnp_DOMException err;
char *variable=NULL, *value=NULL;   // name, value of changed
                                    // state variable
int i;

// lock global data
pthread_mutex_lock(&mutex);

printf("\nBlenderCP: GENA event for subscription id");
printf(" %s, seq number %d.\n",
event->Sid, event->EventKey);

// find out which service it corresponds to; none
// if there's no current blender selected...

if (current == NULL) {
  printf("BlenderCP: No current blender, not interested in");
  printf(" this event.\n");
  // unlock
  pthread_mutex_unlock(&mutex);
  return;
}
else if (! strcmp(current->power.SID, event->Sid)) {
  printf("BlenderCP: Power-related event.\n");
}
else if (! strcmp(current->speed.SID, event->Sid)) {
  printf("BlenderCP: Speed-related event.\n");
}
else if (! strcmp(current->bowl.SID, event->Sid)) {
  printf("BlenderCP: Contents-related event.\n");
}
else {
  printf("BlenderCP: Not related to one of our");
  printf(" subscriptions.\n");
  return;
}
```

At this point, we know which service is responsible for the event. What remains is to parse the XML document represented by event->ChangeVariables to determine what's new. The portion of the GENA message describing the changed variables has the form indicated in the following C comment:

```
// parse supplied document to see what's new.  Changed
// variables are represented as follows in the
// ChangedVariables XML document:
//
```

```
// <e:propertyset ...>
//    <e:property>
//       <variablename>new value</variablename>
//    </e:property>
//    <e:property>
//       <variablename>new value</variablename>
//    </e:property>
//    ...
// </e:propertyset>
```

The key is obviously to grab all the <e:property> elements, since each contains a single variable name and corresponding value. The DOM model provides a method for grabbing all the elements in a document that match a specified tag; this method is exposed in the SDK as UpnpDocument_getElementsByTagName(). As expected, this function takes two arguments, a Upnp_Document, and the tag. The return value is a Upnp_NodeList, containing one element for each element that matched the tag. This function is used here:

```
// find all of the "e:property" tags...
printf("BlenderCP: Getting e:property tags.\n");
props=UpnpDocument_getElementsByTagName(event->ChangedVariables,
     "e:property");
printf("BlenderCP: Done.\n");
```

As long as the length of the list of nodes just obtained isn't zero, we're in business. UpnpNodeList_item() is used to extract each node—this function returns the Upnp_Node at a specified index. We know that each such node is an "<e:property>" node, and that it has exactly one "child" node—a tag containing a variable name. That's what we need, and a call to UpnpNode_getChildNodes() creates a Upnp_NodeList containing exactly one element, the variable description. One more Upnp-NodeList_item() call (with an index of 0, since there is only one node in this list), and we finally have the node representing the variable's name in hand. UpnpNode_getNodeName() returns the variable name, and UpnpNode_getNodeValue() returns the value associated with this tag, which is the state variable's new value. All that remains is to report this value to the user and then laboriously free all the nodes and node lists we've created in the process. Here, perhaps more than anywhere else in the implementation of the control point, we see the serious limitation of using a DOM-style model in a non-object-oriented language with manual memory allocation.

```c
if (props != NULL) {
  // there are some...
  for (i=0; i < UpnpNodeList_getLength(props); i++) {
    // look at them one at a time and just report associated
    // variable and value;
    // we don't store much blender state, preferring to ask
    // for it when we need it
    prop=UpnpNodeList_item(props, i);
    if (prop) {
      children = UpnpNode_getChildNodes(prop);
      if (children) {
        varnode=UpnpNodeList_item(children, 0);
        if (varnode) {
          variable = UpnpNode_getNodeName(varnode);
          varnodechild = UpnpNode_getFirstChild(varnode);
          if (varnodechild) {
            value = UpnpNode_getNodeValue(varnodechild,
              &err);
            printf("BlenderCP: Variable");
            printf(" \"%s\" has value \"%s\".\n",
              variable, value);
          }
          else {
            printf("BlenderCP: Couldn't get value");
            printf(" for variable.\n");
          }
        }
        else {
          printf("BlenderCP: No variable node.\n");
        }
      }
      else {
        printf("BlenderCP: No children for property node.\n");
      }
    }
    else {
      printf("BlenderCP: UpnpNodeList_item() returned");
      printf(" a null node.\n");
    }

    // free, free, free!  But not props.  Not until the end!
    if (children) { UpnpNodeList_free(children); }
    if (varnode) { UpnpNode_free(varnode); }
    if (varnodechild) { UpnpNode_free(varnodechild); }
    if (prop) { UpnpNode_free(prop); }
    if (variable) { free(variable); }
    if (value) { free(value); }
```

```
      }
    }
    else {
      printf("BlenderCP: No changed variables.\n");
    }

    if (props) { UpnpNodeList_free(props); }

    // unlock
    pthread_mutex_unlock(&mutex);

}
```

The following two functions install a signal handler to deal with control-C and perform a graceful shutdown, respectively. In Shutdown(), a call to UpnpUnRegisterClient() is performed followed by a call to UpnpFinish(). It's always better to attempt to cancel subscriptions during a proper shutdown, but no code is required for this—it's one of the things that UpnpFinish() takes care of.

```
////////////////////////////////
// Deal with control-C
void SignalHandler() {

  int sig;
  // signal handling stuff (for handling shutdown)
  sigset_t sigs_to_catch;
  sigemptyset(&sigs_to_catch);
  sigaddset(&sigs_to_catch, SIGINT);
  sigwait(&sigs_to_catch, &sig);
  Shutdown("Shutting down.");
}


////////////////////////////////
// Do a clean shutdown.   Unregister (if we got that far)
// and then call UpnpFinish() before dying.
//
// reason == reason we're shutting down.

void Shutdown(char *reason) {
  printf("Wait...\n");
  if (handle >= 0) {
    // handles unsubscribes for us!
    UpnpUnRegisterClient(handle);
  }
```

```
    UpnpFinish();
    printf("%s\n", reason);
    done=true;
    exit(0);
}
```

The following function is used to compare BlenderDevice objects, based on their unique device name. It is used primarily by the queue package.

```
/////////////////////////////////
// Compare blenders.  Return 0 if Blenders are the same,
// otherwise return non-zero.  This function should never be
// called (indirectly) outside of a thread-safe context.
//
int CompareBlenders(void *b1, void *b2) {

    BlenderDevice *blender1 = (BlenderDevice *)b1;
    BlenderDevice *blender2 = (BlenderDevice *)b2;

    // blenders are the same if their unique names are the
    // same—don't care about anything else

    return strcmp(blender1->UDN, blender2->UDN);
}
```

The last function in the control point implementation, TimerLoop(), runs in a separate thread [created in the main() function]. The sole responsibility of TimerLoop() is to monitor the expiration associated with device advertisements. When a device advertises the location of its description document, an expiration time for this information is also advertised. The TimerLoop() spends most of its time sleeping, but periodically wakes up to decrease the amount of time remaining before information associated with devices is discarded. If the remaining time drops below 2 min, then we do discovery again, in the hopes that the device will renew its information. If the information for a device actually expires, the device is removed from the device list. When the device comes back online, we will then rediscover it. One complication is that an expired device might actually be the currently selected one. If this occurs, then current is set to NULL and the user must choose another blender before any additional blending operations can be carried out.

```
/////////////////////////////////
```

```c
// Watches device expiration times. Spends most of its time
// sleeping, waking up every 45 secs to determine if discovery
// information related to blenders is nearing expiration.
// If so, we discover again to force the blender to
// re-advertise itself.  If it does re-advertise,
// then AddBlender() will update the expiration.   If an
// actual expiration occurs despite our efforts, then information
// about the blender is deleted.  Note that we can be lazy
// and NOT worry about service eventing subscriptions
// expiring—the UPnP library  does autorenewal of eventing
// subscriptions, as long as AUTO_RENEWAL_TIME is positive.
//
// Dies when done == true, since this means the CommandLoop
// has exited.
//
void *TimerLoop(void *args) {

  // pointer to blender info under examination
  BlenderDevice *dev=NULL;
  // need to run discovery?
  int needtodiscover=FALSE;
  while (! done) {
    printf("\nBlenderCP: TimerLoop thread sleeping.\n");
    sleep (45);          // ZZZZzzzzzZZZZZZZzzzzzzz...
    printf("\nBlenderCP: TimerLoop thread awake, checking");
    printf(" for near-expirations...\n");

    // lock global data before walking through the list of
    // known blenders...
    pthread_mutex_lock(&mutex);

    // walk the list of blenders...stop when we realize that
    // a re-discovery is required

    if (queue_length(device_list) == 0) {
      printf("\nBlenderCP: No blenders in list, TimerLoop");
      printf(" going back to sleep.\n");
    }
    else {
      rewind_queue(&device_list);
      needtodiscover=FALSE;
      while (! end_of_queue(device_list) && ! needtodiscover) {
        dev = (BlenderDevice *)pointer_to_current(device_list);
        dev->expiration -= 45;

        // take a look at dev.expiration—if it's less than
        // two minutes to go, then panic and
```

```
        // cause re-discovery.  Breaks if devices advertise very
        // short expiration times, but that's way out of spec
        // anyway.  None of this is particularly exact, but
        // that's not the point—just want to make sure that we
        // don't let expirations happen if the device is
        // still around.
        //
        // If a real expiration occurs, zap all knowledge of the
        // blender.   Don't bother to use RemoveBlender(), because no
        // need to unsubscribe if the device is gone.
        printf("BlenderCP: Expiration for %s is %d\n",
          dev->UDN, dev->expiration);
        if (dev->expiration < 0) {    // bye bye, delete info
          if (current && ! CompareBlenders(dev, current)) {
            printf("BlenderCP: Current blender disappeared, no current");
              printf(" blender is set now.\n");
              current = NULL;
          }
          printf("BlenderCP: Removing expired blender");
          printf(" %s from the discovered list.\n", dev->UDN);
          // automatically advances current to next element!
          delete_current(&device_list);
        }
        else if (dev->expiration < 120) {
          // just want to cause discovery once at the end—don't
          // need to do it every time
          // we notice a near-expiration!
          needtodiscover = TRUE;
        }
        else {
          next_element(&device_list);
        }
      }
      if (needtodiscover) {
        printf("BlenderCP: Causing rediscovery in hopes of");
        printf(" avoiding expirations.\n");
        SearchForBlenders();
      }
    }

    // unlock state before going back to sleep
    pthread_mutex_unlock(&mutex);
  }

  return NULL;

}
```

Code for the "common.c" Library

There are several tasks that are necessary both in the implementation of a device and a control point, including parsing XML documents to find the value related to a single tag, diagnosing return values from UPnP SDK functions, and printing information about events. These functions are bundled together in "common.c" and are used by both the blender device and the control point. The "common.h" includes the function prototypes for the "common.c" functions. This file is reproduced below:

```
"common.h"
// A small library of functions commonly needed by UPnP
// devices/control points
// Written by Golden G. Richard III, Ph.D.  May 2001

#if ! defined(_COMMON_)
#define _COMMON_
#include "upnp.h"
#include "upnptools.h"
#include "domCif.h"

// function prototypes for common.c functions
void Diagnose(char *func, int line, int err);
void ReportEvent(Upnp_EventType type, void *event, int lots);
char *ParseItem(Upnp_Document doc, Upnp_Element element,
  Upnp_DOMString tag);
#endif
```

The first function in "common.c", ReportEvent(), simply prints exhaustive information about a UPnP event. The first parameter identifies the event type, the second is a pointer to the event structure to be described, and the third governs how much information is printed. If the third parameter is nonzero, then all printable fields in the event structure are displayed; otherwise, only the string representation of the event type is displayed. This function is useful as a quick reference for the fields in the various event structures.

```
// A small library of functions commonly needed by UPnP
// devices/control points
// Written by Golden G. Richard III, Ph.D.  May 2001

#include <stdio.h>
#include <stdlib.h>
#include <string.h>
#include <unistd.h>
#include <signal.h>
#include <pthread.h>
```

```
#include "common.h"

// Print a short description of an event and optionally
// lots more information
//
// type == type of event
// event == actual event object—the guts pointed to by 'event'
//          depends on the event type
// lots == false for short description, true for full description

void ReportEvent(Upnp_EventType type, void *event, int lots) {

  printf("\n\nReceived event: ");
  switch (type) {
  case UPNP_CONTROL_ACTION_REQUEST:
    printf("UPNP_CONTROL_ACTION_REQUEST\n");
    break;
  case UPNP_CONTROL_ACTION_COMPLETE:
    printf("UPNP_CONTROL_ACTION_COMPLETE\n");
    break;
  case UPNP_CONTROL_GET_VAR_REQUEST:
    printf("UPNP_CONTROL_GET_VAR_REQUEST\n");
    break;
  case UPNP_CONTROL_GET_VAR_COMPLETE:
    printf("UPNP_CONTROL_GET_VAR_COMPLETE\n");
    break;
  case UPNP_DISCOVERY_ADVERTISEMENT_ALIVE:
    printf("UPNP_DISCOVERY_ADVERTISEMENT_ALIVE\n");
    break;
  case UPNP_DISCOVERY_ADVERTISEMENT_BYEBYE:
    printf("UPNP_DISCOVERY_ADVERTISEMENT_BYEBYE\n");
    break;
  case UPNP_DISCOVERY_SEARCH_RESULT:
    printf("UPNP_DISCOVERY_SEARCH_RESULT\n");
    break;
  case UPNP_DISCOVERY_SEARCH_TIMEOUT:
    printf("UPNP_DISCOVERY_SEARCH_TIMEOUT\n");
    break;
  case UPNP_EVENT_SUBSCRIPTION_REQUEST:
    printf("UPNP_EVENT_SUBSCRIPTION_REQUEST\n");
    break;
  case UPNP_EVENT_RECEIVED:
    printf("UPNP_EVENT_RECEIVED\n");
    break;
  case UPNP_EVENT_RENEWAL_COMPLETE:
    printf("UPNP_EVENT_RENEWAL_COMPLETE\n");
    break;
  case UPNP_EVENT_SUBSCRIBE_COMPLETE:
```

```
    printf("UPNP_EVENT_SUBSCRIBE_COMPLETE\n");
    break;
case UPNP_EVENT_UNSUBSCRIBE_COMPLETE:
    printf("UPNP_EVENT_UNSUBSCRIBE_COMPLETE\n");
    break;
case UPNP_EVENT_AUTORENEWAL_FAILED:
    printf("UPNP_EVENT_AUTORENEWAL_FAILED\n");
    break;
case UPNP_EVENT_SUBSCRIPTION_EXPIRED:
    printf("UPNP_EVENT_SUBSCRIPTION_EXPIRED\n");
    break;
default:
    printf("Yikes.  Don't know anything about event type");
    printf(" %d in ReportEvent().\n", type);
    return;
}

// now print details, if requested

if (lots) {
  switch (type) {
  case UPNP_CONTROL_ACTION_REQUEST:
    {
      struct Upnp_Action_Request *a_event =
        (struct Upnp_Action_Request *) event;
      char *xmlbuff=NULL;
      printf("Printable fields in Upnp_Action_Request:\n");
      printf("ErrCode     = %d\n",a_event->ErrCode);
      printf("Socket      = %d\n",a_event->Socket);
      printf("ErrStr      = %s\n",a_event->ErrStr);
      printf("ActionName  = %s\n",a_event->ActionName);
      printf("DevUDN      = %s\n",a_event->DevUDN);
      printf("ServiceID   = %s\n",a_event->ServiceID);
      if (a_event->ActionRequest) {
        xmlbuff = UpnpNewPrintDocument(a_event->ActionRequest);
        if (xmlbuff) {
          printf("ActionRequest=  %s\n",xmlbuff);
          free(xmlbuff);
        }
        else {
          printf("ActionRequest=  NULL\n");
        }
      }
      else {
        if (a_event->ActionResult) {
          xmlbuff = UpnpNewPrintDocument(a_event->ActionResult);
          if (xmlbuff) {
            printf("ActionResult = %s\n",xmlbuff);
```

```
            free(xmlbuff);
          }
          else {
            printf("ActionResult = NULL\n");
          }
        }
      }
    }
  }
  break;

case UPNP_CONTROL_ACTION_COMPLETE:
  {
    struct Upnp_Action_Complete *a_event =
     (struct Upnp_Action_Complete *) event;
    char *xmlbuff=NULL;
    printf("Printable fields in Upnp_Action_Complete:\n");
    printf("ErrCode     = %d\n",a_event->ErrCode);
    printf("CtrlUrl     = %s\n",a_event->CtrlUrl);
    if (a_event->ActionRequest) {
      xmlbuff =
        UpnpNewPrintDocument(a_event->ActionRequest);
      if (xmlbuff) {
        printf("ActionRequest= %s\n",xmlbuff);
        free(xmlbuff);
      }
      else {
        printf("ActionRequest= NULL\n");
      }
    }
    if (a_event->ActionResult) {
      xmlbuff = UpnpNewPrintDocument(a_event->ActionResult);
      if (xmlbuff) {
        printf("ActionResult = %s\n",xmlbuff);
        free(xmlbuff);
      }
      else {
        printf("ActionResult = NULL\n");
      }
    }
  }
  break;

case UPNP_CONTROL_GET_VAR_REQUEST:
  {
    struct Upnp_State_Var_Request *sv_event =
     (struct Upnp_State_Var_Request *) event;
    printf("Printable fields in Upnp_State_Var_Request:\n");
    printf("ErrCode     = %d\n",sv_event->ErrCode);
```

```
        printf("Socket        = %d\n",sv_event->Socket);
        printf("ErrStr        = %s\n",sv_event->ErrStr);
        printf("DevUDN        = %s\n",sv_event->DevUDN);
        printf("ServiceID     = %s\n",sv_event->ServiceID);
        printf("StateVarName  = %s\n",sv_event->StateVarName);
        printf("CurrentVal    = %s\n",sv_event->CurrentVal);
    }
    break;


case UPNP_CONTROL_GET_VAR_COMPLETE:
    {
        struct Upnp_State_Var_Complete *sv_event =
          (struct Upnp_State_Var_Complete *) event;
        printf("Printable fields in Upnp_State_Var_Complete:\n");
        printf("ErrCode       = %d\n",sv_event->ErrCode);
        printf("CtrlUrl       = %s\n",sv_event->CtrlUrl);
        printf("StateVarName  = %s\n",sv_event->StateVarName);
        printf("CurrentVal    = %s\n",sv_event->CurrentVal);
    }
    break;
case UPNP_DISCOVERY_ADVERTISEMENT_ALIVE:
case UPNP_DISCOVERY_ADVERTISEMENT_BYEBYE:
case UPNP_DISCOVERY_SEARCH_RESULT:
    {
        struct Upnp_Discovery *d_event =
          (struct Upnp_Discovery *) event;
        printf("Printable fields in Upnp_Discovery:\n");
        printf("ErrCode       = %d\n",d_event->ErrCode);
        printf("Expires       = %d\n",d_event->Expires);
        printf("DeviceId      = %s\n",d_event->DeviceId);
        printf("DeviceType    = %s\n",d_event->DeviceType);
        printf("ServiceType   = %s\n",d_event->ServiceType);
        printf("ServiceVer    = %s\n",d_event->ServiceVer);
        printf("Location      = %s\n",d_event->Location);
        printf("OS            = %s\n",d_event->Os);
        printf("Ext           = %s\n",d_event->Ext);
    }
    break;

case UPNP_DISCOVERY_SEARCH_TIMEOUT:
    // no further info
    break;

case UPNP_EVENT_RENEWAL_COMPLETE:
    {
        struct Upnp_Event_Renewal *er_event =
          (struct Upnp_Event_Renewal *) event;
        printf("Printable fields in Upnp_Event_Renewal:\n");
```

```
         printf("SID          = %s\n",er_event->Sid);
         printf("ErrCode       = %d\n",er_event->ErrCode);
      }
      break;

   case UPNP_EVENT_SUBSCRIBE_COMPLETE:
   case UPNP_EVENT_UNSUBSCRIBE_COMPLETE:
   case UPNP_EVENT_AUTORENEWAL_FAILED:
   case UPNP_EVENT_SUBSCRIPTION_EXPIRED:
      {
         struct Upnp_Event_Subscribe *es_event =
           (struct Upnp_Event_Subscribe *) event;
         printf("Printable fields in Upnp_Event_Subscribe:\n");
         printf("SID          = %s\n",es_event->Sid);
         printf("ErrCode      = %d\n",es_event->ErrCode);
         printf("PublisherURL = %s\n",es_event->PublisherUrl);
         printf("TimeOut      = %d\n",es_event->TimeOut);
      }
      break;

   case UPNP_EVENT_SUBSCRIPTION_REQUEST:
      {
         struct Upnp_Subscription_Request *sr_event =
           (struct Upnp_Subscription_Request *)event;
         printf("Printable fields in Upnp_Subscription_Request:\n");
         printf("ServiceID    = %s\n",sr_event->ServiceId);
         printf("UDN          = %s\n",sr_event->UDN);
         printf("SID          = %s\n",sr_event->Sid);
      }
      break;

   case UPNP_EVENT_RECEIVED:
      {
         struct Upnp_Event *e_event =
            (struct Upnp_Event *) event;
         char *xmlbuff=NULL;
         printf("Printable fields in Upnp_Event:\n");
         printf("SID              = %s\n",e_event->Sid);
         printf("EventKey         = %d\n",e_event->EventKey);
         xmlbuff = UpnpNewPrintDocument(e_event->ChangedVariables);
         if (xmlbuff) {
            printf("ChangedVariables = %s\n",xmlbuff);
            free(xmlbuff);
         }
         else {
            printf("ChangedVariables = NULL\n");
         }
      }
```

```
      break;
    }
  }
}
```

The following function prints a human-readable interpretation of a UPnP SDK return value. In this sense alone, Diagnose() duplicates the functionality of UpnpGetErrorMessage(err), but it's nice to have a listing of the error codes because in some cases special processing might be appropriate.

```
// Diagnose a return value from a UPnP function
//
// func == name of function that returned an error
// line == approximate line in source file
// err == return value
void Diagnose(char *func, int line, int err) {

  char errstr[50];

  switch(err) {
  case UPNP_E_SUCCESS :
    strcpy(errstr,"UPNP_E_SUCCESS"); break;
  case UPNP_E_INVALID_HANDLE :
    strcpy(errstr,"UPNP_E_INVALID_HANDLE"); break;
  case UPNP_E_INVALID_PARAM :
    strcpy(errstr,"UPNP_E_INVALID_PARAM"); break;
  case UPNP_E_OUTOF_HANDLE :
    strcpy(errstr,"UPNP_E_OUTOF_HANDLE"); break;
  case UPNP_E_OUTOF_CONTEXT :
    strcpy(errstr,"UPNP_E_OUTOF_CONTEXT"); break;
  case UPNP_E_OUTOF_MEMORY :
    strcpy(errstr,"UPNP_E_OUTOF_MEMORY"); break;
  case UPNP_E_INIT :
    strcpy(errstr,"UPNP_E_INIT"); break;
  case UPNP_E_BUFFER_TOO_SMALL :
    strcpy(errstr,"UPNP_E_BUFFER_TOO_SMALL"); break;
  case UPNP_E_INVALID_DESC :
    strcpy(errstr,"UPNP_E_INVALID_DESC"); break;
  case UPNP_E_INVALID_URL :
    strcpy(errstr,"UPNP_E_INVALID_URL"); break;
  case UPNP_E_INVALID_SID :
    strcpy(errstr,"UPNP_E_INVALID_SID"); break;
  case UPNP_E_INVALID_DEVICE :
    strcpy(errstr,"UPNP_E_INVALID_DEVICE"); break;
  case UPNP_E_INVALID_SERVICE :
    strcpy(errstr,"UPNP_E_INVALID_SERVICE"); break;
```

```
case UPNP_E_BAD_RESPONSE :
  strcpy(errstr,"UPNP_E_BAD_RESPONSE"); break;
case UPNP_E_BAD_REQUEST :
  strcpy(errstr,"UPNP_E_BAD_REQUEST"); break;
case UPNP_E_INVALID_ACTION :
  strcpy(errstr,"UPNP_E_INVALID_ACTION"); break;
case UPNP_E_FINISH :
  strcpy(errstr,"UPNP_E_FINISH"); break;
case UPNP_E_INIT_FAILED :
  strcpy(errstr,"UPNP_E_INIT_FAILED"); break;
case UPNP_E_URL_TOO_BIG :
  strcpy(errstr,"UPNP_E_URL_TOO_BIG"); break;
case UPNP_E_NETWORK_ERROR :
  strcpy(errstr,"UPNP_E_NETWORK_ERROR"); break;
case UPNP_E_SOCKET_WRITE :
  strcpy(errstr,"UPNP_E_SOCKET_WRITE"); break;
case UPNP_E_SOCKET_READ :
  strcpy(errstr,"UPNP_E_SOCKET_READ"); break;
case UPNP_E_SOCKET_BIND :
  strcpy(errstr,"UPNP_E_SOCKET_BIND"); break;
case UPNP_E_SOCKET_CONNECT :
  strcpy(errstr,"UPNP_E_SOCKET_CONNECT"); break;
case UPNP_E_OUTOF_SOCKET :
  strcpy(errstr,"UPNP_E_OUTOF_SOCKET"); break;
case UPNP_E_LISTEN :
  strcpy(errstr,"UPNP_E_LISTEN"); break;
case UPNP_E_EVENT_PROTOCOL :
  strcpy(errstr,"UPNP_E_EVENT_PROTOCOL"); break;
case UPNP_E_SUBSCRIBE_UNACCEPTED :
  strcpy(errstr,"UPNP_E_SUBSCRIBE_UNACCEPTED"); break;
case UPNP_E_UNSUBSCRIBE_UNACCEPTED :
  strcpy(errstr,"UPNP_E_UNSUBSCRIBE_UNACCEPTED"); break;
case UPNP_E_NOTIFY_UNACCEPTED :
  strcpy(errstr,"UPNP_E_NOTIFY_UNACCEPTED"); break;
case UPNP_E_INVALID_ARGUMENT :
  strcpy(errstr,"UPNP_E_INVALID_ARGUMENT"); break;
case UPNP_E_FILE_NOT_FOUND :
  strcpy(errstr,"UPNP_E_FILE_NOT_FOUND"); break;
case UPNP_E_FILE_READ_ERROR :
  strcpy(errstr,"UPNP_E_FILE_READ_ERROR"); break;
case UPNP_E_EXT_NOT_XML :
  strcpy(errstr,"UPNP_E_EXT_NOT_XML"); break;
case UPNP_E_NO_WEB_SERVER :
  strcpy(errstr,"UPNP_E_NO_WEB_SERVER"); break;
case UPNP_E_INTERNAL_ERROR :
  strcpy(errstr,"PNP_E_INTERNAL_ERROR"); break;
}
```

```
// NOTE:  UpnpGetErrorMessage(err) would do the same
// as the above, but it's nice to have a list of the error
// codes for special treatment, etc.

printf("Error %s in function %s at line %d.\n",
   errstr, func, line);
}
```

> This function is used perhaps more than any other in the device and control point implementations: given a Upnp_Document or Upnp_Element and a tag, it returns the value corresponding to the tag. Slightly different processing [a call to UpnpDocument_getElementsByTagName() or to UpnpElement_getElementsByTagName()] is necessary depending on whether a Upnp_Document or Upnp_Element is the source; so the function should be called with exactly one of the first and second parameters set to NULL. Note that ParseItem() always returns the value of the first matching tag.

```
/////////////////////////////
// Given a Upnp_Document or a Upnp_Element, return the
/ corresponding string value for a specific tag.  Uses the DOM
// (document object model) functions provided in
// the UPnP SDK.   The caller is responsible for freeing storage
// associated with the return value using free().
//
// doc == UPnP Document —OR—
// element == UPnP Element
// tag == tag to search for
//

char *ParseItem(Upnp_Document doc,
   Upnp_Element element, Upnp_DOMString tag)   {

   Upnp_NodeList node_list=NULL;
   Upnp_Node node=NULL;
   Upnp_Node tmp=NULL;
   Upnp_DOMException err;
   char *ret=NULL;
   Upnp_DOMString val=NULL;

   // default is an empty string that is free()-able
   ret = malloc(1);
   ret[0]=0;

   // depending on whether a document or element was passed,
   // call the appropriate function to retrieve matches
```

```c
if (doc) {
  node_list = UpnpDocument_getElementsByTagName(doc, tag);
}
else {
  node_list = UpnpElement_getElementsByTagName(element, tag);
}

if (node_list == NULL) {
  // couldn't find anything—just return something that
  // is free-able.
  printf("BlenderCP: Didn't match tag %s, returning \"\".\n", tag);
}
else {
  if ((tmp = UpnpNodeList_item(node_list, 0)) == NULL) {
    // couldn't find anything—just return something that is
    // free-able.
    printf("BlenderCP: Didn't match tag %s, returning \"\".\n",
      tag);
  }
  else {
    node=UpnpNode_getFirstChild(tmp);
    if (node) {
      val = UpnpNode_getNodeValue(node, &err);
      if (val && err == NO_ERR) {
        free(ret);
        ret = malloc(strlen((char *)val)+1);
        if (ret) {
          strcpy(ret, (char *)val);
        }
      }
    }
  }
}

// really have to free stuff here—too many cases where
/ some operations succeeded and  others failed above!  Be *sure*
// to use the appropriate *_free() function.  Failure to do
// so will result in very nasty behavior.

if (tmp) {
  UpnpNode_free(tmp);
}
if (node_list) {
  UpnpNodeList_free(node_list);
}
if (node) {
  UpnpNode_free(node);
}
```

```
  if (val) {
    UpnpDOMString_free(val);
  }

  return ret;
}
```

Code for the "prioque.c" Queue Package

Code for the queue package used in the control point implementation is provided below without further comment, except for documention in the code itself. It's a straightforward implementation of priority queues (plus some extra convenience functions) for arbitrary types that I've been using in various forms for the last 15 years or so. It's not pretty, but it works.

```
"prioque.c"
/**/
/* priority queue header file "prioque.h" */
/* (c) 198x/1998/2001 by Golden G. Richard III, Ph.D. */
/**/

#define   TRUE  1
#define   FALSE 0
#define CONSISTENCY_CHECKING

#if ! defined(QUEUE_TYPE_DEFINED)
#define QUEUE_TYPE_DEFINED

/* type of one element in a queue */

typedef struct _Queue_element {
   void  *info;
   int priority;
   struct _Queue_element *next;
} *Queue_element;

/* basic queue type */

typedef struct Queue {
    Queue_element queue;        /* linked list of elements */
    Queue_element current;      /* current position for sequential
                                   access functions */
    Queue_element previous;     /* one step back from current */
    int queuelength;            /* # of elements in queue */
```

```
      int elementsize;              /* 'sizeof()' one element */
      int duplicates;               /* are duplicates allowed? */
      /* element comparision function */
      int (*compare)(void *e1, void *e2);
  } Queue;


  /********/
  /*
  NOTE: init_queue() must be called for a new queue before
  any other "prioque.c"  functions are called.
  */
  /********/


  /* function prototypes and descriptions for visible
     "prioque.c" functions
  */

  /* initializes a new queue 'q' to have elements of
     size 'elementsize'.  If 'duplicates' is true, then duplicate
     elements in the queue are allowed, otherwise duplicates are
     silently deleted.  The element-comparing function 'compare'
     is required only if duplicates==FALSE or either equal_queues()
     or element_in_queue() are used (otherwise, a null function is
     acceptable).   'compare' should be a standard qsort()-style
     element comparison function:  returns 0 if elements match,
     otherwise a non-0 result (<, > cases are not used).

     NOTE:Only the 'compare' function is used for duplicate
     detection—priority is not considered (i.e., attempting
     to add a "duplicate" element that has a different
     priority than the existing element will have no effect!)
  */
  void init_queue(Queue *q, int elementsize, int duplicates,
    int (*compare)(void *e1, void *e2));

  /* destroys all elements in 'q'
  */
  void destroy_queue(Queue *q);

  /* adds 'element' to the 'q' with position based on 'priority'.
     Elements with lower-numbered priorities are placed closer
     to the front of the queue, with strict 'to the rear'
     placement for items with equal priority [that is, given two
     items with equal priority, the one most recently added will
     appear closer to the rear of the queue].
  */
```

```
void add_to_queue(Queue *q, void *element, int priority);

/* removes the element at the front of the 'q' and places it
   in 'element'.
*/
void remove_from_front(Queue *q, void *element);

/* returns TRUE if the 'element' exists in the 'q', otherwise
   false.  The 'compare' function is used for matching.  As a
   side-effect, the current position in the queue is set to
   matching element, so 'update_current()' can be used to update
   the value of the 'element'.
*/
int element_in_queue(Queue *q, void *element);

/* returns TRUE if 'q' is empty, FALSE otherwise
*/
int empty_queue(Queue q);

/* returns the number of elements in the 'q'.
*/
int queue_length(Queue q);

/* makes a copy of 'q2' into 'q1'.  'q2' is not modified.
*/
void copy_queue(Queue *q1, Queue q2);

/* determines if 'q1' and 'q2' are equivalent.  Uses
   the 'compare' function of the first queue, which should
   match the 'compare' for the second!   Returns TRUE if
   the queues are equal, otherwise returns FALSE.
*/
int equal_queues(Queue q1, Queue q2);

/* merge 'q2' into 'q1'.   'q2' is not modified.
*/
void merge_queues(Queue *q1, Queue q2);

/********************/
/********************/

/* the following are functions used to "walk" the queue like a
   linked list, allowing examination of elements along the way.
   Current position is rewound to the beginning
   by functions above.
*/

/********************/
```

```
/*******************/


/* move to the first element in the 'q' */
void rewind_queue(Queue *q);

/* move to the next element in the 'q' */
void next_element(Queue *q);

/* allows update of current element.  The priority should not
   be changed by this function!
*/

void update_current(Queue *q, void *element);

/* retrieve the element stored at the current position
   in the 'q'
*/
void peek_at_current(Queue q, void *element);

/* return a pointer to the data portion of the current
   element
*/
void *pointer_to_current(Queue q);

/* return priority of current element in the 'q' */
int current_priority(Queue q);

/* delete the element stored at the current position */
void delete_current(Queue *q);

/* has the current position in 'q'  moved beyond the last
   valid element?  Returns TRUE if so, FALSE otherwise.
*/
int end_of_queue(Queue q);

#endif


/*** QUICK REFERENCE ***
void init_queue(Queue *q, int elementsize, int duplicates,
   int (*compare)(void *e1, void *e2));
void destroy_queue(Queue *q);
void add_to_queue(Queue *q, void *element, int priority);
void remove_from_front(Queue *q, void *element);
int element_in_queue(Queue *q, void *element);
int empty_queue(Queue q);
int queue_length(Queue q);
```

```
void copy_queue(Queue *q1, Queue q2);
int equal_queues(Queue q1, Queue q2);
void merge_queues(Queue *q1, Queue q2);
void rewind_queue(Queue *q);
void next_element(Queue *q);
void update_current(Queue *q, void *element);
void peek_at_current(Queue q, void *element);
void *pointer_to_current(Queue q);
int current_priority(Queue q);
void delete_current(Queue *q);
int end_of_queue(Queue q);
 *** QUICK REFERENCE ***/


"prioque.c"

/**/
/* implementation of "prioque.h" priority queue functions */
/* (c) 198x/1998/2001 by Golden G. Richard III, Ph.D. */
/**/

#include <stdio.h>
#include <string.h>
#include <stdlib.h>
#include "prioque.h"

void init_queue(Queue *q, int elementsize, int duplicates,
  int (*compare)(void *e1, void *e2)) {

    q->queuelength = 0;
    q->elementsize = elementsize;
    q->queue = 0;
    q->duplicates = duplicates;
    q->compare = compare;
    rewind_queue(q);
}

void destroy_queue(Queue *q) {

    Queue_element temp;

    if (q != 0) {
      while (q->queue != 0) {
         free(q->queue->info);
         temp = q->queue;
         q->queue = q->queue->next;
         free(temp);
         (q->queuelength)-;
```

```
        }
    }

    rewind_queue(q);

}

int element_in_queue(Queue *q, void *element) {

    if (q->queue != 0) {
        rewind_queue(q);
        while (! end_of_queue(*q)) {
            if (q->compare(element, q->current->info) == 0) {
                return 1;
            }
            next_element(q);
        }
    }

    return 0;
}

void add_to_queue(Queue *q, void *element, int priority) {

    Queue_element new_element, ptr, prev;

    if (q->queue != 0 && ! q->duplicates &&
        element_in_queue(q, element)) {
        return;
    }

    new_element = (Queue_element)malloc(
        sizeof(struct _Queue_element));
    if (new_element == 0) {
        fprintf(stderr,
            "Malloc failed in function add_to_queue()\n");
        exit(1);
    }
    new_element->info = (void *)malloc(q->elementsize);
    if (new_element->info == 0) {
        fprintf(stderr,
            "Malloc failed in function add_to_queue()\n");
        exit(1);
    }

    memcpy(new_element->info, element, q->elementsize);
    new_element->priority = priority;
    (q->queuelength)++;
```

```
    if (q->queue == 0) {
        new_element->next = 0;
        q->queue = new_element;
    }
    else if ((q->queue)->priority > priority) {
        new_element->next = q->queue;
        q->queue = new_element;
    }
    else {
        ptr = q->queue;
        while (ptr != 0 && priority >= ptr->priority) {
          prev = ptr;
          ptr = ptr->next;
        }

        new_element->next = prev->next;
        prev->next = new_element;
    }

    rewind_queue(q);

}

int empty_queue(Queue q) {
    return q.queue == 0;
}

void remove_from_front(Queue *q, void *element) {

    Queue_element temp;

#if defined(CONSISTENCY_CHECKING)
    if (q->queue == 0) {
        fprintf(stderr,
          "NULL pointer in function remove_from_front()\n");
        exit(1);
    }
    else
#endif
    {
        memcpy(element, q->queue->info, q->elementsize);
        free(q->queue->info);
        temp = q->queue;
        q->queue = q->queue->next;
        free(temp);
        (q->queuelength)-;
    }
```

```
    rewind_queue(q);
}


void peek_at_current(Queue q, void *element) {

#if defined(CONSISTENCY_CHECKING)
    if (q.queue == 0 || q.current == 0) {
        fprintf(stderr,
          "NULL pointer in function peek_at_current()\n");
        exit(1);
    }
    else
#endif
    {
        memcpy(element, (q.current)->info, q.elementsize);
    }
}

void *pointer_to_current(Queue q) {

#if defined(CONSISTENCY_CHECKING)
    if (q.queue == 0 || q.current == 0) {
        fprintf(stderr,
          "NULL pointer in function pointer_to_current()\n");
        exit(1);
    }
    else
#endif
    {
      return (q.current)->info;
    }
}

int current_priority(Queue q) {

#if defined(CONSISTENCY_CHECKING)
    if (q.queue == 0 || q.current == 0) {
        fprintf(stderr,
          "NULL pointer in function peek_at_current()\n");
        exit(1);
    }
    else
#endif
    {
        return (q.current)->priority;
```

```
    }
}


void update_current(Queue *q, void *element) {

#if defined(CONSISTENCY_CHECKING)
    if (q->queue == 0 || q->current == 0) {
        fprintf(stderr,
          "NULL pointer in function update_current()\n");
        exit(1);
    }
    else
#endif
    {
        memcpy(q->current->info, element, q->elementsize);
    }
}


void delete_current(Queue *q) {

#if defined(CONSISTENCY_CHECKING)
    if (q->queue == 0 || q->current == 0) {
        fprintf(stderr,
          "NULL pointer in function delete_current()\n");
        exit(1);
    }
    else
#endif
    {

    if (q->previous == 0) {        /* deletion at beginning */
        q->queue = q->queue->next;
        q->current = q->queue;
    }
    else {                         /* internal deletion */
        q->previous->next = q->current->next;
        q->current = q->previous->next;
    }

    (q->queuelength)--;

    }
}

int end_of_queue(Queue q) {

    return (q.current == 0);
```

```
}

void next_element(Queue *q) {

#if defined(CONSISTENCY_CHECKING)
    if (q->queue == 0) {
        fprintf(stderr,
          "NULL pointer in function next_element()\n");
        exit(1);
    }
    else if (q->current == 0) {
        fprintf(stderr,
          "Advance past end in function next_element()\n");
        exit(1);
    }
    else
#endif
    {
        q->previous = q->current;
        q->current = q->current->next;
    }
}


void rewind_queue(Queue *q) {

    q->current = q->queue;
    q->previous = 0;
}

int queue_length(Queue q) {

    return q.queuelength;
}

void copy_queue(Queue *q1, Queue q2) {

    Queue_element temp, new_element, endq1;

    /* free elements in q1 before copy */

    destroy_queue(q1);

    /* now make q1 a clone of q2 */

    q1->queuelength = 0;
```

```
    q1->elementsize = q2.elementsize;
    q1->queue = 0;
    q1->duplicates = q2.duplicates;
    q1->compare = q2.compare;

    temp = q2.queue;
    endq1 = q1->queue;

    while (temp != 0) {
        new_element = (Queue_element)malloc(
            sizeof(struct _Queue_element));

        if (new_element == 0) {
            fprintf(stderr,
                "Malloc failed in function copy_queue()\n");
            exit(1);
        }

        new_element->info = (void *)malloc(q1->elementsize);
        if (new_element->info == 0) {
            fprintf(stderr,
                "Malloc failed in function copy_queue()\n");
            exit(1);
        }
        memcpy(new_element->info, temp->info, q1->elementsize);
        new_element->priority = temp->priority;
        new_element->next = 0;

        (q1->queuelength)++;

        if (endq1 == 0) {
            q1->queue = new_element;
        }
        else {
            endq1->next = new_element;
        }
        endq1 = new_element;
        temp = temp->next;
    }

    rewind_queue(q1);
}

int equal_queues(Queue q1, Queue q2) {

    Queue_element temp1, temp2;
    int same = TRUE;
```

```
   if (q1.queuelength != q2.queuelength ||
     q1.elementsize != q2.elementsize) {
     same = FALSE;
   }
   else {
     temp1 = q1.queue;
     temp2 = q2.queue;
     while (same && temp1 != 0) {
         same = (! memcmp(temp1->info, temp2->info,
           q1.elementsize) && temp1->priority == temp2->priority);
         temp1=temp1->next;
         temp2=temp2->next;
     }
   }

   return same;
}


void merge_queues(Queue *q1, Queue q2) {

   Queue_element temp;

   temp = q2.queue;

   while (temp != 0) {
     add_to_queue(q1, temp->info, temp->priority);
     temp=temp->next;
   }

   rewind_queue(q1);
}
```

POINTERS

At the time this chapter is being written, no other books are available on Universal Plug and Play, and little documentation is available other than the specification on the UPnP website [1]. Since UPnP is based (at least loosely) on popular Internet standards, however, there is a wealth of background information available, although almost all is in electronic form. Reference 3 describes the current HTTP standard. HTTP serves as a foundation for SSDP, SOAP, and GENA. Current HTML standards are addressed at reference 4. Information on XML, which is used to describe UPnP devices and services, to specify SOAP's RPC-like actions, and is used in GENA's eventing mechanism, appears at reference 5. A background in DHCP [6] and ARP [7] is necessary to fully understand UPnP's IP address generation protocol Auto-IP. The references are to the RFCs for these protocols. Reference 8 describes the Xerces-C effort. Xerces-C is the C++-based XML parser used in the Intel SDK. Source code for the Intel SDK is available at reference 2. Reference 9 describes the Document Object Model (DOM) in detail. The DOM is used as a programming interface to XML documents in the Intel SDK.

1. Universal Plug and Play Specification, v1.0, at www.upnp.org.

2. Intel UPnP SDK for Linux, upnp.sourceforge.net.

3. R. Fielding, J. Gettys, J. Mogul, H. Frystyk, L. Masinter, P. Leach, and T. Berners-Lee, "Hypertext Transfer Protocol—HTTP/1.1," RFC 2616, http://www.ietf.org/rfc/rfc2616.txt.

4. "HyperText Markup Language (HTML)," www.w3.org/MarkUp/.

5. "Extensible Markup Language (XML)," www.w3.org/XML/.

6. R. Droms, "Dynamic Host Configuration Protocol (DHCP)," RFC 2131, http://www.ietf.org/rfc/rfc2131.txt.

7. D. C. Plummer, "An Ethernet Address Resolution Protocol (ARP)," RFC 826, http://www.ietf.org/rfc/rfc0826.txt.

8. Xerces-C XML Parser, http://xml.apache.org/xerces-c/.

9. "Document Object Model (DOM)," http://www.w3.org/DOM/.

Bluetooth Service Discovery Protocol

Bluetooth Overview

What Is Bluetooth?

Bluetooth is a low-power, short-range, wireless radio system specification being developed by the Bluetooth Special Interest Group, an industry consortium whose member companies include Ericsson, Nokia, and IBM. The radio has a range of approximately 10 m and provides up to seven links to other Bluetooth devices, with an aggregate bandwidth of about 1 Mbps. Bluetooth operates in the 2.4-GHz industrial, scientific, and medical (ISM) band to maximize international acceptance; employs a frequency-hopping system to minimize interference; and supports isochronous, synchronous, and asynchronous communication. Bluetooth devices periodically sniff for other nearby Bluetooth devices and form personal area networks called *piconets,* connecting devices in a user's personal space. A pair of Bluetooth piconets is illustrated in Fig. 5-1.

Each piconet has a "master" and up to seven "slaves." The master has important responsibilities, including definition of the frequency

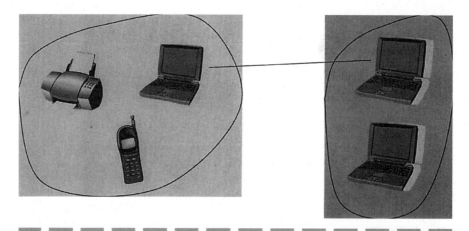

Figure 5-1

A pair of Bluetooth piconets. In the piconet on the left, a laptop is the master and communicates with a cellular phone, which provides a network connection, and a printer. In the piconet on the right, the laptop on top is master, and the other laptop is a slave. When the laptop at the top of the piconet illustrated on the right communicates with the laptop on the bottom on the left, a scatternet is formed. The laptop on the left is now a master in its own piconet and a slave in the piconet on the right.

hopping pattern; but to Bluetooth applications, the master/slave relationship is transparent, and communicating Bluetooth devices have a peer relationship. In general, the master will be the unit that initiates communication, although in some cases master/slave role swaps are performed. Piconets of more than eight devices can be accommodated through "parking," where individual devices enter a nonparticipatory mode for a period of time. It is possible for a piconet to communicate with another piconet—in this case, a master in one piconet is a slave in another. These extended personal area networks are called *scatternets*. The two piconets in the figure form a scatternet if devices (e.g., a laptop on the right and a laptop on the left) begin to communicate across piconet lines.

Bluetooth is defined by a detailed specification [1]. The first part of the Bluetooth specification, called the *core,* defines the characteristics of the various layers in the Bluetooth protocol stack and discusses low-level hardware and communication details. The layers in the stack provide an interface to the Bluetooth radio and also define protocols for telephony, interoperability with RS232 (useful for cable replacement), and object exchange (OBEX) [2,3] which provides interoperability with IrDA [4]. In many aspects Bluetooth is a competitor to IrDA, eliminating line-of-sight requirements and providing longer range. Currently IrDA provides higher bandwidth and IrDA hardware is significantly cheaper, but this may change in the future. The Bluetooth protocol stack is discussed further in the section "Bluetooth Protocol Stack Organization." The other volume of the specification addresses a number of usage scenarios, including the use of cellular phones as point-to-point intercoms, fax over Bluetooth, and the use of Bluetooth for last-hop network access. These usage scenarios are examined in further detail in the section on profiles.

One group of Bluetooth applications targets a range of mobile devices, including PDAs, handheld computers, cellular phones, pagers, and laptops. These devices are increasingly *smart,* capable of storing large amounts of information, but are also necessarily *peripheral-poor,* since functionality must be traded for suitable form factors and low power consumption. Such devices must rely on neighboring devices for services such as input (e.g., a wireless keyboard), storage, faxing, network access, and printing. Bluetooth provides a service discovery protocol (Bluetooth SDP) which can be used to search for needed services, and access to the services can be provided wirelessly. Simple applications of Bluetooth include cable replacement scenarios, e.g., a Bluetooth-capable laptop discovering and then wirelessly accessing a printer; but more complex interactions can be supported, such as the same laptop discovering a cellular phone in the user's briefcase and using the phone to make a call to transfer a document from a remote computer.

Beyond providing access to peripherals, exciting synchronization applications are envisioned which automatically synchronize contact lists, notes, and other collections of personal data stored in devices such as mobile phones and pagers. A highly anticipated Bluetooth application will provide a wireless headset for cellular phones, where the headset and handset (containing the cellular transmitter, keypad, and larger battery) are actually separate Bluetooth devices, communicating over a short-range wireless link. Other benefits for enabled mobile devices will include facilities for on-demand exchange of information such as business cards or calendar entries. Since one goal of Bluetooth is a low-cost radio, with prices expected to eventually dip below $5, many other simple data exchange scenarios can be envisioned. A Bluetooth module on your keychain could activate lights and music, transfer desktop settings, and upload important files when you enter your office. With Bluetooth radios well under 2 cm, they could theoretically be placed into virtually any device. As this book is written, Bluetooth radios are still substantially more expensive than the $5 target, and significant cost reductions must occur before Bluetooth can be widely deployed.

As a cable replacement technology, Bluetooth promises to significantly reduce desktop clutter. While bandwidth limitations in the current specification of Bluetooth make it unsuitable for replacing the cables that connect high-speed peripherals such as scanners, it is suitable for connection of lower-speed devices, such as keyboards, mice, joysticks, modems, and fax machines. Future revisions to Bluetooth will likely provide higher bandwidth, increasing the number of cables that can be safely tucked away in that bottom desk drawer. Of course, for Bluetooth to be adopted widely as a cable replacement technology, the cost of the Bluetooth devices at each end of the connection should not substantially exceed the cost of the replaced cable. Bluetooth will also affect areas beyond computing, communication, and personal information devices. If its potential is realized, Bluetooth technology will allow photographic equipment such as flashes, light meters, and similar peripherals to communicate wirelessly, using a standard radio system. For digital photography, a package of Bluetooth "film" the size of a candy bar, in your back pocket, could store thousands of images wirelessly. Add to this list remote controls for VCRs and other devices which work beyond line-of-sight, a coffee pot that activates the toaster when the coffee is ready, and more.

Goals of the Chapter

The Bluetooth specification comprises about 1500 pages, and several good books exist that summarize the specification [5,6,7]. The goals of this chapter are to provide a basic background on Bluetooth and then to address the service discovery aspects in greater detail. Unfortunately, Bluetooth development tools are generally not yet mature. As the chapter is being written, many Bluetooth stacks [e.g, 8,9] are in a fragile state, either with very specific hardware requirements and/or with APIs for some of the Bluetooth protocols either nonexistent or exposing low-level protocol details. This situation is likely to change within the next year. At least one complete Windows-based Bluetooth stack exists, written by Digianswer [10]. This stack and related applications (such as a Bluetooth version of "Network Neighborhood" called "Bluetooth Neighborhood") are distributed by IBM and several other vendors with their Bluetooth hardware (e.g., IBM's Bluetooth PCMCIA card). The primary problem with including sample code based on the Digianswer stack is that it makes extensive use of Microsoft's COM (Component Object Model) [11]. While this allows an elegant architecture in Windows, it poses a problem in the context of this book. Extensive experience with Microsoft COM would have to be assumed, and there simply isn't space in a single chapter to address COM, details of the SDK, and Bluetooth SDP. Lack of experience in COM, for example, would make any source code quite opaque. So unlike in the Jini, SLP, and UPnP chapters, I have omitted complete examples and will instead describe relevant parts of the Digianswer API to illustrate the character of a typical Bluetooth API. Readers familiar with COM who are interested in doing development under Microsoft Windows should definitely have a look at the Digianswer Bluetooth SDK, which contains extensive documentation. Those interested in tackling Bluetooth on a more "portable" level will have to wait for the open source stacks to mature (especially in supporting a wider array of Bluetooth hardware). All that said, there's a lot of buzz about Bluetooth, and SDP is important enough to warrant discussion in this book. A future edition will address Bluetooth development in greater detail. The next section discusses Bluetooth at a high level, the subsequent section examines SDP, and then the Digianswer SDK is surveyed.

Bluetooth Basics

This section briefly surveys the Bluetooth specification, to provide sufficient background for understanding Bluetooth's Service Discovery Protocol (SDP). Below, some general Bluetooth device characteristics are examined. The next section examines the Bluetooth protocol stack, and the following section surveys Bluetooth profiles, which are included in the specification to define usage scenarios. Most of the profiles depend heavily on SDP to find services of an appropriate type. A brief look at Bluetooth security is included at the end of this section.

The Basics. Each Bluetooth device is identified by a universally unique 48-bit Bluetooth address, which is analogous to the unique MAC address assigned to network interface cards. As we saw in the introduction, groups of up to eight Bluetooth devices can form ad hoc networks called *piconets* to communicate, share services, and synchronize data. In each piconet, a master device coordinates the other Bluetooth devices (including setting the 1600 hops per second frequency-hopping pattern). Extended personal area networks called *scatternets,* which consist of several piconets, are also supported.

A Bluetooth device can be in one of several states. The mechanisms by which Bluetooth devices change state are quite complex and are detailed in the specification, but we discuss the states at a high level here. The various states are as follows:

- *Standby.* The device is conserving power and waiting to connect to another Bluetooth device.

- *Inquire.* The device is searching for nearby Bluetooth devices. This mode is used to learn the Bluetooth addresses of devices in range. The page mode can then be used to contact devices of interest.

- *Page.* The device is trying to contact another Bluetooth device. If the page is successful, the device enters the connected state as a master.

- *Page scan.* The device is responsive to page requests. Devices periodically wake from power-conserving states and enter page scan to see if they are being paged.

- *Inquiry scan.* Devices that are in a discoverable mode periodically enter the inquiry scan mode to determine if other devices in range require a Bluetooth address.

- *Connected.* The device is connected to another Bluetooth device, as either a master or a slave.

- *Sniff, hold, park.* The device is participating in a piconet with varying degrees of power savings. In addition to power savings, the park mode can be used to support more than eight devices per piconet, since when in park mode a device gives up its 3-bit active member address. This 3-bit address is the limiting factor in the number of active members of a piconet. A device can be subsequently unparked to return to active duty.

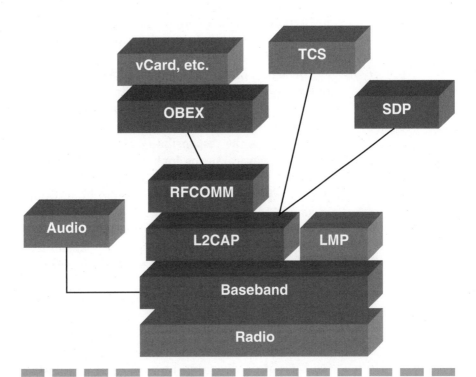

Figure 5-2

The Bluetooth protocol stack. The baseband and radio layers implement a fast frequency-hopping radio platform and provide a robust communication facility to the upper layers. The Link Manager Protocol (LMP) controls link setup and provides encryption and authentication services. The proprietary L2CAP layer provides protocol multiplexed communication to higher-level layers such as RFComm, which emulates an RS-232 interface. The OBEX (object exchange) protocol, running over RFComm, enhances Bluetooth's interoperability with IrDa, allowing exchange of business cards and other objects. TCS handles control for telephony applications.

Bluetooth Protocol Stack Organization. The Bluetooth protocol stack is illustrated in Fig. 5-2. At the bottom, the radio and baseband layers provide the short-range, frequency-hopping radio platform. The baseband layer implements forward error correction (FEC) and data whitening to enhance transmission reliability and supports asynchronous and synchronous (SCO) links. Up to three high-priority SCO links are supported per piconet; these are intended to carry telephone-quality audio data. The Link Manager Protocol (LMP) handles data link setup, sets up authentication and encryption, and handles control, including establishment of power savings modes, bandwidth allocation for L2CAP and audio, and master/slave role switches (e.g., when a master departs a piconet). The LMP does not transmit application data, and LMP packets may be transferred without the interaction of a higher-level protocol.

The logical link control and adaptation protocol (L2CAP) supports multiplexed connectionless and connection-oriented communication, shielding higher layers from the frequency-hopping nature of the Bluetooth radio. L2CAP assumes that a full-duplex, reliable communication facility is provided—this is the responsibility of the lower portion of the stack. L2CAP is used by several of the higher-level Bluetooth protocols, including SDP and RFComm. RFComm emulates an RS232 serial interface and can support many serial-oriented protocols. For example, the simple object exchange protocol (OBEX), which enhances Bluetooth's interoperability with IrDA, runs over RFComm. Hayes "AT" commands, which are used to control devices such as modems, can be transmitted over RFComm, meaning that many communication applications can run over Bluetooth without modification. One of Bluetooth's profiles discusses PPP over RFComm, which provides a natural way to run IP over Bluetooth.

Profiles. The second volume of the Bluetooth specification, weighing in at almost 500 pages, defines profiles for common interactions. A Bluetooth profile defines the characteristics of a particular use case, specifying the capabilities that are made available and defining the communication protocol. Certainly not all Bluetooth devices will implement all profiles. Profiles are examined below, with an eye to the SDP aspects of each. Each profile implemented by a particular service will have the profile's identifier included in the value of its BluetoothProfileDescriptorList attribute.

GENERIC ACCESS PROFILE. This profile defines the use of the baseband and LMP layers, defining how Bluetooth devices discover each other, how security is addressed, and how discoverability (the ability of other devices to find and connect to a particular Bluetooth device) interacts with the power-saving modes. The Generic Access Profile (GAP) is the basis of all other profiles, and it defines standard terminology that is used in describing other profiles. The GAP asserts that even if two Bluetooth devices in radio proximity do not share a common application, it should still be possible to communicate and determine this fact. In general, Bluetooth devices will conform to the GAP to establish basic interoperability.

SERVICE DISCOVERY APPLICATION PROFILE. The Service Discovery Application Profile defines how a service discovery application can support discovery of services by their service classes and by their descriptive attributes. It also describes service browsing. Several primitive service discovery-related operations are defined, including enumerateRemDev( ), serviceBrowse( ), serviceSearch( ), and terminatePrimitive( ). These do not officially define an API, but should map easily to functions provided in an SDP implementation. The enumerateRemDev( ) allows the devices in radio proximity to be enumerated, possibly constrained by their device type. The serviceBrowse( ) allows the services on a specified list of remote devices to be enumerated. The serviceSearch( ) allows searching a group of remote devices for services that match a search pattern. Finally, terminatePrimitive( ) allows the service discovery application to terminate one of the other discovery-related operations. The Service Discovery Application Profile does not define Bluetooth SDP—SDP is defined in the core specification. Rather, it defines how a service discovery application behaves and how the Bluetooth protocol layers are used to support service discovery.

CORDLESS TELEPHONY, INTERCOM PROFILE, AND HEADSET PROFILES. This profile addresses the use of Bluetooth for cordless telephony, including the use of Bluetooth communication between a cellular phone and a local gateway (GW) providing telephony services, the use of Bluetooth-only "walkie-talkies" (without traditional cellular capabilities) that can access the GW for telephony services, and the use of hands-free, TCS-capable headsets. Note that all these device types are rather sophisticated—they must understand telephony protocols. For "dumb" headsets, the Headset Profile (discussed below) is more appropriate. The service classes assigned to Cordless Telephony-compliant GWs are Cordless Telephony and General Telephony. SDP can be used to discover services of these classes in order to use access telephony services. The

Intercom Profile allows Bluetooth-enabled cellular phones to communicate directly in an "intercom" mode. The SDP service classes used are Intercom and Generic Telephony.

The Headset Profile is intended to support a much simpler form of headset than the sort targeted in the Cordless Telephony Profile. A headset device in the context of the Headset Profile merely serves as a wireless audio interface to a phone or some other device—it does not need to support advanced telephony protocols. Of all the Bluetooth use cases mentioned in the press, this is perhaps the most widely discussed. It enables hands-free operation of cellular phones, moving the cellular transmitter away from the user's brain (and out of his hands, a raging debate in the "cellular meets driving an automobile" controversy). Bluetooth headsets might also be used for videoconferencing via a personal computer. In the Headset Profile, AT commands are used to establish calls, control volume, etc. The service classes for the Bluetooth headset are Headset and Generic Audio. For the gateway (the device with which the headset communicates), the service classes are Headset Audio Gateway and Generic Audio.

SERIAL PORT PROFILE. The Serial Port Profile defines requirements for emulated serial connections (using RS232 signaling) between two Bluetooth devices. This profile will be used in most cable replacement scenarios. Legacy applications utilizing the virtual serial ports provided by a Serial Port Profile-compliant Bluetooth service should be able to run unchanged if the emulation provided is sufficiently accurate (e.g., the Serial Port Profile does not mandate the implementation of all RS232 signaling). RFComm is used to transport user data in this profile. The service class is Serial Port.

DIAL-UP NETWORKING PROFILE. The Dial-up Networking Profile supports a "network bridge" abstraction, where devices can use a Bluetooth-enabled modem, cellular phone, or other device as a bridge to the Internet or to a private network. This profile requires authentication and encryption and uses the Serial Port Profile for transfer of data, AT-style modem commands, and modem control signals, since the network bridge is modeled as a modem connected to a serial port (although it's likely that the Bluetooth device providing the service is not a traditional modem). The profile specification contains a complete list of the "AT" commands that should be supported by the gateway. The service classes for services providing the gateway functionality are Dial-up Networking and Generic Networking.

FAX PROFILE. The Fax Profile defines a use case that allows a computer to use a Bluetooth-enabled device (such as a cellular phone) as a fax modem. This profile is based on the Serial Port Profile, and as for the Dial-up Networking Profile, standard "AT" commands are used to control the fax service. Audio feedback (to allow the user to sense the status of a fax in progress) is optional. The service classes for the device implementing the Fax Profile and offering the fax service are Fax and Generic Telephony.

LAN ACCESS PROFILE. The LAN Access Profile describes how to provide LAN access for Bluetooth devices over PPP. The model supports access for a single Bluetooth device, access for multiple Bluetooth devices, and a computer-to-computer mode using PPP over serial emulation. PPP provides a natural mechanism for supporting many higher-level protocols, the most important of which is IP. Authentication and encryption are required in the LAN Access Profile. If multiple users are supported, then the device providing LAN access will always become master of the piconet. LAN Access using PPP is the service class of the device providing network access.

GENERIC OBJECT EXCHANGE, OBJECT PUSH, FILE TRANSFER, AND SYNCHRONIZATION PROFILES. The Generic Object Exchange Profile (GOEP) defines basic requirements for support of point-to-point object exchange using the OBEX protocol and is based on the Serial Port Profile. The GOEP defines the use of OBEX connection establishment, object push, and object pull. Scenarios include object push (e.g., transfer of a business card or an entry in a contact list), file transfer, and synchronization of data located on two devices. Each of these scenarios has its own profile based on the GOEP (i.e., Object Push Profile, File Transfer Profile, Synchronization Profile). The Object Push Profile supports push of an object into the inbox of a Bluetooth device, pushing a business card, and business card exchange (which is a push followed by a pull). A Bluetooth service capable of receiving an object through object push will have service class OBEX Object Push.

The File Transfer Profile provides for more sophisticated functionality than object push, including the ability to browse files or objects stored on a remote Bluetooth device, to create folders, and to push and pull data from the remote device. When a device is put into a mode to support file transfer (possibly via a user action), a service with service class OBEX File Transfer will be listed as available. The Synchronization Profile allows data on two Bluetooth devices to be synchronized. This profile address synchronization of contact lists, calendars, e-mail, and notes. Manual synchronization is mandatory for clients and services implementing this profile, and automatic synchronization support is required for synchronization services but optional for clients. The data formats for the contact lists, etc., must be compliant with the IrMC specification [3]. The service class for synchronization services is IrMCSync.

Security. Security is clearly important for a technology aimed squarely at personal mobile devices, many of which will contain sensitive information. Bluetooth devices provide data security through unique 48-bit identifiers, 128-bit authentication keys, and 8- to 128-bit encryption keys. Strong authentication is used because no international restrictions prevent it, but Bluetooth devices must negotiate encryption strength to comply with laws restricting encryption (thus the support for various encryption key lengths). Note that Bluetooth devices must be paired to provide them with matching secret keys that will support authentication. Once paired, Bluetooth devices can authenticate each other and protect sensitive data from snooping. Regardless of encryption strength, Bluetooth's fast frequency-hopping scheme makes snooping somewhat difficult.

Our Focus: Bluetooth SDP

The Bluetooth SDP provides simple mechanisms for searching the devices in range for needed services and for discovering the characteristics of these services. Much like UPnP, the Bluetooth specification does not define an SDP API, leaving this up to individual implementations. But it does describe a set of operations which provide a neat one-to-one mapping with the functions likely to be provided in an implementation. Client applications use the SDP API designed by an implementer to search for available services by service class or on a limited basis, by other service attribute values. Responses consist of 32-bit *service handles,* each of which uniquely identifies a particular service on a particular device; thus a service handle in conjunction with a device's unique Bluetooth address uniquely identifies a service within a piconet. Clients can use a service handle obtained in a service query to retrieve the attributes of a remote service. The attributes reveal information such as service capabilities and the protocols which must be used to communicate with the service. Unlike more powerful service discovery technologies such as Jini, Bluetooth's SDP does not provide a mechanism for using discovered services—communication must be accomplished with a non-SDP protocol. However, a standard attribute (ProtocolDescriptorList) is defined which enumerates appropriate protocols for communicating with the service. Attributes, service classes, and other important SDP issues are described in greater detail in the following sections.

Service Attributes.   Attributes describe essential characteristics of a service and consist of an attribute identifier (the *name* of the attribute) and an attribute value. The attribute identifier is a 16-bit unsigned integer that uniquely identifies the attribute within a service class. A number of types are supported for attribute values, including signed and unsigned integer, string, boolean, and sequences of other types. An implementation will typically provide functions for manipulating values of each of the supported types (e.g., GetBoolean, PutBoolean). Each service is described by at least two attributes, with distinguished IDs. These are the ServiceRecordHandle (0x0000) and the ServiceClassIDList (0x0001). The ServiceRecordHandle is the service handle associated with a service, and it uniquely identifies the service on a given Bluetooth device. The ServiceClassIDList is a sequence of service class identifiers which indicate the service classes that a service belongs to, beginning with the most specific and ending with the most general. Service classes are discussed in detail in the next section.

In addition to these two required attributes, other attributes will typically be defined. Several are predefined for all service classes in section E.2.3 of the Bluetooth core specification. The ServiceID attribute, if present, contains a UUID that differentiates the service on a global level from all other services. Note that ServiceID is globally unique, while the required ServiceRecordHandle is only unique with respect to a given Bluetooth device. The ServiceRecordState attribute allows clients to monitor the freshness of cached attribute values—if the ServiceRecordState attribute's value is unchanged, then no other attribute values have been modified since the last time ServiceRecordState was sampled. If ServiceRecordState changes, then at least one other attribute value has changed since the last sampling of ServiceRecordState. The ProtocolDescriptorList attribute defines the set of protocols that may be used to access the service. The value for this attribute consists of a sequence of protocol descriptors, each of which defines a specific protocol (identified by a UUID) and provides protocol-specific parameters. The format of these parameters is not defined in the specification. The Bluetooth ProfileDescriptorList attribute identifies the Bluetooth profiles to which the service conforms. The value is a sequence; each element contains a UUID that identifies a profile and a 16-bit quantity that defines the profile version. The high-order bits define the major version number, and the lower-order bits represent the minor version number of the profile.

An interesting attribute, which supports the SDP service browsing mechanism (discussed below), is BrowseGroupList. The BrowseGroup-List attribute's value consists of a sequence of UUIDs that identify *browse groups* to which the service belongs. Other standard attributes include DocumentationURL, which supplies a URL where documentation for the service can be found; ServiceName, which provides a short, human-readable name for the service; and ServiceDescription, which provides a brief human-readable description of the service. All the standard attributes are discussed in section E.2.3 of the specification. Attribute identifiers 0x000D through 0x01FF are reserved so that additional universal attributes can be defined in the future.

Service Classes. A service class defines the attributes that are associated with a particular kind of service, and is uniquely identified by a 128-bit UUID. The ServiceClassIDList attribute's value consists of a sequence of these identifiers. A service may be a member of more than one service class; in this case, some service classes are subclasses of other service classes listed in ServiceClassIDList. For example, a high-resolution, color digital image service might belong to HighResolutionColorDigitalImage, ColorDigitalImage, and DigitalImage. The HighResolutionColorDigitalImage supplements the set of attributes defined by ColorDigitalImage, which in turn supplements the set of attributes defined by DigitalImage. New services classes generally define broad device categories, such as Printer, ColorPrinter, and PostscriptPrinter, while attributes allow a finer level of description, such as indicating whether a printer supports duplex operation, multiple paper trays, or stapling. Manufacturers must eventually standardize these service classes for maximal interoperability between Bluetooth devices.

Service Records. Attributes that describe the services offered by a Bluetooth device are stored in service records, maintained by the device's SDP server. Each Bluetooth device contains at most one SDP server, although devices that never offer services may have no SDP server. Each service record is identified by a service handle, which in addition to the Bluetooth device ID uniquely identifies a particular service during an interaction between two devices. The contents of a service record consist entirely of attributes associated with the corresponding service. These include both universal attributes, applicable to all service classes, and attributes associated with the particular service classes to which the service belongs. Bluetooth SDP operations search the list of service records maintained by a device's SDP server to find matching services.

Bluetooth SDP Operations

The Bluetooth specification defines a few core operations for SDP, leaving "housekeeping" operations such as opening and closing an SDP connection (e.g., OpenSDPSession, CloseSDPSession) to particular implementations. The core operations are

- ServiceSearchRequest (resulting in a ServiceSearchResponse)
- ServiceAttributeRequest (resulting in a ServiceAttributeResponse)
- ServiceSearchAttributeRequest (resulting in a ServiceSearchAttributeResponse)

Each of these operations is discussed in detail below.

ServiceSearchRequest.   ServiceSearchRequest allows a client to find services of interest. Recall that the service classes of which a service is an instance are stored in an attribute (ServiceClassIDList); SDP uses this fact to provide a uniform searching interface across service classes and attribute values. Clients may search the service records on nearby Bluetooth devices using a list of UUIDs, which denote service classes and attribute values. A service record matches if some attribute in the service record has a value matching each of the specified UUIDs. If even one of the UUIDs isn't matched, then the service record does not match the request. Note that while this interface is uniform (e.g., all matching boils down to looking for specified attribute values), it prohibits searching for attribute values that are not UUIDs. Once an interesting service has been located, however, subsequent ServiceAttributeRequests can be used to retrieve non-UUID valued attributes. More on this in a moment, but first an aside about UUID optimizations.

UUIDs are 128-bit quantities, and the entire range of UUIDs represents a vast identifier space. By reserving regions of this space for specific purposes, it is possible to fix some of the 128 bits and eliminate the need for transferring these bits. Bluetooth does exactly this, defining the "Bluetooth Base UUID" to be 0x0000000000001000800000805F9B34FB. Service classes and attribute values can then be represented as either 16- or 32-bit quantities for transmission, and the complete UUIDs can be reconstituted using the following formulas:

$$128\_bit\_UUID = 16\_bit\_UUID*296 + Bluetooth\_Base\_UUID$$

$$128\_bit\_UUID = 32\_bit\_UUID*296 + Bluetooth\_Base\_UUID$$

The 16-bit UUIDs can be compared directly, and so can 32-bit UUIDs, without regenerating the complete UUID (since they are simply offsets from a fixed base). To compare 16- and 32-bit UUIDs, however, the 16-bit UUID must be zero-extended.

The response to a ServiceSearchRequest consists of a ServiceSearchResponse from each SDP server having matching records. The ServiceSearchResponse contains a list of 32-bit service handles for the matching services. These service handles may subsequently be used to learn the values of attributes for the service or to contact the service.

ServiceAttributeRequest. A ServiceAttributeRequest allows a client to determine the value of specified attributes for a service instance. The service instance is identified by the service handle, determined in a previous ServiceSearchRequest. The attribute values to be returned are identified by a sequence of attribute identifiers. For single attributes, these identifiers are 16-bit quantities. For convenience, it is also possible to request the values of ranges of attributes. In this case, 32-bit quantities are specified, with the high order 16 bits determining the beginning of the range and the low-order 16 bits being the end of the range. The response is a ServiceAttributeResponse, which contains a list of attribute name/value pairs for attributes that have a value. Neither the name nor the value of an attribute with a null value is returned.

ServiceSearchAttributeRequest. The ServiceSearchAttributeRequest combines the preceding operations into a single, more complex one. ServiceSearchAttributeRequest allows a client to search for matching services and to specify the list of attribute values that should be returned for each matching service in a single operation. The maximum number of UUIDs that may be required for a service to match (across service classes and attribute values) is 12. This limit is imposed to restrict the size of the search packet. The response to a ServiceSearchAttributeRequest is a sequence of attribute sequences, each of which provides the name/value pairs of the requested attributes for a matching service. Clients should request the value of attribute ServiceRecordHandle in order to learn the service handle for each matching service. As with ServiceAttributeRequest, attribute name/value pairs are not returned for those attributes with a null value.

Service Browsing. ServiceSearchRequest, ServiceAttributeRequest, and ServiceSearchAttributeRequest allow services of specific classes or with specific attribute values to be discovered. Sometimes, however, clients are interested in browsing the space of available services offered by a device. The browsing facility in SDP uses the BrowseGroupList attribute, which is universal (it applies to all service classes). To initiate browsing, a client searches for services using the UUID PublicBrowseRoot. Services defined at the "root" browse level should have this value in their BrowseGroupList attribute—they will be discovered on the initial browsing operation. To create hierarchies of browseable services, additional browse groups must be defined. Service records with a service class of BrowseGroupDescriptor serve to define new browse groups. The BrowseGroupDescriptor service class defines a single attribute, GroupID, which provides an identifier for a browse group. The GroupID of a browse group should be stored in the BrowseGroupList attribute for a service to be browseable at this level of the hierarchy.

A sample browseable hierarchy is depicted in Fig. 5-3. BrowseGroupDescriptor records break the hierarchy of services into Printer and Info(rmation) groups, and within Info, into Weather and Literary service groups. In each case, the GroupID for a BrowseGroupDescriptor creates a new branch, and is placed in the BrowseGroupList attribute of child nodes in the tree. A client searching for PublicBrowseRoot will discover the placeholder services with service classes BrowseGroupDescriptor and GroupIDs PrinterGroupID and InfoGroupID. Subsequent searches may then be formulated to browse other levels of the hierarchy.

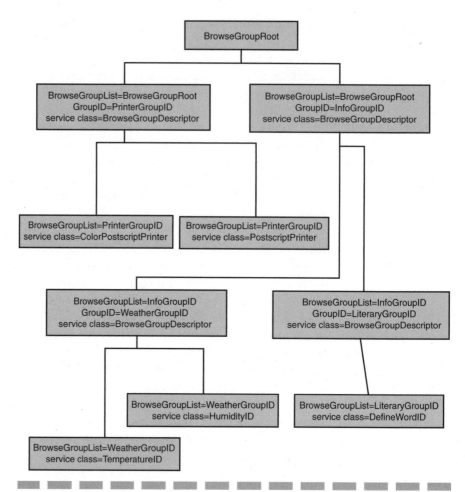

Figure 5-3
An example illustrating a browseable hierarchy of services offered by a Bluetooth SDP
server. Service records with a service class of BrowseGroupDescriptor serve as place-
holders in the hierarchy of services; their GroupID names a branch in the tree. A client
browsing the root level of this hierarchy will encounter a printer and Info branches,
and can browse further to find various printers and a fork in the Info branch that sepa-
rates two weather-based services from a more literary "DefineWord" service.

A Sample API: Digianswer's Bluetooth Software Suite

In this section the SDK for the Digianswer Bluetooth Software Suite is
examined, primarily to provide an example of what APIs provided by

Bluetooth SDKs will look like. Various open source Bluetooth stacks are under development and should become mainstream within the next year. The Digianswer Bluetooth Software Suite is not open source, but is shipped with several Bluetooth devices, including Digianswer's own line of PCMCIA Bluetooth card and IBM's PCMCIA offering, and targets Microsoft Windows. Linux may be supported in the future, and support for other hardware is forthcoming, including the IBM Ultraport adapter. The Bluetooth Software Suite comprises a compliant Bluetooth stack, profiles, and a Windows "Bluetooth Neighborhood" (similar to "Network Neighborhood") application that exposes much of the functionality of the profiles (including file transfer, a network bridge, etc.) without programming. The stack contains L2CAP, RFComm, Audio, and SDP protocols (the radio and baseband are included in the Bluetooth hardware, as usual). As this is written, serial port, file transfer, and object push profiles are included. Limited versions of some of the other profiles, including headset and network access, are provided; and others, like synchronization, are in development. An SDK is available, and representative functions available in the SDK are listed below, to provide a feel for Bluetooth development. Microsoft COM experience is actually required to do development with the SDK, but no knowledge of COM is assumed in the discussion below. The complete SDK documentation is available online at Digianswer's site.

Core Bluetooth.   The methods in this portion of the SDK are intended primarily for controlling the local device and finding other Bluetooth devices. Methods are provided for entering inquiry mode to discover other Bluetooth devices, for determining the names of the local device and of remote devices, and for managing the power savings modes (such as sniff and park). Representative methods are listed below. A complete list appears in the SDK documentation.

IBluetooth::Inquiry

IBluetooth::CancelInquiry

IBluetooth::GetLocalDeviceAddress

IBluetooth::GetLocalClassOfDevice

IBluetooth::SetLocalFriendlyName

IBluetooth::GetLocalFriendlyName

IBluetooth::RequestRemoteFriendlyName

IBluetooth::HoldMode

IBluetooth::SniffMode

IBluetooth::ExitSniffMode

IBluetooth::ParkMode

IBluetooth::ExitParkMode

Events. The SDK defines a number of event types, which are used to alert an application to the discovery of other Bluetooth devices, the discovery of the names of remote devices, etc. Representative event types are listed below. The names are self-explanatory.

IBluetoothEvents::OnInquiryComplete

IBluetoothEvents::OnInquiryResult

IBluetoothEvents::OnInquiryStart

IBluetoothEvents::OnInquiryCancel

IBluetoothEvents::OnConnection

IBluetoothEvents::OnDisconnection

IBluetoothEvents::OnLocalDeviceRemoved

IBluetoothEvents::OnLocalDeviceReset

IBluetoothEvents::OnCloseDown

IBluetoothEvents::OnRemoteNameResult

IBluetoothEvents::OnDeviceListChange

File Transfer Profile. The file transfer profile provides functions that allow transfer of files between Bluetooth devices. Files may be pushed and pulled, the remote directory listed, and authentication settings changed (e.g., to require or not require a password before access to files is allowed). The functions provided by this profile are listed below and are typical of the level of abstraction provided by other profiles in the SDK.

IBTOBEXFileTransferProfile::Connect

IBTOBEXFileTransferProfile::Disconnect

IBTOBEXFileTransferProfile::GetConnections

IBTOBEXFileTransferProfile::GetLocalServices

IBTOBEXFileTransferProfile::GetRemoteServices

IBTOBEXFileTransferProfile::SetRemotePath

IBTOBEXFileTransferProfile::GetRemoteFolderContents

IBTOBEXFileTransferProfile::PushFile

IBTOBEXFileTransferProfile::PullFile

IBTOBEXFileTransferProfile::DeleteRemoteFile

IBTOBEXFileTransferProfile::GetSharedFilesDirectory

IBTOBEXFileTransferProfile::SetSharedFilesDirectory

IBTOBEXFileTransferProfile::GetAccessMode

IBTOBEXFileTransferProfile::SetAccessMode

IBTOBEXFileTransferProfile::GetAuthenticationMode

IBTOBEXFileTransferProfile::SetAuthenticationMode

SDP. The SDP-related functions provided in the SDK allow manipulation of locally stored service records (indicating which services are offered by the local device) and discovery of remote services. The ServiceSearchRequest function provides for service discovery by service classes and attribute values (but again, only those attributes with UUID-typed values). The ServiceAttributeRequestSingle function allows the value of a single attribute for a remote service to be determined, while ServiceAttributeRequest allows the values of both individual attributes and ranges of attributes to be queried. ServiceSearchAttributeRequest provides for combined service discovery and querying of specified attributes.

IBTSDPProfile::OpenSDPSession

IBTSDPProfile::CloseSDPSession

IBTSDPProfile::CreateServiceRecord

IBTSDPProfile::DeleteServiceRecord

IBTSDPProfile::AddServiceAttribute

IBTSDPProfile::DeleteServiceAttribute

IBTSDPProfile::ServiceSearchRequest

IBTSDPProfile::ServiceAttributeRequestSingle

IBTSDPProfile::ServiceAttributeRequest

IBTSDPProfile::ServiceSearchAttributeRequest

POINTERS

The following list includes references to the Bluetooth specifications (both core and profiles) [1], several books that address the Bluetooth specification in detail [5,6,7], and three Bluetooth stacks that are currently under development [8,9,10]. Also included are links to the IrDA website [4] and two of the most important IrDA standards documents [2,3]. Reference 11 provides a good introduction to Microsoft COM, experience in which is necessary to use the Digianswer Bluetooth SDK.

1. Bluetooth specification, available from http://www.bluetooth.org/.

2. "IrDA Object Exchange Protocol IrOBEX v1.2," http://www.irda.org/standards/pubs/IrOBEX12.pdf.

3. "Infrared Data Association Specifications for Ir Mobile Communications (IrMC) v1.1," http://www.irda.org/standards/pubs/IrMC_v1p1Specs&Errata0010 24.zip.

4. Infrared Data Association® (IrDA®, http://www.irda.org.

5. B. Miller and C. Bisdikian, *Bluetooth Revealed: An Insider's Guide to the Open Specification for Global Wireless Communications,* Prentice-Hall, Englewood Cliffs, N.J., 2000.

6. N. Muller, *Bluetooth Demystified,* McGraw-Hill, New York, 2000.

7. J. Bray and C. Sturman, *Bluetooth: Connect Without Cables,* Prentice-Hall, Englewood Cliffs, N.J.2000.

8. BlueDrekar, http://www.alphaworks.ibm.com/tech/bluedrekar.

9. BlueZ, http://bluez.sourceforge.net.

10. Digianswer Bluetooth Software Suite, http://www.digianswer.com.

11. D. Rogerson, *Inside COM: Microsoft's Component Object Model,* Microsoft Press, 1997.

INDEX

Note: Boldface numbers indicate illustrations.

802.11, 13

abort(), Jini, 142–143
ABSOLUTE, leasing, 34
abstract vs. concrete types, in SLP, 153, 187
account creation, Jini, 60–61, 108
action requests in SOAP, UPnP, 243–250
actionPerformed(), Jini, 102, 110
actions, UPnP, 318
active discovery, SLP, 166
addAttributes(), Jini, 80
addGroups(), Jini, 44
addListener(), Jini, 124
addLocators(), Jini, 49–50
Address Resolution Protocol (ARP), UPnP, 223, 236, 358
addressing, Bluetooth SDP, 364
addService(), Jini, 94, 112
advertisement of services, 2–3, 7
  SLP and, 164, 166, 170
  Universal Plug and Play (UPnP) and, 222, 237–242, 264, 333–335
agents, SLP, 150, 163–176
AllPermission, Jini, 126
ANY, leasing, 32–34, 35
APIs:
  Bluetooth Service Discovery Protocol (SDP), 370, 376–379
  Service Location Protocol (SLP) and, 10
AppleTalk, SLP, 154
applications for service discovery, 11–14
asynchronous vs. synchronous processing, 366
  Bluetooth Service Discovery Protocol (SDP) and, 366
  SLP and, 178–179, 185–187,

asynchronous vs. synchronous processing (*Cont.*):
  Universal Plug and Play (UPnP) and, 300
Atomicity,Consistency, Isolation, Durability (ACID), 138, 140, 144
attributes:
  Bluetooth Service Discovery Protocol (SDP) and, 371–372, 374, 379
  Jini, 54–55, 70, 77, 78, 80
  SLP and, 150, 156–157, 165, 168, 169, 173–174, **173**, 180, 182, 184, 202–203
  Universal Plug and Play (UPnP) and, 241, 251
AttributesCallback(), SLP, 202
AttrRqst/AttrRply, SLP, 165, 168–170, 174
augmented Backus–Naur form (ABNF) grammar of URLs, 156, 219
authentication, in SLP, 215 216–217, **216**
authenticator blocks (ABs) in URLs, SLP, 172
Auto IP protocol, UPnP, 10, 224, 236
autoconfiguration, UPnP, 10–11
AWTPermission, Jini, 126

binding, SLP, 176, 212
Blender Service example using Universal Plug and Play (UPnP), 227–229, 232–236, 260–335
Block Structure Descriptor (BSD), SLP, authentication/security, 216–217
blocking protocols, Jini transaction processing, 139–140
Bluetooth and Service Discovery Protocol (SDP), 7, 9, 11–13, 15, 359–380
  addressing in, 364

Bluetooth and Service Discovery
Protocol (SDP) (*Cont.*):
API in, 370, 376–379
asynchronous vs. synchronous
processing in, 366
attributes in, 371–372, 374, 379
Bluetooth explained, 360–363, **360**
browse groups in, 372, 375
BrowseGroupDescriptor in, 375
BrowseGroupList in, 372, 375
browsing for services in, 367, 372,
375, **376**
caching in, 371
classes of services in, 372
CloseSDPSession in, 373
Component Object Model (COM)
and, 363
connected state in, 365
Cordless Telephony Profile in,
367–368
core specification of, 361, 377–378
data types in, 371
Dial-Up Networking Profile in, 368
Digianswer and, 363, 376–379
DocumentationURL in, 372
enumerateRemDev() in, 367
events in, 378
Fax Profile in, 369
File Transfer Profile in, 369–370,
378–379
forward error correction (FEC) in,
366
gateways (GWs) in, 367
Generic Access Profile in, 366–367
Generic Object Exchange Profile
in, 369–370
GroupID in, 375
Headset Profile in, 367–38, 367
industrial scientific and medical
(ISM)_bandwith for, 360
inquire state in, 364
inquiry scan state in, 364
Intercom Profile in, 367–368
IrDA interoperability in, 361
Jini vs., 15, 363, 370
LAN Access Profile in, 369
Link Manager Protocol (LMP) in,
366

Bluetooth and Service Discovery
Protocol (SDP) (*Cont.*):
logical link control and adaptation
protocol (L2CAP) in, 366
master and slave devices in,
360–361
mobile devices and, 361
object exchange (OBEX) in, 361,
366, 369–370
Object Push Profile in, 369–370
OpenSDPSession in, 373
operating systems and, 377
operation of, 373–376
page scan state in, 364
page state in, 364
parking devices in, 361
peripherals and, 361–362
piconets of bluetooth and, 360–361,
360, 364
ProfileDescriptorList in, 372
profiles in, 366–370
protocol layers or stack in, 361,
363, **365**, 366
ProtocolDescriptorList in, 371
PublicBrowseRoot in, 375
records of services in, 372–373
RFComm in, 366
Salutation and, 15
scatternets in, 361, 364
searching for services in, 367,
373–375
security in, 370
Serial Port Profile in, 368
Service Discovery Application
Profile in, 367
service handles in, 370
Service Location Protocol (SLP)
vs., 363
service records in, 11
ServiceAttributeRequest/Response
in, 373, 374, 379
ServiceBrowse() in, 367
ServiceClassIDList() in, 371,
372
ServiceDescription in, 372
ServiceName in, 372
ServiceRecordHandle() in, 371
ServiceRecordState, 371

Bluetooth and Service Discovery
Protocol (SDP) (*Cont.*):
ServiceSearch() in, 367
ServiceSearchAttributeRequest/
Response in, 373, 374–375
ServiceSearchRequest/Response
in, 373–374
SLP and, 150
sniff, hold, park state in, 365
software development kit (SDK)
and, 363, 377
standby state in, 364
state variables in, 371
states of devices in, 364–365
synchronization and, 362, 369–370
Synchronization Profile in,
369–370
terminatePrimitive() in, 367
Universal Plug and Play (UPnP)
vs., 15, 363
URLs in, 372
UUID in, 371, 372–375
web sites of interest for, 380
Windows and, 363, 377
wireless devices and, 362–363
browse groups, Bluetooth SDP, 372,
375
BrowseGroupDescriptor, Bluetooth
SDP, 375
BrowseGroupList, Bluetooth SDP,
372, 375
browsing for services, 7
Bluetooth Service Discovery
Protocol (SDP) and, 367,
372, 375, **376**
Jini, 117–119
SLP and, 174

C API for SLP, 177–184
asynchronous vs. synchronous
behavior in, 178–179,
185–187
attributes in, 180, 182, 184,
202–203
callback functions in, 178–180,
184–187, 189–190, 202–205
configuration in, 184
cookies and, 185

C API for SLP (*Cont.*):
directory agents (DAs) in, 182
echo service client implementation
using, 199–212
echo service using, 187–199
error codes in, 177–178, 189–194
escape characters in, 183
graceful death ritual in, 194
handles in, 178–179, 189
Lightweight Directory Access
Protocol (LDAP) in, 181, 219
main() in, 188, 200
OpenSLP and, 177, 187, 199
operating systems and, 187
refresh in, 182, 189
registration in, 179–180, 190, 191,
200–201
reserved characters in naming in,
183
scopes in, 182–183, 206
search filters in, 181–182, 206
service agents (SAs) in, 182
service discovery in, 180, 181
signal handler in, 188–189, 194
SLPHandle in, 178–179
SLPSrvURL in, 178
sockets connection in, 195–199
source file in, 187
types in, 177
URLs in, 183, 189, 204, 206
C language
SLP and, 152, 176
Universal Plug and Play (UPnP)
and, 223, 225, 259, 267, 290,
358
CACHE CONTROL header, UPnP,
238
caching of services
in Bluetooth Service Discovery
Protocol (SDP) and, 371
in Jini, 119–124, **120**
in SLP and, 150
CALLBACK, UPnP, 252–256
CallbackHandler(), UPnP,
268–270
callbacks:
SLP and, 178–181, 184–187,
189–190, 202–205

callbacks (*Cont.*):
   Universal Plug and Play (UPnP)
        and, 264, 265, 268–269, 298,
        300, 301, 303–305
cancelling subscriptions, UPnP,
        251–255
CannotJoinException, Jini, 141
catalogs of service, 2, 7–8
   Jini and (*See* lookup services)
   Service Location Protocol (SLP)
        and, 10
cell phones, 5, 13
changed(), Jini, 45
check(), Jini, 122
choose(), SLP, 201
classes of services, Bluetooth SDP,
        372
CLASSPATH, Java, 23
client/server systems, 2–4
clients, 4–6
   Jini, 28, 84–124
   SLP and, 175
close() method in Jini, 61–62
CloseSDPSession, Bluetooth SDP,
        373
code mobility, Jini, 20
CommandLoop(), UPnP, 294
commit(), Jini, 142–143
common characteristics of service
        discovery, 6–8
common.c library, UPnP, code,
        336–346
Component Object Model (COM),
        Bluetooth SDP, 363
configuration, 4
   auto, Universal Plug and Play
        (UPnP), 10–11
   device drivers and, 5
   peripheral device, 4–5
   SLP and, 184, 212–214
connected state, Bluetooth SDP, 365
connecting clients to services, 4
connecting with client, Jini, open()
        and close() methods, 61–62
constants, UPnP, 289
CONTENT LENGTH header, UPnP
        and, 242, 244, 255–256
CONTENT TYPE header, UPnP, 244

control points, UPnP, 222–224, 245,
        262, 269–274, 289–335
control URLs, UPnP, 224, 227, 244,
        311
cookies:
   SLP and, 185
   Universal Plug and Play (UPnP)
        and, 263, 269, 294
Cordless Telephony Profile, Blue-
        tooth SDP, 367–368
core specification of Bluetooth
        Service Discovery Protocol
        (SDP), 361
CPU requirements for Universal
        Plug and Play (UPnP), 226
crash counts, Jini transaction
        processing, 140–143
CrashCountException, 140–141
create(), Jini, 108, 140, 142, 144
createLookupCache(), Jini, 121, 122,
        123
createNewBiz(), Jini, 132
createNewReason(), Jini, 132

DA Stateless Boot Timestamp, SLP,
        164–165, 219
DAAdvert, SLP, 164–166, **164**, 170,
        176, 217–219
data structures, Jini object serializa-
        tion, 21–22
data synchronization, 13
   Bluetooth Service Discovery
        Protocol (SDP) and, 362,
        369–370
data types:
   Bluetooth Service Discovery
        Protocol (SDP) and, 371
   SLP and, 156
   Universal Plug and Play (UPnP)
        and, 231–232, 289
DATE header, UPnP, 253
debugging:
   Jini, 75
   Universal Plug and Play (UPnP)
        and, 269
delete(), Jini, 110
description document, UPnP, 226,
        229, 238, 242, 262, 267, 308

description URL, UPnP, 299
designing services in Jini, 57–69,
    77–84
destructive and nondestructive
    copies in JavaSpaces, 129
device chassis, Jini, 27–28, **27**
device defined, 6
device drivers, 5
    Jini and, 9
    Universal Plug and Play (UPnP)
      and, 222
device templates, UPnP, 227
deviceType, UPnP, 227
DHCP servers, 2
Diagnose(), 192
    Jini, 190, 192
    SLP and, 177, 189, 207–210
    Universal Plug and Play (UPnP)
      and, 263, 342
Dial-Up Networking Profile,
    Bluetooth SDP, 368
die(), SLP, 207–210
Diagianswer and Bluetooth Service
    Discovery Protocol (SDP), 363,
    376–379
Digital Signature Algorithm (DSA),
    218
digital signatures, SLP, 216, 218
directories of services, UPnP, 10–11
directory agents (DAs), SLP, 10, 150,
    151, 163–166, **164**, 170, 171,
    175, 176, 182, 215, 217, 218
discard(), Jini, 43, 45, 124
discovered(), Jini, 45, 46, 73, 74, 90
discovery of services, 1–16, **2**
    applications for, 11–14, 11
    Bluetooth Service Discovery
      Protocol (SDP) and
      7, 9, 11, 12–13, 15, 359–380,
      359
    client/server systems in, 2–4
    common characteristics of, 6–8
    data synchronization and, 13
    features of, 4–6
    interoperability issues and,
      14–16
    Jini for, 7–10, 13–15, 17–148
    lookup services in Jini, 42–51

discovery of services (*Cont.*):
    mobile devices and, 13
    networked devices and, 12
    Remote Method Invocation (RMI)
      for, 9
    Salutation for, 9, 15
    Service Location Protocol (SLP)
      7, 8, 10, 15, 149–220
    suites for, 8–11
    Universal Plug and Play (UPnP)
      for, 8, 10–11, 12, 14–15,
      221–358
    XML in, 14–15
DiscoveryEvent in Jini, 46–47, **47**
DiscoveryGroupManagement in Jini,
    43–47, **44**, 50
DiscoveryListener, Jini, 43–47, **46**,
    73–74, 90–91
DiscoveryLocatorManagement, Jini,
    49–51, **49, 51**
DiscoveryManagement, 43–47, **43**,
    49, 50, 79, 81, 120
DiscoveryPermission, Jini, 126
distributed objects, Jini, 23–27
Document Object Model (DOM),
    UPnP, 258–260, 328–330,
    358
DocumentationURL, Bluetooth SDP,
    372
domain name service (DNS), 7
dongle, 12
downloading code, Jini, 22–23
DURATION, leasing, 34
Dynamic Host Configuration
    Protocol (DHCP), 7
    Jini, 28
    SLP and, 163, 166, 170, 175–176,
      215, 219
    Universal Plug and Play (UPnP)
      and, 224, 236, 358

echo service:
    SLP and, using C API, 154, 158,
      187–199
    SLP and, client in C API, 199–212
EchoClient(), SLP, 201, 210–212
element_in_queue() calls, UPnP, 314
enabled services, 2

encryption, SLP, 218–219
entities, Jini, 28–31
Entry objects:
    JavaSpaces and, 54
    Jini, 54–55, 78, 85, 118–119, 130
enumerateRemDev(), Bluetooth SDP,
    367
equals(), 54, 85, 121, 124
Ericsson, 360
error codes and error handling:
    General Event Notification
        Architecture (GENA) and,
        253–257
    Jini, 141
    Simple Object Access Protocol
        (SOAP) and, 246–250
    SLP and, 177–178, 189–194
    Universal Plug and Play (UPnP)
        and, 272, 273, 276, 277, 294,
        342–343
escape characters, SLP, 161, 183
event messages in GENA and
    Universal Plug and Play
    (UPnP), 255–257
event subscription URLs, 250–251
eventing and events, 8
    Bluetooth Service Discovery
        Protocol (SDP) and, 378
    Universal Plug and Play (UPnP)
        and, 230–231, 245, 250–257,
        279, 326–328
exceptions (*See* error codes and error
    handling)
exit(), SLP, 194
expiration of advertisement, UPnP,
    240, 305

Fax Profile, Bluetooth SDP, 369
file storage service example:
    StorageService.java, 58–69
    StorageServiceClient.java,
        88–93
    StorageServiceServerJM.java,
        81–84
file storage, remote (*See* remote file
    storage)
File Transfer Profile, Bluetooth SDP,
    369–370, 378–379

file transfer protocol (FTP), 13
FilePermission, Jini, 126
FindAttributes(), SLP, 202–203, 206
FindEchoServices(), SLP, 201, 206
FOREVER, leasing, 32–33
forward error correction (FEC), Blue-
    tooth SDP, 366
FreeBSD, 152

garbage collection, 2, 8
gateways (GWs), Bluetooth SDP, 367
General Event Notification
    Architecture (GENA), 10
  attributes in, 251
  error codes and error handling in,
    253–257
  event messages in, 255–257
  HandleGENAEvent() in, 302
  state variables in, 251, 302
  subscription cancellation in,
    251–255
  subscription process in, 251–255
  subscription renewal in, 251–255,
    302
  Universal Plug and Play (UPnP)
    and, 224, 231, 232, 250–260,
    302, 328–330, 357
  URLs in, 250–251
  variables and values in, 251, 256
Generic Access Profile, Bluetooth
    SDP, 366–367
generic methods, Jini, 52
Generic Object Exchange Profile,
    Bluetooth SDP, 369–370
GET command (HTTP), UPnP, 242
getAttributes(), Jini, 80
getBytes(), Jini, 104
getDiscoveredLocators(), Jini, 50
getDiscoveryManager(), Jini, 80
getEntryClasses(), Jini, 53, 118–119
getFieldValues(), Jini, 53, 117–118
getFilenames(), Jini, 103, 114
getGroups(), Jini, 44, 46, 52
getHost(), Jini, 48
getIPAddress(), Jini, 122
getJoinSet(), Jini, 80
getLease(), Jini, 70
getLeaseRenewalManager(), Jini, 80

getLeastSignificantBits(), Jini, 57
getLocator(), Jini, 52
getMostSignificantBits(), Jini, 57
getPort(), Jini, 48
getRegistrar(), Jini, 46–48
getServiceID(), Jini, 52, 69, 87
getServiceInfo(), UPnP, 308–311
getServiceItem(), Jini, 87, 94
getServiceTypes(), Jini, 53
getSource(), Jini, 94
getState(), Jini, 144–145
getStorageServiceNames(), Jini,
    103, 113
getTransition(), Jini, 87–88
getUndiscoveredLocators(), Jini, 50
global variables, UPnP, 264, 277
graceful death ritual, SLP, 194
graphic user interfaces (GUIs),
    Jini, 95–117, **96**
    Universal Plug and Play (UPnP)
        and, 257
GroupID, Bluetooth SDP, 375
groups of lookup services, Jini,
    38, 77

HandleCommand(), UPnP, 274, 275,
    280, 283–284
HandleGENAEvent(), UPnP, 302,
    328–330
handles:
    Bluetooth Service Discovery
        Protocol (SDP) and, 370
    SLP and, 178–179, 189
    Universal Plug and Play (UPnP)
        and, 263, 264
HandleSubscriptionRequest(), UPnP,
    270
HandleVariableRequest(), UPnP, 272
hardware provided services, 12
hashCode(), 124
hashtable of discovered services,
    Jini, 97–98, 103, 112–113, 124
Headset Profile, Bluetooth SDP,
    367–38
HOST header, UPnP, 238, 244
HTML, 357–358
    Universal Plug and Play (UPnP)
        and, 222, 224, 257

HTTP, 10
    Simple Object Access Protocol
        (SOAP) and, 243
    Universal Plug and Play (UPnP)
        and, 222, 224, 225, 238,
        242–244, 357

IBM, 360, 363, 377
IDs for lookup services in Jini, 52
incremental registration, SLP, 160
industrial scientific and medical
    (ISM) bandwith, Bluetooth
    SDP, 360
init_queue(), UPnP, 293
initialization, UPnP, 264–265, 294
InitializeStateTable(), UPnP,
    264–265
inquire state, Bluetooth SDP, 364
inquiry scan state, Bluetooth SDP,
    364
insertion of services, 3, 7
installation of services, 4–5
    device drivers and, 5
interacting with services:
    GUI instances for client in,
        95–117, **96**
    Jini, 95–117
    Universal Plug and Play (UPnP)
        and, 223–224, 295
Intercom Profile, Bluetooth SDP,
    367–368, 367
Internet Assigned Naming Authority
    (IANA), 159, 180
Internet Engineering Task Force
    (IETF), 150
interoperability, 3, 14–16
IOException, Jini, 80
IP addresses, 2
    Jini, 28, 48, 122
    lookup services in Jini and, 48
    SLP and, 154
    Universal Plug and Play (UPnP)
        and, 222, 223, 236, 261–262,
        293
IP-based networks, 150, 224–225
IPX, SLP, 154
IrDA interoperability, Bluetooth SDP,
    361

Java:
  CLASSPATH and, 23
  device chassis for, 27–28, **27**
  device drivers and, 9
  downloading bytecode in, 22–23
  Java Virtual Machine (JVM) and, 22–23, 27–28
  Jini and, 14, 15, 20–23, 27–28, 125–127
  Remote Method Invocation (RMI) and, 23–27, **24**, 146, 147
  security and, 125–127
  SLP and, 152, 176
  Universal Plug and Play (UPnP) and, 225
Java Virtual Machine (JVM), 22–23, 27–28
JavaSpace, 9
  destructive and nondestructive copies in, 129
  Entry objects and, 54
  Jini and, 32, 54, 127–138, **128**, 146
  leasing and, 32, 127–128
  main() method in, 130
  read() in, 129
  readIfExists(), 129
  Receipt Handling example using, 129–138
  self healing feature of objects in, 127
  snapshot() in, 129
  take() and takeIfExists() in, 129, 135, 138
  template used in, 135, 137
  Transaction used in, 145–146
  transient vs. persistent objects in, 127
  write() in, 128, 132, 135
Jini, 7–10, 14, 15, 17–148
  aborting or commiting transactions in, 142–143
  account creation for, 60–61, 108
  Atomicity,Consistency, Isolation, Durability (ACID) in transaction processing of, 138, 140, 144
  attributes in, 54–55, 70, 77, 78, 80

Jini (*Cont.*):
  Bluetooth Service Discovery Protocol (SDP) and, 15, 363, 370
  browsing for services using, 117–119
  caching of services in, 119–124
  CannotJoinException in, 141
  client entities in, 28
  clients in, 84–124
  code downloading in, 22–23
  code mobility in, 20
  connecting with client in, open() and close() methods, 61–62
  controlling lookup services via ServiceRegistrar in, 51–53, **52**
  crash counts in, 140–143
  data structures in, 21–22
  debugging in, 75
  deployment of, 146–147
  designing services in, 57–69, 77–84
  destructive and nondestructive copies in JavaSpaces and, 129
  development and history of, 18
  device chassis for, 27–28, **27**
  directories and files for, 146–147
  discovery of lookup services in, 42–51
  discovery of services and, 29–31, **30**
  DiscoveryEvent in, 46–47, **47**
  DiscoveryGroupManagement in, 43–47, **44**, 50
  DiscoveryListener in, 43–47, **46**, 73–74, 90–91
  DiscoveryLocatorManagement in, 49–51, **49, 51**
  DiscoveryManagement in, 43–47, **43**, 49, 50, 79, 81, 120
  distributed objects and RMI in, 23–27, **24**
  distributions of (PDF and Postscript), 147
  Dynamic Host Configuration Protocol (DHCP) and, 28
  entities in, 28–31

Jini (*Cont.*):

Entry objects in, 54–55, 78, 85, 118–119, 130

exceptions in, 141

file storage service example (StorageServiceServerJM.java), 58–69, 81–84, 88–93

finding lookup services in, 38–42

generic methods in, 52

groups of lookup services in, 38, 77

GUI instances for client in, 89, 91, 95–117, **96**

hardware services and, 19

hashtable of discovered services in, 97–98, 103, 112–113, 124

ID for lookup services in, 52

interacting with services using, 95–117

interface vs. implementation in, 19–20

IOException in, 80

IP addresses and, 28, 48, 122

Java and, 14, 15, 20, 21, 22–23, 27–28, 125–127

Java Virtual Machine (JVM) and, 27–28

JavaSpace and, 32, 54, 127–138, **128**, 146

Jini Technology Core Platform Specification for, 77

Join Protocol in, 77, 81

JoinManager in, 57, 78–81, **79**, 119, 120

LeaseRenewalManager for, 34–37, **35**, 72, 76, 79, 80, 81, 89, 92, 120, 131, 132

leasing facilities in, 31–37, 60, 72, 74, 75

listeners in, 102, 124

locations of services in, 38

lookup services in, 18, 20, 21, 28–32, **29**, 37–53, 57–58, 60, 74, 77

LookupCache in, 121, 123–124, **123**

LookupDiscovery in, 43–47, **45**, 73, 90

LookupDiscoveryManager in, 50–51, **50**, 73, 80

Jini (*Cont.*):

LookupLocator in, 47–48, **47**

LookupLocatorDiscovery in, 49, **49**

lost services in, serviceDisappeared(), 103, 104, 106, 114

MAC addresses and, 57

main() method in, 71, 130

managing unicast and multicast discovery of lookup services in, 50–51

Meaning of Life (MOL) service interface in, example of RMI, 24–27

migration of proxy object in, 53–54

multicast announcement protocol to find lookup services in, 41, **41, 42**

multicast lookup service discovery in, 43–47

multicast request protocol to find lookup services in, 39–40, **39, 40**

Network File System (NFS) and leasing in, 31–32

object serialization in, 21–22

overview of, 19–21

pausing services in, 78

permissions for security in, 126–127

persistent objects in JavaSpaces and, 127

persistent state and leasing in, 32, 77

plugging and unplugging services in, 18

policy files for security in, 125, 126–127

proxy objects in, 19–22, 29, 37–38, 53, 57–58, 60, 73, 74, 95–117

public group of lookup services in, 38

public methods in, 52

Receipt Handling example using JavaSpaces in, 129–138

reggie default lookup service implementation, 146

registration in, 25, 29–32, **30**, 38, 53, 60, 69–78

Jini (*Cont.*):
remote file storage and, 13–14
Remote Method Invocation (RMI)
and, 21, 23–27, **24**, 38, 58,
125, 146, 147
RemoteEvent in, 86, **87**
RemoteEventListener in, 53, 86,
87
RemoteException in, 43, 104,
105–106, 114, 141
requirements of, 21, 27–28
searching for services using, 23,
57–58, 84–95
security in, 71, 125–127
SecurityManager in, 125
ServerTransaction in, 143–146, **145**
Service Location Protocol (SLP)
and, 15, 53
ServiceDiscoveryListener in, 122
ServiceDiscoveryManager in, 114,
119–124, **120**
ServiceEvent in, 86–87, **87**
ServiceID in, 52–53, 56–57, 60,
69–80, 84, 87, 124
ServiceItem in, 69–77, **69**, 94
ServiceItemFilter in, 121, 122
ServiceItems in, 121
ServiceMatches in, 86, **86**, 91
ServiceNotifier in, 93–94
ServiceRegistrar in, 21, **30**, 31, 38,
40, **40**, 42–47, 48, 51–53, **52**,
69, 84–95, 117–119
ServiceRegistration in, 69–77, **70**
services, service entities defined
for, 19, 28, 53–84
ServiceTemplate in, 84–95, **85**, 89,
119
Simple Jini Client example (code),
18
SLP and, 150
socket connection in, 22, 28
StorageServiceServer in, 70–77
stream objects vs. serialization in,
22
String argument in, 119
terminating connectivity with
client in, shutdown()
method, 62, 109

Jini (*Cont.*):
Thread objects vs. serialization in,
22
timeout in, 48
Transaction in, 143–146, **144**
Transaction system for, 127,
138–146
TransactionConstants in, 142,
142
TransactionFactory in, 143–146,
145
TransactionManager in, 140–143,
141
TransactionParticipant in,
140–143, **143**
transient objects in JavaSpaces
and, 127
Transmission Control Protocol
(TCP) and, 28, 31, 39, 42, 58
two-phase commit in, 139–140,
139
unicast discovery protocol to find
lookup services in, 41–42
unicast lookup service discovery in,
47–48
Universal Plug and Play (UPnP)
vs., 15, 28, 241, 257
universally unique IDs in, 55–57,
77
UnknownTransactionException in,
141
URLs and, 48
User Datagram Protocol (UDP)
and, 28, 39, 41, 58
window-related events for GUI in,
115–116, 115
Jini Technology Core Platform Specification, 77
Join Protocol, Jini, 77, 81
join(), Jini, 140, 141, 144–145
JoinManager, Jini, 57, 78–81, **79**,
119, 120

key security, in SLP, 215

LAN Access Profile, Bluetooth SDP,
369
laptops, 4–5

LeaseRenewalManager, Jini, 34–37,
    35, 72, 76, 79, 80, 81, 89, 92,
    120, 131, 132
leases and garbage collection, 8
leasing:
    ABSOLUTE constant in, 34
    ANY in, 32–34, 35
    basic Lease interface for, 32–34
    batching of, 34
    DURATION constant in, 34
    duration of, 32–34, 75
    expiration time of, 35
    FOREVER in, 32–33
    JavaSpaces and, 32, 127–128
    Jini, 31–37, 60, 72, 74, 75, 79, 80, 81
    LeaseRenewalManager for, 34–37,
        35, 72, 76, 79, 80, 81, 89, 92,
        120, 131, 132
    listeners and, 36
    Network File System (NFS) and,
        31–32
    persistent state maintenance and,
        32, 77
    renewal of, automatic, 34–37
Lightweight Directory Access
    Protocol (LDAP), SLP, 181,
    219
Linda, 9, 127
Link Manager Protocol (LMP),
    Bluetooth SDP, 366
Linux, 12, 152, 187, 199, 259, 377
listeners:
    Jini, 102, 124
    leasing and, 36
    SLP and, 161
listFiles(), Jini, 103, 114
location changes, 3
LOCATION header, UPnP, 238
location of services, 7
    Jini, 38
    SLP and, 150
locking of device state:
    Network File System (NFS), 31
    Universal Plug and Play (UPnP)
        and, 265–267, 316
logical link control and adaptation
    protocol (L2CAP), Bluetooth
    SDP, 366

lookup services, Jini, 9, 18–21, 28–32,
    29, 37–53, 57–58, 60, 74, 77
control of, via ServiceRegistrar,
    51–53, **52**
discovery of, 42–51
DiscoveryEvent in, 46–47, **47**
DiscoveryGroupManagement in,
    43–47, **44**, 50
DiscoveryListener in, 43–47, **46**,
    73–74
DiscoveryLocatorManagement in,
    40–51, **49, 51**
DiscoveryManagement in, 43–47,
    43, 49, 50, 79, 81, 120
finding, 38–42
IDs for, 52
IP addresses and, 48
LookupDiscovery in, 43–47, **45**, 73,
    90
LookupDiscoveryManager in,
    50–51, **50**, 73, 80
LookupLocator in, 47–48, **47**
LookupLocatorDiscovery in,
    49, **49**
managing unicast and multicast
    discovery of, 50–51
managing unicast discovery of
    multiple, 49–50
multicast announcement protocol
    to find, 41, **41, 42**
multicast lookup service discovery
    in, 43–47
multicast request protocol to find,
    39–40, **39, 40**
reggie default implementation of,
    146
RemoteEventListener in, 53
ServiceDiscoveryListener in, 122
ServiceDiscoveryManager in, 124
ServiceID in, 52–53, 56–57, 77–80
ServiceRegistrar in, 40, **40**, 42,
    43–48, 51–53, **52**
Transmission Control Protocol
    (TCP) and, 39, 42
unicast discovery protocol to find,
    41–42
unicast lookup service discovery in,
    47–48

lookup services, Jini (*Cont.*):
  URLs and, 48
  User Datagram Protocol (UDP)
    and, 39, 41
lookup(), Jini, 53, 84, 90, 91, 121,
  122, 124
LookupCache, Jini, 121, 123–124,
  123
LookupDiscovery, Jini, 43–47, **45**, 73,
  90
LookupDiscoveryManager, Jini,
  50–51, **50**, 73, 80
LookupLocator, Jini, 47–48, **47**
LookupLocatorDiscovery, Jini,
  49, **49**
lost services in Jini, serviceDisap-
  peared(), 103, 104, 106, 114

MAC addresses, Jini, 57
MacOS, 12, 152, 187, 199
main()
  Jini, 71, 130
  SLP and, 188, 200
  Universal Plug and Play (UPnP)
    and, 260–262, 265, 288, 293,
    333–335
master and slave devices, Bluetooth
  SDP, 360–361
matching attributes, SLP, 174
memory requirements for Universal
  Plug and Play (UPnP), 226
message extensions, SLP, 160–161,
  160
message formats in SLP, 159–162,
  159
message header, SLP, 159–160, **159**,
  170
message retransmission policies,
  SLP, 162
migration of proxy object in Jini,
  53–54
mobile devices, 5–6, 13, 361
modifyAttributes(), Jini, 70, 81
multicast announcement protocol to
  find lookup services in Jini,
  41, **41, 42**
multicast convergence algorithm,
  SLP, 162

multicast lookup service discovery in
  Jini, 43–47
multicast request protocol to find
  lookup services in Jini, 39–40,
  39, 40
multicasting, 2
  catalogs of services and, 8
  SLP and, 150, 151, 161, 162, 163,
    170, 176
  Universal Plug and Play (UPnP)
    and, 237–242

Naming Authority, SLP, 153, 154,
  155, 159, 180
naming devices for Universal Plug
  and Play (UPnP), 227
National Insitute of Standards and
  Technology (NIST), 218
National Security Agency (NSA), 218
NetPermission, Jini, 126
Network File System (NFS)
  leasing and, 31–32
  locking in, 31
networked devices, 12
Nokia, 360
Notification Sub Type (NTS) header,
  UPnP, 238
Notification Type (NT) header, UPnP,
  238
NOTIFY message, UPnP, 255–256,
  264
notify(), Jini, 53, 86, 88, 92

Object Exchange (OBEX), Bluetooth
  SDP, 361, 366, 369–370
Object Push Profile, Bluetooth SDP,
  369–370
object serialization:
  Jini, 21–22
  stream objects vs., 22
  Threads vs., 22
opaque types, SLP, 156
open(), Jini, 61–62, 107
OpenSDPSession, Bluetooth SDP,
  373
OpenSLP, 10, 152, 187, 177, 199,
  212, 215
operating systems, 12

object serialization (*Cont.*):
    Bluetooth Service Discovery
          Protocol (SDP) and, 377
    SLP and, 152, 187

page scan state, Bluetooth SDP, 364
page state, Bluetooth SDP, 364
palmtop computers, 4–5
parking devices, Bluetooth SDP, 361
ParseItem(), UPnP, 267, 311–313,
    322–324, 344
passive discovery, SLP, 166
pausing services in Jini, 78
peer-to-peer service discovery, 7
peripheral devices, 4–5, 361–362
permissions for security, Jini,
    126–127
persistent objects in JavaSpaces, 127
persistent state, leasing to maintain,
    32, 77
personal digital assistants (PDAs), 13
piconets, Bluetooth SDP, 360–361,
    360, 364
policy files for security, Jini, 125–127
POST command, UPnP, 243–245
prepare(), Jini, 142–143
prepareAndCommit(), Jini, 143
presentation URLs in Universal Plug
    and Play (UPnP), 224, 257,
    299
previous responder lists, SLP, 162,
    170, 174
prioque.c queue package, UPnP,
    code, 346–357
private key security, SLP, 215
private scope, SLP, 175
ProfileDescriptorList, Bluetooth
    SDP, 372
profiles, Bluetooth SDP, 366–370
PropertyPermission, Jini, 126
protocol layers or stack, Bluetooth
    SDP, 361, **365**, 366
ProtocolDescriptorList, Bluetooth
    SDP, 371
protocols, 14–16
    Universal Plug and Play (UPnP)
        and, 222–224, **225**,
        226–257

prototypes, UPnP, 289
proxy objects, Jini, 9, 19–20, 22, 29,
    53–54, 57–58, 60, 73, 74,
    95–117
    Remote Method Invocation (RMI)
        and, 58
    Transmission Control Protocol
        (TCP) and, 58
    User Datagram Protocol (UDP)
        and, 58
pthread_mutex_lock(), UPnP,
    265–266
pthread_mutex_unlock(), UPnP,
    267
public group of lookup services, Jini,
    38
public key security in SLP, 215
public methods, Jini, 52
public scope, SLP, 175
PublicBrowseRoot, Bluetooth SDP,
    375
publisherhost, UPnP, 252
publisherpath, UPnP, 252
publisherport, UPnP, 252

QueryStateVariable(), UPnP,
    326–328
queueing functions, UPnP, 293

read(), JavaSpaces, 129
ReadAndEcho(), SLP, 198
readIfExists(), JavaSpaces, 129
readvertisement in Universal Plug
    and Play (UPnP), 305
records of services, Bluetooth SDP,
    372–373
ReflectPermission, Jini, 126
refresh, in SLP, 182, 189
refresh(), Jini, 112
reggie default lookup service
    implementation, Jini, 146
register(), Jini, 52, 73–74
registration of services:
    Jini, 25, 29–32, **30**, 38, 53, 60,
        69–78
    SLP and, 160, 165, 166, 169, **169**,
        175–176, 179–180, 190, 191,
        200–201, 217, 218

registration of services (*Cont.*):
  Universal Plug and Play (UPnP)
      and, 263, 268, 288, 294, 300,
      332
remote file storage, 13–14
Remote Method Invocation (RMI), 9
  Jini and, 21, 23–27, **24**, 38, 58,
      125, 146, 147
  proxy objects and, 58
Remote Procedure Call (RPC), UPnP,
      243
RemoteEvent, Jini, 86, **87**
RemoteEventListener, Jini, 53, 86,
      87
RemoteException, Jini, 43, 104–106,
      114, 141
removal of service, 4, 7
removeGroups(), Jini, 44
removeLocators(), Jini, 49–50
renewing leases, 34–37
renewing subscriptions, UPnP,
      251–255, 302
ReportEvent(), UPnP, 269, 336
reserved characters in SLP, 155, 183
retransmission policies in SLP, 162
RFComm, Bluetooth SDP, 366
RuntimePermission, Jini, 126

SAAdvert, SLP, 166, 168–170, **168**,
      176, 218
Salutation, 9, 15
scatternets, Bluetooth SDP, 361, 364
scope, SLP, 150–151, 175–176,
      182–183, 206, 212–214
search filters, SLP, 181–182, 206
searching for services, 7
  Bluetooth Service Discovery Proto-
      col (SDP) and, 367, 373–375
  DiscoveryListener in, 90–91
  Entry objects in, 85
  Jini, 57–58, 84–95
  RemoteEvent in, 86, **87**
  RemoteEventListener in, 86, **87**
  ServiceEvent in, 86–87, **87**
  ServiceID in, 84, 87
  ServiceItem in, 94, 121
  ServiceItemFilter in, 121, 122
  ServiceMatches in, 86, **86**, 91

searching for services (*Cont.*):
  ServiceNotifier in, 93–94
  ServiceRegistrar in, 84–95, 90, 94
  ServiceTemplate in, 84–95, **85**
  Universal Plug and Play (UPnP)
      and, 241, 298–299
Secure Hash Algorithm (SHA),
      218–219
security, 13
  Bluetooth Service Discovery
      Protocol (SDP), 370
  Java, 71, 125–127
  Jini, 125–127
  SLP, 150, 215–219, 215
SecurityManager, Jini, 125
SecurityPermission, Jini, 126
SendAction(), UPnP, 318–322, 324
Serial Port Profile, Bluetooth SDP,
      368
SerializablePermission, Jini, 126
serialization (*See* object serialization)
ServeEchoClients(), SLP, 198
server defined, 4–6
SERVER header, UPnP, 253
ServerTransaction, Jini, 143–146,
      145
service agents (SAs), SLP, 150, **151**,
      163, 166–171, 175, 176, 182,
      215, 217–218
Service Control Protocol Description
      (SCPD), UPnP, 227, 229–236,
      243–244, 262
service defined, 4–6
Service Discovery Application Profile,
      Bluetooth SDP, 367
Service Discovery Protocol (SDP)
      (*See* Bluetooth Service
      Discovery Protocol)
service handles, Bluetooth SDP, 370
service ID, UPnP, 227, 270–273
Service Location Protocol (SLP), 7, 8,
      10, 15, 149–220
  abstract vs. concrete types in, 153,
      187
  active vs. passive discovery in, 166
  advertisement in, 164, 166, 170
  agents in, 150, 163–176
  AppleTalk in, 154

Service Location Protocol (SLP)
(*Cont.*):
asynchronous vs. synchronous
behavior in, 178–179,
185–187
attributes in, 150, 156–157, 165,
168, 169, 173–174, **173**, 180,
182, 184, 202–203
AttrRqst/AttrRply in, 165, 168,
169, 170, 174
augmented Backus–Naur form
(ABNF) grammar of URLs
in, 156, 219
authentication in, 215, 216–217, **216**
authenticator blocks (ABs) in
URLs of, 172
binding in, 176, 212
Bluetooth Service Discovery
Protocol (SDP) vs., 150, 363
browsing for services in, 174
C language and, 152, 176, 177–184
caching services in, 150
callback functions in, 178–180,
181, 184–187, 189–190, 202,
203–205
client configuration and scope in,
175
configuration files in, 184, 212–214
cookies and, 185
DA Stateless Boot Timestamp in,
164–165, 219
DAAdvert in, 164–166, **164**, 170,
176, 217, 218, 219
data types in, 156
digital signatures and, 216, 218
directory agents (DAs) in, 150,
151, 163–166, **164**, 170, 171,
175, 176, 182, 215, 217, 218
Dynamic Host Configuration
Protocol (DHCP) and, 163,
166, 170, 175–176, 215, 219
echo service client implementation
using C API for, 199–212
echo service in, 154, 158
echo service using C API in,
187–199
encryption in, 218–219
error codes in, 189–194

Service Location Protocol (SLP)
(*Cont.*):
error codes in C API for, 177–178
escape characters in, 161, 183
graceful death ritual in, 194
handles in, 178–179, 189
incremental registration in, 160
IP addresses in, 154
IP-based networks and, 150
IPX in, 154
Java and, 152, 176
Jini vs., 15, 53, 150
Lightweight Directory Access
Protocol (LDAP) in, 181, 219
listeners in, 161
locations of services in, 150
main() in, 188, 200
matching attributes in, 174
message extensions in, 160–161, **160**
message formats in, 159–162, **159**
message header in, 159–160, **159**,
170
message retransmission policies in,
162
multicast convergence algorithm
in, 162
multicasting and, 150, 151, 161,
162, 163, 170, 176
Naming Authority in, 153, 154,
155, 159, 180
OpenSLP and, 152, 177, 187, 199,
212, 215
operating system support for, 152,
187
order of request messages in, 170
previous responder lists in, 162,
170, 174
private key security in, 215
private vs. public scope in, 175
public key security in, 215
refresh in, 182, 189
registration in, 160, 165, 166, 169,
169, 175–176, 179–180, 190,
191, 200–201, 217, 218
reserved characters in naming in,
155, 183
SAAdvert in, 166, 168–169, **168**,
170, 176, 218

Service Location Protocol (SLP)
    (*Cont.*):
  scope in, 150–151, 174–176,
      182–183, 206, 212–214
  search filters in, 181–182, 206
  security and, 150, 215–219
  service agents (SAs) in, 150, **151**,
      163, 166–170, 171, 175, 176,
      182, 215, 217, 218
  Service Discovery Protocol (SDP)
      and, 150
  service types in, 153–158
  signal handler in, 188–189, 194
  size of message in, 172–173
  slpd daemon for security in, 215
  SLPFindSrvs() in, 171
  SLPHandle in, 178–179
  SLPSrvURL in, 178
  sockets connection in, 187,
      195–199
  SrvAck in, 166, 167
  SrvReg/SrvDeReg, 165, 166–169,
      167, 169, 217
  SrvRqst/SrvRply in, 165–168,
      170–174, **171, 172**, 218
  SrvTypeRqst/SrvTypeRply in, 165,
      168, 170, 174, **175**, 180, 218
  string comparison rules in,
      161–162
  subclassing of service types in,
      153–154
  templates in, 153, 154–158, 187
  threads and, 184
  time to live (TTL) setting in, 212
  Transmission Control Protocol
      (TCP) and, 150, 156, 158,
      173
  types in C API, 177
  types of messages in, 165, 168
  unicasting and, 161, 170, 176
  Universal Plug and Play (UPnP)
      vs., 150, 241
  URLs and, 150, 153–158, 165–167,
      172, 174, 183, 189, 204, 206
  user agents (UAs) in, 150, **151**, 163,
      170–174, 176, 215, 217, 218
  User Datagram Protocol (UDP)
      and, 150, 156, 172–173

Service Location Protocol (SLP)
    (*Cont.*):
  user selectable scoping in, 176
  versions of (SLPv1, SLPv2), 152
  XID fields in messages in, 162
service records, Bluetooth, 11
service types, SLP, 153–158
ServiceAttributeRequest/Response,
    Bluetooth SDP, 373, 374, 379
serviceBrowse(), Bluetooth SDP, 367
ServiceClassIDList, Bluetooth SDP,
    371–372
ServiceDescription, Bluetooth SDP,
    372
serviceDisappeared(), Jini, 103, 104,
    106, 114
ServiceDiscoveryListener, Jini, 122
ServiceDiscoveryManager, Jini, 114
  caching of services using, 119–124,
      120
ServiceEchoClients(), 191
ServiceEvent, Jini, 86–87, **87**
ServiceID, Jini, 52–53, 56–57, 60,
    69–80, 84, 87, 124
serviceIDNotify(), 78
ServiceItem, Jini, 69–77, **69**, 94
ServiceItemFilter, Jini, 121, 122
ServiceItems, Jini, 121
ServiceMatches, Jini, 86, **86**, 91
ServiceName, Bluetooth SDP, 372
ServiceNotifier, Jini, 93–94
ServiceRecordHandle (), Bluetooth
    SDP, 371
ServiceRecordState, Bluetooth SDP,
    371
ServiceRegistrar, Jini, **30**, 31, 38, 40,
    40, 42, 43–48, 51–53, 69–77,
    90, 94
  browsing for services using,
      117–119, 117
  lookup services in Jini and, 40, **40**,
      42–48, 51–53, **52**
  searching for services using, 84–95
  ServiceID in, 69–77
  ServiceItem in, 69–77, **69**
  ServiceRegistration in, 69–77, **70**
  StorageServiceServer in, 70–77
ServiceRegistration, Jini, 69–77, **70**

services entities, Jini, 28
serviceSearch(), Bluetooth SDP, 367
ServiceSearchAttributeRequest/
    Response, Bluetooth SDP,
    373–375
ServiceSearchRequest/Response,
    Bluetooth SDP, 373–374
ServiceTemplate, Jini, 84–95, **85**, 119
serviceTypes, UPnP, 227
setAttributes(), Jini, 70, 81
setGroups(), Jini, 44
setLocators(), Jini, 49–50
SHA–1 encryption, SLP, 218–219
ShowMenu(), UPnP, 295
shutdown(), 190
    Jini, 62, 109
    SLP and, 187, 189, 194, 207–210
    Universal Plug and Play (UPnP)
        and, 288, 296, 332
signal handler
    SLP and, 188–189, 194
    Universal Plug and Play (UPnP)
        and, 265, 288, 294
SignalHandler():
    SLP, 194, 207–210
    Universal Plug and Play (UPnP)
        and, 288, 294
sigwait(), UPnP, 288
Simple Object Access Protocol
    (SOAP), 10
    action requests in SOAP in,
        243–250
    error codes and handling in,
        246–250
    HTTP and, 243
    Remote Procedure Call (RPC) in,
        243
    state variable requests in,
        248–250
    Universal Plug and Play (UPnP)
        and, 229, 243–250, 258–260
    XML and, 243
    Universal Plug and Play (UPnP)
        and, 224, 324, 357
Simple Service Discovery Protocol
    (SSDP), 10, 237–242
    Universal Plug and Play (UPnP)
        and, 264, 357

SLPAttrCallback(), 186
SLPAttrs(), 202
SLPClose(), 179, 194
slpd daemon, 215
SLPDelAttrs(), 180, 184, 185
SLPDereg(), 180, 184, 185, 187, 194
SLPError(), 191, 199
SLPEscape(), 183
SLPFindAttr(), 182, 184, 186, 203
SLPFindScopes(), 182–183
SLPFindSrvs(), 171, 181, 184, 204,
    206
SLPFindSrvTypes(), 180, 185, 186
SLPFree(), 183, 184
SLPFreeURL(), 183
SLPGetProperty(), 184
SLPGetRefreshInterval(), 182
SLPHandle(), 178–179, 182, 189, 199
SLPOpen(), 179, 185, 187, 189, 201
SLPParseAttr(), 184
SLPParseSrvURL(), 178, 204
SLPReg(), 184, 185, 190, 191
SLPSetProperty(), 184
SLPSrvTypeCallback(), 186
SLPSrvURL, 178
SLPSrvURLCallback(), 186
SLPUnescape(), 183
snapshot(), JavaSpaces, 129
sniff, hold, park state, Bluetooth
    SDP, 365
socket connections:
    Jini, 22, 28
    SLP and, 187, 195–199
SocketPermission, Jini, 126
software development kit (SDK)
    Bluetooth Service Discovery
        Protocol (SDP) and, 363, 377
    Universal Plug and Play (UPnP)
        and, 222, 257–258, **258**, 358
software-provided services, 12
Solaris, 12, 152
sprintf(), UPnP, 280–283
SrvAck, SLP, 166, 167
SrvReg, SLP, 166–167, **167**
SrvReg/SrvDeReg, SLP, 165, 168,
    169, **169**, 217
SrvRqst/SrvRply, SLP, 165–168,
    170–174, **171, 172**, 218

SrvTypeRqst/SrvTypeRply, 165, 168, 170, 174, **175**, 180, 218

ssdp:alive message, UPnP, 237–239, 241–242

ssdp:all messages, UPnP, 242

ssdp:byebye message, UPnP, 239, 240, 317

ssdp:discovery message, UPnP, 240–241

stable vs. transient devices, UPnP, 240

standby state, Bluetooth SDP, 364

state variable:
    Bluetooth Service Discovery Protocol (SDP) and in, 364–365, 371
    SOAP and Universal Plug and Play (UPnP) and, 248–250
    Universal Plug and Play (UPnP) and, 248–251, 264, 267, 272, 302, 326–328

StorageService.java, Jini, 58–69

StorageServiceClient.java in Jini, 88–93

StorageServiceServer in Jini, 70–77

StorageServiceServerJM.java, Jini, 81–84

store(), Jini, 104

stream objects vs. serialization, 22

string comparison rules, SLP, 161–162

subclassing of service types in SLP, 153–154

SUBSCRIBE message, UPnP, 253–254

SubscribeService(), UPnP, 316

subscribing to events, UPnP, 224

subscription cancellation, UPnP, 251–255

subscriber ID (SID), UPnP, 253, 255–256, 316

subscription process, UPnP, 251–255

subscription renewal, UPnP, 251–255, 302

subscription requests, UPnP, 270–271

subscription URLs, UPnP, 227, 250–251, 311

subtyping, 7

suites for service discovery, 8–11

synchronization (*See* data synchronization)

Synchronization Profile, Bluetooth SDP, 369–370

synchronous SLP, 178–179, 185–187

tag values, UPnP, 344–345

take() and takeIfExists(), JavaSpaces, 129, 135, 138

templates for services 10
    JavaSpaces and, 135, 137
    SLP and, 153, 154–158, 187
    Universal Plug and Play (UPnP) and, 227, 229–231

terminate(), Jini, 81, 121, 124

terminatePrimitive(), Bluetooth SDP, 367

terminating connectivity with client, Jini, shutdown() method, 62, 109

threading:
    Jini, 22
    SLP and, 184
    thread objects vs. serialization in Jini, 22
    Universal Plug and Play (UPnP) and, 265–265, 294, 296, 311, 324, 333–335

time to live (TTL) values:
    SLP and, 212
    Universal Plug and Play (UPnP) and, 237, 241, 242

timeout, Jini, 48

TIMEOUT, UPnP, 252

TimerLoop(), UPnP, 294, 305, 333–335

toolkit for Universal Plug and Play (UPnP), 222

Transaction, Jini, 143–146, **144**

Transaction processing in Jini, 127, 138–146
    abort() in, 142–143
    Atomicity,Consistency, Isolation, Durability (ACID) in, 138, 140, 144
    blocking protocols in, 139–140

Transaction processing in Jini
(*Cont.*):
CannotJoinException in, 141
commit() in, 142–143
crash counts in, 140–143
CrashCountException in, 140–141
exceptions in, 141
RemoteException in, 141
ServerTransaction in, 143–146, **145**
Transaction in, 143–146, **144**
TransactionConstants in, 142, **142**
TransactionFactory in, 143–146,
145
TransactionManager in, 140–143,
141
TransactionParticipant in,
140–143, **143**
two-phase commit in, 139–140,
139
UnknownTransactionException in,
141
TransactionConstants, Jini, 142, **142**
TransactionFactory, Jini, 143–146,
145
TransactionManager, Jini, 140–143,
141
TransactionParticipant, Jini,
140–143, **143**
transient objects in JavaSpaces, 127
Transmission Control Protocol (TCP):
Jini, 28, 31, 39, 42, 58
multicast request protocol for
lookup services and, 39
proxy objects and, 58
SLP and, 150, 156, 158, 173
unicast discovery protocol for
lookup services and, 42
Universal Plug and Play (UPnP)
and, 223–225, 251
two-phase commit, Jini, 139–140,
139

unicast discovery protocol to find
lookup services in Jini,
41–42
unicast lookup service discovery in
Jini, 47–48
unicasting, SLP, 161, 170, 176

uniform resource identifiers (URIs),
UPnP, 238
unique device name (UDN), UPnP,
267, 270–273, 299, 313–314
unique identifiers, UPnP, 238, 264
Unique Service Name (USN) header,
UPnP, 238
Universal Plug and Play (UPnP), 7,
8, 10–12, 14–15, 221–358
action requests in SOAP in,
243–250
actions in, 318
Address Resolution Protocol (ARP)
and, 223, 236, 358
advertisement in, 222, 237–242,
264, 333–335
asynchronous vs. synchronous
processing in, 300
attributes in, 241, 251
Auto IP protocol for, 224, 236
Blender Service example using,
227–229, 232–236, 260–335
Bluetooth Service Discovery
Protocol (SDP) vs., 15, 363
C language and, 223, 225, 259,
267, 290, 358
CACHE CONTROL header in, 238
CALLBACK in, 252–256
CallbackHandler() in, 268, 269, 270
callbacks in, 264, 265, 268–269,
298, 300, 301, 303–305
CommandLoop() in, 294
common.c library in, code for,
336–346
constants in, 289
CONTENT LENGTH header in,
242, 244, 255–256
CONTENT TYPE header in, 244
control points in, 222–224, 245,
262, 269, 270, 272, 274,
289–335
control URLs in, 224, 227, 244,
311
cookies in, 263, 269, 294
CPU requirements for, 226
data types in, 231–232, 289
DATE header in, 253
debugging in, 269

Universal Plug and Play (*Cont.*):
  describing devices and services in, 226–235
  description documents in, 226, 229, 238, 242, 262, 267, 308
  description URL in, 299
  device drivers and, 222
  device templates in, 227
  devices using, 226
  deviceType in, 227
  Diagnose() in, 263, 342
  discovery of services in, 223
  Document Object Model (DOM) and, 258–260, 328–330, 358
  Dynamic Host Configuration Protocol (DHCP) and, 224, 236, 358
  element_in_queue() calls in, 314
  error codes and error handling in, 253–257, 272, 273, 276, 277, 294, 342–343
  error codes and handling in SOAP and, 246–250
  event messages in GENA and, 255–257
  event subscription URLs (*See* subscription URLs)
  eventing in, 230–231, 245, 250–257, 279, 326–328
  expiration of advertisement in, 240, 305
  General Event Notification Architecture (GENA) and, 224, 231, 232, 250–260, 302, 328–330, 357
  GET command (HTTP) in, 242
  GetServiceInfo() in, 308–311
  global variables in, 264, 277
  HandleCommand() in, 274, 275, 280, 283–285
  HandleGENAEvent() in, 302, 328–330
  handles in, 263, 264
  HandleSubscriptionRequest(), 270
  HandleVariableRequest() in, 272
  HOST header in, 238, 244
  HTML and, 222, 224, 257, 357–358

Universal Plug and Play (*Cont.*):
  HTTP and, 222, 224, 225, 238, 242–244, 357
  implementation of, 226
  init_queue() in, 293
  initialization in, 264–265, 294
  InitializeStateTable() in, 264, 265
  interacting with services in, 223–224, 295
  interfaces from DOM in, 259–260
  IP addresses and, 222, 223, 236, 261–262, 293
  IP networks and, 224–225
  Java and, 225
  Jini vs., 15, 28, 241, 257
  LOCATION header in, 238
  locking of device state in, 265–267, 316
  loops in, 285, 305, 333–335
  main() in, 260–262, 265, 288, 293, 333–335
  memory requirements for, 226
  multicasting in, 237–242
  naming devices for, 227
  Notification Sub Type (NTS) header in, 238
  Notification Type (NT) header in, 238
  NOTIFY message in, 255–256, 264
  ParseItem() in, 267, 311–313, 322–324, 344
  POST command in, 243–245
  presentation URLs in, 224, 257, 299
  prioque.com queue package in, code for, 346–357
  protocols and, 222–257, **225**
  prototypes in, 289
  pthread_mutex_lock() in, 265–266
  pthread_mutex_unlock() in, 267
  publisherhost/path/port in, 252
  QueryStateVariable(), 326–328
  queueing functions in, 293
  readvertisement in, 305
  registration in, 263, 268, 288, 294, 300, 332
  Remote Procedure Call (RPC) in, 243
  ReportEvent() in, 269, 336

Universal Plug and Play (*Cont.*):
requirements for, 224–225
SDK return value, 342
searching for services in, 241,
298–299
SendAction() in, 318–322, 324
SERVER header in, 253
Service Control Protocol Description (SCPD) in, 227,
229–236, 243–244, 262
service IDs in, 227, 270–273
Service Location Protocol (SLP)
vs., 241
serviceTypes in, 227
ShowMenu() in, 295
shutdown() in, 288, 296, 332
SignalHandler() in, 288, 294
sigwait() in, 288
Simple Object Access Protocol
(SOAP) and, 224, 229,
243–250, 258–260, 324,
357
Simple Service Discovery Protocol
(SSDP) in, 237–242, 264,
357
SLP and, 150
software development kit (SDK)
for, 222, 257–258, **258**, 358
ssdp:alive message in, 237–239,
241–242
ssdp:all messages in, 242
ssdp:byebye message in, 239, 240,
317
ssdp:discovery message in,
240–241
stable vs. transient devices in, 240
state variable requests in SOAP
and, 248–250
state variables in, 251, 264, 267,
272, 302, 326–328
SUBSCRIBE message in, 253–254
SubscribeService() in, 316
subscribing to events in, 224
subscription cancellation in,
251–255
subscription ID (SID) in, 253,
255–256, 316
subscription process in, 251–255

Universal Plug and Play (*Cont.*):
subscription renewal in, 251–255,
302
subscription requests in, 270–271
subscription URLs in, 227, 311,
250–251
tag values in, 344–345
templates for, 227, 229–231
thread processing in, 265–265,
294, 296, 311, 324, 333–335
time to live (TTL) values in, 237,
241, 242
TIMEOUT in, 252
TimerLoop() in, 294, 305, 333–335
toolkit for, 222
Transmission Control Protocol
(TCP) and, 223, 224, 225, 251
uniform resource identifiers (URIs)
in, 238
unique device name (UDN) in, 267,
270–273, 299, 313–314
unique identifiers in, 238, 264
Unique Service Name (USN)
header in, 238
UNSUBSCRIBE message in, 254
UPC codes for devices using, 227
UPNP_CONTROL_ACTION_COM
PLETE, 303–305
UPNP_CONTROL_GET_VAR_CO
MPLETE, 303–305
Upnp_Document in, 289–290, 324,
328–330, 344
Upnp_Element, 344
UPNP_EVENT_RENEWAL_
COMPLETE, 303–305
UPNP_EVENT_SUBSCRIBE_
COMPLETE, 303–305
UPNP_EVENT_UNSUB-
SCRIBE_COMPLETE,
303–305
Upnp_Node in, 290
Upnp_NodeList in, 290
UpnpAcceptSubscription() in, 272
UpnpActionRequest() in, 274,
275–277
UpnpActionResult() in, 274,
278–279
UpnpAddToAction() in, 324

Universal Plug and Play (*Cont.*):
UpnpClientHandle() in, 294
UpnpDevice_Handle in, 263
UpnpDocument, 330
UpnpDocument_freed(), 324
UpnpDocument_getElementsBy-
TagName(), 330
UpnpElement() in, 308
UpnpFinish() in, 288–289, 332–333
UpnpGetErrorMessage() in, 342
UpnpGetServiceVarStatus() in,
300, 326–328
UpnpGetServiceVarStatusAsync()
in, 300
UpnpInit() in, 262–263, 294
UpnpMakeAction() in, 324
UpnpNode_free() in, 290
UpnpNodeList() in, 308, 330–331
UpnpNotify() in, 279
UpnpPDocument(), 308
UpnpRegisterClient() in, 294, 300
UpnpRegisterRootDevice() in, 263,
268, 269, 288, 294
UpnpSearchAsync() in, 298–301
UpnpSendAction() in, 300, 322, 324
UpnpSendActionAsync() in, 300
UpnpSendAdvertisement() in,
264
UpnpSetWebServerRoot() in, 263
UpnpSubscribe() in, 315–316
UpnpUnRegisterClient() in, 332
UpnpUnRegisterRootDevice(), 288
UpnpUnsubscribe() in, 317
URLs in, 223, 224, 226, 227, 242,
244, 250–251, 262, 299, 311
User Datagram Protocol (UDP)
and, 223, 225, 237, 241
UUID in, 238, 253
variables and values in, 231, 251,
256, 272–273, 300,
326–328
web servers and, 263
web sites of interest to, 229, 358
Xerces and, 258–260, 358
XML and, 14–15, 222–226, 229,
242–245, 257–260, 267,
278–279, 289, 290, 308,
324, 358

universally unique IDs (UUIDs)
Bluetooth Service Discovery
Protocol (SDP) and, 371–375
Jini, 55–57, 77
Universal Plug and Play (UPnP)
and, 238, 253
UnknownTransactionException, Jini,
141
UNSUBSCRIBE message, UPnP, 254
UPC codes for devices using
Universal Plug and Play
(UPnP), 227
UpnpAcceptSubscription(), 272
UpnpActionRequest(), 274–277
UpnpActionResult(), 274–279
UpnpAddToAction(), 324
UpnpClientHandle(), 294
UPNP_CONTROL_ACTION_
COMPLETE, 303–305
UPNP_CONTROL_GET_VAR_
COMPLETE, 303–305
UpnpDevice_Handle, 263
Upnp_Document, 308, 324, 328–330,
289–290, 344
UpnpDocument_freed(), 324
UpnpDocument_getElementsByTag-
Name(), 330
UpnpElement(), 308
Upnp_Element, 344
UPNP_EVENT_RENEWAL_
COMPLETE, 303–305
UPNP_EVENT_SUBSCRIBE_
COMPLETE, 303–305
UPNP_EVENT_UNSUBSCRIBE_
COMPLETE, 303–305
UpnpFinish(), 288–289, 332–333
UpnpGetErrorMessage(), 342
UpnpGetServiceVarStatus(), 300,
326–328
UpnpGetServiceVarStatusAsync(),
300
UpnpInit(), 262–263, 294
UpnpMakeAction(), 324
UpnpNode_free(), 290
Upnp_Node, 290
Upnp_NodeList, 290
UpnpNodeList(), 308, 330–331
UpnpNotify(), 279

UpnpDocument(), 308
UpnpRegisterClient(), 294, 300
UpnpRegisterRootDevice(), 263, 268,
    269, 288, 294
UpnpSearchAsync(), 298–300
UpnpSendAction(), 300, 32, 324
UpnpSendActionAsync(), 300
UpnpSendAdvertisement(), 264
UpnpSetWebServerRoot(), 263
UpnpSubscribe(), 315–316
UpnpUnRegisterClient(), 332
UpnpUnRegisterRootDevice(), 288
UpnpUnsubscribe(), 317
URLs for services, 10
    augmented Backus–Naur form
        (ABNF) grammar of, 156, 219
    authenticator blocks (ABs) in, 172
    Bluetooth Service Discovery
        Protocol (SDP) and, 372
    Jini, 48
    lookup services in Jini and, 48
    SLP and, 150, 153–158, 165–167,
        172, 174, 183, 189, 204, 206
    Universal Plug and Play (UPnP)
        and, 223, 224, 227, 226, 242,
        244, 250–251, 262, 299, 311
user agents (UAs), SLP, 10, 150, **151**,
    163, 170–174, 176, 215, 217, 218
User Datagram Protocol (UDP)
    Jini, 28, 39, 41, 58
    multicast announcement protocol
        for lookup services and, 41
    multicast request protocol for
        lookup services and, 39–40
    proxy objects and, 58
    size of message in, 172–173
    SLP and, 150, 156, 172–173

User Datagram Protocol (UDP)
    (*Cont.*):
    Universal Plug and Play (UPnP)
        and, 223, 225, 237, 241
user selectable scoping in SLP, 176

valueChanged(), Jini, 111
variables and values, UPnP, 251,
    256, 272–273, 300, 326–328

web servers, UPnP, 263
web sites of interest
    Bluetooth Service Discovery
        Protocol (SDP) and, 380
    Universal Plug and Play (UPnP)
        and, 229, 358
Windows, 12, 152
    Bluetooth Service Discovery
        Protocol (SDP) and, 363, 377
wireless devices, 12
    Bluetooth Service Discovery
        Protocol (SDP) and, 362–363
wireless LANs, synchronizatioin, 13
write(), JavaSpaces, 128, 132, 135
writeBytes(), Jini, 57

Xerces, UPnP, 258–260, 358
XID fields in messages, SLP, 162
XML, 14–15
    Universal Plug and Play (UPnP)
        and, 10–11
    Simple Object Access Protocol
        (SOAP) and, 243
    Universal Plug and Play (UPnP)
        and, 222–229, 242–245,
        257–260, 267, 278–279, 290,
        308, 318, 324, 358

About the Author

Golden G. Richard III is currently an Associate Professor of Computer Science at the University of New Orleans. He is the creator of a popular tutorial on service discovery, presented at several leading conferences, including Mobicom. He is primarily a "systems guy," working in mobile computing and wireless networking. His current major interest is interoperability for service discovery.

Professor Richard received a B.S. degree in computer science with a minor in philosophy from the University of New Orleans and an M.S. and Ph.D. in computer science from The Ohio State University. When he's not hacking, he can be found consuming jazz, cooking, or covered in dirt, in his garden.